The Westminster
to Karl Barth

Other books in The Westminster Handbooks to Christian Theology series

THE WESTMINSTER HANDBOOKS
TO CHRISTIAN THEOLOGY

The Westminster Handbook to Karl Barth

Edited by RICHARD E. BURNETT

WESTMINSTER
JOHN KNOX PRESS
LOUISVILLE · KENTUCKY

© 2013 Westminster John Knox Press

First edition
Published by Westminster John Knox Press
Louisville, Kentucky

13 14 15 16 17 18 19 20 21 22—10 9 8 7 6 5 4 3 2 1

Book design by Sharon Adams
Cover design by Cynthia Dunne
Cover art: Monks Copying Manuscripts
(Corbis/ © Archivo Iconografico)

Library of Congress Cataloging-in-Publication Data

The Westminster handbook to Karl Barth / Richard E. Burnett, Editor. — First edition
        pages cm. — (The Westminster handbooks to Christian theology)
    Includes bibliographical references.
    ISBN 978-0-664-22530 8 (alk. paper)
    1. Barth, Karl, 1886–1968. I. Burnett, Richard E., 1963–
    BX4827.B3W45   2013
    230'.044092—dc23

2012048003

∞ The paper used in this publication meets the minimum requirements of the American National Standard for Information Sciences—Permanence of Paper for Printed Library Materials, ANSI Z39.48-1992.

Contents

Series Introduction

The Westminster Handbooks to Christian Theology series provides a set of resources for the study of historical and contemporary theological movements and Christian theologians. These books are intended to assist scholars and students in finding concise and accurate treatments of important theological terms. The entries for the handbooks are arranged in alphabetical format to provide easy access to each term. The works are written by scholars with special expertise in these fields.

We hope this series will be of great help as readers explore the riches of Christian theology as it has been expressed in the past and as it will be formulated in the future.

The Publisher

Introduction

Defining Karl Barth's terms has been the task of at least two generations of scholars and, given the increasing number of books, articles, and dissertations on Barth's theology that have appeared more and more each year over the last two decades, it is clear that this task is far from over. Indeed, notwithstanding the efforts made here, most of the contributors to this volume would say that the task in earnest has only just begun, especially in the English-speaking world. The task of defining Barth's terms has remained a challenge because of the level at which he sought to rethink the theology of the Christian church. As "the greatest theologian since Thomas Aquinas," according to Pope Pius XII, Barth's theology has forced the reconsideration, if not the redefinition, of the vast majority of terms in the theological encyclopedia. Recognizing the breadth and depth of Barth's contribution has taken time. And it continues to take time because the crater left by the "bombshell which exploded on the playing field of theologians"—as the Roman Catholic theologian Karl Adam famously described the first edition of Barth's *Römerbrief*—continues to be measured, as does the magnitude of the impact of his subsequent theological revolution.[1]

As some of the smoke and debris of Barth's bombshell began to clear throughout the twentieth century, it became apparent that Barth's work anticipated debates that many theologians have had only in recent decades, for example, over how theology is to be studied in a modern or postmodern, foundationalist or nonfoundationalist, postfoundationalist or post-Christian context. More importantly, closer analysis of Barth's engagement of most of the major theologians and movements throughout nearly every period in church history: patristic, medieval, Reformation, post-Reformation, and modern, including his vigorous engagement of the history of biblical interpretation, has helped to clarify significant points of continuity and discontinuity between his theology and the church's theological tradition. In particular, deeper insight into Barth's massive critique of philosophical and theological movements and figures of the eighteenth and nineteenth centuries has shown not only the depths of his engagement, but also the enormous power and scope of the intellectual tradition he sought to overcome. Of course, it did not happen all at once or without several "false starts,"

---

1. Karl Adam, "Die Theologie der Krisis," *Hochland: Monatsschrift für alle Gebiete des Wissens, der Literatur und Kunst* 23 (1926/1927): 271–86. Also: *Gesammelte Aufsätze zur Dogmengeschichte und Theologie der Gegenwart* (Augsburg: Literar. Institut P. Haas, 1936), 319–37. "Barths Römerbrief schlug gleich bei seinem ersten Erscheinen (August 1918) wie eine Bombe auf dem Spielplatz der Theologen ein" (325).

as he acknowledged. But so thoroughgoing was Barth's effort to overcome so much of his own theological inheritance and to reinterpret the entire Christian theological tradition in light of christological and Trinitarian categories that it is only now becoming clear what he meant and how serious he was when he said after his break with liberalism that he had to learn his "theological ABCs all over again."[2]

Defining Barth's terms remains a challenge therefore because of the necessity of understanding the intellectual context out of which the meaning of so many of his terms emerged. For if the meaning of terms is determined by use, as Barth believed, then it is important to understand how he used specific terms in light of the history of their interpretation, that is, in the context of various long-standing theological debates and over and against various theological opponents and alongside various theological allies. This is the basic material challenge of trying to define Barth's terms. Yet if this is the basic material challenge, then the basic formal challenge is that there is simply so much material to assess. Those who have tried to understand Barth seriously on his own terms according to his own intratextual world know this. They know that the basic challenge is: Life is short. Barth is long.

The sheer length and breadth of Barth's contribution can be overwhelming (and there is still a good bit that has not yet been published and an enormous amount that has not yet been translated into English). It has been suggested that Barth wrote so much that he wrote himself out of our times. In times such as ours, particularly here in America, so dominated by sound bites, e-mail, text messaging, and media outlets for people with busy lives and short attention spans, this should not surprise us. Given such times, perhaps more surprising should be not only that so much interest in Barth's theology persists, but that it also seems to be on the rise. Nevertheless, many otherwise serious students of theology find Barth, the great theological monolith of the twentieth century, easier to walk around than to try and walk through.

Barth's capaciousness is daunting, and there is probably truth in the claim that he expected too much from his readers. Yet compared to most modern theologians, Barth is relatively easy to understand. Though he does not avoid technical terminology, nor fail to discuss the most intricate theological nuances, and often cites references in their original languages, there is a lively, colloquial, and sometimes even sermonic quality about his prose in the *Church Dogmatics*. In fact, Barth was awarded by the German Academy of Language and Poetry the distinguished Sigmund Freud Award in 1968 for the eloquence of his "scientific prose." Still, reading Barth is challenging. To paraphrase George Hunsinger, it is like entering a medieval cathedral. At first it appears dark and can feel perhaps a bit foreboding. But after one's eyes have had time to adjust to the light, one begins to see all sorts of lights, colors, and shapes.[3] The difference, it seems to me, is that there usually comes a day, even for most interested viewers, when the conceptual insights gleaned from looking at a cathedral come to an end, whereas for most interested readers of the *Church Dogmatics* Barth's insights into the Christian faith and tradition seem almost inexhaustible.

It was Hans Frei who gave perhaps the most compelling rationale for the vastness of Barth's project. Barth sought to overcome the dominant theological program of his day, Protestant liberalism, by exposing and uprooting its spiritual and intellectual seeds that were sown and had been growing for more than two hundred fifty years. As his own project grew he sought to expose and uproot not only the seeds of unbelief and confusion over the revelation of God in Jesus Christ that had flourished throughout the history of the church, but to retill the soil of the church's theological

2. Karl Barth, "Postscript," 264.
3. George Hunsinger, *How to Read Karl Barth: The Shape of His Theology* (New York: Oxford University Press, 1991), 27–28.

past and recast theology according to a better understanding of God's Word by cultivating more attention to the Bible's and theology's central subject matter, content, and theme. And, according to Frei, the basic means by which Barth sought to do so was by way of "redescription." So comprehensive was the scope of this program that "Barth had as it were to recreate a universe of discourse, and he had to put the reader in the middle of that world, instructing him in the use of that language by showing him how—extensively, and not only by stating the rules or principles of discourse." This accounts for Barth's prolixity and the "lengthy, even leisurely unfolding" of so many concepts, themes, and doctrines. Barth sought to create a world that was at the same time "a world with its own linguistic integrity" on the one hand and to ensure on the other hand that "unlike any other depicted world it is the one common world in which all live and move and have our being."[4]

Yet, however internally coherent one may find Barth's universe of discourse and however much it may correspond to the one real world that Barth claimed is the world the Bible depicts, Frei points out a problem that bears significantly on the efforts represented in this volume. He refers to it as "the difficulty of second-hand restatement." There is no doubt that in elaborating his theological universe of discourse in all its intricacy and grandeur Barth possessed "astonishing descriptive powers," Frei says. "But then, as one tries to restate it afterwards the material dies on one's hands. It can be done, but there is nothing as wooden to read as one's own or others' restatement of Barth's terms, his technical themes and their development. . . . For that reason reading 'Barthians,' unlike Barth himself, can often be painfully boring."[5]

This suggests something of the challenge that was presented to the contributors to this volume in trying to define Barth's terms. The challenge, on the one hand, was to try to define terms that derive from a world so large, comprehensive, autocratic, self-absorbing (as Auerbach might have described it),[6] and self-consistent that it seems practically self-contained, as Frei says, "to the point of being virtually hermetic, except for those who are already 'in' on it."[7] On the other hand, the challenge was to do so in a way that avoided wooden recapitulation.

Of course, there is an extent to which this could be said of the effort to define terms from most any discipline or field of knowledge. Most fields of knowledge, such as biology, chemistry, or physics, have specialized vocabularies that require a broad context to understand. To understand a discrete technical term among them usually requires more than simply abstract reasoning, but knowledge of other technical terms or constellations of terms that form what is often called today a "web of meaning." Apart from an understanding of these other terms or a specific web of meaning, it is difficult if not impossible to understand any single term properly or sufficiently. This is as true of theology in general and Barth's theology in particular as it is of many other fields of knowledge. To borrow an image I once heard George Hunsinger use to try and disabuse a confused critic on a particular point, Barth's theology is like a complex machine with many moving, interconnected parts. There are wheels within wheels. Sometimes readers become confused when they focus on one part and fail to see its connection with other parts. Unaware or unaccustomed to the workings of the larger structure, a reader can go round and round on one wheel—and often enough

---

4. Hans W. Frei, "An Afterword: Eberhard Busch's Biography of Karl Barth," in *Karl Barth in Re-View: Posthumous Works Reviewed and Assessed*, ed. H. Martin Rumscheidt (Pittsburgh: Pickwick, 1981), 111ff.

5. Ibid., 109.

6. Erich Auerbach, *Mimesis: The Representation of Reality in Western Literature*, trans. Willard R. Trask (Princeton: Princeton University Press, 1953), 14ff.

7. Frei, "Afterword," 109.

it is a smaller wheel turning in an opposite direction—without seeing its connection to larger wheels at work. Thus, understanding any single term in Barth's theological vocabulary often requires an understanding of other terms or sometimes an entire complex of terms. And it is this interconnectedness that is well illustrated in this project as one observes how often other key terms—which we have placed in boldface and italic to indicate their treatment elsewhere—are needed in the attempt to define a single term.

Yet recognizing the larger context and interconnectedness of Barth's theological vocabulary is only one aspect of the challenge of trying to define his terms. Given the limited space in which contributors were asked to do so and the range of readers for whom this volume was intended (viz., students, pastors, scholars, and others), the constant dilemma throughout has been to try to capture the rich complexity of Barth's terms without sacrificing intelligibility. The temptation has been, on the one hand, to sacrifice nuance for simplicity or, on the other hand, to satisfy the precision and rigor of specialists at the expense of the accessibility and clarity demanded by nonspecialists. The temptation has been to provide a thicker description of the larger context from which a given term emerges and thereby risk obscuring its meaning or to provide a thinner description of a term that is perfectly clear yet risks greater misunderstanding because its larger context is obscure. Either way there are risks of misunderstanding. And, of course, there is an extent to which this is true of every effort to define large terms. But my hope has been that this book will not contribute to what my teacher, David Willis, has referred to as one of the greatest threats to the church today, namely, the "Gerberization of theology." I do not recall my beloved teacher ever offering a precise definition of this phrase (he often used such phrases and left it up to us to figure them out), but it has something to do with the chopping up and smoothing out of rich, complex, high-fiber theological concepts into some bland mush that is tasteful and perhaps somehow nourishing only to theological infants who wish to be fed forever by teaspoons. I share this concern. Yet if it turns out that the terms defined in this book tend to be tasteful only to the refined palettes of Barth scholars who have written more for one another than for its intended readers, then this book will have failed to fulfill its purpose.

Suffice it to say, there are many risks taken in producing a volume such as this. Those who have read Barth for themselves will recognize at once that defining his terms too tightly risks sucking the blood out of them, not to mention the joy so characteristic of Barth's theology. Stale or sterile definitions thus can do more harm than good. And if in defining some terms we must "murder to dissect," then it is probably better to leave them alone until better insights and methods become available. Nevertheless, if we keep in mind the ancient Chinese proverb, "Books do not exhaust words; words do not exhaust thoughts," and if, as Terrence Tice says, "Definitions are the shortest distance between ignorance and understanding,"[8] then there is a chance that this book may do some good.

Several fine works have been produced over the years to introduce Barth's theology. Geoffrey Bromiley's *Introduction to the Theology of Karl Barth* provides a rich and comprehensive overview of each major section of the *Church Dogmatics*.[9] George Hunsinger's *How to Read Karl Barth: The Shape of His Theology* focuses carefully on six key motifs that pervade Barth's theology and reflect "its inner logic or coherence."[10] Other introductions examine various themes, survey the intellectual landscape

8. Terrence Tice, *Schleiermacher* (Nashville: Abingdon, 2006), 47.

9. Geoffrey W. Bromiley, *Introduction to the Theology of Karl Barth* (Grand Rapids: Eerdmans, 1979).

10. Hunsinger, *How to Read Karl Barth*, 20.

from which Barth's theology arose, or place him in dialogue with other theologians or theological currents. More recently, Eberhard Busch has produced an extraordinarily lively study along the lines of a classic loci approach in *The Great Passion: An Introduction to Karl Barth's Theology*.[11] Each of these studies has their strengths and has been very helpful. However, since the task of understanding Barth continues, it seems additional tools may still be needed, and owing to the editorial genius of Donald McKim we may now have another. He created and designed the *Westminster Handbook Series* in order to help scholars and students to "find concise and accurate treatments of important theological terms" in their efforts to understand major Christian theologians and movements. And if ever there was a theologian whose terms needed "concise and accurate" treatment it is Barth. Therefore, I owe a great debt of gratitude to Donald McKim for asking me to help forge this tool and for his patience and encouragement along the way. At one point, he wrote to me: "Just think how useful this work would have been when you (or I) were starting out trying to wrap our minds around Barth's great 'cathedral'!"

Yet, to be sure, like all tools this one has its limitations. In fact, some tools can be dangerous. If any book ever deserved a warning label, this one does. So let the reader beware. These definitions may be hazardous to one's theological health if misused. Barth himself was concerned to issue such a "warning" in light of attempts to interpret his theology in more concise terms. In prefaces to the German and English editions of Otto Weber's *Karl Barth's Church Dogmatics: An Introductory Report*, Barth acknowledged the need for a "Compendium" such as Weber's to help readers get if not a grasp then at least an accurate glimpse of Barth's "Moby Dick" (Barth's nickname for the volumes of the *Church Dogmatics*, which were originally published in white covers). Yet Barth worried about "lazy people who are always in a hurry to get things done, the glib talkers and superficial writers on this and the yon side of the Atlantic, who, if possible, will merely scan through even this volume." In particular, given all the insipid, "neo-orthodox" caricatures and half-truths of "hasty theological journalism" to which his theology had been subjected, Barth asked: "Am I in error when I have the impression that quite extensively in the world of Anglo-Saxon theology there is a definite aversion to voluminous books as such, and a certain preference for summaries that are easily understandable and may be repeated in simple catchwords?" Barth scorned "hoary summations . . . hastily dashed off by some person at some time, and for the sake of convenience, just as hastily accepted, and then copied endlessly, which, of course, can easily be dismissed." Yet, for all his "reservations," Barth expressed gratitude for Weber's efforts to promote understanding even while emphasizing the express warning: "*abusus non tollit usum*," which roughly translates: "wrong use does not preclude proper use."[12]

I am not at all sure that Barth would have approved of a project that attempted to define his major terms so succinctly, that is, in 500, 1000, 2,000, or 2,500 words. I am not even sure he would have imagined a world in which anyone would ever want seriously to try. But I certainly have been keenly aware of the warning he issued to readers of Weber's work, and I can only hope that readers of this work will take this same warning to heart. Readers should also know that most of the contributors to this project found it extremely difficult to try and define Barth's terms so concisely. In fact, some said it was among the most difficult theological challenges they had ever

---

11. Eberhard Busch, *The Great Passion: An Introduction to Karl Barth's Theology*, trans. Geoffrey Bromiley (Grand Rapids: Eerdmans, 2004). For a shorter yet no less lively introduction, see Busch's *Barth*, trans. Richard and Martha Burnett (Nashville: Abingdon, 2008).

12. Otto Weber, *Karl Barth's Church Dogmatics: An Introductory Report*, trans. Arthur C. Cochrane (Philadelphia: Westminster, 1953), 5–10.

undertaken. It is not because Barth or his writings on a particular topic were unfamiliar to them. On the contrary, almost all of them are recognized authorities on Barth's theology. Indeed, most were chosen precisely because they had contributed a major book, article, or dissertation on the topic they were assigned. In other words, most of them were chosen because they had already lived a long time with the term they had been asked to define and understood it as well as anyone else in the world. But summing up Barth is never easy, and often the more one knows the more difficult it is to do. So if readers find themselves dissatisfied by the inadequacy of these definitions and want to complain to me that justice was not done to this or that term, my response to them is: *Get in line!* Get in line behind those of us who tried to write these definitions. You will find it is already a long one.

This is the fruit of the labor of the largest team of Barth scholars that has ever been gathered to interpret Barth's theology. Some chose a more genetic approach to define their assigned terms, others adopted a more synthetic approach. Many utilized a combination of both. Few were entirely satisfied with what they could do in the space they were provided and many expressed frustration about it. Yet, in the end, many said that being forced to define a given term in Barth's theology so concisely had proven to be a very helpful exercise and that the results would be beneficial to both new and seasoned readers of Barth. I am deeply grateful to each contributor. I am particularly grateful to several who were—and who in many respects continue to be—my teachers. I owe a special debt of gratitude to my *Doktorvater*, Bruce McCormack, who gave me many good suggestions in selecting the best scholars for many of the terms treated in this volume.

Apart from my wish that more terms could have been included, my greatest regret is that instead of including Barth scholars almost exclusively from the Western hemisphere, I did not include Barth scholars—of which there is a growing number—from what has been called the "New Christendom," namely from Africa, Asia, Central and South America. I trust if there is a second edition of this volume, it will include not only more terms, but also fresh insights and perspectives from more people and perhaps even revisions. This would help to demonstrate that real theology is always *theologia viatorum*, "theology on the way," and that, because real theology is simply an ongoing response to the Word of God, the task of defining theological terms is not a matter of producing square, finely chiseled hunks of granite, but an ongoing process, as Barth once described it, of "Starting Out, Turning Around, and Confessing."[13]

A special word of thanks goes to my remarkably gifted student assistant, Jacob Thielman, and his remarkably gifted wife, Erin. Jacob's help in editing and his input throughout and Erin's work on the abbreviations were invaluable. Since my father was a seminary classmate and friend of both Jacob's grandfather and Erin's grandfather and I was a student assistant of Jacob's grandfather, I have had a special sense of joy and satisfaction in having the help of these two children of the covenant. Their dedication and fellowship has been a great blessing to me, as has the theological and ecclesial heritage we share. I also thank another one of my students, the Reverend Matthew Waldron, for his encouragement and feedback in reading some of the entries to this volume. I am also deeply grateful for the keen editorial eyes of Julie Tonini of Westminster John Knox Press and for the help of my friends Clifford Anderson, former curator of the Center for Barth Studies at Princeton Theological Seminary, and Fred Guyette and Sara Morrison of McCain Library at Erskine Theological Seminary, who were a great help to me in tracking down valuable information. And, as always and in everything, I must thank my wife, Martha, whom I have reason

13. Karl Barth, "Starting Out, Turning Round, Confessing," in *Final Testimonies*, trans. Geoffrey Bromiley (Grand Rapids: Eerdmans, 1977), 52–62.

to believe works harder and loves more sacrificially than any other wife and mother in the world.

Finally, I dedicate this volume to two of my beloved mentors, the Reverend Dr. Donald R. Mitchell, former president of King College, who in his life and work and in his death, demonstrated to all who knew him the value of words and the importance of using them properly, and the Reverend Dr. Richard A. Ray, former managing editor of John Knox Press, who has been a wise coach, counselor, and cornerman to me throughout this project and, more profoundly, throughout my entire adult life.

Contributors

Clifford B. Anderson
Director, Scholarly Communications
   in the Jean and Alexander Heard
   Library
Vanderbilt University
Nashville, Tennessee

Michael Beintker
Professor of Systematic Theology
University of Münster
Münster, Germany

Kimlyn J. Bender
Associate Professor of Theology
George W. Truett Theological
   Seminary
Baylor University
Waco, Texas

Andrew Burgess
Vicar
All Saints Anglican Parish
Nelson, New Zealand

Richard E. Burnett
Professor of Systematic Theology
Erskine Theological Seminary
Due West, South Carolina

Bryan Burton
Associate Professor of Theology
   and Ministry
Fuller Theological Seminary
Seattle, Washington

Eberhard Busch
Professor Emeritus of Systematic
   Theology
University of Göttingen
Göttingen, Germany

Michael D. Bush
Field Director
Office of Presbyterian Ministries
Gordon-Conwell Theological
   Seminary
Charlotte, North Carolina

Christophe Chalamet
Professor of Systematic Theology
University of Geneva
Geneva, Switzerland

David Clough
Professor of Theological Ethics
University of Chester
Chester, United Kingdom

Thomas W. Currie
Dean and Professor of Theology
Union Presbyterian Seminary–
   Charlotte Campus
Charlotte, North Carolina

R. Dale Dawson
Adjunct Professor of Theology
Tyndale University College
Toronto, Ontario, Canada

Gary W. Deddo
Senior Editor
InterVarsity Press
Downer's Grove, Illinois

Michael T. Dempsey
Assistant Professor of Theology
St. John's University
Queens, New York

David E. Demson
Professor Emeritus of Systematic
  Theology
Emmanuel College, University of
  Toronto
Toronto, Ontario, Canada

Gregor Etzelmüller
Professor of Systematic Theology
University of Heidelberg
Heidelberg, Germany

Matthias Gockel
Professor of Systematic Theology
University of Jena
Jena, Germany

T. J. Gorringe
Professor of Theological Studies
University of Exeter
Exeter, England

Garrett Green
Professor Emeritus of Religious Studies
Connecticut College
New London, Connecticut

Daniel M. Griswold
Pastor
Trinity Reformed Church
Rochester, New York

Darrell L. Guder
Professor of Missional and Ecumenical
  Theology
Princeton Theological Seminary
Princeton, New Jersey

Martin Hailer
Professor of Systematic Theology
Heidelberg University of Education
Heidelberg, Germany

John W. Hart
Pastor
Liberty Presbyterian Church
Delaware, Ohio

Trevor Hart
Professor of Divinity
University of St. Andrews
St. Andrews, Scotland

Kevin W. Hector
Assistant Professor of Theology
  and of the Philosophy of Religions
The University of Chicago Divinity
  School
Chicago, Illinois

Alasdair I. C. Heron
Professor Emeritus of Reformed
  Theology
University of Erlangen
Erlangen, Germany

I. John Hesselink
President and Professor of Theology,
  Emeritus
Western Theological Seminary
Holland, Michigan

Christopher R. J. Holmes
Senior Lecturer in Systematic
  Theology
University of Otago,
Dunedin, New Zealand

George Hunsinger
Professor of Systematic Theology
Princeton Theological Seminary
Princeton, New Jersey

J. Christine Janowski
Professor Emerita of Dogmatics
  and History of Philosophy
University of Bern
Bern, Switzerland

Merwyn S. Johnson
Professor Emeritus of Systematic
  Theology
Erskine Theological Seminary
Due West, South Carolina

Paul Dafydd Jones
Associate Professor of Religious
  Studies
University of Virginia
Charlottesville, Virginia

William Klempa
Principal Emeritus
Presbyterian College, McGill University
Montreal, Quebec, Canada

Dietrich Korsch
Professor of Systematic Theology
University of Marburg
Marburg, Germany

Wolf Krötke
Professor of Systematic Theology
Humboldt University
Berlin, Germany

David Lauber
Associate Professor of Theology
Wheaton College
Wheaton, Illinois

Friedrich Lohmann
Professor of Systematic Theology
  and Ethics
Bundeswehr University
München-Neubiberg, Germany

Joseph L. Mangina
Professor of Systematic Theology
Wycliffe College, University of Toronto
Toronto, Ontario, Canada

Amy Marga
Associate Professor for Systematic
  Theology
Luther Seminary
St. Paul, Minnesota

Lidija Matosevic
Lecturer for Systematic Theology
Theological Faculty Matija Vlacic Ilirik
Zagreb, Croatia

Bruce L. McCormack
Professor of Systematic Theology
Princeton Theological Seminary
Princeton, New Jersey

John C. McDowell
Professor of Theology
University of Newcastle
Newcastle, England

Paul C. McGlasson
Pastor
First Presbyterian Church
Sullivan, Indiana

Alexander J. McKelway
Professor Emeritus of Religious Studies
Davidson College
Davidson, North Carolina

Paul Louis Metzger
Professor of Christian Theology and
  Theology of Culture
Multnomah Biblical Seminary
Portland, Oregon

Daniel L. Migliore
Professor Emeritus of Systematic
  Theology
Princeton Theological Seminary
Princeton, New Jersey

Paul D. Molnar
Professor of Systematic Theology
St. John's University
Queens, New York

Adam Neder
Associate Professor of Theology
Whitworth University
Spokane, Washington

Paul T. Nimmo
Lecturer in Theology
University of Edinburgh
Edinburgh, Scotland

Russell W. Palmer
Professor of Philosophy and Religion
University of Nebraska at Omaha
Omaha, Nebraska

Amy Plantinga Pauw
Professor of Doctrinal Theology
Louisville Presbyterian Theological
  Seminary
Louisville, Kentucky

Georg Pfleiderer
Professor of Systematic Theology
 and Ethics
University of Basel
Basel, Switzerland

William C. Placher†
Professor of Philosophy and
 Religion
Wabash College
Crawfordsville, Indiana

Andrew Purves
Professor of Reformed Theology
Pittsburgh Theological Seminary
Pittsburgh, Pennsylvania

H. Martin Rumscheidt
Professor Emeritus of Theology
Atlantic School of Theology
Halifax, Nova Scotia, Canada

Gerhard Sauter
Professor Emeritus of Systematic
 and Ecumenical Theology
University of Bonn
Bonn, Germany

Stephanie Mar Smith
Independent Scholar
Seattle, Washington

Katherine Sonderegger
Professor of Theology
Virginia Theological Seminary
Alexandria, Virginia

Bryan D. Spinks
Professor Liturgical Studies and
 Pastoral Theology
Yale University Divinity School
New Haven, Connecticut

Günter Thomas
Professor of Systematic Theology
Ruhr-Universität Bochum
Bochum, Germany

Katja Tolstaja
Professor of Theology
University of Amsterdam
Amsterdam, Netherlands

Edwin Chr. van Driel
Associate Professor of Theology
Pittsburgh Theological Seminary
Pittsburgh, Pennsylvania

Francis Watson
Professor of New Testament
Durham University
Durham, England

John Webster
Professor of Systematic Theology
Aberdeen University
Aberdeen, Scotland

David Willis
Professor Emeritus of Systematic
 Theology
Princeton Theological Seminary
Princeton, New Jersey

Abbreviations

KARL BARTH'S WORKS IN ENGLISH

Anselm   *Anselm: Fides Quaerens Intellectum.* Translated by I. W. Robertson. Richmond, 1960.

AS   *Against the Stream: Shorter Post-War Writings 1946–52.* Translated by E. M. Delacour and S. Godman. London, 1954.

C&A   *Christ and Adam.* Translated by T. A. Smail. New York, 1956.

"C&S"   "Church and State." In *Community, State, and Church.* Translated by G. R. Howe. Edited by W. Herberg, 101–48. 1968. Repr., Eugene, OR, 2004.

"C&T"   "Church and Theology." In *Theology and Church: Shorter Writings 1920–1928.* Translated by L. P. Smith, 286–306. London, 1962.

"CCCC"   "The Christian Community and the Civil Community." In *Community, State, and Church.* Translated by S. Godman. Edited by W. Herberg, 149–89. 1968. Repr., Eugene, OR, 2004. Also in *Against the Stream: Shorter Post-War Writings 1946–52.* Translated by S. Godman. Edited by R. G. Smith, 12–50. London, 1954.

CD   *Church Dogmatics* (4 vols. in 13 parts). Translated by G. W. Bromiley, et al. Edited by G. W. Bromiley and T. F. Torrance. Edinburgh, 1936–1977. Cited by volume, part number, and page or section (e.g., *CD* I/2:8 or *CD* 1/2:§1). Throughout, the revised edition of I/1 (1975) is cited.

CL   *The Christian Life.* Translated by G. W. Bromiley. Grand Rapids, 1981.

"Concept of the Church"   "The Concept of the Church." In *Theology and Church: Shorter Writings 1920–1928.* Translated by L. P. Smith, 272–85. London, 1962.

Credo	*Credo: A Presentation of the Chief Problems of Dogmatics with Reference to the Apostles' Creed.* Translated by J. S. McNab. New York, 1936.	
CSC	*Community, State, and Church.* Edited by W. Herberg. 1968. Repr., Eugene, OR, 2004.	
DiO	*Dogmatics in Outline.* Translated by G. T. Thomson. London, 1949.	
ER	*The Epistle to the Romans.* Translated by E. C. Hoskyns. Oxford, 1933.	
Eth	*Ethics.* Translated by G. W. Bromiley. New York, 1981.	
EvT	*Evangelical Theology: An Introduction.* Translated by G. Foley. New York, 1963.	
"F&I"	"Fate and Idea in Theology." In *The Way of Theology in Karl Barth: Essays and Comments.* Translated by G. Hunsinger. Edited by H. M. Rumscheidt, 25–61. PTMS 8. Allison Park, PA, 1986.	
FCh	*The Faith of the Church.* Translated by G. Vahanian. New York, 1958.	
FGG	*Fragments Grave and Gay.* Edited by H. M. Rumscheidt. Translated by E. Mosbacher. London, 1971.	
FT	*Final Testimonies.* Edited by E. Busch. Translated by G. W. Bromiley. Grand Rapids, 1977.	
"G&L"	"Gospel and Law." In *Community, State, and Church.* Translated by	

A. M. Hall. Edited by W. Herberg, 71–100. 1968. Repr., Eugene, OR, 2004.

GD	*Göttingen Dogmatics.* Translated by G. W. Bromiley. Grand Rapids, 1991.
HC	*The Heidelberg Catechism for Today.* Translated by S. Guthrie. London, 1964. Reprinted as *Learning Jesus Christ through the Heidelberg Catechism.* Grand Rapids, 1981.
"Herrmann"	"The Principles of Dogmatics According to Wilhelm Herrmann." In *Theology and Church: Shorter Writings 1920–1928.* Translated by L. P. Smith, 238–71. London, 1962.
HG	*The Humanity of God.* Translated by T. Wieser and J. Thomas. Richmond, 1960.
Hom	*Homiletics.* Translated by G. W. Bromiley and D. E. Daniels. Louisville, KY, 1991.
HS&CL	*The Holy Spirit and the Christian Life.* Translated by R. B. Hoyle. Louisville, KY, 1993.
HSGML	*How to Serve God in a Marxist Land.* Translated by T. Wieser. New York, 1959.
KGSG	*The Knowledge of God and the Service of God According to the Teaching of the Reformation.* Translated by J. L. M. Haire and I. Henderson. New York, 1939.
L61–68	*Letters 1961–1968.* Translated by G. W. Bromiley. Grand Rapids, 1981.

LGB	*Letter to Great Britain from Switzerland.* Translated by E. H. Gordon. London, 1941.		*Essays and Comments.* Translated by R. Palma. Edited by H. M. Rumscheidt, 79–95. PTMS 8. Allison Park, PA, 1986.
LKB–RB	*Karl Barth–Rudolf Bultmann: Letters 1922–1966.* Translated by G. Bromiley. Grand Rapids, 1981.	"Postscript"	"Concluding Unscientific Postscript on Schleiermacher." In *The Theology of Schleiermacher.* Translated by G. W. Bromiley, 261–79. Grand Rapids, 1982.
"Luther's Doctrine"	"Luther's Doctrine of the Eucharist: Its Basis and Purpose." In *Theology and Church: Shorter Writings 1920–1928.* Translated by L. P. Smith, 74–111. London, 1962.	Pr	*Prayer: 50th Anniversary Edition.* Translated by S. F. Terrien. Louisville, KY, 2002.
Moz	*Wolfgang Amadeus Mozart.* Translated by C. K. Pott. Grand Rapids, 1986.	PTh	*Protestant Theology in the Nineteenth Century.* Translated by B. Cozens and J. Bowden. London, 1972.
"Need and Promise"	"The Need and Promise of Christian Preaching." In *The Word of God and the Word of Man.* Translated by D. Horton, 97–135. 1928. Repr., Gloucester, MA, 1978.	"RB—AUH"	"Rudolf Bultmann—An Attempt to Understand Him." In *Kerygma and Myth: A Theological Debate.* Volume 2. Translated by R. H. Fuller, 83–132. London, 1962.
"New World"	"The Strange New World within the Bible." In *The Word of God and the Word of Man.* Translated by D. Horton, 28–50. 1928. Repr., Gloucester, MA, 1978.	RD	*The Resurrection of the Dead.* Translated by H. J. Stenning. New York, 1933.
OR	*On Religion: The Revelation of God as the Sublimation of Religion.* Translated by G. Green. London, 2006.	RevTh	*Revolutionary Theology in the Making.* Translated by J. D. Smart. Richmond, 1964.
"P&A"	"Protestantism and Architecture." *Theology Today* 19, no. 2 (1962): 272.	"Righteousness"	"The Righteousness of God." In *The Word of God and the Word of Man.* Translated by D. Horton, 9–27. 1928. Repr., Gloucester, MA, 1978.
PGos	*The Preaching of the Gospel.* Translated by B. E. Hooke. Philadelphia, 1963.	"Roman Catholicism"	"Roman Catholicism: A Question of the Protestant Church." In *Theology and Church: Shorter Writings 1920–1928.* Translated by L. P. Smith, 307–33. London, 1962.
"Philosophy"	"Philosophy and Theology." In *The Way of Theology in Karl Barth:*		

"Schleier-macher" "Schleiermacher." In *Theology and Church: Shorter Writings 1920–1928.* Translated by L. P. Smith, 159–99. London, 1962.

"Society" "The Christian's Place in Society." In *The Word of God and the Word of Man.* Translated by D. Horton, 272–327. 1928. Repr., Gloucester, MA, 1978.

SPr *Selected Prayers.* Translated by K. Crim. Richmond, 1965.

T&C *Theology and Church.* Translated by L. P. Smith. London, 1962.

"Task" "The Word of God and the Task of the Ministry." In *The Word of God and the Word of Man.* Translated by D. Horton, 183–217. 1928. Repr., Gloucester, MA, 1978.

TB *The Teaching of the Church Regarding Baptism.* Translated by E. Payne. London, 1948.

ThC *The Theology of Calvin.* Translated by G. W. Bromiley. Grand Rapids, 1995.

ThRefC *The Theology of the Reformed Confessions.* Translated by D. Guder and J. Guder. Louisville, KY, 2002.

ThS *The Theology of Schleiermacher.* Translated by G. W. Bromiley. Grand Rapids, 1982.

TT *Karl Barth's Table Talk.* Edited by J. Godsey. Richmond, 1962.

"Vistas" "Biblical Questions, Insights, and Vistas." In *The Word of God and the Word of Man.* Translated by D. Horton, 51–96. 1928. Repr., Gloucester, MA, 1978.

WGWM *The Word of God and the Word of Man.* Translated by D. Horton. 1928. Repr., Gloucester, 1978. (Time constraints did not allow us to cite the new edition, *The Word of God and Theology.* Translated by Amy Marga. New York: T. & T. Clark, 2011.)

WWorld *The Word in This World: Two Sermons.* Ed. K. Johanson. Vancouver, 2007.

KARL BARTH'S WORKS IN GERMAN

B–1961–1968 *Karl Barth: Briefe, 1961–1968.* Edited by J. Fangmeier and H. Stoevesandt. Zurich, 1979.

BarThE *Texte zur Barmer theologischen Erklärung.* Edited by M. Rohkrämer. Zurich, 1984.

B–B Br *Karl Barth–Rudolf Bultmann: Briefwechsel, 1911–1966.* 2nd edition. Edited by B. Jaspert. Zurich, 1994.

B–Br Br *Karl Barth–Emil Brunner: Briefwechsel 1916–1966.* Edited by E. Busch. Zurich, 2000.

B–R Br *Karl Barth–Martin Rade: Ein Briefwechsel.* Edited by C. Schwöbel. Gütersloh. 1981.

B–Th Br I *Karl Barth–Eduard Thurneysen: Briefwechsel 1913–1921.* Edited by E. Thurneysen. Zurich, 1973.

B–Th Br II	*Karl Barth–Eduard Thurneysen: Briefwechsel 1921–1930.* Edited by E. Thurneysen. Zurich, 1974.	*P-1915*	*Predigten 1915.* Edited by H. Schmidt. Zurich, 1996.
B–Th Br III	*Karl Barth–Eduard Thurneysen: Briefwechsel 1930–1935.* Edited by C. Algner. Zurich, 2000.	*P-1916*	*Predigten 1916.* Edited by H. Schmidt. Zurich, 1998.
ChrD	*Die Christliche Dogmatik im Entwurf* (1927). Edited by G. Sauter. Zurich, 1982.	*Rom* I	*Der Römerbrief* (1919). Edited by H. Schmidt. Zurich, 1985.
G-1959–1962	*Gespräche 1959–1962.* Edited by E. Busch. Zurich, 1995.	*Rom* II	*Der Römerbrief* (1922). Zurich, 1954.
G-1963	*Gespräche 1963.* Edited by E. Busch. Zurich, 2005.	*ThF&A*	*Theologische Fragen und Antworten.* Zurich-Zollikon, 1957.
G-1964–1968	*Gespräche 1964–1968.* Edited by E. Busch. Zurich, 1996.	*Unterricht* I	*Unterricht in der christlichen Religion* I. Edited by H. Reiffen. Zurich, 1985.
KD	*Kirchliche Dogmatik.* 4 vols. in 13 parts. Zurich, 1942–1970. Cited by volume, part number, and page (e.g., *KD* I/2:8).	*Unterricht* II	*Unterricht in der christlichen Religion* II. Edited by H. Stoevesandt. Zurich, 1990.
Konf	*Konfirmandenunterricht, 1909–1921.* Edited by J. Fangmeier. Zurich, 1987.	*Unterricht* III	*Unterricht in der christlichen Religion* III. Edited by H. Stoevesandt. Zurich, 2003.
Lutherfeier	*Lutherfeier 1933.* Theologische Existenz heute 4. Munich, 1933.	*VkA* I	*Vorträge und kleinere Arbeiten 1905–1909.* Edited by H.-A. Drewes and H. Stoevesandt. Zurich, 1992.
"Nachwort"	"Nachwort." In *Schleiermacher-Auswahl.* Edited by H. Bolli, 290–312. Munich, 1968.	*VkA* II	*Vorträge und kleinere Arbeiten 1909–1914.* Edited by H.-A. Drewes and H. Stoevesandt. Zurich, 1993.
P-1913	*Predigten 1913.* Edited by N. Barth and G. Sauter. Zurich, 1994.	*VkA* III	*Vorträge und kleinere Arbeiten 1922–1925.* Edited by H. Finze. Zurich, 1990.
P-1914	*Predigten 1914.* Edited by U. Fähler and J. Fähler. Zurich, 1999.	*VkA* IV	*Vorträge und kleinere Arbeiten 1925–1930.* Edited by H. Schmidt. Zurich, 1994.

GENERAL ABBREVIATIONS

AThR	*Anglican Theological Review*		Translated by K. Crim and L. De Grazia. Richmond, 1968.
Beginnings	*The Beginnings of Dialectic Theology.* Edited by J. M. Robinson.	ET	English translation
		EvTh	*Evangelische Theologie*

IJST	*International Journal of Systematic Theology*	PSB	*Princeton Seminary Bulletin*
JREth	*Journal of Religious Ethics*	PTMS	Pittsburgh Theological Monograph Series
JRT	*Journal of Religious Thought*	rev.	revised
Karl Barth	E. Busch, *Karl Barth: His Life from Letters and Autobiographical Texts*. Translated by J. Bowden. 1976. Repr., Grand Rapids, 1994.	SJT	*Scottish Journal of Theology*
		TEh	Theologie Existenz heute. Munich, 1933–1941
MTh	*Modern Theology*	ThSt	Theologische Studien. Zurich. 1938–present
ns	new series	ThT	*Theology Today*
NTh	E. Brunner and K. Barth, *Natural Theology.* Translated by P. Fraenkel. London, 1946.	ThZ	*Theologische Zeitschrift*
		TJT	*Toronto Journal of Theology*
		TynBul	*Tyndale Bulletin*
PrTMS	Princeton Theological Monograph Series	ZDTh	*Zeitschrift für dialektische Theologie*
		ZZ	*Zwischen den Zeiten*

List of Articles

Articles

Actualism "Actualism" is a term used to indicate one of the most significant characteristics of Barth's mature *theology*. The term alludes primarily to the way in which Barth, following the *witness* of Scripture, conceives of *God* and *Jesus Christ*, and (derivatively) of human beings, as beings-in-action, existing in a *covenant* relationship in which the dialectical concepts of "*history*" and "event" are important. These conceptions have vital ramifications for Barth's understandings of *preaching*, the *Bible*, and the *church*.

The basis of Barth's actualism is found in his doctrine of God. Barth's confession of the existence of God is based on *revelation*, the divine event in which God acts to reveal Godself to human beings. Revelation attests that God is a living God operative in the history of the covenant, in respect of whom words such as "event" and "act" cannot be avoided. Central to Barth's understanding of revelation at this point is his view that "God is who He is in His works" (*CD* II/1:260). In other words, the Trinitarian activity of revelation involves God declaring who God really is: God's being and action *ad extra* correspond to God's being and action *ad intra*.

Barth happily calls upon the dynamic vocabulary of the theological tradition to describe God as a being-in-action: God is *vita, actuositas, actus*, even *actus purissimus*. This act is not *general* or *abstract*, however, but is shown in revelation to be *concrete* and *particular*: not just *actus purus*, then, but "*actus purus et singularis*" (II/1:263). First, it is God alone who exists absolutely in act, in a conscious, willed, and executed decision, and who is thus properly "event," "act," and "life": "When we know God as event, act, and life, we have to admit that generally and apart from Him we do not know what that is" (II/1:264). Second, this act of the living God has a particular content, which is the free and gracious decision of God to be for *humanity* in Jesus Christ: "before [Jesus Christ] and above Him and beside Him and apart from Him there is no election, no beginning, no decree, no Word of God" (II/2:95).

This eternal *election* of Jesus Christ is an act of *love* that is free of compulsion or necessity: "In so far as God not only is love, but loves, in the act of love which determines His whole being God elects" (II/2:76). For Barth, Jesus Christ is the Subject and Object of this election. In the history that is thereby elected, "the Son of God becomes identical with the man Jesus of Nazareth, and therefore unites human essence with His divine essence" (IV/2:107).

This history entails the humiliation of God and the exaltation of humanity in the concrete existence of Jesus Christ, the God-human in divine-human unity, and represents the actualization of the eternal will and decree of God. Barth writes correspondingly that Jesus Christ is himself "*actus purus*, the actualisation of being in absolutely sovereign spontaneity" (IV/3.1:40). Jesus Christ is thus also a being-in-action, whose divine-human history demonstrates a perfect correspondence of person and work. In the one history of Jesus Christ, the divine essence reveals and gives while the human essence serves and attests and mediates, without confusion or distinction but in a perfect relationship of action. Indeed, Barth's explicit "actualisation" of the doctrine of the hypostatic union leads him to write: "we have left no place for anything static at the broad center of the traditional doctrine of the person of Christ" (IV/2:106).

As Barth derives his theological anthropology directly from his *Christology*, he also construes human persons in general as beings-in-action. The history of each person has its **determination** in light of the history of Jesus Christ; and in correspondence with the being of Jesus Christ, each person "is active, engaged in movement" (III/2:195). As one is determined in this way by God, the question also arises of one's self-determination (II/2:511). Actualism thus also becomes a crucial dimension of Barth's construal of theological *ethics*, in which obedience to the divine command of *grace* can only take place as an event in the history of the covenant. There is also dissimilarity between Jesus Christ and humanity in general, of course: the being of the individual exists by grace alone and is not self-positing or self-determining; the presence of *sin* means that there is no perfect correspondence between the being of the individual and one's actions; and the presence of grace means that the self-determination of the individual is ultimately subordinate to one's

divine determination. Nevertheless, for Barth, it is axiomatic that "To exist as a [hu]man means to act" (II/2:535).

To write of God and of human beings in this actualistic way is to make profound ontological claims: Barth's actualism is therefore not simply a formal description of one aspect of his *theology*, but carries with it profound material content. Indeed, the phrase "actualistic ontology" is found synonymously for "actualism" in much secondary literature; the major alternative would be a "substantialistic ontology" in which God and human beings would be construed as fixed and determinate quantities in a certain abstraction from their histories, acts, and relationships. In implicitly rejecting this view, Barth believes himself to be guided by the witness of divine revelation. Barth is aware that terms such as *ontology* and *actualism* are part of the vocabulary of secular *philosophy*; but he is consequently determined at every stage to ensure that "ontology will have its norm and law in [Jesus Christ], not *vice versa*" (IV/1:757). It is in such a sense that Barth happily speaks of a "strong actualism" in his theology (G-1964–1968, 90), while stoutly opposing any engagement in speculative metaphysics.

The ramifications of Barth's actualism extend beyond these immediate corollaries into other theological loci, of which three deserve brief mention. First, Barth's understanding of proclamation as the **Word of God** is dependent upon human words *becoming* the Word of God in the gracious event of divine revelation (I/1:94). Second, and similarly, Barth conceives Scripture to be the Word of God only as it *becomes* the Word of God through an event of the gracious activity of God (I/1:108). Finally, the being of the church, which is dependent on the work of Jesus Christ through the **Holy Spirit**, is conceived explicitly as a being in action: "Its act is its being, its status is dynamic, its essence its existence" (IV/1:650). In each of these loci, ready evidence of Barth's actualism is further apparent.

G. Hunsinger, *How to Read Karl Barth* (1991); E. Jüngel, *God's Being Is in Becoming*, trans. J. Webster (2001); B. L. McCormack, *Orthodox and Modern* (2008); P. T. Nimmo, *Being in Action* (2007).

PAUL NIMMO

Analogy Analogy is a way of thinking that is of utmost importance to Barth. It enables authentic human speech about *God*, but at the same time safeguards God's mystery. The reality (*Wirklichkeit*) of the triune God is categorically different from human reality. This raises the question whether human words and concepts can ever approach the mystery of God, or, more pertinently, whether human words and concepts can serve adequately for any discussion of God at all. This question can be answered positively with the help of analogy. Although the reality of God is of necessity always to be distinguished from the reality of humans, and therefore also from the reality of human speech, words and concepts are able to express adequately the mystery of God under certain conditions, that is, at that moment when these words and concepts correspond (in an analogical way) with him, according to the stipulations of the *analogia fidei*.

Barth distinguishes between analogy as opposed to parity and disparity. Analogy means "*similarity*, i.e., a *partial* correspondence and agreement (and, therefore, one which limits both *parity* and *disparity* between two or more different entities)" (*CD* II/1:225). Barth particularly emphasizes the aspect of "similarity" ("partial correspondence and agreement" (227), "correspondence and comparableness" (III/3:102). One may venture to speak in *theology* about "similarity and therefore analogy" in the sense that "we find likeness and unlikeness between two quantities: a certain likeness which is compromised by a great unlikeness; or a certain unlikeness which is always relativized and qualified by a certain existent likeness" (102).

In the *CD* Barth uses analogy as a way of thinking in three fundamental fields of application. First, human speech about God and his relation to humans proceeds according to the rules of analogy, that is, according to the *analogia fidei* in the narrower sense, which, in classical terms, means the *analogia attributionis*. The fields of recognition and speech are mentioned in this context. The relationship of human words to God's being is one of neither parity nor disparity. Barth does not orient himself to a general epistemology in the unfolding of these thoughts. He prefers to follow as closely as possible the event of *revelation*. The concept of *disparity* is unsuitable because God reveals himself in his revelation and consequently gives "veracity" to human words that describe him (II/1:233). By God's **grace** they are "awakened" and "taken into service" (235). But the concept of *parity* is equally unsuitable. "That God also veils Himself in His revelation certainly excludes the concept of parity as a designation of the relationship between our words and God's being" (235). This classical definition of "analogy," which occupies a middle point between parity (univocity) and disparity (equivocity), is too formal and abstract. We are confronted with the revelation of the *living* God. The living God always encounters us in his revelation in "both His veiling and His unveiling" (236).

Second, the relationships within the inner Trinitarian being of God, his revelation in the man Jesus, and the existence of human beings in their interrelationship with God and with one another, are arranged in an analogical way. These respective relationships are neither in a relation of identity nor in a relation of difference toward the *I-Thou* relationship in the triunity of God, but rather in a relation of correspondence. Since the characteristic feature in view is the comparable relationship between "I and Thou," Barth uses the concept of *analogia relationis*, which, in classical terms, means the *analogia proportionalitatis*. The relationship in the inner being of God between the Father, the Son, and the **Holy Spirit** is the "source of every I and Thou" (III/2:218). This relationship is repeated and copied in God's eternal **covenant** with **humanity**, as it is revealed in the humanity of Jesus in our age (cf. 218–19). The man Jesus repeats is his being for humans the inner being, the essence (*Wesen*), of God himself, thereby making his being true for God. In this way the *analogia relationis* allows for the only adequate understanding of Jesus' humanity. Between the humanity of Jesus that belongs to the created world (the relationship of God to the reality that differs from him) and the inner sphere of the reality of God (the relationship of God to himself), there is correspondence and similarity, but no identity (cf. 219; IV/1:126–27, 203–4; IV/2:43–44). With the *analogia relationis*, Barth relates the differing levels of Trinitarian theology, **Christology**, anthropology, and ethical propositions in such a way that their respective mutual relationships, as well as their categorical differences, are guaranteed. To cite an example: "The relationship between the summoning I in God's being and the summoned divine Thou is reflected both in the relationship of God to the man whom He has created, and also in the relationship between the I and the Thou, between male and female, in human existence itself" (III/1:196).

Third, divine action and human action must be clearly distinguished. Nevertheless, certain analogies arise between divine action and human action when humans try to respond to God's turning toward us with corresponding acts of **love**. One finds such analogies, for instance, in the description of Christian discipleship (cf. IV/1:634ff.) or in love (cf. IV/2:776–79, 785–86) or in characterizing the nature of the church (cf. IV/3.2:728–29). Barth's **ethics** are also

determined by the formation of such analogies. He characterizes the correspondence between divine work and human works as an *analogia operationis* (III/3:102). According to Barth, while there is between the work of God and that of the creature "no identity . . . there is a similarity, a correspondence, a comparableness, an analogy" (III/3:102). Furthermore, the highly valued idea of *Gleichnis* (which cannot be translated adequately in its comprehensive sense, but is similar to "likeness," "resemblance," or "parable") appears quite often in contexts like these (cf. III/3:49–50; IV/3.1:110–65). Due to its structure, the *analogia operationis* is concerned with the application of the *analogia relationis* or *proportionalitatis* because particular relationships are also always portrayed here.

Barth orients the structure of analogy to the mystery of God's **incarnation** in **Jesus Christ**, which has to be comprehended as the original image of parity and disparity. The parity between the Father and the eternal Son corresponds with the disparity between the Father and the man Jesus: on the one hand "unity of essence," on the other hand "complete disparity between the two aspects" (III/2:219). An analogy exists between the relationship of Father-Son (unity) and the relationship of Father-man Jesus (disparity), which is constituted by the incarnation of the Son. The inner being of God adopts "this form *ad extra* in the humanity of Jesus, and in this form, for all the disparity of sphere and object, remains true to itself and therefore reflects itself" (220). It does this, however, *per analogiam relationis*, because "repetition" and "reflection" signify neither identity with nor difference from the divine and the human being of the Son. For Barth, therefore, the humanity of Jesus as it relates to the divine being concerns the prototype of the formation of analogy, "the true and original correspondence and similarity" (219).

The essence of Barth's use of analogy discloses itself in the contemplation of the incarnation of God. It is not deduced from a metaphysical principle, which seeks to safeguard the center between the thought categories of "logic" and "dialectic" with the help of "analogy." This was the approach of Erich Przywara in his work *Analogia entis* (1932), through which he specifically sought to respond to questions initiated by Barth with his **dialectical theology** of the 1920s. Przywara founded his use of analogy on the logical law of contradiction, upon which the three steps of *Logic, Dialectic,* and (in the center of both) *Analogic* consequently follow. With this approach to analogy, Przywara wanted to express formal ontological structures, not only of the relationship between Creator and **creation**, but also of the created world itself. Faithful to his metaphysical approach, he saw analogy as a general principle of metaphysics as such. Barth rejected his expansion of the concept of analogy to a grammar of being because of his suspicion that, in so doing, the cause of theology was subordinated to an already evident philosophical principle. This explains his sharp rejection of *analogia entis* "as the invention of Antichrist" (I/I:xiii). For Barth, analogy should be based from the outset on the foundation of a *theology of revelation*—in a certain sense, as the grammar of God's persistent care for humanity, which itself is founded in the inner relations of his triune being. Analogy as a way of thinking is justified and required by the fact that God, in the words of human speech and in the Word incarnate (John 1:14), comes in the being of a man, which is of necessity to be distinguished from God's being. The God who reveals himself in Jesus Christ is the foundation and standard of analogy. For this reason Barth speaks emphatically about an *analogia fidei.*

Barth's desire to maintain the difference and, at the same time, the relationship between the Creator and the creature is admittedly in accord with Przywara's intentions. Barth's critique aimed at a way of thinking in which Creator and creature are tacitly subsumed under a concept of being that is common to both, and is thereby placed above them (cf. II/1:79ff., 103). Barth had evidently misjudged Przywara, because Przywara consequently claimed an analogical way of thinking about the "being" of the creature as well as the being of the Creator in order to rule out any univocity. Although Creator and creature come together in "being," they are also simultaneously infinitely separated from each other in "being." For this conviction, Przywara referred to the famous statement of the Fourth Lateran Council (1215): "inter creatorem et creaturam non potest tanta similitudo notari, quin inter eos maior sit dissimilitudo notanda" ("between creator and creature no likeness can be recognized that would be greater than the unlikeness that is to be recognized between them"). From the perspective of an understanding of analogy schooled in the gospel's movement into human language, the problem of the *analogia entis* for Przywara is less a matter of leaning toward a kind of **natural theology**, as Barth suspected, but rather that the distance between Creator and creature becomes too great.

Eberhard Jüngel has explained that Przywara's concept of analogy inevitably results in an unavailability (*Unverfügbarkeit*) of God, since similarity is always eliminated by an ever greater distance between God and humans. The later Barth also recognized this. That is, he was afraid that the *analogia entis* misses the distinction between God and humans precisely because it overlooks God's nearness. But the *with-each-other* and *in-each-other* "veiling and unveiling of God" in the process of revelation, which is already characteristic of Barth's doctrine of God in the *CD*, is neither shaped symmetrically nor oriented onesidedly to the veiling. The unveiling in this case corresponds with the parity, the veiling with the disparity. The relationship of unveiling/parity/*similitudo* and veiling/disparity/*dissimilitudo* is determined by "an ordered dialectic, and indeed one which is teleologically ordered" (II/1:236). This "teleological order" in the concept of analogy is grounded in the fact that both unveiling and veiling are an expression of God's grace. Thus the grace of God determines the gradient between unveiling/parity/ *similitudo* and veiling/disparity/*dissimilitudo*. The unveiling claims precedence; contrary to the statement of the Fourth Lateran Council and Przywara, the similarity for Barth is still greater than the dissimilarity.

In his *CD*, Barth's concept of analogy attained its final shape and most mature expression. In the 1920s his theological epistemology was dominated by an awareness of the problem of dialectics. As in the case of the *analogia fidei*, Barth's dialectics maintained the qualitative distinction between God and humanity and was directed against a correlation of identity between the **Word of God** and human speech about the Word of God. The difficulty centers on the issue of the human ability to authentically express the Word of God. We are humans and, as such, cannot speak about God. God alone can speak about himself authentically. The resulting dialectical contradiction between our *having-to-speak* and our *not-being-able-to-speak* is overcome at the level of analogy by the correspondence between God's speaking and humans' speaking about God's speaking.

It is therefore understandable that Hans Urs von Balthasar characterized the changes in Barth's thought on dialectics from *Rom* II (1922) to his *CD* as a "turning towards analogy." Although some arguments could be offered in support of such a "turn," this characterization does not do justice to the complexity of the developments in Barth's thought. An affinity for an analogical way of thinking can already be observed in Barth's early works and during the 1920s. One finds in his early work many examples of the *analogia proportionalitatis* as well as *relationis*.

Even the motif of the *Gleichnis* is significant in which the events and relationships of this aeon foreshadow the laws of the kingdom of heaven. However, there is just as little warrant for simply concluding that Barth has replaced a dialectical way of thinking with an analogical way of thinking. Barth's mature theology exhibits logical, dialectical, as well as analogical lines of argumentation. They can be independent of one another, but they may also overlap or be interconnected. It is therefore necessary to speak of a coexistence of analogy, logic, and dialectic in Barth's theology (Eberhard Mechels). Only in such a way can theological thought continue to do justice anew to the activity of a living God.

H. Urs von Balthasar, *The Theology of Karl Barth*, trans. J. Drury (1971); E. Jüngel, *God as the Mystery of the World*, trans. D. Guder (1983); B. L. McCormack, *Karl Barth's Critically Realistic Dialectical Theology* (1995); E. Mechels, *Analogie bei Erich Przywara und Karl Barth* (1974); W. Pannenberg, *Analogie und Offenbarung* (1977); E. Przywara, *Analogia Entis* (1932).

MICHAEL BEINTKER

Angels Barth's extensive and creative theological treatment of angels is unique in twentieth-century Protestant thought. At a time when most of his theological contemporaries were disinclined to engage the subject at all, Barth devoted a long section to angels in the third part of his doctrine of **creation** in *CD* III/3, following his treatment of divine **providence** and **evil**. He titled this section, "The Kingdom of Heaven, the Ambassadors of God and Their Opponents." Barth finished this part of the *CD* in the summer of 1949, in the wake of Rudolf Bultmann's call to demythologize the New Testament, including its depictions of the supernatural activity of **God** and his angels, in order to make the gospel comprehensible to modern people. In his angelology Barth exuberantly went against the grain of such modern sensibilities.

Barth was not content simply to re-pristinate earlier Christian treatments of angels, because he found that "a lot of hampering rubbish has accumulated in this field in both ancient and more modern times" (III/3:xi), requiring him to do much ground clearing before even the right questions could emerge. Barth pushed aside the ornate, speculative angelologies of the medieval tradition that, in his view, had forgotten that angels appear as only marginal figures in Scripture. The scriptural treatment of angels must guide dogmatic approaches: "Angels are not independent and autonomous subjects like God and man and *Jesus Christ*. They cannot, therefore, be made the theme of an independent discussion" (III/3:371). Instead of concerning himself with names and hierarchies of angels, Barth located his reflections at the intersection of angelic presence and the divine economy of *grace*.

Angels are creatures of heaven, the realm "of all that which in creation is unfathomable, distant, alien and mysterious" (III/3:424), and the terminus a quo for God's redemptive action on earth. Guided by the description of angels in Heb. 1:14 as spirits "sent to serve for the sake of those who are to inherit *salvation*," Barth emphasized the mission of angels rather than their ontological nature. In *CD* IV Barth would take the same actualist approach to ecclesiology. The function of angels is to praise and bear *witness* to God, making God's purposes "open and perceptible" to creatures on earth (III/3:485). "Place is found for them in the Bible where the consummating action of God Himself is not yet or no longer visible to man directly" (III/3:502). As such, angels are liminal figures, always appearing on the edges of human knowledge and perception.

In the aftermath of World War II, contemporaries of Barth such as Hans Asmussen and Gustaf Wingren attempted to grapple with its horrors by giving

theological attention to the demonic realm. By contrast, Barth's treatment of demons is markedly short and dismissive. He emphatically rejected the theological tradition that posited demons as fallen angels, deriding it as "one of the bad dreams of the older dogmatics" (III/3:531), without secure foundation in Scripture. Barth chose the daring theological alternative of denying that Satan and his minions were creatures at all. In a tongue-in-cheek reference to *Bultmann*, he asserted that angels and demons are related "as kerygma and myth" (III/3:520). While angels are creaturely agents of divine providence, demons are a mythological personification of nothingness. Demons exist "only as God affirms Himself and the creature and thus pronounces a necessary No" (III/3:523). They inhabit "a sphere of contradiction and opposition which as such can only be overthrown and hasten to destruction" (III/3:522). Since Christ has already triumphed over the forces of nothingness, it would be perverse to give demons sustained theological attention. In Barth's view, the "supposedly very realistic demonology" of the Christian tradition must be discarded, "not out of any desire for demythologization, but because [demons] are not worth it" (III/3:xii).

Unlike earth, heaven is a morally unambiguous realm. According to Barth, "its being is an obedient being.... The presence of God in heaven, the origin and commencement there of His action in the *world*, makes it necessary that He should find there the obedience of His creature; that His creature in heaven should do His will" (III/3:371). As wholly obedient creatures, angels "have no history or aims or achievements of their own. They have no profile or character, no mind or will of their own" (III/3:480). They are "pure witnesses" who point to God in an "utterly selfless and undemanding and purely subservient" way (III/3:484). What appears as angels' ontological weakness is really their glory. Barth made a similar argument about women earlier in his doctrine of creation. Woman is the glory of man (1 Cor. 11:7); like the angels, she exercises no choice of her own, choosing only "that for which God has chosen her" (III/1:303).

As a form of creaturely existence immune from the threat of *sin* and destruction, angels reveal the eschatological destiny of human creatures: "they are in an exemplary and perfect way that which constitutes the essence of all creatures and characterises earthly creatures as their origin and goal" (III/3:480). In particular, angels disclose that the eschatological *freedom* God has determined for all creatures is not "the so-called *liberum arbitrium*, i.e., the freedom to become fools" (III/3:531), but rather a free obedience in which "the possibility of deviation or omission does not arise" (III/3:493).

K. Barth, *CD* III/3:§51; D. Heidtmann, *Die Engel* (2005); A. N. S. Lane, *The Unseen World* (1996); A. P. Pauw, "Where Theologians Fear to Tread," *MTh* 16, no. 1 (2000): 39–59.

AMY PLANTINGA PAUW

Apologetics "Apologetics is an attempt to show," according to Barth, "that the determining principles of *philosophy* and [the results] of historical and scientific research at some given point in time certainly do not preclude, even if they do not directly require, the tenets of *theology*, which are founded upon *revelation* and upon *faith* respectively. A bold apologetics proves to a particular generation the intellectual necessity of the theological principles taken from the *Bible* or from church *dogma* or from both; a more cautious apologetics proves at least their intellectual possibility" (*PTh*, 439–40). Barth rejects either type on the grounds that both betray revelation, which is as such always free, self-grounded, and self-authenticating. Whereas *dogmatics* seeks "to measure its talk about

God by the standard of its own being, i.e., of divine revelation" (*CD* I/1:28), apologetics seeks to establish first how human knowledge of revelation is possible on external grounds, or proceeds "as though there were doubt whether revelation is known, or as though insight into the possibility of knowledge of divine revelation were to be expected from investigation of human knowledge" (I/1:29). Thus, as "the attempt to establish and justify theological thinking in the context of philosophical, or, more generally and precisely, nontheological thinking" (*Eth*, 21), apologetics succeeds precisely where the theme of *grace* is lost (II/2:521).

If treated as one *possibility* among others, then revelation becomes an idea, abstract theory, general concept, or relatively benign, neutral principle, that is, something to be deduced, proven, posited, or prescribed. It falls under human control and becomes a matter of scrutiny, a fact at our disposal, a truth that *can be* judged and chosen rather than one that *actually* judges and chooses. By allowing revelation and the conditions for its possibility to be predetermined and defined by "alien principles of explanation in the form of metaphysical, anthropological, epistemological or religio-philosophical presuppositions" (IV/3.2:849), apologetics circumscribes and therefore domesticates and falsifies both the form and content of revelation. It denies its unique, singular, concrete particularity and assumes that revelation can be measured by standards other than its own. It betrays the fact that God is known only through God and that such knowledge is a gift that cannot be grasped by unaided *reason* but only received by grace through faith. As such, apologetics assumes that the work of dogmatics is somehow "complete" and that there is "the time and the authority to abandon" its concerns (I/1:30), even if only temporarily and tactically.

Falsification of the human *witness* to revelation occurs in apologetics with the adoption of a posture of neutrality. "This white flag, which the theologian must carry as an apologist," means he "must take his point of departure (standpoint) above Christianity" and suspend "his judgment of the *truth* or even absoluteness of the Christian revelation" and take up the position of "a moral philosopher and philosopher of religion" (*PTh*, 444). Though the goal is to lead the unbeliever to knowledge of the real God, the "initial aim is to disguise this and therefore to pretend to share in the life-endeavor of natural man" (II/1:94). On the basis of a certain natural knowability of God (see *point of contact*), a "preliminary decision" is presented that is supposedly connected to "the real decision of faith or unbelief." But whereas the latter decision "can and will occur only in and with man's encounter with God's revelation," here "a game is played with natural man with a view to leading him beyond this preliminary stage and placing before him the actual decision itself" (II/1:88–89). However well meaning, this "is an error which not only injures truth but also and directly *love*. . . . The unbeliever who is partner in this conversation is not a child playing games, to whom we are in the habit of speaking down in order the more surely to raise up" (94). "We are not taking him seriously because we withhold from him what we really want to say and represent." Despite the "friendly intention," it will be "not without justice" if the unbeliever sees himself as "despised and deceived" and "hardens himself against" such a "masked faith" that "does not speak out frankly, which deserts its own standpoint and merely pretends to take up the contrary standpoint of unbelief" (93). "Neutrality is really a decision of unbelief" (*Die Souveränität des Wortes Gottes* [ThSt 5; Zollikon: Evangelische Buchhandlung, 1939], 18). "We cannot experiment with unbelief, even if we think we know and possess all sorts of interesting and very promising possibilities and recipes for it." The believer "is the one who will find unbelief first and foremost in himself. . . .

How can he fail to know that there is only one remedy against unbelief, and that is faith taking itself seriously, or rather taking the real God seriously?" (II/1:95). If we are going to address another seriously "from faith" we must do so "out of faith" (92).

Nevertheless, since faith must speak *against* unbelief, dogmatics *will have* an "apologetic character" (*TT*, 62). Indeed, to the extent that dogmatics "must prepare an exact account of the presupposition, limits, meaning and basis of the statements of the Christian confession," apologetics will serve as "a necessary function of dogmatics" (IV/3.1:109) not by providing arguments for belief from unbelief, but by refuting arguments for unbelief from belief. Explaining the *gospel* to itself and the *world*, the Christian community can and should try to take away "the illusion that knowledge [of faith] is possible only in the form of a *sacrificium intellectus*. . . . While the community will not presume to try to accomplish what is not its work, it can show . . . that even from the human standpoint this knowledge is quite as much in order as any other human knowledge" (IV/3.2:848).

Yet apologetics in service of dogmatics can only be "ad hoc" (Frei, 114). It cannot be "deliberately planned" but "simply happens as God Himself acknowledges the witness of faith" (I/1:30). Since the community "cannot do more than this, it will spare both the world and itself the pain of a specific apologetic, the more so in view of the fact that good dogmatics is always the best and basically the only possible apologetics" (IV/3.2:882). Barth's bottom line: "'Except the Lord build the house, their labor is but lost that build it. Except the Lord keep the city, the watchman waketh but in vain. . . .' Good apologetics is distinguished from bad by its responsibility to these words" (II/1:9).

K. Barth, *CD* II/1:§26; D. Bloesch, *A Theology of Word and Spirit* (1992), 212–49; H. W. Frei, "An Afterword," in *Karl Barth* in *Re-View*, ed. M. Rumscheidt (1981), 95–116; G. Hunsinger, *How to Read Karl Barth* (1991); W. Placher, *Unapologetic* (1989).

RICHARD E. BURNETT

Ascension   The ascension of Jesus is a doctrine Barth strongly affirms without giving it any extended treatment per se. Clearly the commentaries on the Apostles' Creed (*Credo* and *DiO*) necessarily involve brief discussion of "He ascended into heaven," but it is in the overall development of some key themes in *CD* that the import of Barth's belief in ascension bears fruit.

In describing Jesus' ascension Barth steers a path away from notions of "space travel," or a physical flight into a heaven situated above the earth. The key to understanding both Jesus' destination and the *meaning* of Jesus' ascension is the cloud that hides Jesus from sight. This cloud signifies the "hidden presence" of *God* within the *creation* (à la the Sinai theophany, Elijah's experience, and both Jesus' *baptism* and transfiguration—the last being particularly significant as a *revelation* of the glory of the heavenly one). Jesus disappears into the cloud and is taken from sight, and this indicates that his destination is "heaven," which Barth describes as "the hidden place where God takes space within the creation." The movement of Jesus' (genuinely physical) resurrection is complete in his arrival at the "Father's right hand," from whence we expect his return. Ascension is one with the movement of resurrection, with the forty days of resurrection appearances as a particular revelation of Jesus' glory and divinity that reaches its goal in Jesus' removal from our immediate perception (see *resurrection of Jesus Christ*). That the New Testament descriptions of Jesus' ascension as event vary considerably does not cause undue concern, as they point to a reality beyond straightforward representation, and such a reality will necessarily be

portrayed enigmatically and provisionally (see *CD* III/2:451ff.).

First, we must note that Jesus' ascension *reveals* (and does not create) the union of God with *humanity* and humanity with God that is the reality of Jesus himself (see, e.g., IV/2:153). Beyond this, it is the removal of Jesus from the immediacy of our space and the expectation of his return that are key, as together they provide the conditions that frame the present age—an age Barth names the "time-between"— specifically the *time* between ascension and Parousia. At the heart of this designation is the understanding of the way that this age is shaped and determined by the dynamic of Jesus' presence and absence. Jesus' ascension in the first instance creates his absence—he is simply not available to be heard, seen, touched or smelled in the way he was before, even in his risen body. Yet Jesus is not purely absent, for he does have a form of availability in the "time-between" as he comes in the Spirit. (Barth describes a threefold Parousia: the forty days of resurrection appearances, Jesus' coming in the Spirit, and the final *parousia* at the end of the age. See IV/3.1:295ff.)

Consonant with his broader (Chalcedonian) christological determinations, Barth rejects the common reading of Jesus' ascension as his exaltation in glory having suffered humiliation for a time (see, e.g. IV/2:150). The glory revealed in Jesus' ascension—his place at the "right hand" of the Father—is the glory that has always been his. (We may note at this point Barth's commitment to the "*extra-calvinisticum.*")

What then is the purpose of the ascension, particularly as it is worked out in the "heavenly session," or Jesus' heavenly reign, while the present age is extended, and the eschaton seemingly delayed? Why must Jesus be absent, and come in the Spirit?

These conditions define the current time as the "time of the *church*," and hence the time of *mission*. Ecclesiology is to be shaped by the horizons imposed by Jesus' ascension. The *ecclesia* is the "earthly-historical" form of Jesus' ongoing existence—his earthly form of availability. However, the church is not permitted to dominate here, as Jesus ascended, he is still embodied within the creation (his "heavenly-historical" existence) and the church can only ever be a secondary and derivative form of availability. Nonetheless, the derivative identity of the church with Jesus' body is not vacuous, for the present age is to be understood as the time of the church, and thus of mission. Any sense of a "delay" of the Parousia is to be understood as the establishment of a time for the mission of Jesus to be worked out in the mission of the church. (See IV/1:725ff.; IV/3.2:724.)

Thus Barth's doctrine of Scripture is tied up with his apprehension of Jesus as ascended. The ascended Lord exercises authority *over* the church via the external rule of Scripture, which is a concrete form of his presence to and for the church in the age between (IV/1:718). In this way Barth disallows any move to reduce Jesus' authority over the church to the authority of the church (I/2:512). Barth's critique of both **Roman Catholicism** and Neo-Protestantism on this point refers directly to the fact of Jesus' ascension and expected Parousia (e.g., I/2:692).

Similarly, the being of Christians is shaped by the tension of the present age as the time of Jesus' absence and coming in the Spirit, and by the expectation of his return. This can be seen especially clearly in Barth's exposition of **ethics** in the command of God to **love** both God and the "neighbour," which is worked out very strongly on the basis of the present age as that in which Jesus is ascended. (See *CD* §18, especially I/2:408.)

Within all this, pneumatological considerations are key. The **Holy Spirit** is identified as the agent of Jesus' genuine presence in the age between, and it is on this basis that the dynamic of presence and absence functions. The Spirit mediates the ascended **ministry** of Jesus, but

at the same time this mediate presence is not the same as the immediacy awaited in Jesus' eschatological return. (See, e.g., sections such as IV/3.1:395ff.)

Here is the point at which Barth has been most strongly criticized for failing as an ascension theologian, most notably by Thomas Torrance and Douglas Farrow. Farrow in particular is highly critical of Barth for failing to have an adequate **theology** of Jesus' activity as ascended, particularly in relation to a high-priestly role, which Farrow tracks into a poor pneumatology, concomitant with a lack of regard for earthly-historical reality. Farrow sees Barth as curtailing Jesus' ministry by having nothing fresh to achieve in his continuing **history**, and therefore as restricting the role of the Spirit to representing a somewhat static heavenly Lord. (For an opposing view see Burgess.)

A. Burgess, *The Ascension in Barth* (2002); D. Farrow, *Ascension and Ecclesia* (1999); T. F. Torrance, *Space, Time and Resurrection* (1976).

ANDREW BURGESS

Atonement   As every first-year **theology** student knows, there are three "types" of atonement theory: the substitution type, the moral exemplar type, and the Christus Victor type. (And as every second-year theology student knows, there is also a fourth type: the incarnational or "ontological" type.) It is hard to say whether this typology does more harm than good. On the one hand, it tempts us to deal with the types themselves rather than with Christians' actual reflections on the atonement, and it tempts us to think that the most interesting question one can ask about a thinker is where he or she belongs in the typology. On the other hand, by gathering a wealth of material under a handful of manageable categories, the typologizing approach has encouraged would-be atonement theorists to consider the adequacy of their views relative to some alternatives. Several criteria of adequacy emerge from such consideration: Does a particular view explain how Christ's there-and-then work suffices for the *forgiveness of sins*? Can it explain how Christ's there-and-then work "reaches" us here-and-now? Does it understand the atonement as an act of *God* from first to last, rather than as an act of, say, Christ's *humanity* alone? Finally, does it see Christ's life and resurrection as integral to his atoning work, and not just his death? In what follows, I will elaborate a reading of Barth's mature understanding of the atonement according to which it meets each of these criteria.

Barth's view can be summarized rather simply: in *Jesus Christ*, God assumed sinful human flesh, thereby abolishing sinful flesh and exalting humanity to *covenant* partnership with God. To understand this view, we need to understand each element in this formulation.

We begin, then, with the assertion that in Jesus Christ, *God* assumed sinful flesh: Barth insists that "we have to do with God Himself as we have to do with this man. . . . God Himself acts and suffers when this man acts and suffers as a man. God Himself triumphs when this One triumphs as a man" (*CD* IV/2:51). God assumes sinful flesh, according to Barth, by repeating *ad extra* the triune act of God's being: because God is triune, "his Godhead embraces both height and depth, both sovereignty and humility, both lordship and service." Hence "He does not become a stranger to Himself when in His Son He also goes into a far country" (IV/2:84). Barth's view, briefly stated, is that God is eternally a Father who wills to *love* and be loved by a Son, a Son who perfectly fulfills the Father's will by loving him wholeheartedly, and a Spirit who is the bond of their love. God's being is, accordingly, a communion of love, which means that God does not have to change in order to be God-with-us: the Father corresponds to himself in willing to love us as sons and daughters; the incarnate Son corresponds to himself in fulfilling the Father's will and returning his love wholeheartedly; and the Spirit corresponds to himself in binding us to the Father through the Son. In redeeming us, therefore, the triune God "lives in the repetition and confirmation of what He is in Himself" (IV/2:346). For our purposes, we must pay special attention to the Son's self-correspondence: eternally in Godself, the Son's being is a being-in-response—the Father loves, and the Son returns this love; the Father wills, and the Son mirrors this will. The Son becomes incarnate precisely by repeating this being-in-response in *history*: each moment of Christ's life returns the Father's love and mirrors his will, such that each moment incarnates the Son's eternal being. Hence the *incarnation* is "the strangely logical final continuation of the history in which He is God. . . . He simply activates and reveals Himself *ad extra*, in the world. He is in and for the world what He is in and for Himself" (IV/1:203–4). This is what Barth means, then, when he claims that in Jesus Christ, *God* assumed flesh.

Not just any flesh, though. God assumed *sinful* flesh, the flesh of disobedient, unfaithful, condemned humanity (IV/1:171–74). As we will see, that God assumed this flesh is crucial to Barth's understanding of the atonement. We will return to this claim momentarily; for now, we must note Barth's insistence that the Son became incarnate "to expose himself to the accusation and sentence which must inevitably come upon us," which is why he took on human nature "as it is determined and stamped by human *sin*" (IV/1:236; IV/2:25). Hence to say that God assumed flesh is, for Barth, to say that God assumed flesh that had been handed over to disobedience.

So then: in Jesus Christ, *God* assumed sinful flesh, and God assumed *sinful* flesh. In order to understand Barth's view of the atonement, we must understand the way in which these two formulations hang together—we must see, that is, what it means to say that God *assumed* sinful flesh. As we have seen, the Son's eternal being is being-in-response; the Son becomes incarnate by repeating this being in human history. We have also seen that the human history in which the Son becomes incarnate is a history of disobedience and unfaithfulness. To these claims, we can now add the following: just as every moment of Jesus Christ's life is an incarnation of the Son's being-in-response, so every moment of his life is an overcoming of human disobedience. As Barth claims, "the sinlessness of Jesus was not a condition of His being as man, but the human act of His life working itself out in this way from its origin" (IV/2:92). "It was the act of his being in which he defeated temptation in his condition which is ours, in the flesh" (IV/1:259). The Son of God eternally loves the Father and mirrors his will; he becomes incarnate by repeating this loving and mirroring in human history. More precisely: the incarnate*ness* of the Son should be understood as a continuous incarnat*ing*—that is, as the Son's moment-by-moment act, as a human being, of loving and mirroring the Father (cf. IV/2:109). In the same way, every moment of Christ's life takes on, and overcomes, the disobedience and unfaithfulness of humanity; Christ's sinlessness, and the overcome*ness* of sin, must be understood as a continuous overcom*ing* of sin. Because the Son took on flesh that had been handed over to disobedience, he "had to achieve His **freedom** and obedience in the chain of an enslaved and disobedient humanity" (IV/1:216). Moment by moment, then, the Son of God takes on flesh that has become enslaved in disobedience, and moment by moment he perfectly obeys the Father's will, thereby overcoming this disobedience. God's assumption of sinful flesh is, accordingly, the ongoing activity in which the Son repeats his being-in-response in human history, and is therefore the ongoing activity of defeating human disobedience.

Christ likewise assumes, and thereby fulfills, the judgment to which we sinners are liable. God judges sin, according to Barth, by handing us over to its consequences: in addition to enslaving ourselves to sin, we have become alienated from God and have given ourselves over to nonbeing (cf. II/2:449–50). The Son takes this judgment upon himself by entering into this alienated existence-toward-nonbeing; every moment of his life is a taking on of this alienation and nonbeing. God hands us over to the consequences of our sin, and Christ takes this handing over to its bitter conclusion: death on a cross. In dying on the cross, Christ endures fully the alienation and nonbeing to which we have been handed over; but in rising again, this alienation and nonbeing have been defeated. As Barth writes, "it was to fulfill this judgment on sin that the Son of God took our place as sinners. He fulfills it—as man in our place—by completing our work in the omnipotence of the divine Son, by treading the way of sinners to its bitter end in death, in destruction, in the limitless anguish of separation from God, by delivering up sinful man and sin in his own person to the non-being which is properly theirs, the non-being, the nothingness to which man has fallen victim as a sinner and toward which he relentlessly hastens" (IV/1:253). By assuming sinful flesh, therefore, Christ has overcome both sin *and* judgment.

One consequence of Christ's assumption of sinful flesh is that sinful humanity has been abolished. We are sinners in that we have chosen that which God has rejected, namely, being-apart-from-covenant. In Christ, however, God has assumed this being-apart-from-covenant so that it too is taken up into God's covenant love. As a result, "the rejected man exists in the person of Jesus Christ only in such a way that he is assumed into his being as the elect and beloved of God; only in refutation, conquest, and removal by him" (II/2:453). Our being-apart-from-covenant is precisely what God does *not* will—and in

Christ, God rejects this being-apart-from-covenant precisely by taking it into the covenant: Barth asserts that "in virtue of what was determined in the *election* of Jesus Christ and what took place in his death and resurrection, this non-willing is enclosed and surpassed and excelled by, and subordinated and made subservient to, that which (even in his non-willing) he positively wills—his loving-kindness, the loving-kindness of his election" (II/2:458). There is no longer any such thing as being-apart-from-covenant, therefore, at least not in an absolute sense, because being-apart-from-covenant is itself now included in the covenant. Strictly speaking, there is no longer anything "outside" the covenant, which means that in choosing to be-apart-from-covenant, we sinners remain within the bounds of the covenant; the sinner who rejects God still stands "in the sphere of the eternal covenant of divine *grace*; he is as such surrounded by the election and kingdom of Jesus Christ, and as such confronted by the superiority of the love of God" (II/2:450). Humanity-apart-from-covenant has accordingly been abolished.

God's assumption of our flesh is also the exaltation of humanity. On the one hand, the Son became incarnate by loving God and mirroring his will; on the other hand, humanity's highest good is to love and obey God. The incarnation thus achieves humanity's highest good: in Christ, humanity is exalted "to that harmony with the divine will, that service of the divine act, that correspondence to the divine grace, that state of thankfulness, which is the only possibility in view of the fact that this man is determined by this divine will and act and grace alone" (IV/2:92). In this way, "he is true to his own nature as the creature of God, the creature which is appointed in its own decisions to follow and correspond to the decisions of God, to follow and correspond to the decisions of God which are its own" (IV/1:257). Christ has brought about something new in human history: the human being who

wholeheartedly loves and obeys God—and this is humanity's highest exaltation. As we are united to Christ by the *Holy Spirit*, we begin to love and obey God wholeheartedly too, thereby sharing in the first fruits of Christ's exalted humanity (IV/2:59–60).

Briefly stated, then, this is Barth's understanding of the atonement. With this account on board, we return to the criteria with which we began. On Barth's view, every moment of Christ's life, including his death and resurrection, takes on and overcomes our sin; this taking on is the activity of the eternal Son; he takes our judgment upon himself by being handed over to alienation, enslavement, and nonbeing, and he thereby abolishes sinful humanity; and his work includes us both there-and-then, when he put an end to being-apart-from-covenant, and here-and-now, when his Spirit unites us to his new humanity. The criteria that emerge from the popular "typologizing" approach thus provide some support for Barth's understanding of the atonement.

Probably some readers still wonder where Barth's view belongs in the typology. If I were forced to answer, I would say that he understands substitution, exemplarity, and Christ's triumph over sin in terms of an incarnational model—but I think we would be better off sticking to Barth's views themselves.

D. Bloesch, *Jesus Is Victor!* (1976); H. Küng, *Justification*, trans T. Collins, et al. (2004); D. Lauber, *Barth on the Descent into Hell* (2004); B. L. McCormack, "The Ontological Presuppositions of Barth's Doctrine of the Atonement," in *The Glory of the Atonement*, ed. C. Hill and F. James (2004), 346–66; J. Webster, *Barth's Ethics of Reconciliation* (1995).

KEVIN W. HECTOR

Baptism Barth's mature position on baptism, which represents a break with traditional Reformed *theology*, was heralded in the publication of the Gwatt lecture of May 7, 1943 (*TB*), and subsequently in *CD* IV/4. In the latter he drew attention to the work on Ephesians of his son Markus, and claimed that this had made him change his mind. Indeed, Barth seems to have sat lightly to baptism in many of his earlier writings, and in some respects IV/4 represents less a change of mind than a return to his own earlier preference for a Zurich approach to sacraments over against the Genevan approach (Spinks, 261–88).

In *Rom* I (1919) Barth had used the Augustinian-Calvinian terminology, in which sacraments are visible words. Baptism is the objective, creative **Word of God** that not only signifies but is the new creation. Through baptism God speaks the redeeming word through which the objective **truth** of his **grace** is disclosed (*Rom* I, 212). The Word is effective and incorporates the individual into Christ. In *Rom* II (1922) sacraments remain only significant of fellowship with God, as do all impressions of *revelation*. They are signs, but the decision of God eternally precedes the sign, and the purpose of God stretches eternally beyond it. Baptism mediates a new *creation*, and though itself is not grace, is from first to last a means of grace. But the sign and the thing signified are not the one and the same. In spite of Barth's appeal to **Calvin**, missing is Calvin's appeal to the **Holy Spirit** as the mediating link between sign and signified. Barth sided with the "symbolic parallelism" of Bullinger rather than the "symbolic instrumentalism" of Calvin (Gerrish, 245–58). In the same year as the revised edition of *Der Römerbrief* appeared, Barth became professor of Reformed *dogmatics* at Göttingen, and lectured on the theology of Calvin, though only until the latter's stay in Strasbourg. After contrasting Calvin with **Luther** and Zwingli, he noted that Calvin calls a sacrament an appendix of the promise by which God seals the promise and makes it more credible to us. The water of baptism is not itself our cleansing and **salvation**, but simply the instrument of

these, mediating to us the knowledge and assurance of this gift of God that takes place through the Word (*ThC*, 173–74). Calvin gave a much greater significance to the term *instrumenta* than Barth admitted, and the later Calvin had far more to say on baptism. In the *Göttingen Dogmatics* Barth contended that the sacraments have no inherent power to confer anything by themselves, but are signs of the grace of God given in Christ by the power of the Holy Spirit. Faith is needed for reception. In *CD* I/1, appearing in 1932, sacraments are a form of proclamation, and baptism testifies to the objectivity of grace. In *The Knowledge of God and the Service of God* (1938), which was based on the Scots Confession of 1560, Barth describes sacraments as an action in which God acts and humanity serves. Though they are God's signs of the divine promise, humanity's part is simply obedience (*Gehorsam*). By the time of *CD* IV/1, Barth confined the term *sacrament* to the one *mysterium*, the one sacrament of **Jesus Christ**. Although appointed by God, baptism and the **Lord's Supper** are at best attestations to the one single sacrament, and are in fact obedient human responses. Once the knot that tied together the outward and inward had been cut, then baptism can only be a human attestation. Thus what was perhaps implicit in previous writings, but ambiguous because of the Augustinian-Calvinian terminology, was made explicit in the Gwatt lecture, and honed in *CD* IV/4.

In the Gwatt lecture Barth called for "responsible baptism" in place of "half baptism," which had become the norm (*TB*). He distinguished carefully between the temporal act of the **church** and the eternal act of Christ of which it is a depiction or representation (*Abbild*). It is "baptism with the Holy Spirit" that unites a person with the work of Jesus Christ, and accomplished full **justification** before God. Water baptism is the visible sign of the invisible *nativitas spiritualis*. Barth made it quite clear that as such, water baptism is a human act in which the church obeys the mandate of Jesus Christ. It is a symbol of the fact that we have been redeemed, and not itself a means of redemption. It is because baptism is an active obedient response, needing in humans an active partner, that infant baptism (passive baptism) must be deplored. Quoting *Schleiermacher*, Barth agrees that infant baptism can only be complete baptism with a profession of *faith* later in life. Behind this lurked Barth's suspicion of the *Volkskirche* in all its forms, but especially as manifested in the German Christian Movement. In this work, there is a clear distinction between water baptism and Spirit baptism, the churchly rite and God's saving redemption.

In *CD* IV/4 this earlier objection to infant baptism was pursued and expanded. No longer could the term *sacrament* be applied to baptism, which was limited to Jesus Christ. Under the title "Baptism with the Holy Spirit," Barth took up the discussion of how what took place in the saving work of Christ *extra nos* and *pro nos* can be also *in nobis*; that is, from the ontological to the ontic to the noetic. For Barth the change necessary for the *in nobis* is faith. Through God's initiative, baptism of the Spirit justifies and sanctifies, and summons to obedient *gratitude*. When Barth turns to "Baptism with Water," he urges that it is Spirit baptism that makes water baptism possible. Water baptism is the obedient response to the grace of God that has come upon a human by the *history* of Jesus Christ that has taken place for him or her. It is thus a human response to the *in nobis* work of the one sacrament, Jesus Christ. Infant baptism becomes an impossibility. Barth claimed that his view might be termed "Neo-Zwinglian," but striking parallels with Menno Simons and Dirk Philips suggest "Neo-Anabaptist" as more appropriate.

K. Barth, *TB*; B. A. Gerrish, "The Lord's Supper in the Reformed Confessions," in *Major Themes in the Reformed Tradition*, ed. D. McKim (1992), 245–58; E. Jüngel,

Karl Barths Lehre von der Taufe (1968); D. L. Migliore, "Reforming the Theology and Practice of Baptism," in *Toward the Future of Reformed Theology*, ed. D. Willis and M. Welker (1998), 494–511; B. D. Spinks, "Karl Barth's Teaching on Baptism," *Ecclesia Orans* 14 (1997): 261–88.

BRYAN D. SPINKS

Barmen Declaration   The founding document of the Confessing Church in Germany unanimously adopted by representatives of the Reformed, Lutheran, and United churches at the First Confessional Synod of the German Evangelical Church in the town of Barmen on May 29–31, 1934, the Barmen Declaration (officially titled "Theological Declaration Concerning the Present Situation of the German Evangelical Church") arose "in view of the errors of the 'German Christians' of the present Reich Church government which are devastating the *Church*." One of the most defiant public statements made by any group within Germany after 1933, Barth, the primary author, insisted: "It was not the new political totalitarianism," nor racism, nor "German Christianity," nor religious intolerance, as popularly construed, "which precipitated this event" (*CD* II/1:176). Rather it was directed "against the same phenomenon which for more than two hundred years had slowly prepared for the devastation of the Church" (Hans Asmussen), that is, "the problem of *natural theology*" (II/1:172–73).

Without denying the possibility of natural theology as such or the existence of other events and powers, figures and truths, alongside the one *Word of God*, Barmen's first article announced: "*Jesus Christ*, as he is attested for us in Holy Scripture, is the one Word of God which we have to hear and which we have to trust and obey in life and in death"; and "We reject the false doctrine, as though the Church could and would have to acknowledge as a source of its proclamation, apart from and besides this one Word of God, still other events and powers, figures and truths, as God's *revelation*." "The protest was without doubt directed against *Schleiermacher* and Ritschl" (175), but also against past and present conservative and liberal theological programs "in England and America, in Holland and Switzerland, in Denmark and Scandinavian countries," among others, which "demanded that side by side with its attestation in Jesus Christ and therefore in Holy Scripture the Church should also recognize and proclaim God's revelation in *reason*, in conscience, in the emotions, in *history*, in *nature*, and in *culture* and its achievements and developments" (174–75).

Yet, "if we want to really understand the genesis of Barmen," Barth claimed, "we shall be obliged to look finally neither to the Confess[ing] Church as such nor its opponents. For there is not much to be seen here." The Confessing Church simply uttered "a cry of need and of joy" in face of "a remarkable revelation, . . . a fresh confirmation of the one old revelation of God in Jesus Christ." It noticed "the fact of the unique validity of Jesus Christ as the Word of God spoken to us for life and death. The repudiation of natural theology was only the self-evident reverse side of this notice." "When nothing else was left for the Church, the one Word of God who is called Jesus Christ remained." Though he later regretted it did not address the so-called Jewish question (see *Israel*), Barth called Barmen "one of the most notable events in modern Church history" (176–77).

Widely regarded as "the most significant Church document that has appeared since the Reformation Confessions and Catechisms of the sixteenth and seventeenth centuries" (Cochrane, 14), Barmen's six articles have to do with revelation (the source and norm of the church's proclamation); the extent of God's claim upon our lives; the nature, form, and order of the church and its message; the church's relation to the *state*; and the nature of the church's *mission* and *ministry*. Each article begins with Scripture, followed by an affirmation. It then reintroduces into modern Protestantism the ancient *damnamus* ("We reject"), not independently but for the sake of the Yes that is in Jesus Christ and "as a particular work of love" (I/2:630). Against the "happy little hyphens" of medieval, modern, natural, mediating, or apologetic theologies, Barmen recapitulated the Reformation *solas* for its time.

K. Barth, *CD* II/1:172–78; idem, *BarThE*; E. Busch, *The Barmen Theses Then and Now*, trans. D. and J. Guder (2010); A. C. Cochrane, *The Church's Confession under Hitler* (1976); K. Scholder, *The Churches and the Third Reich*, trans. J. Bowden, 2 vols. (1988).

RICHARD E. BURNETT

Bible The Bible *is* the *Word of God* and is only rightly understood as such. But this equation is only rightly understood, according to Barth, by keeping two things together: the Bible's "distinctiveness from" and its "unity with" *revelation* (*CD* I/2:463). To put it sharply: "On the one hand *Deus dixit*, on the other *Paulus dixit*. These are two different things. And precisely because they are not two things but become one and the same thing in the event of the Word of God, we must maintain that it is by no means self-evident . . . that revelation should be understood primarily as the superior principle and the Bible primarily as the subordinate principle" (I/1:113–14). It is not self-evident that revelation is the superior principle in relation to the Bible because of the Bible's indirect identity with revelation. Yet to understand the Bible we must understand this relation and follow the path of revelation. Barth's understanding of the Bible therefore cannot be understood apart from the wider canvas of *Christology*.

The Bible is a human document like any other, "the literary monument of an ancient racial *religion* and of a

18   Bible

Hellenistic cultus religion of the Near East" ("Vistas," 60) and must be studied as such (see *historical criticism*). Yet, "as the *witness* of witnesses directly called in and with revelation itself . . . it too can and must—not as though it were *Jesus Christ*, but in the same serious sense as Jesus Christ—be called the Word of God" (*CD* I/2:500). "As the Word of God in the sign of this prophetic-apostolic word of man Holy Scripture is like the unity of *God* and man in Jesus Christ. It is neither divine only nor human only. Nor is it a mixture of the two or a *tertium quid* between them. But in its own way and degree it is very God and very man, i.e., a witness of revelation which itself belongs to revelation, and historically a very human literary document" (501).

Barth summarizes his teaching on the nature of Holy Scripture (§19) in *CD* I/2 with eight propositions (527–35): (1) The Bible is the Word of God because it is the Word of *God*, that is, not because of anything about the Bible as such but because of a being and event beyond our control (527). (2) The Bible is the Word of God because it is the work of God, that is, because of "a divine disposing, action and decision" (502) "continually made in the life of the *Church*" (535). (3) The Bible is the Word of God not as a fact that can be deduced but as a miracle to be confessed (528). (4) The Bible is the Word of God notwithstanding the offense of its human form. The biblical authors were real and therefore fallible men. As such, in their *language* and thought forms and "even in their function as witnesses," they were not only "capable" but also "actually guilty of error" not in some but in every word they spoke or wrote. Nevertheless, by the miracle of *inspiration*, they spoke "the infallible Word of God" (III/1:23) "in their fallible and erring human word" (I/2:529–30). (5) The Bible is the Word of God but the Word of God is not the Bible nor "an attribute inhering once for all in this book as such" (530). "God is not an attribute of something else, even if that something else is the Bible" (513). (6) The Bible is the Word of God and word of humans, "but we are completely absolved from differentiating in the Bible between the divine and the human, the content and the form, the spirit and the letter, and then cautiously choosing the former and scornfully rejecting the latter" (531). Even if biblical authors contradicted themselves "in the realm of human self-contradiction," God does not contradict himself in what he says through them (II/1:106), and "we must be careful not to be betrayed into taking sides into playing off the one biblical man against the other, into pronouncing that this one or that has 'erred.' From what standpoint can we make any such pronouncement?" (I/2:510). (7) The Bible is the Word of God, though not "alongside or behind" the text, nor "in some place which we have first to attain to or even create beyond the text," but in and through the text itself. God "says what the text says" and "the work of God is done through the text" (532–33). The Bible does not "contain" the Word of God or "include" revelation. "To say this would be to imply that the Bible is a more or less thick husk enclosing a sweet kernel and that it is up to us to decide, on the strength of our *reason* (eighteenth century), or our religious experience (nineteenth century), where revelation is to be found" (*AS*, 218). (8) The Bible is the Word of God not because of our *faith* in it but because it is. Yet we would not know this except in faith (I/1:110; I/2:534).

Barth writes twice as much about the Bible's authority as he does about its nature (§§20–21), and it is easy to see why some deemed him a "biblicist" (see *biblicism*). The Bible "constitutes the working instructions or marching orders by which . . . the very Church itself stands or falls" (I/1:101); its authority is "absolute and material authority" (I/2:538, passim); "To say that Jesus Christ rules the Church is equivalent to saying that Holy Scripture rules the Church. The one explains the other, the one can be understood only through the other" (693).

Yet for all the church could say and has said about Scripture, Barth says, "To say 'Lord, Lord' is not enough." Belief in the inspiration and authority of the "Bible stands or falls by whether the concrete life of the Church and of the members of the Church is a life really dominated by the *exegesis* of the Bible" (533). And despite the "violence" of its interpreters (which the study of church history is), "Scripture is in the hands but not in the power of the Church" (682). Because it exists by the power of the resurrection (678ff.), the Bible has "the power sooner or later to throw off every foreign sense attributed to it," to expose the "perversity" of misinterpretations, and to assert its own meaning, and thereby comfort yet also confront, contradict, and attack the church to the extent that the church rejects the freedom it has under it, which is the only true freedom it has (715ff.).

K. Barth, *CD* I/2:§§19–21; R. E. Burnett, *Karl Barth's Theological Exegesis* (2004); H. Kirschstein, *Der souveräne Gott und die heilige Schrift* (1998); T. F. Torrance, "Karl Barth, Theologian of the Word," in *Karl Barth* (1990), 82–120; F. Watson, "The Bible," in *Cambridge Companion to Karl Barth*, ed. J. Webster (2000), 57–71.

RICHARD E. BURNETT

Biblicism   Labeled a "biblicist" by reviewers of *Rom* I (1919), Barth responded: "For this some have blamed and some have praised me. The word is not mine, but I accept it, provided I am allowed to explain what I mean by 'Biblicism'" (*Rom* II, xv). At first, he simply stated: "Taken precisely, all the 'Biblicism' which I can be shown to have consists in my having the prejudice that the *Bible* is a good book, and that it is worthwhile to take its thoughts at least as seriously as one takes one's own."

Later in the *Göttingen*, *Christian*, and *CD*, Barth distinguished between two types of biblicism. "Material biblicism" assumes that all the questions and concerns of Christians can be answered by direct appeal to individual Bible verses without the *church* or its confessions, *history*, *dogmatics*, or *exegesis*. "The Bible individually read and autonomously understood and expounded" is alone authoritative (*CD* I/2:608), as if we had never heard the voice of the church (its teachers or pupils) or that we could read the Bible *de novo*, "as spaceless and timeless monads" (607), or as if the mere repetition of the biblical words as such were sufficient and their meaning self-evident. "Are we not dealing with a pious, but in its audacity no less explicitly modern leap into direct immediacy?" (608). "Will those who will have the Bible alone as their master, as though Church history began again with them, really refrain from mastering the Bible?" (609). Biblicists have sometimes provided a "necessary reminder of the Evangelical Scripture principle," but they have more often betrayed it by confusing their own thoughts with the Bible's. "In actual fact, there has never been a Biblicist who for all his grandiloquent appeal directly to Scripture against the fathers and tradition has proved himself so independent of the spirit and *philosophy* of his age and especially of his favorite religious ideas that in his teaching he has actually allowed the Bible and the Bible alone to speak reliably by means or in spite of his anti-traditionalism" (609). "The Biblicism of the Reformers," however, is different. It is "second-degree Biblicism," which consists of a "biblical attitude, that of the prophets and apostles," the attitude of a *witness*, "the attitude that put the Scriptures in the canon and called their text holy, the attitude not of spectators or reporters or thinkers, but of people who come down from the absolute presupposition, the *Deus dixit*, with all the irresistible momentum of a boulder rolling down a mountain side" (*GD*, 288–89). "It is a human attitude which we can learn and exercise and study, which we can grow accustomed to, in which the more or less of any human attitude will always play a part.

Biblicism is not identical with *faith* and obedience. It is a rule of thought [*Denkregel*] resulting from them" (291–92), and "the first concrete requirement which is made of dogmatics, and in obedience to which . . . its investigations, formulae and demonstrations must have a biblical character" (I/2:816). Barth describes such biblicism as a "formal," "relative," yet "formative principle" that keeps "the text of the Bible continually and constantly in view in [light of] its content" (821).

In contrast to this "right and necessary and central Biblicism, there is a scattered and peripheral" biblicism. "This does not know that the Bible is a totality and that it is meant to be read in all its parts in the light of its unity, that is, of the One of whom it everywhere speaks. On the contrary, it regards *Jesus Christ* merely as one object of its witness among others. It regards the Bible as a repository of all sorts and degrees of pious knowledge." It thinks ("with or without the lame hypothesis of the 17th century doctrine of *inspiration*") it can understand and expound its truths apart from or alongside rather than from the *truth* of its living center, Jesus Christ, who "is the primary and ultimate object of its witness." "A word of warning is required against this type of Biblicism" because it refuses "to be taught by Scripture, i.e. the whole of Scripture" (III/1:24).

K. Barth, *CD* I/2:606–7, 816–17; *GD*, 288–95; C. Baxter, "Barth a Truly Biblical Theologian?" *TynBul* 38 (1987): 3–27; R. E. Burnett, *Karl Barth's Theological Exegesis* (2004), 57–58; T. F. Torrance, "Barth's Biblicism," in *Karl Barth* (1990), 115–18; K. Vanhoozer, "A Person of the Book?" in *Karl Barth and Evangelical Theology*, ed. S. W. Chung (2006), 26–59.

RICHARD E. BURNETT

Brunner   Emil Brunner was Barth's theological ally in the *dialectical theology* movement in the 1920s and a

mediator of Barth's *theology* to the English-speaking world in the 1930s and 1940s.

Three years younger than Barth, Brunner was also a Swiss Calvinist, a supporter of Christian Socialism, and a small-town pastor (Brunner was pastor at Obstalden in Canton Glarus from 1916 to 1924). Barth and Brunner were introduced in the early 1910s by their common friend, Eduard *Thurneysen*. In 1916 they began an extensive correspondence that sheds light on their respective theological development and their personal relationship (see B–Br Br).

Brunner was first affiliated publicly with Barth through his glowing review of *Rom* I (1919). With the launch of ZZ (1923) and the publication of Brunner's anti-Schleiermacher polemic *Die Mystik und das Wort* (1924), Thurneysen formally brought Brunner into the dialectical theology circle by soliciting articles for ZZ. Brunner always remained a peripheral player in the dialectical theology group, however, as can be first detected in Barth's mixed review of *Die Mystik* in ZZ (1924).

Nonetheless, Brunner was easily associated with Barth in the theological public's mind due to their common central emphases: an energetic No! to nineteenth-century theology; a theology centered on *revelation*; a dynamic understanding of Scripture's *inspiration* (not "it is written" but "God speaks"); a theology centered on the divine-human *Jesus Christ* who is himself the *Word of God*; and the conviction that Protestant theology was in critical need of a fresh grounding.

By the late 1920s the differences within their similarities became apparent. Barth's first systematic work, *Die christliche Dogmatik im Entwurf* (1927), surprised his dialectical friends by positively appropriating Reformation and Catholic scholastic sources. Brunner, on the other hand, understood himself to be a theologian in service of the church by interacting with and challenging modern thought that was antagonistic to Christianity; he was a theologian "on the offensive," taking on existentialism, relativism, and atheism. In a 1929 ZZ article, Brunner argued that, in addition to theology's dogmatic task, there was a task that he labeled "eristics," from the Greek word *erizein* ("to debate"): "[It is the] task of eristic theology to point out how, through the Word of God, human reason is exposed partly as the source of a life-threatening error, and partly as the source of an incomplete human quest. . . . It is the most essential task of eristic theology to point out to *humanity* that it can only rightly understand itself in faith, that only through the Word of God does it receive what it seeks, that what it seeks in a distorted manner is known only in Christian faith" ("Other Task of Theology," 260).

From 1929 to 1933 Brunner and Barth engaged in an escalating "footnote war" over the proper task of theology and the nature of revelation: Brunner: "Other Task of Theology" (ZZ 7 [1929]: 255–76), *God and Man* (1936), *The Word and the World* (1931), "The Question of the 'Point of Contact' as a Problem for Theology" (ZZ 10 [1932]: 505–32); Barth: *CD* I/1/§2.1 (1932), "Abschied" (ZZ 11 [1933]: 536–44). Their argument boiled over in 1934 with Brunner's publication of "Nature and Grace: A Conversation with Karl Barth" and Barth's reply, "No! Answer to Brunner" (see *NTh*).

In "Nature and Grace," Brunner summarized Barth's position on natural theology and provided his own countertheses. For Brunner, the issue at stake was the church's ability and responsibility to be engaged with the modern person. Thus Brunner argued that there must be a *"point of contact"* between God and *humanity*, between *creation* and redemption: "Not even Karl Barth can deny that there is a *problem* concerning Christianity and *Culture*, Commandment and Ordinances, *Reason* and Revelation, and that this problem requires thoroughgoing theological treatment" (*NTh*, 19). But Barth did deny this problem. He rejected

Brunner's summary of his position, stating that he had no interest in natural theology, which Barth defined as "every (positive or negative) *formulation of a system* which claims to be theological, i.e. to interpret divine revelation, whose *subject*, however, differs fundamentally from the revelation in Jesus Christ, and whose *method* therefore differs equally from the exposition of Holy Scripture" (74–75). Barth asserted that the trajectory of Brunner's argument inevitably undercut and compromised the action of God's sovereign *grace*.

In 1938, Brunner announced a new direction in his theology with the publication of *Wahrheit als Begegnung*, which stated as his new theme the overcoming of the "subject-object opposition in Western thought."

While there would be further published arguments between the two theologians over the Oxford Group Movement (1936), communism (1948), and anthropology (1951), their theological and personal relationship essentially ended in 1934 over the natural theology debate. Nonetheless, their names remained linked in the English-speaking world due to the extremely slow pace of translating Barth's works. By 1946 only Barth's *Romans*, *CD* I/1, Gifford Lectures, and some other lectures had been published in English. By that time not only had seven major works and four lecture series by Brunner been translated, but he had also made lecture tours to the United States in 1928, to Great Britain in 1931, and served as visiting professor at Princeton Theological Seminary from 1938–1939.

Despite their common commitments, the Barth-Brunner theological alliance was unable to endure due to five fundamental differences: (1) Brunner's thinking always sought relationships in a "both/and" fashion, while Barth's thinking was more decisively "either/or" (what Brunner constantly complained about as Barth's "one-sidedness"); (2) Brunner did *theology* with explicit attention to *philosophy*, while Barth focused on reclaiming the task of *dogmatics*; (3) Brunner's intellectual engagement was primarily with contemporary thought, while Barth plumbed the depths of the theological tradition; (4) Brunner's "eristic" style displayed confidence in dispatching opponents (which Barth dismissed as Brunner's "school-marmish" attitude), while Barth always sought to "begin again at the beginning"; and (5) Brunner focused on the end benefit of theology for Christian living (a more subjective emphasis), while Barth focused on the end benefit of theology for Christian teaching (a more objective emphasis).

In the end, Barth and Brunner were not equal partners. In both their influence and personal relationship, Barth was always dominant. Brunner never became a decisive conversation partner in Barth's theological development; rather, he was one of many acquaintances who helped Barth clarify and enunciate his own theological insights.

K. Barth, *B–Br Br*; J. W. Hart, *Karl Barth vs. Emil Brunner* (2001); F. Jehle, *Emil Brunner* (2006); C. W. Kegley, ed., *The Theology of Emil Brunner* (1962).

JOHN W. HART

Bultmann One of the towering figures in New Testament studies and systematic *theology* in the twentieth century, Bultmann was born near Oldenburg on August 20, 1884. His father was a Lutheran minister. After studying at Tübingen and Berlin, he completed his degree in Marburg, where some of the leading New Testament scholars (Johannes Weiss and Adolf Jülicher) and one of the most respected Lutheran theologians of the time, Wilhelm **Herrmann**, were teaching. Encouraged by Weiss to pursue a doctoral degree, Bultmann stayed in Marburg, where he met Barth sometime in 1908. This was the beginning of a (mostly) friendly relationship spanning six decades, with peaks and valleys, depending to a large extent on the state of their theological (dis)agreements.

Their friendship developed at the home of Martin Rade, professor at Marburg and editor of *Die christliche Welt*, the popular journal affiliated with Ritschlianism. Both Bultmann and Barth participated in the evening conversations organized by Rade. As Barth left Marburg for Geneva (1909), the signs of their burgeoning friendship became infrequent: Bultmann sent him his first postcard in June 1911 with his best wishes on Barth's marriage. They probably saw each other only infrequently until the religious-socialist conference at Tambach in September 1919. Alongside Tillich, **Thurneysen**, Gogarten, and others, Bultmann was present in part because of his growing interest in socialism. By then, *Rom* I had been published. In September 1920, in a lecture on "Ethical and Mystical Religion in Primitive Christianity," Bultmann succinctly accepted Barth's critique of *culture* but forcefully rejected what he saw as an enthusiastic (*schwärmerisch*) and "arbitrary adaptation" and "renewal" of the "Pauline myth" classically summarized in the hymn of Philippians 2 (*Beginnings*, 232).

With *Rom* II a fruitful conversation and collaboration began. Indeed, Barth had toned down the romantic enthusiasm and was seeking to emphasize more strongly God's otherness. Bultmann taught in Breslau (1916–1920), Giessen (1920/1921), then in 1921 came to Marburg, where he remained until his death (1976). It was a surprise to many, including Barth, when Bultmann expressed agreement with much of *Rom* II. Bultmann's detailed review, published in *Die christliche Welt* (*Beginnings*, 100–120) was the beginning of a relatively close, but not very long, theological friendship. Barth's talk of God's "immediacy" in *Rom* I had been replaced by his emphasis on "indirectness," God's hiddenness in his *revelation*, his judgment in his *grace*. Many liberals and conservatives disliked such use of dialectical tensions, but not Bultmann, who had become sensitive through Herrmann to the unavoidability of paradoxical statements in theological discourse. Bultmann also welcomed Barth's overall approach to biblical interpretation, especially his focus on the subject matter itself rather than on historical-critical details. But Barth's deeply theological *exegesis* lacked one final step, namely, a critique of Paul's text from the standpoint of the subject matter, since even the apostle had been unable to always adequately say what he meant to say. What Bultmann advocated would mature into his demythologization program of 1941.

Another critique from 1922 that is also related to the program of demythologization and that would haunt the debates between the two theologians was Bultmann's critique of Barth's theological objectivism. As a Herrmannian, Bultmann took issue with any talk of a purely "objective reality," be it *God, faith, love*, or human existence. That does not mean that Bultmann "subjectivized" God. What mattered to him was reality insofar as it encounters someone or as it is "for" someone, as the Reformers had stressed in some of their writings. Despite these criticisms, which foreshadowed deeper disagreements, there seemed to be enough agreement for both theologians to perceive themselves as working in the same direction.

Barth further stimulated Bultmann's reflection with his lecture on "The Word of God as the Task of Theology" (ET: "Task"), in which Barth spoke of the impossibility yet necessity of speaking of God. Bultmann was enthralled by the lecture. In January 1925, Bultmann published an article, "What Does It Mean to Speak of God?" in which he raised the same basic question, but which he answered in a way that began to trouble Barth. Indeed, one of Bultmann's theses stated that one cannot speak of God without speaking of one's human existence. This sort of correlation between God and *humanity* worried Barth, for it seemed to reopen the door to the kind of theological confusions he had witnessed in the fall of 1914. Barth was even more puzzled by Bultmann's small book on *Jesus* (1926), in which Barth found a very partial presentation centered on Jesus' teachings to the exclusion of his deeds, his crucifixion and resurrection, as well as the projection, so typical of the modern lives of Jesus, of the author's personal ideas and ideals onto the person of Jesus (in Bultmann's case, Jesus had become a dialectical theologian!). Bultmann read the New Testament selectively, and as a historical source rather than as a *witness*. Despite these worries, the two theologians maintained a public appearance of unity. And when in 1925 Erik Peterson issued his pamphlet against them, they viewed their responses as fitting neatly together and were hoping to publish them together (see "C&T").

The conversation became more difficult after 1926, as Bultmann sought to convince Barth of the importance of Heidegger's phenomenology for theology to avoid a crudely objectifying, abstract conceptuality (Heidegger had arrived in Marburg in 1923 and soon began conversing with Bultmann). In a letter from June 1928, Bultmann expresses both disappointment and gratitude: "You have a sovereign scorn for modern work in philosophy, especially phenomenology. . . . It seems to me that you are guided by a concern that theology should achieve emancipation from philosophy. You try to achieve this by ignoring philosophy. The price you pay for this is that of falling prey to an outdated philosophy. . . . I need hardly stress that I have learned, and learn, and hope still to learn many decisive things from you. In relation to you I am the recipient, the student, albeit a critical student. More important than the criticisms are the thanks that I owe you, and the criticisms themselves have their source in the conviction that I am at one with you in the concern that you represent in your *Dogmatics*" (*LKB–RB*, 38–39).

Barth was unmoved by Bultmann's invitation to learn from Heidegger's existential-ontological approach, for he could only see it as leading back to *liberalism*'s anthropocentrism. The root of the problem had to do with differing views of what constitutes the proper subject matter of theology. Bultmann tended to consider faith, rather than God's Word, to be the object of theology. In other words, he could not follow Barth's stricter theological objectivism (an objectivism that was nevertheless inherently oriented toward the human subject). The two men maintained friendly relations even as they realized their respective paths were leading them in different directions. But Barth's distrust deepened in 1930, as two other members of the dialectical school, Gogarten and *Brunner*, were publishing articles that revealed interest in anthropology and *natural theology*. In Barth's mind, their talk of faith as a human possibility pointed to a possible end of their collaboration. Bultmann, for his part, was not certain these differences were basic. But the breakup took place in the fall of 1933 when the journal *Zwischen den Zeiten* was dissolved.

Still, Barth and Bultmann met several times in each other's homes. They belonged to a group of theologians from Bonn and Marburg who were appalled by the "brown wave" that had taken over Germany. Bultmann expressed in a letter his solidarity with Barth's energetic response to the events in his pamphlet *TEh* (July 1933). Barth, however, had expected that Bultmann would eventually join the "Deutsche-Christen," that is, German Protestants who welcomed Hitler's "revolution" and sought to apply its anti-Semitic laws to Protestant churches. Bultmann was quite shocked when he heard that from Barth himself (*LKB–RB*, 75). In Barth's opinion, anyone who engaged in some sort of natural theology was likely to join those who saw the hand of God

in the historical events of 1933. Bultmann's interest in natural theology was clear, since he claimed that a preunderstanding of revelation is given universally with human existence and that this preunderstanding represents a point of contact for revelation in human existence. But Bultmann had no inclination to support the Nazi regime or to apply its ideology to the church and thus was comforted in his impression that Barth had somehow misunderstood him.

Barth's dismissal from Bonn (1935) greatly limited the possibility of dialogue. Only after World War II did they meet again. By then, collaboration was unlikely. Bultmann's demythologization campaign and his existential interpretation of the New Testament (1941), in which he responded to what he saw as the rise of a rigid *biblicism* and doctrinalism among pastors and theologians who had opposed the Nazi regime, was soon at the center of theological debates and would remain there for two decades. Barth, for his part, could only lament the fact. He was largely unaware that, despite Bultmann's different stance with regard to the authority of Scripture (a stance that had something to do with Bultmnann's Lutheran identity, whereas Barth, in conformity with his Reformed roots, maintained the human and divine character of Scripture in its entirety), Bultmann was, like him, trying to express the idea that God's revelation is an event that no one can master and that faith alone discerns. Revelation disrupts our attempts at securing ourselves and calls us to trust in God. *Science* and myth, with their objectifications, support our natural desire for security, whereas the message of the New Testament compels us to give up the chimera of security and to trust in God. This is the meaning of *justification* by faith alone.

Bultmann's aim was never simply destructive but also constructive: he attempted to recover the truly miraculous and indeed supranatural character of revelation, beyond its immanentization and objectification in mythological and scientific discourses, so that the *gospel* might encounter people anew and become meaningful in their existence. For Bultmann, this was essentially a hermeneutical task: the kerygma had to be translated in order for it to become relevant again. For the true scandal of the gospel to become apparent, the false scandal, created by the fact that our worldview is radically different from the worldview presupposed by the biblical authors, had to be eliminated. In other words, as Bultmann already advocated in 1922, the text of the New Testament has to be criticized from the standpoint of the subject matter to which it points. Barth was certainly willing to criticize the theological tradition from the standpoint of the subject matter of theology, but he was opposed to a critique of the *Bible* itself.

A thorough but belated exchange took place in 1952, as Barth wrestled with Bultmann in his doctrine of *reconciliation* (*CD* IV/1:9–10). Barth published his "attempt to understand" ("RB–AUH"), to which Bultmann replied with a long, fascinating letter (*LKB–RB*, 87–102). According to Bultmann, to argue that one must first give one's assent to the proposition that Christ's cross is salvific in order then to trust in God is an objectification that only reveals one's need to secure oneself. After Bultmann's letter, Barth realized that the heart of their disagreement had to do with the notion of "objectification," with the fact that for Bultmann anything meaningful existentially is bound to be relational and never merely an "objective" reality (*LKB–RB*, 93 and 106). But this is ultimately where Barth and Bultmann came closest to each other: both rejected mere "objectivity" and wanted to focus on the relation between God and his creature. As Barth later wrote: "Since God in His deity is human, this culture must occupy itself neither with God in Himself nor with man in himself but with the man-encountering God and the God-encountering man and with their

dialogue and history, in which their communion takes place and comes to its fulfillment" (*HG*, 55). In his mature theology, as a consequence of his radical Christocentrism, Barth suggested that the word *theology* should be replaced by *theo-anthropology* (*EvT*, 9). He was aware that such statements were not too distant from Bultmann's existential theology. But he also wondered whether this proximity could lead to an agreement. Barth was concerned that "neither the people of *Israel* nor the Christian community appears to have constitutive meaning" in Bultmann's theology (*HG*, 56). Barth was also concerned that a theo-anthropology could easily be reversed and become an anthropo-theology. Indeed, despite important convergences, some equally important divergences on the starting point of theology but also on Scripture, Christology, and Trinitarian theology made it impossible for Barth to see real promise in Bultmann's existential theology.

—————

R. Bultmann, "New Testament and Mythology," in *New Testament and Mythology and Other Basic Writings*, ed. and trans. S. M. Ogden (1984), 1–43; idem, "What Does It Mean to Speak of God?" in *Faith and Understanding* I, ed. R. W. Funk, trans. L. P. Smith (1969), 53–65; C. Chalamet, *Dialectical Theologians* (2005); J. D. Smart, *The Divided Mind of Modern Theology* (1967).

CHRISTOPHE CHALAMET

Calvin Barth's theological engagement with John Calvin was deep, complex, and sustained throughout his *preaching* and teaching career. Fundamentally dipolar in character, it combined the highest regard for and agreement with Calvin on the one hand and the most incisive critique and disagreement with him on the other. This dipolarity can be illustrated by the following two quotations: "there is hardly a better teacher apart from the biblical prophets and apostle than he," Barth said on the occasion of the four hundredth anniversary of Calvin's death in 1964 (*FGG*, 109). On the other hand, Barth told a group of Wuppertal students in 1968, "my theology has, let's say, seven or eight differences from Calvin's" (*G-1964–1968*, 489).

A study of Barth's theological relationship with Calvin by Sung Wook Chung appeared in 2002. It helpfully emphasizes this dipolarity but is vitiated, first, by wrongly ascribing a central role to Kant in Barth's *theology* and then accusing Barth of using Kant to critique Calvin; and second, by arguing and putting forward a nonsensical conclusion: "Calvin's role in Barth's theology was not only formative, constitutive, and determinative but at the same time subsidiary and even negligible and dismissible" (223). How can one have it both ways?

Before considering Barth's complex relationship with Calvin, it is necessary to recount the historical background of his encounter with Calvin, which began in the first semester of his theological studies in Berne in 1905 when he was formally introduced to Calvin's theology. Barth's father, Fritz, lectured on the Reformation and set forth Calvin's theology by dealing with Calvin's life from beginning to end (*ThC*, xiii, 131). Yet the youthful Barth did not immerse himself in Calvin as he did in Kant and *Schleiermacher* until his vicarship at St. Peter's Church in Geneva, 1909–1911 when, as he tells us, he plunged into Calvin's *Institutes*. The impact was profound. But as Barth confessed later, he read Calvin "with the peculiar glasses of [his] student years." Indeed, he admitted that "Calvin would hardly have been very pleased at the sermons which I preached in his pulpit then." He toyed with the idea of combining idealist theology with the reformation but later abandoned the project as not feasible (*Karl Barth*, 53–54, 57).

The move to the Safenwil pastorate in 1911; his close association with Eduard *Thurneysen*, who shared his interest in Calvin; and the use of Calvin's commentaries for the preparation of his sermons, all contributed to a greater familiarity with Calvin's theology. Barth's growing involvement with the Socialist movement during his Safenwil village pastorate was nourished in part by Calvin's concept of God's kingdom. His 1910 and 1911 essays "Der christliche Glaube und die Geschichte" (*VkA* II, 155–212) and "Jesus Christus und die soziale Bewegung" (*VkA* II, 380–417; ET: *JCMSJ*) reflect the influence of both Calvin and Zwingli. Later, Barth's intensive study of Romans was facilitated by Calvin's systematic interpretation of Paul's epistle. When he rewrote *Rom* I (1919), he spent much time studying Calvin (*Karl Barth*, 114). *Rom* II was even more Calvinian, Barth stated.

A more evident and intensive engagement with Calvin occurred in 1922 during the first year of his professorship at Göttingen. Barth gave a summer semester course on "The Theology of John Calvin." He described his encounter with Calvin to Thurneysen in highly expressionistic language: "Calvin is a cataract, a primeval forest, a demonic power, something directly down from Himalaya, absolutely Chinese, strange, mythological; I lack completely the means, the suction cups, even to assimilate this phenomenon, not to speak of presenting it adequately" (*RevTh*, 101).

Calvin's inaccessibility spurred Barth on. He carried forward his interest in Calvin in his lectures, "The Word of God and the Task of the Ministry" (1922), "The Doctrinal Task of the Reformed Churches" (1923) (ET of both in *WGWM*), and in the *Göttingen Dogmatics* (1924–1926), which, following Calvin, he called "Instruction in the Christian Religion." Thereafter, the time and space he devoted to Calvin in the *CD*, special lectures on Calvin, Calvin's *Geneva Catechism*, and the numerous seminars on Calvin's *Institutes* exceeds the attention given to any other theologian, with *Luther* running a close second. Yet critical appropriation rather than repristination was Barth's chief aim. One needs to learn from theologians like Calvin, Barth said, but the primary binding of a Reformed theologian is to the *Bible*.

A few aspects of Barth's agreement and disagreement with Calvin can now be set out, but we should keep in mind that there is always a measure of accord and discord in each area or doctrinal *loci*.

First, the disagreements. Barth differed dramatically from Calvin with regard to *election*. Yet this doctrine mirrors both his appreciation of and major difference from Calvin. Like Calvin, Barth affirmed the "eternal, unconditional and twofold" character of election, its importance and its great mystery. But he differed from Calvin on the *exegesis* of Romans 9–11, Calvin's wrong emphasis (in Barth's unfair estimation) on experience and Calvin's inadequate christological grounding of election. Barth replaced Calvin's *decretum absolutum* with the *decretum concretum*, that is, God's self-*determination* in Christ, to make election good news, "the sum of the *gospel*" (CD II/2:798; see "Calvin" in Name Index). Barth also disagreed with Calvin's platonic view of immortality (III/2:384), his formal rather than Trinitarian concept of God in *providence* (III/3:115), his abstract concept of *sin* (IV/1:367–68), his particularistic doctrine of *salvation* (IV/2:520; IV/3.1:17–18), his overemphasis on mortification (IV/2:574–75), his aristocratic view of ministerial office (IV/3.1:33), and his doctrine of infant *baptism* (IV/4:114–15).

Second, his agreements with Calvin: Barth took his cue from Calvin on the Scripture principle, the *knowledge of God*, the one *covenant* of *grace, gospel and law*, Christ's threefold office, *justification* and *sanctification*, the *Christian life*, to name only a few *loci*. Yet what he took he reworked and renewed in his inimitable, unique, and creative way. Barth was a truly ecumenical theologian who embraced the whole theological tradition of the Western and Eastern churches and of both Protestantism and **Roman Catholicism**. Yet he gave Calvin an especially significant place in his theology. Under Calvin's influence his theology became a biblical theology. As Eberhard Busch comments: "Because of the characteristic concentration on the '*Word of God*,' this theology has aptly been called a 'theology of the Word'; the term '*dialectical theology*' is less apt, but it does describe its characteristic forms" (143–44). It was also under Calvin's influence, as distinguished from Luther's, that Barth's theology was given its ethical turn, emphasizing that dogmatics is *ethics* and ethics is *dogmatics*.

Yes, "notwithstanding all the necessary criticisms and corrections, there is hardly a better teacher apart from the biblical prophets and apostles than he" (*FGG*, 109). It is not surprising then that Barth placed the portrait of Calvin on the same level on his study wall as the portrait of his beloved composer, Mozart. Both men, in his view, were special ministers of God for whom he was grateful.

K. Barth, *ThC*; E. Busch, *Karl Barth*, trans. J. Bowden (1994); S. W. Chung, *Admiration and Challenge* (2002); D. Gibson, *Reading the Decree* (2009); W. Klempa, "Barth as a Scholar and Interpreter of Calvin," in *Papers Presented at a Colloquium on Calvin Studies*, ed. J. H. Leith (1994), 31–44.

WILLIAM KLEMPA

Christian Life   A passion for the Christian life was a hallmark of Barth's *theology* from the very beginning. The phrase embraces a complex range of ideas, all having to do with human existence as a response to and as energized by God's *grace*. These include *justification*, *sanctification*, *ethics*, conversion, *witness*, personhood, the *church*, *salvation*, and even religious experience or affectivity. Quite simply, "the Christian life" denotes the life that is God's gift to us in *Jesus Christ* by the power of the *Holy Spirit*.

Barth's concern for questions of Christian living may be traced to his days as a student of Wilhelm **Herrmann**. For a liberal such as Herrmann, what Christianity was finally all "about" was not ecclesiastical *dogma*, but personal religious experience—"the communion of the Christian with God"—mediated by a living relationship with the Savior. Not knowledge about the historical Jesus, but life in Jesus; not proofs of God's existence, but *prayer* to the Father in heaven. Although Barth would eventually move very far from Herrmann and modernist Protestantism, he remained in important ways a faithful pupil of his teacher. Theology itself presupposes involvement in the Christian life. It is an activity of the church—thus, *CD*. Theology is really just a form of intellectually reflective prayer, as underscored by the many places where Barth offers extended reflection on prayer as the quintessential act of *faith* (e.g., *CD* I/2:453–54; III/3:264–88; IV/2:703–6; *EvT*, 159–70). Barth's entire theology, we might say, is a performance designed to direct the reader to a point beyond all talk about *God*, to the place where God himself speaks, disclosing himself to us as our *gracious* Lord. The primarily practical rather than speculative character of theology was a major theme of the Protestant Reformers, and it was a conviction that Barth shared.

A simple concept Barth often used to talk about the Christian life was that of "eccentricity." We do not, he believed, learn who we are or what must do by introspecting. The Christian person is determined not by self-consciousness in the manner of Descartes, but by a word that comes from outside the self, in an unscripted encounter with Another. The ek-centric person is one who has been displaced from the center of his or her moral universe: "Your life is hidden with Christ in God" (Col. 3:3). Moreover, since the **Word of God** names an eschatological happening, the Christian life must be understood as a life in motion, realized in event, decision, action,

history, a "hastening"—as Barth put it in a conscious echo of Christoph Blumhardt—"that waits."

The themes just cited were much in evidence in Barth's early mature theology—for instance, in the two great Romans commentaries of 1919 and 1922. Nor did Barth ever abandon them: in his late lectures on ethics, aptly titled *The Christian Life*, the eschatological note sounds out just as clearly as ever. But to the extent that *eschatology* in the earlier Barth was determined by a dialectic of death and **resurrection, time** and **eternity**, his depiction of the Christian life was likewise constrained. The ethical practice implied by *Rom* II would be a kind of imitation of Jesus' own death and resurrection in our own lives, a perennial "dying to self." Again, it is not that the later Barth rejected this view, though he did come to see it as abstract and one-sided.

Barth's later, more nuanced accounts of the Christian person were a function of his new insights concerning the being and action of God. For if the God of **revelation** is really the triune God, then his intrusion into the **world** in Jesus and the Spirit means the constitution of human beings as real agents in time and history. "Because I live, you also will live" (John 14:19). Barth expresses the positive correspondence between God's being and that of the Christian using the important concept of "acknowledgment" (*Anerkennung*; for this idea, see I/1:205–8).

"Acknowledgment" is both a relational and a self-involving notion. On the one hand, to acknowledge another person is to recognize or make space for that person in our lives. The person who acknowledges God yields to God's authority, understood not as raw power but as the authority of his grace. On the other hand, one does not rightly acknowledge grace by being absolutely passive. As genuine faith is a form of obedience (Rom. 1:5), so the acknowledgment of God cannot help but issue in new thoughts, new actions, even new experiences. It is telling that Barth's treatment of *Anerkennung* unfolds under the heading: "The Word of God and Experience," in an obvious challenge to those critics who said he had no room for experience in his theology (209). The new life of the believer is also marked by transformed affections. Barth was as unwilling to deny this aspect of Christian existence as he was to make a fetish of it.

Barth's first truly great writing on the Christian life, however, occurs later in I/2, in the section titled "Das Leben der Kinder Gottes," "The Life of the Children of God" (§18). Significantly, this section appears under the larger heading, "The Outpouring of the Holy Spirit." It is as the revelation of God is enacted not just by the Father and the Son but by the Spirit that it becomes an event in which human beings actively participate. The thesis preceding this section is lapidary in its precision: "Where it is believed and acknowledged in the Holy Spirit, the revelation of God creates men who do not exist without seeking God in Jesus Christ, and who cannot cease to testify that he has found them" (I/2:362).

Barth's initial formulation of the matter is negative because he wants to head off any suggestion that seeking God and testifying to him is something we are capable of on our own. Only by virtue of God's gracious act are there Christians at all: men and women who seek God. They seek him, only because he has first found them. Nevertheless, *there are Christians*, people whose lives are determined in a twofold way as a seeking and a testifying, a being and a doing. Barth unpacks the "being" aspect in §18.2 as "The Love of God," and the "doing" aspect in §18.3 as "The Praise of God." The first takes the form of an exposition of the commandment to "love the Lord thy God with all thy heart, and with all thy soul, and with all thy mind, and with all thy strength." The second explores the ethical imperative that arises from this, the command to "love thy neighbor as thyself" (Mark 12:29–31). Both these sections will repay careful study.

Barth borrowed the title "The Life of the Children of God" from his former teacher, Adolf von **Harnack**, noting: "without any change in material significance we might just as well use the title 'The Life of the Church'" (I/2:368). Just that alternate title, however, marks the distance between Harnack's liberal individualism and Barth's ecclesial vision of the Christian life. For Barth, there is no Christian life that is not at the same time a life in the church. The reason for this is the universal scope of God's saving action. God acts in Christ for the *salvation* of all humankind. The church exists as "the provisional representation of the whole world of *humanity* justified in him" (IV/1:643). This means that every Christian is called to a life of building up the *ecclesia*, precisely so that it may fulfill its responsibilities toward those who have not yet heard the gospel; or toward those who, having once heard it, have turned away; or toward those who have heard it, but failed to realize that it is good news for them too. The Christian life is necessarily ecclesial, not because Christians are called to turn their back on the world, but precisely for the world's sake. In short, there is no clear line dividing soteriology and ecclesiology. While Barth finds Cyprian's formula *extra ecclesiam nulla salus*, "outside the church there is no salvation," to state the matter too strongly, he does defend it in a modified form. While it is not the case that all those outside the church are necessarily lost, it is certainly the case that the Christian life of faith, *hope*, and *love* is unthinkable apart from the church. "What is true is that the typical and ministerial separation of an individual, in virtue of which he is distinguished and marked off from other men as one who believes and knows, is as such his separation to life and *ministry* in and with the community. If he does not have it as such, he does not have it at all. . . . What is true is that there is no legitimate private Christianity" (IV/1:689).

Barth is sometimes criticized for a certain idealism in matters of ecclesiology, ethics, and the Christian life. There is some merit to this accusation. At times one longs for him to descend from those long, looping trains of thought in the large print, and even from the riches of Scripture in the small print, into the realm of the empirical and practical. In short, there often seems to be less concrete display of the Christian life than one might hope for. At one level, this is simply a question of the way his mind worked. The task of *dogmatics* as he saw it is primarily a matter of conceptual description and analysis, not the giving of examples. Yet there are many exceptions to this rule. In the farewell lectures he gave at the end of his teaching career, for instance, he sought to give an account of the "existentials" of the theological life, marked as it is by wonder, concern, commitment, faith, solitude, doubt, prayer, and love (*EvT*). While Barth is writing specifically about the *vocation* of the theologian, he could be describing the actions and passions of Christian existence more generally. Finally, we should note that Barth might question the notion of concreteness being employed by his critics. Which is more concrete and practical, he would ask—our own social and psychological perceptions, or the testimony of Holy Scripture?

Of the many set pieces on the Christian life in the *CD*, among the more remarkable is the part-section titled "The Direction of the Son" in IV/2. This extraordinary treatise is designed to show how knowledge of the risen Lord issues in self-knowledge on the part of the Christian. If Christ (ontologically) be raised from the dead, then we (noetically, spiritually, and practically) cannot but know ourselves as those who live with him and in him, receiving concrete "direction" (*Weisung*) for our lives. This text shows how easily Barth's thought approaches to a doctrine of participation in God's own being: "In what takes place between the man Jesus and us

when we become Christians, God himself lives. Nor does he live an alien life. He lives his own most proper life"—to wit, the life of the *Trinity* (IV/2:342). The treatments of sanctification, of the upbuilding of the church, and of Christian love in this same volume add further precision to Barth's conception of the new person.

Barth may be said, then, to have an extremely high doctrine of the Christian life. Yet the extravagance of the claims should not detract from what is finally the deeply personal character of Christian existence. As a disciple of Jesus Christ I am not called to live some generic life of saintliness, but precisely *this* life, with its joys and sorrows, its possibilities and limitations, its ordinary duties and extraordinary encounters. "I came that they may have life and have it abundantly" (John 10:10). It is for me, a sinner, that Christ has come in the flesh, thereby sanctifying the limited time of my life, and setting me free for the active love of God and neighbor. Living out of the abundant grace of God, bearing *witness* of that grace to others, the Christian presents to the world the image of "a strangely human person" (*CL*, 204).

K. Barth, *CL*; idem, *Pr*; S. Hauerwas, "On Honor," in *Dispatches from the Front* (1994), 58–79; D. Lauber, *Barth on the Descent into Hell* (2004); J. Mangina, *Karl Barth on the Christian Life* (2001); J. Webster, *Barth's Moral Theology* (1998).

JOSEPH L. MANGINA

Christology

Christology While Barth is renowned for promoting a *dogmatics* that is "christologically determined as a whole and in all its parts" (*CD* I/2:123), his actual Christology presents readers with a daunting interpretive challenge: coming to grips with an account of Christ's person that is manifestly traditional in some respects but staggeringly innovative in others. On one level, Barth rejects the supposition that religious experience, cultural and moral development, or historical-critical research—mainstays of late-nineteenth- and early-twentieth-century European theological *liberalism*—set the terms for dogmatic reflection. Drawing inspiration from a range of patristic, medieval, and scholastic sources, he instead develops a Christology that harks back to the Chalcedonian Definition (451 CE). Indeed, every section of the *CD* expresses Barth's conviction that Christ is the "Word made flesh": one person, in whom divinity and *humanity* unite inconfusedly, unalterably, undividedly, and inseparably. On another level, Barth's Christology is no restatement of patristic wisdom, much less a "neo-orthodox" rehearsal of classical Protestant claims. An array of bold exegetical ventures, a coordination of insights drawn from both wings of the magisterial Reformation, a distinctive brand of *actualism* that connects the doctrines of Christ and *God*, and, finally, a powerful treatment of the threefold office: all this marks Barth's determination to think novelly about Christ in a late modern context.

The famous second edition of his commentary on Romans showcases Barth's conviction that christological reflection begins and ends with the *Bible*. Appropriately so: what Barth discovers in Paul's letter is not the bare fact of an "infinite qualitative distinction" but Christ himself—one "who exposes the gulf which separates God and man, and, by exposing it, bridges it"; one who reveals the faithfulness of God through "the inferno of His complete solidarity with all the *sin* and weakness and misery of the flesh" (*ER*, 31 and 105). This emphasis on Scripture continues in the *CD*. Granted the shift in genre and a newfound delight in scholastic distinctions (of particular note being the *anhypostasia*/*enhypostasia* pairing, which emphasizes that the divine Son forms the subject of Christ's person), Barth continues to insist that Scripture alone supplies christological inquiry with its source and norm. On some occasions,

then, one finds lengthy expositions of a single verse or phrase—thus the important §15 of *CD* I/2, which analyzes John 1:14, and the thrilling discussion of Christ as the "Light of Life" in IV/3.1. On other occasions, the biblical narratives are put front and center—thus the identification of the tripartite plot of the Synoptics as normative for reflection on Jesus' atoning *history* and the remarkable excursus on Gethsemane in IV/1. What motivates this constant recourse to Scripture? Well, certainly not naive *"biblicism"*—an approach to *exegesis* that exchanges a reductionistic brand of *historical criticism* for its equally troubling supernatural twin. It is rather that, as Barth understands it, Christ just *is* the cutting-edge of God's *revelation* to humankind. He is not a word that God spoke; he is the Word that God graciously speaks. And it is he, with the *Holy Spirit* and before the Father, who indwells the human words of Scripture, rendering them witnesses to God's saving work. The theologian's task, accordingly, is to respond to God's self-presentation: to conform one's thought and writing to the person one meets in the "strange new world" of the Old and New Testaments.

With respect to the dogmatic yield of this engagement with Scripture, one finds a treatment of Christ that often recalls *Calvin* and his followers. Barth posits, for instance, a "sharp distinction and even antithesis" (IV/2:61) between Christ's divine and human essences, and staunchly resists construals of the *communicatio idiomatum* that suggest a deification of Christ's humanity. Further, and in line with the finale of the second book of the *Institutes*, Barth offers a vivid account of Christ's decision to suffer and die on behalf of sinners. Divinely *and* humanly, Christ assents to the will of the Father and sets his face toward Jerusalem; divinely *and* humanly, Christ enacts an identity that culminates in his being the "Judge Judged in our Place" (IV/1:§59.2). The dogmatic payoff here is significant. One of the more worrying features of liberal Protestant thought—a bland commendation of Christ's moral decency that seems unrelated to the gospel narratives—is replaced with a striking exposition of Christ's obedience-unto-death.

Barth's Christology also has connections with the other wing of the magisterial Reformation. Initial hints of a "Lutheran" sensibility are present in the Romans commentary: Barth coordinates talk of the "hidden" Son with a description of the "blessed exchange," hailing Christ's death as that which reveals "the faithfulness of God in the depths of *hell*" (*ER*, 97). The *CD* intensifies this emphasis—so much that Luther's 1535 commentary on Galatians may have exerted as much influence on Barth as works by Calvin and the Reformed. The Word's assumption of "flesh," for instance, reveals God's decision to exist "in the sequence and fellowship of men who had fallen victim to the judgment of God" (IV/4:54); it makes plain God's willingness to stand in solidarity with those who disregard and violate the law. And Barth does not shrink from the claim that the divine Son suffers and dies on the cross. There is of course no endorsement of the *genus tapeinoticum*, much less an anticipation of Moltmann's overblown *theopaschitism*. Yet Barth follows **Luther** and others in refusing to restrict suffering to Christ's human essence. Because the *indivise* and *inseperabiliter* adverbs of the Chalcedonian Definition must be taken seriously, because Christ is *one* person in two essences, the cross is "the passion of God Himself" (IV/1:245). On Calvary, the Son endures God's crushing rejection of sin; he "lets a catastrophe which might be quite remote from Him approach Him and affect His very heart" (III/3:357).

These claims about the cross connect with Barth's abiding belief that the economic activity of God ought to control reflection on God's immanent, Trinitarian relationships. Nowhere is this more evident than in IV/1. In the pivotal §59, Barth refuses to avoid "the astounding conclusion of a divine obedience" (IV/1:202) and insists on "the offensive fact that there is in God Himself an above and a below, a *prius* and a *posterius*, a superiority and a subordination" (200–201). The logic is compelling: since divine revelation is *self*-revelation, the economic relationship between Christ and the Father articulates the immanent relationship that obtains between God's first and second ways of being. Obedience can therefore neither be restricted to Christ's humanity nor deemed a temporary condition of the Word incarnate; one must posit a relationship between Father and Son that, for all **eternity**, involves an act of fatherly begetting and an act of filial obedience. Precisely for this reason, in fact, Barth's striking treatment of Christ's humanity is complemented by a robust affirmation of Christ's divinity. There is no disconnect between God's eternal being, God's revelatory self-communication qua Son, and the concrete fact of Christ's obedient life-unto-death. With the **incarnation**, we have the "genuine article . . . God Himself in His true deity. The humility in which He dwells and acts in **Jesus Christ** is not alien to Him, but proper to Him" (193).

What does Barth mean, though, when he claims that "the inward divine relationship between the One who rules and commands in majesty and the One who obeys in humility is *identical* with the very different relationship between God and one of His creatures, a man" (203)? One answer is that Christ's history is only the economic outworking of God's eternal decision to relate lovingly to humankind, and does not affect God's being as such. On this reckoning, while the *logos asarkos* (the disincarnate Word) is not other than the obedient *logos incarnandus* and *logos ensarkos* (the Word who will incarnate, the Word enfleshed), these modes of existence must be differentiated. The Son's **mission** can be correlated with his procession from the Father, but this temporal event does not impinge upon its eternal antecedent. The incarnation is an event that stands apart from God's immanent life. Another possible answer is that God's second way of being, for all eternity, becomes and *is* the *logos ensarkos*—Jesus Christ, *vere deus vere homo*. On this reckoning, Barth's references to divine "self-*determination*" do more than underscore God's pretemporal decision to incarnate. They point up the most radical implication of Barth's doctrine of *election*—namely, that God lifts the concrete history of Jesus Christ into the *time* and space of the divine life; that God defines Godself, as Son, in terms of the Son's actual journey into the "far country." For sure, it remains important to parse out the Son's various modes of existence and, more generally, to differentiate the immanent and economic *Trinity*. Failure to do so risks suggesting that God's being is reducible to God's action in and for the *world*—an obvious mistake. But dogmatic distinctions of this kind must be understood in light of God's decision to assign himself an identity, as Son, that is always already bound to the concrete history of Jesus Christ. The doctrines of Christ, election, and God coinhere in an ontologically significant way.

While this issue has proven controversial, the second answer strikes me as the most compelling way to approach the later stages of *CD*. Barth's acclamation of the "humanity of God" is not a poetic turn of phrase. It is a statement about God's inclusion of the concrete history of Jesus Christ in the divine life; it is a way of signaling that God's *love* for humankind has a depth that "classical theism" cannot imagine. To read Barth in this way, moreover, does not require the supposition that God's being is unavoidably conditioned by God's economic activity. The point is simply that God freely wills to be God in *this* way; that *Gottes Gnadenwahl* (God's election of *grace*) is God's sovereign decision to draw the concrete person of Christ into the time and space of God's eternal being, so as to establish an everlasting

covenant between God and humankind. What else, after all, does it mean for Barth to say that "in the pre-temporal eternity of God, the eternal divine decision as such has as its object and content the existence of this one created being, the man Jesus of Nazareth" (II/2:116); that Jesus Christ "is God as He takes part in the event which constitutes the divine being" (IV/1:129)?

Granted that Christ is the subject of election, he is also the *object* of election. Because he lives for God and others, enacting an identity perfectly correspondent with the Father's gracious direction, Jesus' history is "ontologically decisive" (III/2:135) for every one of us. The covenant really is fulfilled. We have been released from hostility toward God and the slothful negligence of our fellows; we are propelled, now and forevermore, toward lives characterized by *gratitude*, responsibility, and joyful obedience. Just as Christ is the key for understanding who God is, so Christ— *not* Adam and Eve—is the key to understanding who we are.

How exactly, though, does Christ displace the "old" human, corrupted and plagued by sin? This question animates the christological sections of IV/1–3, which ground Barth's account of *reconciliation*. Guiding Barth's exposition is a creative appropriation of the *munus triplex* motif—Christ's threefold office of priest, king, and prophet—and an intriguing understanding of the two "states" of humiliation and exaltation. Christ's priestly work is the starting point for IV/1, albeit with a figurative switch: Barth follows earlier Reformed thinkers in conceptualizing *atonement* in forensic terms and treating Christ's death as the pivot around which *justification* turns. Christ's identity as the "royal man" is explicated in IV/2; the prior descriptions of Christ's justifying death in IV/1 are now complemented with an account of his sanctifying life. There is another shift of focus, too: while IV/1 associated the state of humiliation with the divine Son, IV/2 balances this emphasis with a careful description of Jesus as the exalted human. Finally, in IV/3.1 Barth identifies Christ as the ultimate prophet, decisive in his victory over falsehood and brilliantly declarative of God's kingdom. Christ's divinity and humanity are treated together, and Barth writes movingly about Christ's guidance of his church and Christ's lordship in the world.

While Barth's soteriology is examined elsewhere in this volume (see forgiveness of sins, justification, reconciliation, resurrection of Jesus Christ, *salvation, sanctification*), notice that this exposition of reconciliation brings into view an implication of everything said thus far: for Barth, reflection on Christ's person means reflection on Christ's work. Put a bit differently, thinking rightly about Christ's identity as the "electing God" and the "elected human," one person in two essences, requires attending to the life that Christ leads before God, with and for his fellows. What is the content of this life? Nothing other than the perfect realization of God's exuberant love; nothing other than God's insistence that humanity be released from sin and fitted to participate in joyful covenantal fellowship with God. To say "Jesus Christ," then, is to identify a divine and human *history* that passes from cradle to cross to resurrected glory, and that renders every human being a child of God. Christology and soteriology are two sides of the same coin

It need hardly be noted that these remarks only scratch the surface of Barth's account of Jesus Christ. More could be said about the relationship between Christology and the doctrines of God, election, *creation*, and the human; more could be said too about Barth's engagement with historical-critical scholarship, his treatment of patristic materials, and his relationship to various medieval, modern, and contemporary authors. My goal has been only to sketch how Barth's Christology maintains classical standards while breaking significant new ground. One might even say, a touch mischievously, that Barth fulfills Schleiermacher's call for a reforming theology that incorporates orthodox and heterodox (*not* heretical) insights. Certainly one finds in *CD* a much-needed riposte to liberal equivocations about Christ's deity. Noteworthy, too, is Barth's willingness to draw on the insights of others when developing his Christology—a salutary rebuke to those who condemn any reliance on "tradition" as an exercise in false consciousness. Yet neither a critique of liberal Christology nor a respect for past masters ever overwhelms what Barth described as the "quite specific *astonishment* [that] stands at the beginning of every theological perception, inquiry, and thought, in fact at the root of every theological word" (*EvT*, 64)—an astonishment that enabled this often-misunderstood author to buck the allure of mere convention and to produce a dogmatics that moves Christian thinking forward, while not losing touch with time-honored convictions. It follows too that those who delight in this Christology must beware any slavish reiteration of their hero's arguments. As Barth would doubtless remind us, "the image of the invisible God" and the "firstborn of all creation" (Col. 1:15) is no academic object of interest but a life-defining provocation of inexhaustible importance—the *new* reality to which Christian *faith* and thought must always turn.

G. Hunsinger, *Disruptive Grace* (2000); P. D. Jones, *The Humanity of Christ* (2008); B. L. McCormack, *Orthodox and Modern* (2008); A. Neder, *Participation in Christ* (2009); J. Thompson, *Christ in Perspective* (1978).

PAUL DAFYDD JONES

Church   The centrality of the church in Barth's *theology* is evinced in the very title of his magnum opus, the *CD*. Barth's doctrine of the church is rich and complex, taking the local and concrete body of believers gathered by the Spirit's call through the **Word of God** as its primary referent. Indeed, Barth thinks of the church more in terms of a people than an institution, as a concrete and personal congregation rather than as a bureaucratic organization, reflected in his preference for the term *community* (*Gemeinde*) rather than the term *church* (*Kirche*). This view of the church developed over time, as an early period marked by a predominantly critical evaluation of the church gave way to one of positive constructive ecclesiology.

The Development of Barth's Ecclesiology: Barth's negative evaluation of the church during the critical phase is preeminently displayed at its apex in *Rom* II (1922), a work marked by a relentless critique of the church as standing on the side of human religious ambitions and thus under divine judgment. Barth's consistent eschatological perspective in that work, which emphasized the radical *diastasis*, or separation, between **God** and the *world*, as well as his emphasis upon the nontemporality of the **kingdom of God**, accompanied and undergirded a trenchant attack upon the contemporary church-*culture* synthesis of Protestant *liberalism*. In the commentary, Barth emphasizes that the church, like all historical events and realities, stands on the side of the world over against God, and thus falls under divine condemnation for its attempt to domesticate God (*ER*, 332–33). The church is not an exception to but a demonstration of this general rule.

Yet even in Barth's critical phase and *Rom* II itself, Barth had a place for *hope* and *grace* with regard to the church, for as the zenith of human ambitions, it is also the climax of human failure, and thus points beyond itself and from its own failure to God's own action. This is so because it is the church that dares to speak of the relation of God and *humanity*, and in its stuttering and inadequate speech of proclamation, God himself may choose to speak. This divine speak-ing thus condemns the church but also establishes it so that the church is both killed and made alive (*ER*, 340–41). God's judgment of the church thus serves the larger purposes of his grace.

Nevertheless, while Barth's evaluation of the church in *Rom* II was not wholly negative, the church's positive role was so limited as to make a coherent ecclesiology impossible. Barth's radical *eschatology* effectively protected against any direct identification between the church in *history* and the kingdom of God, whether propounded by ecclesial conservatism or liberalism, and thus against any form of ecclesiastical triumphalism, but it came with a steep price, for it could provide no positive evaluation of the church as a new community existing in the world, a deficiency that mirrored Barth's inability to provide a developed and rich notion of the *incarnation*. This critical period thus failed to produce either a constructive **Christology** or ecclesiology, and these deficiencies were intrinsically related, as Barth himself observed in his later evaluation of this period and its theology (see *HG*, 37–65). It must also be noted, however, that Barth never advocated an escape from the church at any time, for, as he could write to his friend Eduard **Thurneysen**, his early protest against the church was at the same time a protest put forth from within its parameters and for its renewal (*RevTh*, 216).

Barth's conversion from predominantly critical to positive ecclesiology followed his new attempt at constructive *dogmatics* during his Göttingen professorate. In Barth's dogmatic lectures beginning in 1924, a turn from a *time*-eternity dialectic to a christological one allowed for the development of a constructive doctrine of the incarnation, and this was mirrored in the development of a constructive ecclesiology and a conception of the church as embodied in though not subsumed into history. It was in the Göttingen lectures that Barth took up the church as a material doctrine of theology for the first time, and his ecclesiology bears the significant marks of Barth's newfound Trinitarian and christological discoveries (see, *Unterricht* III, §34). Barth's positive ecclesiology begun in these early lectures would come to full fruition in his later definitive work, the *CD*; and while Barth never left his early criticisms of cultural Christianity behind, he did develop a rich doctrine of the church in conversation with the dialogue partners of **Roman Catholicism** on his right and Neo-Protestantism on his left, rejecting both of their answers to the question of the church and advancing an alternative in light of his own Reformed theological and christological commitments (for the development of Barth's ecclesiology, see Bender, chaps. 2–3).

Barth's Christological Ecclesiology— Its Nature and Formal Structure: Barth's mature doctrine of the church may be described as christological in both its material content and formal construction (see Bender, *Karl Barth's Christological Ecclesiology*, 1–13, passim). In regard to content, Barth's ecclesiology is centered on the image of the church as the body of Christ, his "earthly-historical form of existence" ("irdish-geschichtliche Existenzform"; IV/1:661). Barth does not see this image as simply symbolic or metaphorical, but as an ontic description of the church's true nature and reality (IV/1:666). Barth's mature ecclesiology can be seen as an attempt systematically to examine and describe the meaning and significance of the central dogmatic conviction that the church is the body of Christ; and while Barth does attend to other biblical and traditional images for the church, these take a secondary position to this christological one. Indeed, Barth states: "All ecclesiology is grounded, critically limited, but also positively determined by Christology" (IV/3.2:786). This intentional christological focus has been criticized by some who believe Barth has slighted other Trinitarian and pneumatological concerns. Nevertheless, while Barth places the doctrine of the

church under the subjective side of the work of the **atonement**, and therefore under the third article of the creed as a doctrine of the **Holy Spirit** (IV/1:643), this discussion itself takes place under the more inclusive doctrine of **reconciliation**, and thus within the framework of the second article (i.e., IV).

The close affiliation between **Christology** and ecclesiology in Barth's thought is further made evident in that mistaken ecclesiological positions are construed by Barth in terms of christological heresies. For Barth, to consider the true church to be an invisible reality behind the visible institution, and indeed opposed to and in contradiction with it, is to succumb to a docetic ecclesiology. On the opposite side, to conceive of the church solely and purely as a historical phenomenon and as one human society among others, without regard to its grounding in the activity of the Holy Spirit as an eschatological event, is to fall into an ebionitic **heresy**. While Barth explicitly identifies these errors as docetic and ebionitic, he also speaks implicitly of a third error: that of confusing the historical institution, life, and practices of the church with **revelation** itself, what might be termed a Eutychian heresy. Here the dialectical relation itself is sacrificed so that history is divinized and revelation is historicized in a confused and amalgamated relation. The first error sacrifices the historical form to the divine event, whereas the second sacrifices the divine event to the historical form. The third sacrifices the dialectical character and confuses the realities, so that the asymmetrical and irreversible character of the relation is lost, the correspondence of the church giving way to synergism.

Barth's own position is to speak of the church as both divinely constituted and historically situated, a reality composed of both an inner mystery of the Spirit and a society of human persons in fellowship and joint activity. Barth seeks neither to confuse nor to separate the divine event and the historical and sociological form, presented in a highly dialectical construal of the relation between divine action and historical duration. He regularly defines the church dialectically with reference to rejected and opposing dyads—the church is neither docetic nor ebionitic, neither idealized nor historicized, neither antinomian nor legalistic, neither sacralized nor secularized.

The Material Content of Barth's Doctrine of the Church: Barth's mature ecclesiology is found in the doctrine of **election** in II/2 as well as in the doctrine of reconciliation in IV/1–3, though the church is a recurrent theme throughout Barth's magisterial work. In the second volume of the *CD*, Barth grounds the church not in a historical event but in the eternal will of God, so that the church stands under the election of Christ while preceding the election of the individual. The church thus stands, by eternal decree, between Christ and the Christian, and correspondingly, between Christ and the world (II/2:196; cf. 205–6).

By grounding the church in the doctrine of election (and thus within the doctrine of God, for Barth places election itself there), Barth preserves the divine initiative in relation to the church. He thereby ensures that the church is viewed as part of God's eternal covenantal intention and decision, and not simply as a corporate body composed of individuals who willingly join themselves together on the basis of a shared religious experience. For this reason, Barth insists that the proper descriptive mode for understanding the church must be theological, rather than sociological or historical.

If the doctrine of election provides the basis and ground for the doctrine of the church, it is the doctrine of reconciliation that gives Barth's ecclesiology its primary material content. There Barth presents his most detailed description of the church under three headings: "The Holy Spirit and the Gathering of the Christian Community" (IV/1); "The Holy Spirit and the Upbuilding of

the Christian Community" (IV/2); and "The Holy Spirit and the Sending of the Christian Community" (IV/3.2:§72). In IV/1 Barth's primary (though not sole) focus is on the *being and nature* of the church. Central to this discussion is Barth's conception of the church as both invisible and visible. Barth does not think of these terms along traditional Augustinian and Calvinist lines (in which the organized visible church on earth is contrasted with the body of true believers known only to God). Rather, the invisible church is the miraculous working of the Spirit that gives rise to a visible congregation in history (IV/1:652–56). Barth rejects both an exclusively invisible church that takes flight from history (docetic ecclesiology), as well as a solely visible church in which the unique spiritual reality of the church is sacrificed and exchanged for a purely historical and sociological explanation of the church's existence (ebionitic ecclesiology). The church consists as the unity of both an inner spiritual activity and reality and a visible manifestation and embodiment. The church is thus the union of a divine work of the Spirit and a historical, concrete, visible life in *analogy* to the singular, unparalleled, and irreplaceable miracle of the incarnation. To confess *faith* in the church is thus to confess "faith in the invisible aspect which is the secret of the visible. . . . Faith in His community has this in common with faith in Him, that it, too, relates to a reality in time and space, and therefore to something which is at bottom generally visible. If, then, we believe in Him, we cannot refuse—however hesitantly or anxiously or contentiously—to believe in His community in its spatio-temporal existence, and therefore to be a member of it and personally a Christian" (IV/1:654).

The relationship between the invisible and visible church is thus tied to the highly dialectical notion of the church as both event and institution, as both an ever-recurrent calling of the church into existence by the Spirit, and an ongoing historical corporate life that exists through time. The relationship between these is one of the most complex and controversial aspects of Barth's ecclesiology, and a common criticism of Barth is that he has sacrificed the latter reality to the former within the pairs.

In IV/2 Barth turns to questions pertaining to the church's *form and order* (though, again, not exclusively to such questions). There he takes up the theme of the nature of the church's life in the world. A central aspect of the church's concrete historical existence is the question of church law (IV/2:676ff.). With regard to such law, Barth rejects both a formless ecclesiastical antinomianism and a rigid ecclesiastical jurisprudence. He refuses either to absolutize such law (such that it becomes a binding universal norm that cannot be revised) or to relativize it (so that the church becomes formless and void of visible organization and structure). Barth's markedly dialectical conception of church law is therefore akin to his dialectical understanding of church *dogma*. Both church doctrine and ecclesiastical law are relative rather than absolute authorities, the latter type of authority belonging to Christ alone (and secondarily to his living voice in Scripture, which stands above both the church's dogma and law and serves as their criterion). Church dogma and law are seen as necessary yet provisional, authoritative yet reformable, both understood as a response of human obedience to divine revelation, rather than equated with revelation itself (I/2:585–660). Barth maintains that the church's law should be derived from the "christologico-ecclesiological concept of the community" (IV/2:681). It is thus christologically grounded and construed (IV/2:682).

Such law serves not only to give shape to the church's own life in *worship* and service, but should exist as a pattern upon which all other human law may be predicated. Church law is, in Barth's memorable term, "exemplary law," and as such is paradigmatic "for

the formation and administration of human law generally, and therefore of the law of other political, economic, cultural, and other human societies" (IV/2:719).

In the last major section on the church (IV/3.2:§72), "The Holy Spirit and the Sending of the Christian Community," Barth turns to the church's *mission and vocation.* The church does not exist for itself, but in service to God and for the world. While the community lives within the world, it is also set apart from the world by God in order to carry out its divinely appointed task, which is to *witness* to the world regarding its own alienation and point it to God's reconciliation and *salvation* in Christ (762–63). Barth can go so far as to say that the church has no independent existence apart from its Christ-appointed *ministry* to the world (786, 795–96, 830–31).

Barth's ecclesiology is thus considerably determined by a teleological, rather than purely ontological, concern, and Barth defines the church's nature by its activity. Indeed, for Barth these are inseparable, for the church's being is determined in and by its action. Moreover, the church is defined not solely by its self-constituting practices (as it is by the Augsburg Confession, for example), but by its missionary and evangelistic task. It must be stated that this task is predominantly described by Barth in terms of *witness* rather than *mediation.* Barth does not see the church's ministry and mission as either an extension or supplement of Christ's own salvific work, but as a witness and proclamation of a prior event, Christ's finished and perfect atonement. Likewise, the church is not an extension of the incarnation, nor does the church replace Christ in the economy of salvation following the *ascension.* Barth insists that even with regard to its "invisible essence," the church "is not Christ, nor a second Christ, nor a kind of extension of the one Christ" (729). Because Christ is the sole redeemer and Lord of the world, the church's ministry is always the humble ministry of service and proclamation, never one of lordship or coredemption. It is therefore not surprising, given Barth's proclivity for speaking of the church as witnessing to, rather than bearing, God's grace, that the church is portrayed as most closely aligned with the prophetic, rather than priestly or kingly, form of Christ's threefold office (790). Its ministry is undertaken by means of "concrete forms of ministry" in the twofold witness of speech and action that both determine the particular identity of the church and serve its witness to the world (865–901).

Conclusion: Barth's ecclesiology is one that strives to preserve both the superiority and uniqueness of God's activity in Christ through the Spirit on the one hand, and the integrity of the church and its activity on the other (IV/2:59–60; cf. I/2:348; and IV/2:655). For Barth, the church and its work have no independent existence apart from the divine initiative, but at the same time the church does have a real and true existence and activity in the *covenant* of grace, which Barth sees preeminently in terms of witness to God's gracious act in Christ by the Spirit. As noted above, the church and its action cannot in any way be seen as a substitute for Christ (Barth eschews all notions of a vicarious role for the church and indeed eschews church offices themselves, evident already in his first dogmatic lectures—see *Unterricht III*, 372–77). Nor can the church's work be seen as a supplement to Christ's own (Barth rejects all such synergistic accounts of salvation), for Christ and the church exist in an irreversible and asymmetrical relationship. Nevertheless, the church does have its own true identity and role, a unique dignity established by Christ. Though the church exists on a different plane from its Lord, and its work is better described as a witness and correspondence to a completed work rather than a mediation of salvation itself, it nonetheless possesses a real and concrete task in service to God and to the world, one that Barth

can even refer to as a form of cooperation with Christ if rightly qualified and understood (IV/3.2:777). So while there is nothing insufficient in Christ's work of atonement that requires completion in the church's life, the church does by grace accompany and serve this atonement as a witness to the world. In sum, the church is to attempt and bear within its life and in the life of each member "an imitation and representation of the love with which God loved the world" (III/4:502).

K. J. Bender, *Karl Barth's Christological Ecclesiology* (2005); idem, "Karl Barth's Doctrine of the Church in Contemporary Anglo-American Ecclesiological Conversation," *ZDTh* 21, no. 1 (2005): 84–116; N. M. Healy, "Karl Barth's Ecclesiology Reconsidered," *SJT* 57 (2004): 287–99; R. Hütter, "Karl Barth's 'Dialectical Catholicity,'" *MTh* 16, no. 2 (2000): 137–57; J. Mangina, "Bearing the Marks of Jesus," *SJT* 52 (1999): 269–305.

KIMLYN J. BENDER

Confession   To be a Christian means more than confessing with one's lips, Barth insists, but it does not mean less. "It is in his spoken word that man, like *God*, comes out into the open, making himself clear, intelligible and in some way responsible, venturing forth and binding and committing himself. . . . Just as Jesus has bound Himself to speak and still speaks for men, so without doubt they on their side are bound to speak of Him" (*CD* III/3:75). Confessing *faith* is never a "private matter," but "in the most general sense is the accounting and responding which in the *Church* we owe one another and have to receive from one another in relation to the hearing and receiving of the *Word of God*" (I/2:588). Confession in this general sense is dependent upon "the confession of the Church in the narrower meaning of the concept, i.e., the voice of others in the Church reaching me in specific agreements and common declarations and as such preceding my own faith and the confession of it" (593). "A Church confession is a formulation and proclamation of the insight which the Church has been given in certain directions into the *revelation* attested by Scripture, reached on the basis of common deliberation and decision" (620).

Barth claims that a genuine church confession: (1) "explains Scripture." It is, at best, "a commentary" (621). It does not merely repeat biblical texts. "It can point to them in order to make clear in what connection it wishes to explain Scripture. But at bottom it must speak in its own words . . . in the speech of its age" (621). (2) It represents not the interests of one group or party in the church but takes responsibility "to speak from and to the one universal Church" (623). (3) It is born not of good ideas or convictions or sound theological reflection or biblical inquiry, but is a gift, a miracle, an *event* "born out of a need of the Church, out of a compulsion . . . imposed on the Church by the Word of God" (624). "We cannot confess because we would like to confess in the belief that confession is a good thing. We can confess only if we must confess" (624). In face of new or old questions, conflicts, or temptations, the church confesses not because it wants to say more than Scripture says but only because it does not want to say less. It arises because of an either-or decision of faith, which, though not by force, "challenges everyone to take up a position" as to whether its pronouncements stand contrary to or in agreement with the Word of God (625). In doing so it calls for both affirmation and rejection: "If the Yes does not in some way contain the No, it will not be the Yes of a confession" (631). (4) It "always involves the statement and expression of the insight given to the Church in definite limits" (625–26), for example, geographic, temporal, and material limitations. A confession is always a human word and as such is only partial, preliminary, and provisional. It "can never be a final word, but only a word which is impera-

tive and binding and authoritative until it is succeeded by something else" (657). Confession is thus "an eschatological concept." In accord with the Reformed Scripture principle, a confession's authority cannot be "absolute" but only "relative." "If it wished to be more, it would be less, for it would then be a hindrance to the Word of God" (*KGSG*, 184). A "confession cannot in any sense stand beside Holy Scripture, claiming the same divine authority, the same character as the source and norm of Church proclamation. In substance, no express or tacit obligation to a confession can ever be anything but an obligation to Holy Scripture" (649). But "wherever the Church really is, this obligation to Holy Scripture will have a [concrete] form determined by the particular guidance and history of the Church (through its continuity with the earlier Church and its connection with Churches elsewhere)" (649), and it will seek to learn and follow in that direction respectfully (665–66). And if it is real, its confession (5) "will have the power to continue speaking even at a great distance from its own geographical and temporal and historical place" (653). Tested in light of the Word, "Church confession acquires a character which does not belong to it in virtue of its limitation" when "the power of His Word . . . breaks through human error and falsehood" and provides "a definite perception of the truth" (636). As such its authority is binding. But "what really decides its authority is simply its content as scriptural exposition, which is necessarily confirmed or judged by Scripture itself" (637–38). (6) It also must be important (though its importance may not be "immediately apparent"), public, and "speak concisely and in thesis form" and "in such a way that without any knowledge of technical *theology* the whole Church can understand it" (639–41).

A confession "is necessarily a challenge, an unsettling factor, a disturbing of the environment, so that that environment inevitably wishes to silence it";

and those who confess will necessarily be brought "by that environment into a struggle, into suffering and therefore into temptation" (643). If it does not question and thereby exert some sort of pressure that evokes counterpressure, if it involves no risk, danger, or venture, it is a harmless theory and not a true confession (645). Resistance by the confessors to such counterpressures "is the true ratification of a confession" (646). Yet *joy* is "the secret of the power of a Church confession" (625). "The particular *humanity* of the Church's confession consists in the *freedom*, the joy of responsibility, the certainty and the *love*, in which it has always taken place in spite of the limits of those who make it" (634).

While the above criteria were written in the immediate aftermath of the *Barmen Declaration* and during the public dissolution of the Confessing Church in Germany (ca. 1937), Barth later elaborated his understanding of church confession under the rubric, "The Praise of God," which he called "the larger field to which belongs the narrower confession" (III/4:74ff.). There he emphasized that confession takes place not in order to have an effect or bring about certain results, but solely for "God's honor" (77–78). "Its critical protest against unbelief, superstition and *heresy* will always be to the effect that God is for us, that He is with us and not against us. The same 'for' and 'with' will always include those whom it must first attack." The confessor must not forget "that the God whose partisan he may and must be is the gracious God." The confessor is not "God's detective, policeman, and bailiff" (79–82). "The one infallible test" of genuine confession is "whether and to what extent it is concerned with what Scripture sets before us as its all-controlling theme, and therefore with *Jesus Christ*, with the *covenant* fulfilled in Him. . . . The other infallible test . . . is whether and to what extent the word of the confessor commits him to a specific public action" (83–85). Finally, "Confes-

sion is a free action" and not an act of "special courage or valor" (85–86).

———

K. Barth, *CD* I/2:585–649; III/4:77–88; idem, *KGSG*; idem, *ThRefC*; A. C. Cochrane, *The Church's Confession under Hitler* (1976).

RICHARD E. BURNETT

Covenant   The theme of covenant is central to both the substance and form of the Christian canon of Scripture and prominent within the Reformed theological heritage. It may seem unsurprising, then, that a theologian so self-consciously biblical and Reformed as Barth should find a significant place for it in the articulation of his own *dogmatics*. Barth, though, never believed that faithfulness was had by mere reiteration, and his systematic appropriation and deployment of the covenant concept departs markedly at points from earlier Reformed versions of it, and travels a considerable distance along trajectories that he certainly judged to be indicated by the pattern of Scripture but that, as we shall see, take the reader far beyond any simple surface *exegesis* of the biblical text.

Most distinctively of all, perhaps, Barth traces the significance of the covenant of *grace* between *God* and human beings back from the historic acts of God *ad extra* into his account of God's eternal acts *ad intra* so that it becomes essential to the very definition of who God is or, in more familiar theological terms, of God's eternal "being." Thus, while for Barth the covenant is the central and most significant fact in the relationship between God and the creature, equally it is his eternal choice of and commitment to this same covenant that determines God's own existence as Father, Son, and *Holy Spirit*. The eternal relations of hypostatic procession (generation and spiration) in the triune life of God are grounded in and orientated toward God's first work *ad extra*, namely, his eternal decision not to be God alone but to be "God for us" in *Jesus Christ*. God chooses fellowship with us for himself, and fellowship with himself for us, despite the fact that nothing necessitates this choice and despite what the choice will cost him (*CD* II/2:10). The form of such fellowship is the covenant of grace; its concrete content is Jesus Christ, and us in and together with him. This is what Barth means when in his treatment of the doctrine of *election* he insists that Jesus Christ is the object of the divine decree (II/2:103–4). What God decrees eternally is precisely the existence of Jesus Christ, the one in whose life and death and resurrection the covenant of grace will eventually be fulfilled and established from the human side as well as from God's side. Jesus, in other words, is the one true covenant partner in whose creaturely response the Father finds a faithful correspondence to his own divine character and action (III/2:203), and this is a matter of an eternal choosing in the light of which all God's actions are oriented. For Barth, though, Jesus Christ himself is the subject as well as the object of the eternal divine choice (II/2:103). At first blush this is an odd way of putting the matter. Surely it would be more precise to insist simply that the one who in due time took flesh and entered our world as the man Jesus Christ was none other than the eternal Word, and thus identical with the God who chooses covenant fellowship with his human creature? For Barth, though, this is insufficient, because it permits us to imagine a *Word of God*, a second person of the *Trinity* whose identity in *eternity* is somehow detachable from the concrete identity of Jesus Christ. This, Barth insists, is not so: God ordains himself eternally to be the bearer of this particular name, the subject of this concrete human *history* (II/2:100), and we must therefore think of the Word's eternal identity as characterized already by the identity of the man he will in due course become and be. God has no existence prior to or apart from the covenant eternally chosen and historically realized in Jesus Christ (II/2:509).

Precisely because the covenant of grace is a matter of God's eternal choosing and to that extent constitutive of who God himself eternally is, it also shapes and orientates every other act of God from first to last. Thus we find one of Barth's most sustained discussions of the concept of covenant arising at the heart of his doctrine of *creation*, that primal act whereby in the *freedom* of his *love* God calls into being a *world* genuinely other than himself. Creation, Barth insists, is the "external basis" of the covenant (III/1:94ff.). Chronologically prior to the covenant, it is nonetheless logically subsequent and subordinate to it, since its very purpose is to furnish a fitting theater for the occurrence of the divine drama that will have the establishment and fulfillment of the covenant as its high point and eventual denouement (III/1:99).

Accordingly, Barth understands God's evaluation of the finished creation as "very good" (Gen. 1:31) as a teleological rather than an empirical judgment. The world is "good" not in any abstract or absolute sense, but because it is adapted well to its purpose as the stage on which the covenant history will now be played out (III/1:213). Correspondingly, Barth describes the covenant as the "internal basis" of creation (228ff.), the meaning and reason behind the creature's contingent existence. This is very important because it leads Barth to reject traditional Reformed notions of a distinct "covenant of nature" lying somehow outside the sphere of God's grace (414). Grace, Barth insists, characterizes all of God's works, and creation itself is its first concrete manifestation. It is not itself the covenant (97), but it participates fully in it as its presupposition and condition. This means that creation and redemption must be held closely together too, for if the creature's making is essential to the existence of the covenant, it is nonetheless *sinners* with whom God chooses to enter into fellowship, and therefore the costly remaking of the creature through the economy of *incarnation*, cross, and resurrection is essential to its establishment and fulfillment. Creation and new creation alike are thus part of the wider economy of grace through which God's eternal decision for the creature is realized in *time*.

If God's own eternal being is effectively determined and defined by the covenant, so too, for Barth, is that of God's human creature. To be human means, above all, to be made capable of and called to share in that covenant fellowship that God has purposed eternally and established historically in the life, death, and *resurrection of Jesus Christ* (III/1:185). While this covenant clearly involves two parties, from the perspective informed by the doctrines of Trinity and incarnation, God himself nonetheless appears as the subject of the relevant action from first to last, humanly as well as divinely. Thus the covenant confronts us in the first instance as business already transacted, closed from the human side (IV/1:32–33) because Christ has substituted himself for us and already fulfilled all of its terms on our behalf. Here, though, the logic of grace is not to displace us entirely, as it might at first appear, but to set us on our feet and draw us in to share actively and freely in the dynamics of covenant living (IV/3.2:941–92). The God of the covenant of grace, Barth insists, "wills and expects and demands something from His covenant-partner" (II/2:11) and creates humankind in his own image precisely in order to be "a real partner . . . which is capable of action and responsibility in relation to Him" (III/1:184–85). God, then, desires not Jesus Christ alone, but *us together with him* (the human creature whose "flesh" the eternal Son assumed and indwelt) as his covenant partner. That is the meaning of *humanity* as such, and the reason for the existence of human beings. God also knows that, left to our own devices, we shall not fulfill this calling but, beset by *sin* and dragged down by guilt, live in denial of it instead. By establishing his covenant objectively in Christ in an

act of sheer grace (IV/1:33), therefore, he liberates us (forgiving sin and thereby lancing the poisonous fear of failure) to throw ourselves gladly into Spirit-generated acts of covenantal response. Whatever their substance in particular contingent contexts, the appropriate mood of these acts, Barth observes, will always be one of *gratitude* and *joy* (and therefore obedience) (IV/1:41–42), and their characteristic form (and thus that of all truly human action) will be one of *prayer* (III/4:93).

Thus it is in terms of the covenant of grace—originating eternally in the self-determining choice of God, prepared for in the ordering of the world created by God, and wrought in the flesh of our historical existence in *Israel*'s Messiah, who is also God's Word and only begotten Son—that human life and action in the here and now too is granted its true shape and orientation. Indeed, at every point of God's dealings with humankind from beginning to end, Barth insists, it is in terms of this same covenant and not otherwise that the glorification of God and the *salvation* of humankind are to be found and made sense of (II/2:125). Little wonder, then, that in Barth's own theology its traces are to be identified on more or less every page, and not simply where more traditional *exegesis* and dogmatic classification might have expected to find them.

E. Busch, *The Great Passion*, trans. G. W. Bromiley (2004), 82–105; J. Mangina, *Karl Barth* (2004), 57–85; B. L. McCormack, "Grace and Being," in *Cambridge Companion to Karl Barth*, ed. J. Webster (2000), 92–110; J. Webster, *Barth's Ethics of Reconciliation* (1995).

TREVOR HART

Creation   Barth's placement of the doctrine of creation in *CD* is rather conventional. It stands between the doctrine of *God* and *Christology* and is divided into four parts or sub-volumes: III/1, "The Work of Creation" (1945);

III/2, "The Creature" (1948); III/3, "The Creator and His Creature" (1950); and III/4, "Command of God the Creator" (1951). In spite of his traditional placement of the doctrine of creation, Barth presents one of the most radical reconstructions of the doctrine in the nineteenth and twentieth centuries. With his specifically *christological* doctrine of creation, published eleven years after the *Barmen Declaration*, Barth continues to confront **natural theology** on territory that throughout long stretches of theological history have been considered the "home" of diverse variants of such natural theology. In present discussions over intelligent design, religious naturalism, principles of dialogue between the natural sciences and *religion*, as well as in interreligious dialogues, this doctrine of creation still presents an open provocation to theological "common sense" and a strident alternative to it. Half a century later, we are still openly debating whether it is an ingenious renewal or a theological aberration.

Barth himself admits to some uncertainty, undoubtedly with an amount of understatement: "In taking up the doctrine of creation, I have entered a sphere in which I feel much less confident and sure" (III/1:ix). And yet Barth's teaching on creation is based on a simple, basic and consequential insight: No Christian discussion of God's creation can ignore God's self-revelation in *Jesus Christ*. It must *emanate* from the event of this self-revelation.

This basic insight has several substantive and methodological implications. First, Barth concedes that he is not seeking to confront the natural sciences. A specifically theological and christologically determined doctrine of creation does not evolve from dialogue with the natural sciences. The uncoupling of Christian teaching of creation from scientific statements about the *world* from the outset does not mean the immunization of *theology* from *science*, but promotes the freedom of natural science: "There is free scope for natural science beyond what theology describes as the work of the Creator. And theology can and must move freely where science which really is science, and not secretly a pagan *Gnosis* or religion, has its appointed limit. I am of the opinion, however, that future workers in the field of the Christian doctrine of creation will find many problems worth pondering in defining the point and manner of this twofold boundary" (III/1:x).

Second, Barth aims from the beginning at a doctrine of creation that goes beyond a purely epistemic orientation on Jesus Christ. Thus Christ is not only where the intentions of an otherwise dark or seemingly ambivalent God the Creator becomes clear or where an opaque perception of God is "enlightened," refined, or simply surpassed. For Barth, Christ is more than merely where *knowledge* of the Creator is revealed. In other models of *revelation* the biblical presentation of the created world is based on observations of order, feelings of dependence, or the sublime, which have found and still find surpassing corroboration. Yet however such models may vary, Christ himself plays no role in the event of creation.

However, in Barth's radical reconstruction, Christ is the inner rationality of creation with respect to both substance and knowledge. The foundation of this reconstruction is already found in Barth's doctrine of the *Trinity* in *CD* I and again in his doctrine of *election* in *CD* II. With the rather difficult formulation of an "eternal election" of Jesus Christ, Barth expresses that Christians may assume God's self-determination according to which all acts of God are determined through Jesus Christ—and prior to any creation. God's *covenant*, which is made apprehensible through Christ, surpasses not only the *sin* of humankind, but also the event of creation. God's will to form a relationship as manifest and visible in Christ, as well as his *freedom* and rationality, already characterize the act of creation. God's will to create already demonstrates his will to form a partnership with humankind. In and through Christ and therefore as part of divine life, creation has always been "present in God."

At the same time, humans encounter no one but the creator in Jesus Christ. This creation, which refers to Jesus Christ, is a first act in the covenant of *grace* that aims at the story of Jesus Christ. This approach leads Barth to formulations that have again become classic themselves and that he develops based on the two creation stories in Genesis. This is how we should see "creation as the external basis of the covenant" (III/1:94–228) with reference to the first account with its focus on God's "Sabbath *joy*" (98). With reference to the second account in which creation already prepares for the covenant, the covenant must be regarded "as the internal basis of creation" (228–329).

While Jesus Christ and his time reflect a basic acknowledgment of *time* and *history*, God's creation demonstrates God's readiness for time. Creation itself is as temporal as the story of Jesus Christ. Creation as an event in time borders on God's specific time and, in Barth's opinion, can only be unfolded in the narrative. It is not that Christ's story develops from the story of creation, but, on the contrary, the story of Christ encompasses and contains all other history in a nutshell.

In its complexity, Barth's doctrine of creation is not without circularity. Against the background of the eternal election of God's Son and the eternal election of grace, the covenant—as an event culminating in the self-abasement of the Son on the cross—exists in the last analysis only for the sake of creation, for the sake of humankind. It is the internal reason for creation. At the same time, creation exists so that the covenant can happen, so that this covenant process has "a concrete extra-divine object" (III/1:230). "Thus . . . creation is . . . the way to the covenant. . . . The covenant is the goal of creation" (97). The inherent difficulties become obvious when

we follow another of Barth's basic decisions owing to his Christology. He wants to understand creation as an elective event, that is, strictly speaking, an event that can be chosen or rejected. Based on his exegesis of Genesis 1 and 2, Barth considers God's creative activity to be consistently relational, as an act of differentiation, where both possibilities arise only as the differentiation is made! Therefore, creating means choosing *and* rejecting. Thus chaos "is that which is denied by God's will and act" (101). It is therefore not something against God's will that has to be overcome, an antecedent principle, but the other side of the differentiation or act of distinction that, in a certain sense, only coproduces the decision or that is produced with the differentiation—although God only *follows up* on the side of the created and chosen. In a sense, that which was rejected in the differentiation remains appended to what was chosen and created, although the differentiation itself is not symmetrical. The being of the rejected is a "creation of wrath" (III/3:78). What was excluded in the act of creation is chaos and darkness. "Only in its separation from light is darkness also created, and therefore the creature of God" (III/1:117).

Barth observes that in contrast to chaos, darkness has a firm place in creation in the form of night; it is called neither explicitly good nor created. Now the night has two sides in creation, insofar as God protects the cosmos "assailed and threatened by chaos," and yet "not permitting to chaos more than the nature of a threat at the edge of the cosmos" (127). Certainly we will have to argue with Barth that seen exegetically the night is not at the edge of the cosmos but at its center as part of the night and day rhythm. For Barth, the night also has a creaturely existence "in a danger zone" (128).

The point of Barth's approach to creation as an elective process is that creation cannot be understood without a fundamental instability and inevitable shadow. God's *providence* constantly aims at *maintaining* the basic distinctions of creation in view of the permanent threat of being overwhelmed by nothingness in the form of chaos. "Creation itself . . . is menaced by the chaos which to some extent borders it, couching at the door" (74), namely by what was created "in the negative power . . . of this divine creating, approving and calling" (77). Barth emphasizes the appreciation of humankind being present in overcoming chaos, but at the same time he underlines the "actual subjection and impotence in face of that negation" (III/3:81). Given that the creation is "menaced by nothingness" so that it desperately needs "a divine preservation and sustaining and indeed deliverance" (75–76), creation is fundamentally directed toward the covenant in Christ. However, Barth is very careful to avoid the conclusion, which is very much evident in Hegel's philosophy of religion, that chaos or nothingness is a "necessary part" of the covenant event as a whole (299–300). Creation does *not* have this dangerous threat for the self-glorification of God. This shows, finally, the logical problem that creation is at the same time the "result" of as well as the "prerequisite" for the Christ event in terms of covenant theology.

Barth claims to fundamentally redesign the traditional doctrine of **analogy** (*analogia entis*), namely, that in the last analysis there is no continuous connection between God and the creature—a connection that traditionally was often based on humans being in the image of God. To Barth, the alternative of an "analogy of being" is an "analogy of relatedness" (*analogia relationis*) (III/I:220, 226). "The relationship between the summoning I in God's being and the summoned divine Thou is reflected both in the relationship of God to the man whom He has created, and also in the relationship between the I and the Thou, between male and female, in human existence itself" (196). The inner-divine relationship finds a parallel in the relationship between God and creation and most prominently and instructively in the human relationship between man and woman. If the relationship between man and woman, which is given in God's creation, is indeed analogous to the relationship between Creator and creature, this will inevitably lead to two questions. First, why within the whole story of creation and the covenant is it the relationship between man and woman that is the outstanding and single analogy to the relationship between God and the world? Second, if the relationship between God and creation as well as the underlying relationship between Christ and the community is fundamentally asymmetrical, does this not place a lopsided domination into the relationship between man and woman that is theologically unacceptable? Does Barth himself not vigorously practice natural theology when in his interpretation of the second story of creation he claims: "In virtue of his nature man must be formally prepared for grace" (III/1:290)? These are the points against which feminist theologians have directed astute criticism, and rightly so. As impressive as this very innovative creation theology may be, at least three questions cannot be overlooked with regard to Barth's doctrine of creation.

1. How can the explicitly and consistently christologically conceived doctrine of creation be translated into extratheological discourse? How can its findings become acceptable to those who do not confess Jesus Christ?

2. Taking a look at Barth's entire magnum opus, one can note that the Christology that is "written into" the doctrine of creation is not really adopted in the revised Christology of *CD* IV, *The Doctrine of Reconciliation*. How does the Christology that is oriented toward overcoming chaos relate to

the Christology of the doctrine of reconciliation, which is explicitly based on juridical categories?

3. Today, religious naturalists are confronting Barth's doctrine of creation with the question of how, within his association of creation with the covenant, the horrendous evils of biological evolution can be understood. Do such teleologically justified evils serve the purpose of creation or do they represent the (necessary) nothingness in creation? Of course, Barth would not assign any redeeming quality to the suffering of creation. But do they reveal, as is expressed in currents of panentheism, the "cruciform shape" of all creation?

However, these inquiries cannot diminish Barth's achievement. Given its christological orientation, Barth's doctrine of creation has often been accused of having devalued creation. It is said that creation, apart from being a stage for the covenant, has no purpose of its own for Barth and only serves the covenant. Surely this is the result of a somewhat anthropocentrically narrow approach in Barth's doctrine of creation.

But, at the same time, creation can serve as an allegory to the covenant event. That is why Barth is adapting the old teaching of *vestigia trinitatis* to include signs of God's loyalty, benevolence, and "creative joy" in the covenant of grace. According to Barth, creation occurs only *after* God's benevolence culminates in Christ.

Against the horizon of present debates about theism, creation, and theodicy, it must be noted with Barth that the goodness of creation is revealed in Christ, that is, "theology has to recognize and confess creation as benefit because it is the work of God in Jesus Christ" (III/1:343). Thus, in the final analysis, the goodness of creation is revealed in the humiliation and exaltation of Jesus Christ, but also in the special

shape of its dignity *and* poverty. The last justification and appreciation of creation is that the Creator "endures" it (380) and thereby bears the contradiction of creaturely existence. Undoubtedly, the potential of Barth's theology of creation has not been sufficiently elaborated for our time. Paradoxically, it is the relative autonomy of his theology that allows for productive discussion with the cosmology of natural science.

B. Janowski, *Die Welt als Schöpfung* (2008); C. Link, *Schöpfung* (1991); S. McLean, "Creation and Anthropology," in *Theology beyond Christendom*, ed. J. Thompson (1986), 111–42; R. J. Sherman, *Shift to Modernity* (2005); Kathryn Tanner, "Creation and Providence," in *Cambridge Companion to Karl Barth*, ed. J. Webster (2000), 111–26; G. Thomas, "Chaosüberwindung und Rechtsetzung Schöpfung und Versöhnung in Karl Barths Eschatologie," *ZDTh* 21, no. 3 (2005): 259–77.
GÜNTER THOMAS

Culture While Friedrich *Schleiermacher* is generally known as an apologist to religion's "cultured despisers," people commonly perceive Barth as an unapologetic despiser of culture. Nothing could be further from the truth. Certainly, Barth was severe in his critique of "Culture Protestantism" and later the "German Christians." But part of his critique stemmed from his conviction that such movements did not allow culture the loving *freedom* to be the human entity *God* created it to be.

"Culture" stands for the totality of human enterprise and activity. While Barth certainly gave special attention to high culture, he did not limit himself exclusively to that sphere. That being said, Barth's concern for humanness led him to make significant judgments in the two realms he loved beyond the sphere of *theology* proper—political theory and Mozart. Barth's humane theology led him to critique vigorously Aryan

Christianity and National Socialism on the one hand and to affirm the all-too-human and very Germanic composer Mozart on the other hand.

Barth's appreciation for Mozart—while exceptional—is by no means an exception to the rule in his thought. Rather, it is illustrative of what occurs elsewhere. For all the lofty grandeur of Barth's theological structure and discourse, Barth's theology has a very earthy and humane quality to it. Thus, even though his thought certainly undergoes development and transformation over the years, the attention he gives to "the *humanity* of God" in his later work is a corrective that reflects his best theological instincts throughout his career. Barth's intent was always to safeguard proper attention for humanity's distinctive glory through rightful consideration of divine glory disclosed in Christ.

With this in mind, it is important to note that though Barth's admiration for Mozart developed over time, it did not begin with Barth's more incarnational theology. The incarnational turn in Barth's theology and what it spelled for Barth's doctrine of *creation* certainly set the stage for a better hearing. The same Mozart who serves as the aesthetic height of transient reality in *Rom* II later serves as a resounding *witness* to God's promise to preserve and perfect creation's transformation in the period of the *CD*.

For all the growth and dialectical development in Barth's thought, his basic instincts remained unchanged. Thus it should come as no surprise that Barth would say concerning his varying responses to politics over time that different contexts require different responses. Although he was by no means a situation ethicist, Barth was a contextual theologian who ever remained true to his theology's most deeply held convictions in very diverse settings. Thus, regardless of whether he was right or wrong in remaining silent on the evils committed under Soviet communism,

the charge that he was inconsistent in attacking National Socialism and remaining silent on Soviet communism is certainly incorrect. Perhaps to a fault at this point, Barth was all-too consistent. As he sees it, unlike National Socialism, Soviet communism is not "anti-Christian" but blatantly "non-Christian" (part of his rationale for remaining silent regarding the latter was that unlike National Socialism it did not seek to reinterpret Christianity).

Given the centrality of the *incarnation* in Barth's thought, it would be a disservice to approach Barth in a non-enculturated manner. Just as the Word became flesh in a given cultural context in the fullness of *time*, so Barth's theology is enfleshed and enculturated, even timely. Even his great doctrine of eternal *election* was timely in its prophetic import. It is no coincidence that *CD* II/2, beginning with chapter VII, "The Election of God," was written and published during Nazism's reign of terror: the *Jewish* Jesus of Nazareth is the electing God and the elect human.

Moreover, while some detractors portray Barth's employment of classic theological categories as a regressive preservation of outdated thought forms, Barth was too radical a thinker to simply borrow concepts; he commandeered and reframed them for his own *Sitz im Leben*. While Barth was a constructive theologian, he was by no means a conserver of previous cultural motifs. He was too Protestant and too Reformed for that—*semper reformanda*. And as a truly Reformed theologian, Barth sought to return daily to discover anew the strange new *world* within the *Bible*—a world that sheds light on our own world in fresh and faithful ways. Whereas the great theologian of culture Paul Tillich sought to discern humanity's ultimate concern in culture, Barth sought to view culture in light of humanity's ultimate concern—*Jesus Christ*, the eternal Word made flesh.

It is not possible to classify Barth as a theologian of culture per se given his lack of systematic analysis and structuring of theological categories from this vantage point. Nor is it possible to neatly classify Barth's approach to cultural engagement. This calls to mind H. Richard Niebuhr's classic text on the subject, *Christ and Culture*. Niebuhr's work has received its fair share of criticism over the years. One point of critique is that its categories are too static and are not able to account for the complexities in the theologians he surveys. Barth's theology, including his engagement of culture in its various manifestations, defies static categorization. How could it be otherwise given Barth's attempt to remain true to the Word made flesh?

In view of the incarnation, Barth returned daily to the Word to bear witness within the *church* to the culture at large in a dynamic and multifaceted (over against monolithic) manner; for God's incarnate Word always requires prophetic witness in culture that is ever particular and never generic, ever contemporary and never distant, always engaged and never disconnected, always alive to the Spirit's voice through attentiveness to the Scripture's own primary witness in pointing to Christ Jesus. We are speaking here of Barth's dynamic doctrine of the threefold form of the liberating **Word of God** and its import for contemporary culture.

Part of the enduring influence of Barth's theology is its emphasis on the loving freedom of the Word and what that entails for the church and human culture. For Barth, a church that demands rights from the *state* and that condemns society is a spiritually unfree church, whereas a church that is secure in its calling to appeal and not compel bears witness to the Word of *grace*, offering a word of judgment grounded in *hope*. The God of the Bible does not envy *humanity*, and so secures the creation and human culture in that freedom circumscribed by *love* to be what it is created to be in service to the liberating Word. Far from despising culture,

we find here in Barth's thought the basis for culture's high calling, worth, and esteem.

K. Barth, *Moz*; T. Gorringe, *Karl Barth* (1999); idem, "Culture and Barbarism," in *Conversing with Barth*, ed. J. C. McDowell and M. Higton (2004), 40–52; P. Metzger, *The Word of Christ and the World of Culture* (2003); R. Palma, *Karl Barth's Theology of Culture* (1983).

PAUL LOUIS METZGER

Determination   *Bestimmung*, as Barth uses it, carries a wealth of overtones not readily transferred into English. It is translated "determination" in the *CD*, which may be as versatile a rendering as several alternatives: "destiny," "predestination," "foreordination," "intention," "lot," "role," or "purpose." What counts is seeing how his use of "determination" sheds light on his anthropology.

It comes as no surprise that the starting point for Barth's treatment of the doctrine of **creation**, including **humanity**, is God's sovereign call in *Jesus Christ*. From beginning to end this call is good news: the *election* of *grace*. Under the rubric, "The Election of Jesus Christ" (*CD* §33), Barth elaborates the *Leitsatz*: "The election of grace is the eternal beginning of all the ways and works of **God** in Jesus Christ. In Jesus Christ God in his free grace determines Himself for sinful man and sinful man for Himself. He therefore takes upon Himself the rejection of man with all of its consequences, and elects man to participation in his own glory" (II/2:94).

Barth switches the order customarily used by most of Reformed orthodoxy to deal with election and the doctrine of God. He gives priority throughout to election as grace; indeed, he defines God as the graciously electing one revealed in Jesus Christ. That particularity cuts short idle speculation about the content of a so-called *decretum absolutum* guessed at abstractly. Instead, Barth insists on speaking of *gracious election* because Jesus Christ is the electing God and electing human—one person in whom humans find their true determination. Jesus Christ is the content of the eternal decree—the *decretum concretum*—in whom the promises of God to *Israel* no less than to the **church** find their ratification and fulfillment. God does not go back on the promises made to Israel anymore than he does the promises made to the church. It is by utterly free grace that the community joined to Christ by the power of the **Holy Spirit** proclaims the gospel. It is by firmly holding to Christ and his promises that we as sinners, and not just as good creatures, can begin to experience the fruits of Christian **freedom.**

There is a noteworthy parallel between what **Calvin** and Barth teach regarding the totality and all sufficiency of Christ's person and work. Calvin also taught that it is by the "whole course of Christ's obedience" that humans are saved. Barth pushes the implications of this particularity further and radically redefines predestination. According to Barth, there is a sense in which predestination is double: Jesus Christ is fully God, fully human, one person—the elected one and the rejected one. Rejection is included in the cost of the reality of being chosen. Barth does not flinch from the implication that all men and women share, idiosyncratically, yes, but truly, in Christ's singular election.

Barth argues that the **covenant** is that for which creation comes about so there will be **time** and place for the covenant. Humanity's destination includes being created for relationship, of which the relationship between man and woman is an index. His argument is concentrated in §45, "Man in His Determination as the Covenant-Partner of God," under the *Leitsatz*: "That real man is determined by God for life with God has its inviolable correspondence in the fact that his creaturely being is a being in encounter—between I and Thou, man and woman. It is human in this encoun-

ter, and in this humanity it is a likeness of the being of its Creator and a being in *hope* in Him" (III/2:203).

With this christological specificity in place, Barth is free to use a rich variety of terms besides "correspondence." They include "original, copy, parity, likeness, similarity," and "mystery." Being for others is the ontology presupposed in real humanity, referred to in varieties of *analogy* of relation. Barth offers this definition of his usage: "We must press straight on from the fact that the humanity of man consists in the determination of his being as a being with the other," and then tries "to clarify three of the terms employed in this definition" as follows:

1. *We describe humanity as a determination of human being.* Man is, as he is created by God for God, as this creature of God for covenant-partnership with God. But this being is a wholly definite being. It corresponds in its own way to its particular creation and to the meaning and goal of the particularity of its creation. The manner of its being is a likeness of its purpose and therefore of the fact that it is created by God for God. *This parabolic determination of human being, this correspondence and similarity of its nature in relation to its being as such, is humanity.*

2. *We describe humanity as a being of man with others. With this cautious expression we distinguish humanity generally from the humanity of Jesus. . . .* There can be no question of a total being for others as the determination of any other men but Jesus.

3. *We describe humanity as a being of the one man with the other. . . .* We are not thinking here in terms of individualism. But the basic form of humanity, the determination of humanity, according to its creation in the light of the humanity

of Jesus— . . . it is of this that we speak.

(III/2:243–44, italics added).

Barth draws a distinction between being a covenant partner with God by *nature* and by *grace*. We are the covenant partners of God by nature: this is the determination under which we are created with the gracious meaning of our existence and nature—not a human attribute. It does not belong to us in virtue of the fact that this particular man defines what it means to be creatures of God. It is by grace that we are partners in the *history* that is the goal of his creation and in which his work is created and finds continuation and fulfillment (III/2:320). Moreover, that which defines the fullness of the man-woman relationship is not a general pattern but is elucidated and set forth, in Ephesians, as the relationship between Christ and the church.

K. Barth, *CD* II/2:§§32–35; III/2:§45; D. Gibson, *Reading the Decree* (2009).

DAVID WILLIS

Dialectical Theology Barth himself did not use the term *dialectical theology* as a programmatic expression of a new style of *theology*. Rather, as he pointed out in 1933, the term represented a kind of comprehensive description, coined by a "spectator," for a theological movement that surfaced in the 1920s, which attempted to set the whole of Protestant theology up against the tradition influenced first and foremost by Friedrich *Schleiermacher* ("Abschied," ZZ 11 [1933]: 536). Barth's attempt to distance himself from the term was surely motivated by the fact that the group of theologians who had met for the purpose of constructing a new type of theology (and who had gathered around the periodical *Zwischen den Zeiten* since 1922) had almost completely disintegrated with the

beginning of the Nazi era. The question for Barth became whether there was any positive consent within this "new" theology other than its critical attitude toward the liberal theology of the nineteenth century. The tension between Barth and Friedrich Gogarten made Barth especially hesitant to use the term in a positive sense.

Yet references to "dialectical theology" were not completely absent from the texts Barth himself had published. The famous Tambach lecture, "The Christian's Place in Society" (1920; ET "Society"), used the terms *thesis, antithesis,* and *synthesis* so extensively that the allusion to dialectics could not be avoided. (Of course, Barth used these terms in an unusual and quite non-Hegelian manner.) In *Rom* II (1922) he made the term *dialectic* one of the most significant expressions of the relation between *God* and *humanity*. He used the term 43 times in *Rom* II and only 8 times in *Rom* I (1919). Finally, in his speech "The Word of God and the Task of Theology," Barth clearly appeared to view the "dialectical way of theology" as the most suitable way of doing theology—if there is any at all.

Of course, the term *dialectics* needs to be specified. Regarding the notion of "dialectical theology," the comparison with Hegel's use of "dialectic" is most useful here. Following Hegel's conception, it is the movement of the Spirit as such that leads to dialectics. When we are thinking, we experience being confronted with the "object" we think *of*. But at the same time we have a complementary experience whereby we also know the *relation* of our thinking of the "object"—and so we know more than merely the object; we are aware of the relation that surpasses the simple structure of "subject" and "object." In this way, our thinking, our experience, takes part in spirit, which is the living structure of the whole. In the final dimension we become aware of the total coherence of everything, its mediation through the Spirit, which is expressed and condensed in the term *God*.

However, in sharp contrast to the omnipresence of mediation in the Hegelian concept of dialectics, the term *dialectics* in "dialectical theology" tries to interrupt the Hegelian tendency toward bringing about the synthesis in which God and humanity are linked to each other. Instead of combining God and humanity, in dialectical theology there rules a "sheer otherness" or an "infinite distance." God may only be known by this difference, experienced as the negation of everything that counts as specifically human—but, so it is claimed, it is exactly this complete negation that is the way that God's presence in human life becomes real. We thus can regard the concept of dialectical theology as a kind of negative dialectics (to use a term that was developed later by the philosopher Theodor Adorno). In place of the synthesis we find mere actuality; the spirit is the thorough negation of all finite pretension; the movement from one extreme to the other is the only way of identity.

If we understand dialectical theology in this way, we can see how this form of dialectics sprang up and was embraced in the years immediately following World War I. There was no longer any traditional ground to take root in. All that remained was a constant movement focused on God, a movement that promised a new understanding of human identity. And we can also understand why such a theology negates the earlier kind of theology, which had put forward the concept of *religion* as grounded in social and affective life (as expressed in Schleiermacher).

Though Barth's theology found its first specific expression in *Rom* I, it must not be regarded as some sort of "sudden idea" nor as being induced only by World War I, as is sometimes reported. Surely, Barth's work on Romans started already in 1916, and it represented a shift to a new, biblically grounded theological *language*. But Barth's early theology already exhibits certain indications of this later turn. Indeed, there appear to be at least three decisive traits of Barth's early theology that are relevant to our purposes here. The first trait is a basic intuition he inherited from Wilhelm **Herrmann**, his teacher in Marburg in 1908–1909, namely that religion is a matter of life, not a matter of doctrine. Herrmann was committed to showing that the antinomies of *ethics* move one to find and to understand religion; Barth changed the medium: it is within religious life and by means of religious language that the immediacy of the Divine is experienced. This experience forms the second element of Barth's early theology, namely a specific understanding of *history*. History must not be regarded as a process that relativizes individual life. As far as religion is experienced, we find a connection to the "unconditioned" that contains within itself a historical element (see "Der christliche Glaube und die Geschichte" [1910] in *VkA* II, 155–212), and this so-called inner form of history is indubitable. This is also the reason the theological way of expressing religion does not fear antinomies. On the contrary, the immediateness of religion must be preserved by contradictory sentences (see "Der Glaube an den persönlichen Gott" [1913] in *VkA* II, 494–554). It is only one step further to the third insight that this condition of religion stems from the living impression of God himself. Barth's social and political experiences as well as his duties as a pastor at Safenwil likely caused him to take this decisive step forward. The social conflicts he noticed in his parish made him sensitive to the fact that the reality of religion is no longer a product of human wishes, but a divine reality by itself. People get moved "from above." That is why mere reflection on the possibilities and limits of religion as a human phenomenon would not suffice but had to be criticized. In understanding the movement of people's beliefs as a result of God's own action, Barth was obliged to the Swabian pietist, Johann Christoph Blumhardt, whom he knew from his semester at Tübingen and to whom he was reintroduced by his friend and colleague Eduard *Thurneysen*. Together with Thurneysen, Barth's theological language became more biblical—which meant, on the other hand, a theological adjustment of religious language as well. His *Römerbrief* is the decisive work in which the new shape of his theology found its place.

When Barth started his commentary on Romans in the summer of 1916, he wanted to convey the flow of the divine life in his *exegesis* of Paul's letter. He wanted to make Paul's text diaphanous regarding the movement by which it was inspired. This is why the dominant language follows the metaphors of revolution and change—a change that has begun from above and that reaches out into human life, which becomes totally new by the divine spirit. The methodological background of the book is hardly explained at all. It makes use of the metaphorical power of biblical language with a kind of reflective immediacy, thereby affirming the religious value of the orthodox doctrine of *inspiration*. Thus the critical standards of historical exegesis, which live by the distance of historical texts and the present interpreter, are regarded as insufficient or inadequate. This attitude, however, well understandable from Barth's intentions and premises, cannot avoid using categories that stem from specific contexts as well. Barth does not hesitate to utilize terms from a kind of philosophical language focusing on organic growth and metamorphosis. Expressions taken from this type of language are intended to serve as a description of the divine transformation of the *world* in an eschatological dimension. The *analogy* to revolutionary language as well as to expressionist language is obvious.

Rom I was a literary success and paved the way for Barth to Göttingen University. But there was a severe ambiguity in his approach to Romans.

Regardless of how strongly Barth's metaphorical language of change and transformation was worded, it still reflected presuppositions that did not totally fit his theological intention of eliminating the human sphere of religion from the divine movement. If something is changed, there must be some *thing* that undergoes this change. Barth, always a severe critic of himself, soon became aware of this ambiguity, and when he began to work on *Rom* II, he set the figure of negation directly in the middle of his exegesis. *Judgment* and *grace*, law and gospel (see *gospel and law*) are solely connected by a profound negation, and only insofar as God can be understood as the active cause, leading into this negation and even beyond it, can the transition be said to be real. On this revised view, the utmost negation becomes the decisive element for *faith*. "Man is nothing," Barth can state—but we must read this "nothing" not as a simple affirmation of something lacking or something taken away: we must understand it as a qualified negation that is full of content because the negator is none other than God himself. All the dialectical movements of *Rom* II revolve around this theo-logical figure. To see the methodological impact of the book, the foreword of *Rom* II is crucial. In a rather unusual manner, Barth elucidates the convictions he had when writing the book. He is especially clear regarding the questions of theological exegesis, but he treats these questions with a certain irony as well.

The Tambach lecture, "The Christian's Place in Society" (1920; ET: "Society"), marks the transition from *Rom* I to *Rom* II. Here we explicitly find the claim that there is a primary movement in history that leads beyond history: "Christ" does not mean a Christian, as it could be understood in German, but rather means "*Jesus Christ*." And it is the *kingdom of God* that will come to change the world. We, as humans, only have to follow this great movement—and we do so by affirming the world as having its origin in God (the "thesis"), by criticizing the actual shape of the world as having deteriorated from its original state ("antithesis"), and by trusting that both thesis and antithesis are linked to each other by the "synthesis," which is unreachable and can only be understood as a placeholder for God himself. The Tambach lecture is also important insofar as it represents Barth's first speech in postwar Germany as a dialectical theologian. It is also remarkable that, even on this first occasion, Barth set himself up in contradiction to German religious socialists, who strived to realize the kingdom by means of theologically guided politics.

In his Göttingen years, Barth was able to enrich and enlarge his new conception of (dialectical) theology, especially in conferences with pastors, but also in his academic teaching. The lecture "The Need and Promise of Christian Preaching" (1922; ET: "Need and Promise") made the Sunday church service the offspring of the dialectical structure. People who gather for the church service ask for the divine whole, whether they are conscious of this demand or not. And the *Bible* represents the divine answer, which leads the participants of the service much further than they could expect. The pastor is the person in which the two lines, the human question and the divine answer, intersect—but one is obliged to fulfill one's duty by witnessing that the coincidence of the two lines is only a matter of God's will and grace, as they are spoken in God's Word.

To explain the divine ground of this coincidence, the debate centers on the adequate form of theology. In the famous lecture "The Word of God and the Task of the Ministry" (1922; ET "Task"), Barth outlined, in a more heuristic manner, three types of theology: first, the dogmatic way, which highlights the divine root of God's Word; second, the critical way, which stresses the negative function of God's Word in regard to the human life and experience; and, third, the dialectical way, which is concentrated on the intersection of God's Word and human existence. Especially—and only—this dialectical method of theology is able to respect the categorical difference between God himself and all our human attempts to talk about him and his word. Therefore the ultimate goal of theology is to praise and honor God, that is, to give him the glory (which might underline the specifically reformed character of Barth's theology).

In his lecture "The Problem of Ethics Today" (1922; ET in *WGWM*, 136–82), Barth laid out the consequences of dialectical theology for ethics. We find in ethics a conception that starts from the subject and his duty (the Kantian option); we find a conception oriented toward the ultimate goal of history (which is taken up by the socialist option). However, the most fitting conception for theological ethics is based on the insight that our entire life is challenged by God's Word, negating our own competence of realizing the ultimate good, but maintaining the real end of the world and of history in God's promise. Thus his ethical advice is to attempt a kind of obedient cooperation.

Starting with his academic lectures at Göttingen, Barth was transforming his dialectical theology. His lectures on *dogmatics* (*Unterricht* I–III, 1924–1926), finished at Münster, especially opened up a way for him to clarify the very open question of dialectical theology, namely, the insight into the specifically divine origin of the negation. To explain this origin, Barth was forced to enlarge his notion of "the *Word of God*," as he did in the *CD*, beginning in 1932. Nevertheless, the *CD* can only be understood if we keep in mind that it has its origin in the dialectical issues; that is, the *CD* responds, in its own unique way, to the questions of liberal theology. "Dialectical theology" thus remains both an important stage in Barth's theology as well as a fundamental structure that cannot be ignored.

M. Beintker, *Die Dialektik in der "dialektischen Theologie" Karl Barths* (1987); D. Korsch, *Dialektische Theologie nach Karl Barth* (1996); B. McCormack, *Karl Barth's Critically Realistic Dialectical Theology* (1995); G. Pfleiderer, *Karl Barths praktische Theologie* (2000).

DIETRICH KORSCH

Dogma On the one hand, in his debate with Neo-Protestantism, Barth decisively affirms the role of dogma in the life of the *church*. On the other hand, in his debate with **Roman Catholicism**, Barth rejects the traditional notion of dogma as a systematic arrangement of Latin propositions sealed with divine authority. Barth seeks rather to offer a fresh vision of the very meaning of dogma for the life of the church.

Barth distinguishes between dogmas and dogma. Dogmas are theological statements in the public documents of the church; dogma is the aim of the church of the present in its search for the will of **God**. Dogmas are truths to be accepted and pondered critically; dogma is the *truth* itself by which the church is guided and illuminated. Dogmas are in the past; dogma is an eschatological concept, always on the horizon of the church's struggle to discern the way of God in the *world*. Genuine dogma is not a static given; it is not already there to be confirmed, but waiting to be discovered and affirmed.

Dogma is not a neutral or abstract truth; dogma is a concept of relation, in two equally important senses. First, dogma constitutes the relation between the contemporary proclamation of the *gospel* and the *revelation* of God attested in Holy Scripture. All true dogma is derived from Holy Scripture, which alone bears truthful *witness* to *Jesus Christ*. Dogma is not a critical standpoint by which Scripture is judged; on the contrary, Scripture is always free to correct dogma for the sake of the gospel. There can never be any retreat into the past; dogma always entails the present responsibility of the church in the interpretation of Scripture. True dogma is a norm and guide for the living church.

Second, dogma entails the relation between the living command of God and the obedient response of *humanity*. Dogma is not a thing; dogma is an event. Dogma is an act of God, in which the living reality of God commands, requiring the response of obedience. The true content of God's living will is known only in the decision of *faith*; dogma is just this relation between command and decision. Barth therefore undoubtedly keeps the notion of a true content in his understanding of dogma; yet he also insists that truth and obedience are necessarily correlative.

Jesus Christ is the true substance of all dogma. For that reason, the dogmas of the church are not about an It, but about a he; not about a something, but about a someone. The *language* of dogma is therefore not speech about God, but speaking to God; to the one from whom comes all things and to whom all things belong. The study of dogma is therefore undertaken with a deep sense of responsibility, yet is at the same time permeated with the *joy* of its object. Pure doctrine (dogma) is only possible on one basis: the supplication of the promised presence of the **Holy Spirit**, who guides the church in each new age.

H. Urs von Balthasar, *The Theology of Karl Barth*, trans. J. Drury (1971); K. Barth, *CD* I/1:248–92; I/2:758–82; E. Busch, *The Great Passion*, trans. G. W. Bromiley (2004), 39ff.; B. Lohse, "Introduction," in *A Short History of Christian Doctrine*, trans. F. E. Stoeffler (1966), 1–22.

PAUL C. McGLASSON

Dogmatics Dogmatics constitutes the ongoing attempt of the **church** to test self-critically the content of its proclamation of the *gospel*. The energy and focus of the attempt come from within the community of *faith* itself; or rather, from the dialogue of the community with the living *God* whom it serves. The ultimate test becomes whether the words and deeds of the church conform to the one who is the source and goal of its very existence: *Jesus Christ*.

Barth sharply rejects every form of *apologetics*: any effort to ground the message of the church in the alien thought form of a philosophical system, ontology, anthropology, aesthetic, or political ideology. He rejects the attempt to correlate the gospel with any *point of contact* in human *culture*, even to argue for its truthfulness. The *freedom* and autonomy of dogmatics as a discipline of human inquiry is guaranteed, not by any conceptual foundation, but by the promise of the risen Christ, who calls each new generation of the church to fresh responsibility.

The primary focus of dogmatic responsibility is on the humanly impossible task of church proclamation. Through the miraculous presence of the *Holy Spirit*, the word of the preacher becomes God's own word in the world. And yet, as a human word, it is always subject to the temptations of human frailty and fallibility. The ongoing task of dogmatics is to test current proclamation of the gospel; to ask whether it is speaking the *Word of God* in the *world*. Dogmatics is not summoned to critique *preaching* as a hostile opponent; but to aid preaching, as a helping partner in the economy of churchly scholarship. Preaching comes first; dogmatics is there to lend a hand.

In carrying out its task, dogmatics has both a negative and a positive dimension. The negative task—vividly demonstrated by Barth's role in the German Church struggle—is the drawing of boundaries outside of which the gospel is not rightly preached. Outside these boundaries lies not the genuine teaching of the church but false doctrine. Dog-

matics does not have the role of naming heretics: that belongs to the gathered church; nor does it ever attack individuals, but only theological positions. Nevertheless, dogmatics is accountable to the church to speak loudly and clearly when error (see *heresy*) becomes so widespread that the health and well-being of the church are at stake.

The positive dimension is the unfolding of church doctrine. Church doctrine is derived exclusively from Holy Scripture, which alone is the absolute norm for dogmatics. However, the point is not to summarize the teaching of Scripture (biblical theology), but rather to summarize the message of the church on the basis of Scripture. Alongside the primary dialogue with Scripture, dogmatics undertakes a secondary dialogue with the creeds and confessions of the church, which command respect and attention. A third dialogue is also crucial: the dialogue with the contemporary world. Dogmatics is not a propositional summary of timeless truths; every new generation of the church must begin at the beginning and win the truths of the gospel afresh in each new age.

Barth is willing to call dogmatics a *science*, though he did not mean that dogmatics must in any sense borrow from the human or natural sciences universal criteria of meaning or *truth*. This approach Barth repeatedly rejected out of hand. Nevertheless, in its own modest way, there is no reason why dogmatics should not count as a science, and even stand out as a model for scientific endeavor. First, it is oriented wholly toward its object, and strives above all else to maintain serene objectivity even in the storm and stress of the times. Second, it strives for a comprehensive, coherent, and orderly discernment of the inner logic of its subject matter. Third, it involves a community of inquiry stretching out across cultural and linguistic boundaries, in the ecumenical church.

Dogmatics is open-ended on the question of method. The secret of dogmatics is therefore not to be found in the methodological approach, but rather in the final capacity of the results to illuminate Holy Scripture. Still, there is in Barth a broad framework that is unyielding: and that is the standpoint of faith seeking understanding. Dogmatics begins from within the confessional stance of the church; from that standpoint it rigorously inquires concerning the meaning and truth of what the church believes. Dogmatics is not a blind assertion of faith; quite the opposite, the whole point is not only to believe, but carefully to explore and to reflect upon the content of what we believe. Barth proceeds dialectically; while denying a philosophical foundationalism, philosophical tools can and should be used insofar as they aid the project of faith seeking understanding.

In terms of the broad organization of dogmatics, Barth rejects the modern Neo-Protestant approach of isolating an "essence" of *religion* anthropologically, and then using that essence as a critical norm for adjusting the content of faith. Barth likewise rejects the "analytical" method of Protestant scholasticism, which sought to determine the "end" of religion, and then coordinate and arrange all theological propositions systematically toward that end. Rather, Barth returns to the older loci method of the Reformers, in which each locus of doctrine points to the whole truth of the divine word; there is no higher unity than the Word of God itself. Barth divided dogmatics into the locus on God, on *creation*, on *reconciliation*, and on redemption; he prefaced these with a prolegomena on the Word of God as part of dogmatics, not as a preconfessional point of orientation. Also, because the truth of God cannot be separated from the claim of God, dogmatics necessarily includes theological *ethics*.

Above all, the task of dogmatics as a discipline of the church is to ask the question of truth. The question is not one the church asks itself; rather, the church is called by the one whom it serves to ask the question, and it gives its answer with *joy* and humility in prayerful obedience to the Word.

K. Barth, *CD* I/1:3–24; I/2:797–884; E. Jüngel, *Karl Barth*, trans. G. E. Paul (1986); G. Sauter, *Gateway to Dogmatics* (2003); C. Schwöbel, "Theology," in *Cambridge Companion to Karl Barth*, ed. J. Webster (2000), 17–36.

PAUL C. McGLASSON

Election Barth narrates the story of *God* and *humanity* from the perspective of God's eternal election. Everything that is and happens traces its origin to the first decisions of the divine council. And at the beginning of these was *Jesus Christ*: "In the beginning, before *time* and space as we know them, before *creation*, before there was anything distinct from God which could be the object of the *love* of God or the setting for His acts of *freedom*, God anticipated and determined within Himself (in the power of His love and freedom, of His knowing and willing) that the goal and meaning of all His dealings with the as yet non-existent universe should be the fact that in His Son He would be gracious towards man, uniting Himself with him.... This choice was in the beginning. As the subject and object of this choice, Jesus Christ was in the beginning. He was not at the beginning of God, for God has indeed no beginning. But He was at the beginning of all things, at the beginning of God's dealings with the reality which is distinct from Himself. Jesus Christ was the choice or *election* of God in respect of this reality. He was the election of God's *grace* as directed towards man. He was the election of God's *covenant* with man" (*CD* II/2:101–2).

A close reading of this passage helps us to identify six characteristics of God's elective actions. These characteristics, some inferentially connected, all closely interrelated, together form a pattern that, for Barth, governs all further divine activity: God's election of Jesus Christ is primal in order, self-giving in nature, graceful in its motivation, creative in its effect, all-inclusive in its scope, and supralapsarian in character.

God's election of Jesus Christ is primal in order—"at the beginning of God's dealings with the reality which is distinct from Himself." When God decides to reach outside Godself, to call into being what is not God, the first he establishes is Jesus Christ. He is "the beginning of God before which there is no other beginning apart from that of God within Himself. Except, then, for God Himself, nothing can derive from any other source or look back to any other starting point. He is the election of God before which and without which and beside which God cannot make any other choices" (II/2:94).

God's election is self-giving in nature. "God anticipated and determined . . . that . . . He would be gracious towards man, uniting Himself with him." God's first decision has a twofold **determination**. It is a choice of the other, an election that chooses "the other to fellowship with himself." But it is also and foremost "a self-election [by God] in favour of this other" (II/2:10). God "determines man for Himself, having first determined Himself for man" (II/2:91). God determines "that He should not be entirely self-sufficient as He might be," to reach out to what is not God, and the character of this divine reaching out is one of self-giving. "He constitutes Himself as benefit or favour" (II/2:10). God determines to unite Godself with the other, the embodiment of which is the **incarnation**.

God's election is graceful in its motivation. Jesus "was the election of God's grace as directed towards man." God does not elect out of necessity. It is an act of grace, in that "God owes his grace to no one, and no one can deserve it. . . . [G]race cannot be the subject of a claim or a right on the part of the one upon whom it is directed" (II/2:10–11). The structure of God's graceful acts is not such that something outside God relates

to God and triggers a graceful response in and from God; it works the other way around. God, in divine freedom and love, decides to elect, and as such establishes a relationship with what is not God. "God in his love elects another to fellowship with Himself. First and foremost this means that God makes a self-election in favour of this other. He ordains that He should not be entirely self-sufficient as He might be. He determines for Himself that overflowing, that movement, that condescension. He constitutes himself as benefit or favour. And in so doing He elects another as the object of His love" (II/2:10). Love precedes election; election precedes the elect.

The consequence thereof is that *God's election is creative in its effect.* "In the beginning, . . . before there was anything distinct from God." In establishing a relationship with what is not God, God does not just establish a relationship but also establishes the very entities that are at the receiving end of this relationship. The structure of election is not one in which God, from a range of already existing entities, elects some and rejects others. Election is not a function of a more general relationship that God has with the *world*, but every further relationship that God has with the world finds its starting point in the act of election (see II/2:78). In other words, the relationship God establishes in election with what is not God precedes the relationship God has with what is not God in creation. This latter point underscores the freedom of God's grace expressed in election: "Free grace is the only basis and meaning of all God's ways and works *ad extra*. For what *extra* is there that the ways and works could serve, or necessitate, or evoke? There is no *extra* except that which is first willed and posited by God in the presupposing of all his ways and works. There is no *extra* except that which has its basis and meaning as such in the divine election of grace" (II/2:95).

God's election is all-inclusive in its scope—"the goal and meaning of all his dealings with the as yet non-existent universe." Given the priority of election over creation, all that God's creative act establishes is included in God's election. This should, however, not be understood as if "man as such" or "the human race as a whole" is the object of election, "nor indeed a large or small total of individual men." Election is particular. Elected is "the one man Jesus and the people represented in him. Only secondary, and for his sake, is it 'man,' and 'humanity' and the whole remaining cosmos" (II/2:8). In other words, election is addressed and applied to every individual, but "every 'individual' in himself and as such would be rejected if it were not that his election is incorporated in that of Jesus Christ" (II/2:351).

Finally, God's election is supralapsarian in character—"As the subject and object of this choice, Jesus Christ was in the beginning." God's electing act is supralapsarian in the twofold sense of the word. It is supralapsarian, both predestinatarian and christological. Divine predestination is not a first step in a divine response to human *sin*, and neither is the incarnation. Although the foregoing would already be enough ground to draw this conclusion, Barth adds a new element. Christ is not only the object of the election—not even the premier object of divine choice—but he is also its subject. To say that Jesus Christ was in the beginning does not only mean that he is the object of God's decree, but also that he is "himself the plan and decree of God, himself the divine decision with respect to all creation and its *history* whose content is already determined" (II/2:104). He is both elected and elector—"from the very first He participates in the divine election; that election is also His election; it is He Himself who posits this beginning from all things; it is He Himself who executes the decision which issues in the establishment of the covenant between God and man" (II/2:105).

At least since Augustine, theologians have spoken of Christ as the paradigmatic object of election. Reformed scholastics added to this that Christ's election is the foundation of all other divine acts of election. Barth underwrites this notion: Christ is the one who, "[f]rom the very beginning (from eternity itself), as elected man He does not stand alongside the rest of the elect, but before and above them as the One who is originally and properly the Elect. From the very beginning (from eternity itself), there are no other elect together with or apart from Him, but, as Eph. 1:4 tells us, only 'in' Him" (II/2:116). However, central to Barth's doctrine of election is that Christ is not only the first elected human, but that he is this precisely because he is also the electing God. "Jesus Christ is not merely one object of the divine good-pleasure side by side with others. On the contrary, he is the sole object of this pleasure, for in the first instance he himself is this good-pleasure, the will of God in action" (II/2:104). Jesus Christ is, from the beginning, with the Father and the Spirit the subject of election (II/2:101, 105, 107).

To establish this point, Barth develops several arguments. Whereas the further volumes of the *CD* can be read as one sustained theological argument to support his doctrine of election, Barth supports his actual discussion of the doctrine in II/2 by a series of exegetical arguments. He concentrates on three groups of biblical passages, each group representing a particular pattern of thinking about Christ. Together these patterns form a cumulative case for Barth's position. The first pattern is found in a cluster of texts that refer to Jesus Christ as active subject from before the foundation of the world. Barth refers to Eph. 1:4, 11, and 3:11, as well as Rom. 8:29ff. and Col. 1:15–20 (II/2:60). Barth's *exegesis* of these texts highlights two features. First, Barth emphasizes that none of these texts makes a distinction between the Son as λόγος ἄσαρκος, the preincarnate Word, and as Jesus Christ, the embodied Word. The one in whom all are elect and created, the one who is in the beginning, the one who is from before the foundation of the world is not referred to as λόγος ἄσαρκος, but as Jesus. An exegesis that does not take this point into account erodes the content of these texts (II/2:107). Second, Barth interprets the role of Jesus in these texts as one of an active agent. This receives particular emphasis in those texts that speak of an activity δι' αὐτου or ἐν αὐτῷ as divine acts of election and creation. Barth does not interpret these phrases as "through him" or "in him," but in the stronger sense of "by him." On this reading, Jesus is not just the instrument but the active subject in election and creation. "'In Him' does not simply mean with Him, together with Him, in His company. Nor does it only mean through Him, by means of that which He as elected man can be and do for them. 'In Him' means in His person, in His will, in His own divine choice, in the basic decision of God which He fulfils over against every man" (II/2:116–17).

Whereas these texts indeed give Barth good grounds to reject an interpretation of their object as the λόγος ἄσαρκος, Barth has a harder case defending his strong reading of the δι' αὐτου and ἐν αὐτῷ. He legitimates this last move by his exegesis of the second and third cluster of texts. The second cluster concerns texts from the prologue to the Gospel of John. Barth argues that the notion of Logos functions in the entire prologue as a placeholder, "a preliminary indication of the place where later something or someone quite different will be disclosed," namely Jesus (II/2:96). He supports this reading by an exegesis of the clause in John 1:2, "The same was (οὗτος ἦν) in the beginning with God." Barth suggests that this clause is not a recapitulation of verse 1, but a reference forward to the declaration of John the Baptist in verse 15, who, with use of the same expression οὗτος ἦν, says: "This was he of whom I said, 'He who comes after me ranks ahead of me because he was before me.'" The "he" the Baptist refers to is clearly Jesus, the incarnate

Logos; and if verse 2 of the prologue refers forward to the same "he," so must, given the flow of the argument in this section, the "he" of verse 1, who was "in the beginning," and the "he" of verse 3, "through whom all things were made" (II/2:98).

The third cluster of texts concerns those passages that speak of Jesus as the one who elects his disciples: John 13:18, 15:16, and 19. Barth insists that these texts should not be understood "loosely" but in the "strictest and most proper sense: the electing of the disciples ascribed to Jesus must be understood not merely as a function undertaken by him in an instrumental and representative capacity, but rather as an act of divine sovereignty, in which there is seen in a particular way the primal and basic decision of God which is also that of Jesus Christ" (II/2:106). This too would support Barth's strong reading of the δι' αὐτου or ἐν αὐτῷ in the first cluster of texts.

Finally, in addition to these readings, Barth puts forward an exegetical argument of somewhat different nature. This argument aims to bring out the logical presuppositions of the notion of Christ as the object of election and the Pauline formula that we are elected "in Christ." The Pauline formula means that Christ is more than a mere illustration of election; he is its focal point and the head of all the elect. But for him to have such standing before God and such power among humankind, he needs to be more than the object of election. "For where can Jesus Christ derive the authority and power to be the Lord and Head of all others, and how can these others be elected 'in Him,' and how can they see their election in Him the first of the elect, and how can they find in His election the assurance of their own, if He is only the object of election and not Himself its subject, if He is only an elect creature and not primarily and supremely the electing Creator?" (II/2:116).

Having thus established the nature of the "him" in whom we are elected,

Barth is now ready to turn to the nature of the "in." Just as he reads the "him" in the strongest way possible, so does he read the "in": "From the very beginning (from eternity itself), there are no other elect together with or apart from Him, but, as Eph. 1:4 tells us, only 'in' Him. 'In Him' does not simply mean with Him, together with Him, in His company. Nor does it mean only through Him, by means of that which He as elected man can be and do for them. 'In Him' means in His person, in His will, in His own divine choice, in the basic decision of God which He fulfils over against every man. . . . And so they are elect 'in Him,' in and with His own election . . . His election is the original and all-inclusive election" (II/2:116–17). Barth describes the relation expressed by the word "in" as participation: "What can this election be . . . but . . . a participation in the grace of the One who elects, a participation in His creatureliness (which is already grace), and a participation in His sonship (which is eminently grace)?" (II/2:121). In later volumes, Barth unpacks the "in him" in terms of an ontological connection. There is "an ontological connection between the man Jesus on the one side and all other men on the other" because "an ontological declaration about their own being under His sovereignty" was made. "It belongs to the distinctive essence of the Jesus Christ of the New Testament that as the One He alone is He is not alone, but the royal Representative, the Lord and Head of many," because they are "in Him" (IV/2:275).

"In him" becomes thus virtually a technical term. In conformance with the logic of election, it suggests that we are before we come to exist. We are objects of election, participating and ontologically—in being—connected in and to Christ before we receive embodied existence. The relationship God establishes, in election with what is not God, precedes the relationship God has in creation with what is not God. Note also how the relationship between Christ

and those elected in him mirrors the relationship between God and Christ. When God decides to give Godself to what is not God, that which is not God is established: Jesus Christ. He does not yet have embodied existence, but he still was in the beginning with God, "beyond time and beyond the nexus of the created world and its history," in "the sphere where God is with Himself, the sphere of His free will and pleasure" (II/2:100). Likewise, Christ establishes those who are elected in him, and who now have existence in him "before they were" (III/3:88).

M. K. Cunningham, *What Is Theological Exegesis?* (1995); E. C. van Driel, *Incarnation Anyway* (2008), 63–124; D. Gibson, *Reading the Decree* (2009); B. L. McCormack, *Orthodox and Modern* (2008), 183–200, 261–77.

EDWIN CHR. van DRIEL

Eschatology Barth never wrote his eschatology, which he had intended to be the fifth volume of his *CD*, titled "The Doctrine of Redemption." Nevertheless, the basic outline of Barth's eschatology can be reconstructed from the earlier volumes. Moreover, the publication of Barth's early lectures on eschatology from Münster (1925/1926), part of the *Göttingen Dogmatics*, makes it possible to describe the design of Barth's eschatology.

Barth's eschatology differs from previous publications on the subject in that he does not begin with the question of the immortality of the soul and its whereabouts after death. For what happens to the human being is not the subject of eschatology, but only what *hope* sees in "*Jesus Christ*, and everything else that must be mentioned, as *his* deed, as a predicate of *this* subject" (*Unterricht* III, 437). Jesus Christ's Parousia is at the very center of eschatology. According to Barth, it must not be understood in *analogy* to the *incarnation*. True, the redeemer is none other than the reconciler, but the manner of his presence is entirely different. He comes "entirely *unconcealed*" (444) and will be visible to all eyes.

At the same time, Barth emphasizes that Christ's visible coming will take place on a particular day in a particular place, thus making clear that we are dealing with the redemption of none other than this *world*. The reminder of Christ's coming day prevents us from falling into a wrongheaded dualism, one that does not expect anything new in the *history* of the world, but instead hopes for the new only in some fabricated world. The new event for which Christians hope will take place within the history of this world.

Construing the Parousia as an event within *time*, however, means neither that our time is closer to the Parousia than any present that has passed nor, or much less, that our time or the future brings about Christ's Parousia. Indeed, the Parousia-Christ will appear at a particular hour, yet he reaches "all generations in all places" at the same time (448). Any boasting is excluded especially because it is not history that brings about the Parousia. Instead, the day of Parousia arrives because Christ arrives. The Parousia-Christ "remains the *subject*, he does not become the predicate of history" (450). Precisely for this reason, humans cannot bring about this day—that is, neither by any supposed history of progress initiated by them nor by their tendency to waste the environment in a way that leads *creation* to the brink of destruction. Christians do not hope for the perfection of this world's processes, but for Christ "to relinquish his concealment in heaven and reveal . . . the glory of human nature in *his* person directly, visibly" (469).

Of course this *revelation* cannot be understood as a merely noetic apocalypse, as Barth has often been charged of espousing. For Jesus Christ's new presence corresponds to his new and perfecting work: the resurrection of the dead. The concept that characterizes the doctrine of *reconciliation*, that is, that the person and work of Jesus Christ cannot be separated in *Christology*, is valid also for eschatology. The person of Christ cannot be conceived without his work, nor can the Parousia be understood without the resurrection of the dead.

The unity of the Parousia with the resurrection of the dead can be illustrated with the pneumatological insight that Christ cannot be conceived of without his congregation. Being called by Christ, Barth writes, means "nothing less than: *belonging* to him, even being one with him through the *Holy Spirit* in a way that, apart from this, only the persons of the *Trinity belong* to each other, are even *one*" (467). For this reason the unconcealed revelation of Jesus Christ in his Parousia means that our lives will become revealed and those, who belong to him, will rise from the dead.

In accordance with 1 Corinthians 15, Barth conceives of the lives of the risen ones as in continuity with their present lives, but also in discontinuity with them. Eternal life involves individual lives as well, which the risen ones will live as subjects. Eternal life neither means the dissolution of our individual life into an all-fulfilling divine life nor the conservation of our individual lives in God's memory. The redeemed will lead their individual lives as subjects of this life.

In contrast to our present lives, however, we will live our eternal lives as the reconciled, which we already are now in Christ. Yet in the resurrection of the dead, the contradiction that characterizes our present existence will be eliminated, that is, being children of Adam and, in Christ, children of God. The identity as children of Adam, which we still are, will come to an end, so that we can live as children of God. That is why the coming of Christ and the resurrection of the dead at the same time imply the Last Judgment.

According to Barth, the meaning of judgment becomes clear only when we keep in mind that the coming judge is none other than Jesus Christ. Since he who has been judged in our place is the judge, the judgment means "a passing to corruption, but also a becoming new; and both are for the whole world and for all men" (*ER*, 69). Barth repeatedly uses the image of the purifying fire to describe the process of waning and becoming new in judgment: In the Last Judgment, humans will be faced with the purifying fire of God's *love*, by which God wants to sanctify humans for the eternal life that they were already freely given in Jesus Christ. But since quite a few works "will be . . . destroyed" in this crucible "as if . . . it had never been" (*CD* IV/2:637), redemption does not take place without the most severe "reduction and subtraction" (IV/3.2:928). We—and with this Barth always means all of *humanity*—will have to forfeit parts of our lives. This also shows that the Last Judgment is not about dividing humanity up in two parts. Instead, it is about judging the world in such a way that humans can live together in the *kingdom of God*.

This expectation of Christ's coming, of the resurrection of the dead, and of the Last Judgment shapes the life of Christ's congregation. In his doctrine of the redemption, Barth would likely have brought this fact to bear in a twofold way. The doctrine of reconciliation discusses not only reconciliation in Jesus Christ, but also presents how the Holy Spirit appropriates reconciliation for individual Christians. In a similar vein, Barth's doctrine of redemption would have shown how the Holy Spirit leads the congregation to the coming one. In this way Barth would certainly have clarified that the time in which we are waiting for Christ's coming is not a time of darkness. Instead, as the time of the Holy Spirit it is blessed with a variety of lights. Still we have to wait for the great light of the Parousia, but the preceding lights inspire us to do so in confidence.

Just as Barth's doctrines of creation and reconciliation lead to chapters about the *ethics* of creation and reconciliation,

Barth would also have finished his doctrine of redemption with an ethics of redemption. The coming Christ asks us if our actions sufficiently reflect the new that we are awaiting—or if we adapt our deeds too much to those old structures and forms that are bound to pass away.

————

C. Asprey, *Eschatological Presence in Karl Barth's Göttingen Theology* (2010); I. Dalferth, "Karl Barth's Eschatological Realism," in *Karl Barth*, ed. S. W. Sykes (1989), 14–45: G. Etzelmüller, . . . *zu richten die Lebendigen und die Toten* (2001): J. C. McDowell, *Hope in Barth's Eschatology* (2000): G. Sauter, *What Dare We Hope?* (1999).

GREGOR ETZELMÜLLER

Eternity In Barth's theology, "eternity" is a theological term, not a philosophical or scientific concept. It describes theological realities; it says something about *God*. Barth has no *doctrine* of eternity, for it is not a doctrine, not as Barth uses the word *doctrine*. Rather, Barth's understanding of eternity grows out of and helps explicate matters that are themselves doctrines. Among such doctrines, the foremost are that of the *Trinity, Jesus Christ*, and *revelation*. Eternity speaks of the nature of the triune God who is revealed in Jesus Christ.

What Barth meant by "eternity" changed and developed throughout his theological career. Because of the changes one finds in Barth's thought, a single definition of eternity likely cannot be offered. Rather, two broad definitions suggest themselves, loosely corresponding to Barth's early and later work.

In the early period, particularly in *Rom* II, Barth typically speaks of "eternity" alongside "*time*" to express the distinction between *humanity* and divinity. This is illustrated from the famous statement that occurs in the foreword: "If I have a 'system,' it consists in this, that I keep in mind as firmly as possible what Kierkegaard called *the 'infinite qualitative distinction' between time and eternity*, in its negative and positive significance. 'God is in heaven, and you are on earth'" (*ER*, 10; translation revised, and italics added). Time and eternity thus together demarcate the border separating two radically distinct realms, a border that cannot at all be crossed by human initiative, but may be crossed only by the **grace** of God. In *Rom* II, Barth characteristically places these terms in antithesis, in order to highlight the crisis of human pretensions to holiness, a crisis brought about by the righteousness of God revealed in Jesus Christ.

In Barth's later period, starting around the time of the *Göttingen Dogmatics* and coming to full expression in the *CD*, eternity is an attribute of God or, rather, as Barth prefers, a "perfection." Moreover, eternity as well as time have in the *CD* a much greater christological and Trinitarian focus, with the result that these terms no longer are typically deployed to express separation between Creator and creature, but rather to express the way in which that separation is not only established but also gracefully mediated by the triune God.

The earlier usage of eternity and time, then, was one primarily of opposition, whereas Barth later came to use these terms in a way that did not stress the opposition but understood it as an important, first, and yet subordinate note to be sounded. Although he never abandoned the theological convictions that underlay the opposition of time and eternity, Barth later became more convinced that the dominantly negative emphasis in *Rom* II was not sufficient. An adequate theological understanding of eternity as well as of time required greater attention to the revelation of God in Jesus Christ, which pointed not only to opposition between eternity and time but to an overcoming of that opposition by God in Christ.

Barth articulated this refocused understanding of eternity in *CD* II/1, in his lengthy discussion of the **perfections of God**. There he describes God's eternity as having a threefold structure: God's pre-temporality, supra-temporality, and post-temporality. That is, God is the origin of all time, God accompanies or contains all time, and God is there after time as its goal and **hope**.

In so structuring his concept of divine eternity, Barth sought to express a distinction and yet a positive *relationship* between eternity and time. Eternity is described not as merely atemporality, but rather, in this threefold way, with each aspect having time in view, as pre-, supra-, and post-*temporal*. The terms by which Barth defines eternity (pre-temporality, supra-temporality, post-temporality) point to a conception of eternity that is oriented to time rather than alienated from it. However, as a "temporality" that is before, above, and after time, eternity is clearly distinct from time as it is typically understood and experienced. The temporal cast to Barth's construction notwithstanding, eternity is not the same as time.

In giving eternity this threefold structure, Barth thereby connects eternity with his doctrine of the Trinity. The connection is demonstrated not simply in eternity's threefold form. The mere occurrence of a pattern of three does not a Trinity make. Rather, the connection of Barth's concept of eternity with his doctrine of the Trinity is seen in a much more substantive, and doctrinal, focus. This conception of eternity, with its threefold cast, is understood *perichoretically*.

The doctrine of *perichoresis* in traditional **dogmatics** is a means of describing the relations between the persons of the Trinity. Those relations, the doctrine insists, are mutual and cooperative, unified yet distinct. Father, Son, and **Holy Spirit** exist and work together in such a way that they are both united with and distinct from one another. To say that Barth's threefold conception of eternity is perichoretic is to say that the relations among the three aspects of eternity are construed much as are the relations among the persons of the Trinity.

"At this point, as in the doctrine of the Trinity itself, we can and must speak of a *perichoresis*, a mutual indwelling and interworking of the three forms of eternity" (II/1:640).

Pre-, supra-, and post-temporality, therefore, are to be understood as describing divine realities that may be distinguished but not ultimately separated from one another, and that must be understood in their relation to one another. "God is equally truly and really pretemporal, supra-temporal, and post-temporal. But since He is God, He is all this in divine perfection. Thus 'before' in Him does not imply 'not yet'; 'after' in Him does not imply 'no more'; and above all His present does not imply any fleetingness. In each of the distinctions of perfection He has a share in the others" (640).

In Barth's mature articulation of the concept, then, eternity is an attribute of God's being, expressing the nature of God with regard to time and temporality as demonstrated in God's revelation.

K. Barth, *CD* II/1:608–40; D. Griswold, "Perichoretic Eternality" (PhD diss., Southern Methodist University, 2010); G. Hunsinger, "*Mysterium Trinitatis*," in *Disruptive Grace* (2000), 131–47.

DANIEL M. GRISWOLD

Ethics Barth believed that the task of guiding the church and its members in how to live was inseparable from the rest of the task of *theology*. For this reason, understanding the ethical implications of his theology requires an understanding of his theology as a whole. His discussion of suicide, to pick one example (*CD* III/4:401–13), is unlikely to persuade unless the reader is already convinced by his account of God's *election* of human beings and the implication that they are called to lives of responsibility before *God*, set out in CD II/2. Barth's primary aim in writing about ethics is not to persuade his readers to share one or two of the ethical positions he holds, but to help them to recognize the revolutionary implications of God's claim on their lives.

The integration of theology and ethics in Barth's thought does not mean that he saw ethical issues as being of secondary importance to doctrinal questions. In Rom II he commented that "it is our pondering over the question 'What shall we do?' which compels us to undertake so much seemingly idle conversation about God," and it is pressing practical questions, the wickedness on the streets, and the daily newspapers that drive us to reading the letters of Paul (*ER*, 438). In the *CD*, he is even bolder: "the dogmatics of the Christian Church, and basically the Christian doctrine of God, is ethics," and doctrine is "the answer to the ethical question" (II/2:515). For Barth, therefore, the whole theological enterprise can be seen as driven by the need to answer questions of ethics, and theology is sterile unless it informs us about how to live.

Barth's fundamental insight in relation to ethics is that the *church* should seek to follow the will of God. This may seem uncontroversial to the point of banality, but its implications are far-reaching. First, it is rooted in the claim of God on the people of God, grounded in God's gracious *election* in *Jesus Christ* of all *humanity*. Those elected by God are called to a joyful response to this initiative of *grace* by living as God's children according to God's will. Second, this task of seeking to follow God's will means that God has a will for how the church and its members are to live out their lives. God does not leave us to find our own way in a neutral space, but places us within a good *creation* and wills that we live lives in accordance with our identity as those elected by God. Third, the task of following the will of a gracious God means that we are not left to guess what it is God wants of us, but rather that we can expect to be guided by God. This is the reason Barth uses divine command as the primary way of understanding theological ethics: God's will for us is definite, specific, and communicated to us. The moral task is therefore to hear the divine command and obey (see II/2:509–42).

Barth is not unaware of the ways in which the *language* of divine command could be misunderstood. Many possible misunderstandings are ruled out by the context of his theological ethics in the broader structure of his theology. For example, one standard objection to divine command ethics is often discussed in relation to the dilemma presented in Plato's *Euthyphro*: Does God command actions because they are right, or are actions right because they are commanded by God? Taking the first horn of the dilemma seems to make God redundant to morality; taking the second suggests morality is potentially the whim of a despot. This is not a dilemma in the context of Barth's theology because God's commanding takes place within a *covenant* of grace that precedes creation. All things, including morality, have their origin in God; the basis of morality in God does not make morality vulnerable but makes clear its only possible secure foundation. Another standard critique of divine command theories in a post-Enlightenment context is that they fail to allow sufficient autonomy to mature moral agents. Again this concern is defeated in relation to Barth as a result of his wider theological framework. Because this command comes from the God who is gracious in Jesus Christ, it is a permission that does not compel but bursts open the door of the compulsion under which human beings live (II/2:586). It is the command of our true best friend, against us only insofar as we are against ourselves (595). Barth stands here in a long theological tradition that defines true *freedom* not as arbitrary choice but as liberation to be the persons we are meant to be before God.

In setting out his view of the task of theological ethics, Barth engages in a stern denial of some alternative construals. Ethics as a theological task has nothing to do with a general conception of ethics, which, insofar as it is human beings seeking to provide their own answers to the ethical question rather than subject themselves to the divine command, "coincides exactly with the conception of *sin*." Christian ethics is not one disputant in a debate with others, but is the final word (II/2:517–18). There are no other sources of ethical knowledge beyond the command of God, and any attempt to build an alternative route through *natural theology* and natural law is dangerous in setting the limited light of *reason* against God's revealed will (533). Theological ethics must be always open to hearing God's command, which means it cannot operate by expounding God's law and applying it to individual cases, as moral casuistry does (III/4:6). None of this means for Barth that Christian ethics is a *truth* only for the church, however. Jesus is Lord of the whole *world*, and Christian ethics must recognize the human situation before God to be that of everyone (II/2:643). Once Barth has established the basic mode in which Christian ethics is to operate, he is also clear that ethics can be Christian even if not explicitly based in theology—suggesting the novels of Balzac, Dickens, Dostoevsky, and Tolstoy as examples (542)—and that God's will has always been fulfilled outside the church as well as within it (569).

In using the language of divine command, Barth should not be interpreted as believing that ethics is merely responding to divine intuitions, as some critics have suggested. He is clear that we have no unmediated access to God's will. The divine command is not a voice in our head: if God did not speak to us through the objects in our world, we would not be able to hear. God's command is always veiled in some other kind of claim: an insight gained from reading the *Bible*, or a sermon, or a piece of advice, or a felt necessity of action (II/2:584–85). We will normally learn of God's word to us through the Bible and the teaching of the church, but "God may speak to us through Russian Communism, a flute concerto, a blossoming shrub, or a dead dog" or "through a pagan or atheist" (I/1:55). This raises the question of how we are to distinguish God's command from all others. Barth's response is that this question narrows down "to that of distinguishing Jesus Christ from all other lords and ultimately and decisively from the lord that each of us would like to be over himself" (II/2:608).

Given Barth's insistence that Christians should do ethics only by hearing and obeying the command of God, it may seem strange that he devoted such attention to the discussion of particular issues instead of stopping at recommending that Christians listen for God's word. Barth believes that while each person is responsible for attending to God's command, it is possible to speak of continuity in God's commanding. God's commands are not merely multiple and diverse, but are moments in a single divine order and plan. Similarly, human action is not merely a series of individual cases, but the actions of a single subject. God will always address human beings as their creator, reconciler, and redeemer; the human being will always encounter the command of God as creature, sinner, and child of God. Because of these continuities, Barth argues that it is possible to give a "formed reference" providing "instructional preparation" for the divine command (III/4:16–18, 26). This is the task of theological ethics, and it should aim to give as intensive, direct, and binding an approximation to the divine command as possible, while still respecting the truth that it can never substitute for the divine command. True ethics, like true *dogmatics*, Barth says, "steer a middle course—between what they must not be and what they cannot be" (31).

Barth addressed ethical issues throughout his career. In his pastorate in Safenwil he took up the cause of low-paid industrial workers in the vil-

lage, leading the owners of local factories and mills to resign from his church. During this period he published "Jesus Christus und die soziale Bewegung" (*VkA* II, 380–417; ET: *JCMSJ*) and gave addresses on the war and the relationship between socialism and Christianity. In *Rom* II he took up questions of *love* and community, war and peace and revolution, and soon after its publication wrote on Christian social ethics. He lectured on ethics in 1928–1929 in Münster and again in 1930–1931 in Bonn. In the *CD*, as well as discussing questions of ethical method in II/2, he planned to treat particular ethical topics under the headings of creation, *reconciliation*, and redemption, though only the first of these was fully completed. In III/4, discussing the ethics of creation, he considers the Sabbath, *confession*, and *prayer* before turning to relationships between men and women, parents and children, and nations. Under the heading of "Freedom for Life" (§55), he considers human responsibility for plant and animal life, and then health and sickness, suicide, abortion, euthanasia, killing in self-defense, capital punishment, and warfare. Finally, he considers the active life of the Christian before God, focusing on the ethics of work. The unfinished fragment of the ethics of reconciliation, IV/4, is devoted to the question of *baptism*. The most distinctive common characteristic of these discussions is Barth's respect for his own stipulation that ethics should not preempt the event of hearing the divine command. In many cases, Barth refers to the *Grenzfall* (borderline) case, the possibility that God may command something beyond where his discussion has led. Toward the end of the Second World War Barth argued for rebuilding relationships with Germany, and in the years after the war he advocated nuclear disarmament.

In addition to criticisms of his ethical method, Barth has been taken to task for some of his discussions of ethical topics. His long account of relationships between men and women rejects hierarchy between the sexes but retains an ordering in which female follows male and is at odds with almost all more recent theological accounts (III/4:116–240). John Howard Yoder among others noted the strangeness of Barth's consideration of war in the CD (450–70), and particularly his aside that any attack on Switzerland would be sufficient evidence for him to consider it a divine command to kill in defense of his country (462). Others have wished that he had provided more detailed justification of his position at several points. Barth's emphasis on the openness that is necessary in listening for the command of God means that theologically appropriate revisions here or elsewhere to his work would be entirely in accordance with his vision of the task of theological ethics.

N. Biggar, *The Hastening That Waits* (1993); D. Clough, *Ethics in Crisis* (2005); P. T. Nimmo, *Being in Action* (2007); J. Webster, *Barth's Ethics of Reconciliation* (1995).

DAVID CLOUGH

Evil   Barth's most sustained treatment of "evil" is to be found in CD III/3:§50, titled "God and Nothingness" ("Gott und das Nichtige"). The material here was composed in the context of the physical, diplomatic, and psychological sufferings of postwar central Europe, and is significantly located within Barth's celebration of the creativity of God in CD III. As Barth claimed in the late 1940s, "It is easy to be afraid anywhere in the world today. The whole of the Western world, the whole of Europe is afraid, afraid of the East. But we must not be afraid. . . . Everything is in the hands of God" (*AS*, 99).

Barth worried about the modern "theodicy" project that makes evil a "problem" to be solved, and that "systematizes" nothingness so that it is domesticated. Theology's proper business is only to provide a "report" of the "Creator, creature and their co-existence, and

the intrusion upon them of the undeniable reality of nothingness" (III/3:365). This account has three broad theological implications. First, evil can only be known in and through the act of God in resisting it (specifically at the cross). It is neither caused by God, nor is it the necessary product of God's creating and thus the very existence of the creature as creature, even of the "shadow-side" of *creation*. Barth forcefully portrays evil as an "enemy" of God and the creature.

Second, evil as "nothingness" is not the first or ultimate thing that has to be said about the creature. Evil as "nothingness" is an "alien" factor, an intrusion into the primordial relations of God with the creature. Barth understands it primarily in terms of wickedness or *sin*—as both the expression of sin and the perverse conditions that subsequently give rise to sinning. It involves the misshaping of creaturely becoming that results from the disobedience of the creature against the Creator, even though the creature has no "right," "*freedom*" (freedom is the creature's-freedom-for-God), or "*reason*" (what has been created is good) for disobedience. It is, therefore, absurd and "inexplicable" (III/1:354).

Third, evil can only be spoken of in terms that do not make it ontologically necessary and thereby mitigate the intolerableness or, to use Rosmary Radford Ruether's phrase, the "evilness of evil." Specifically, Barth rejects Schopenhauerian pessimism (III/1:335ff.); and anti-dualistic differentiations between "the nothingness" and creation's shadow side. He equally hesitates to discuss demonology in view of the temptation to fit Satan into a legitimate and proper place within creation. "The nothingness" is "detrimental," and harmful to the creature in that it disturbs, injures, and destroys "the creature and its [God-given] nature" (III/3:310). In a broadly Augustinian fashion, Barth describes evil through the general term *the nothingness* (the language also reflects the work of Martin Heidegger and Jean

Paul Sartre a few years earlier). By this he means: "Nothingness is not nothing. . . . [I]t 'is' nothingness" (III/3:349). It has no ontological substance or reality—"the real" is that which God elects Godself to give. Consequently, using dialectical terms, Barth further speaks of it as the "ontological impossibility" (III/2:146), the "impossible possibility" (III/3:351), the "absurd (irrational) possibility of the absurd (irrational)" (178), an "inherent contradiction" (351), a possibility passed over and rejected as a legitimate reality by God.

K. Barth, *CD* III/3:§§50, 51.3; W. Krötke, *Sin and Nothingness in the Theology of Karl Barth*, trans. P. G. Ziegler (2005); J. McDowell, "Much Ado about Nothing," *IJST* 4, no. 3 (2002): 319–35; R. R. Ruether, "The Left Hand of God in the Theology of Karl Barth," *JRT* 25 (1968–1969): 3–26; J. Webster, *Barth's Moral Theology* (1998), chap. 4; N. Wolterstorff, "Barth on Evil," *Faith and Philosophy* 13 (1996): 584–608.

JOHN C. McDOWELL

Exegesis Barth's theological revolution was born of exegesis, and as "the decisive presupposition and source of all *dogmatics*" (*CD* I/2:821), it was the basis of his *theology*. "If I have become a dogmatician," he once remarked, "it is because I long before have endeavored to carry on exegesis" (*Das Evangelium in der Gegenwart* [TEh 25; Munich: Kaiser, 1935], 17). It was due to exegesis that he was called to Göttingen in 1921, and his courses there in New Testament exegesis (nearly half of those he taught) became very popular among students. It was to a professorship in dogmatics *and* New Testament exegesis that he was later called to Münster, and exegesis that he continued to pursue at Bonn. So important was exegesis to him that at the height of the *Kirchenkampf* in February 1935, upon his dismissal from his teaching post at Bonn, his "final piece of advice" to his students was: "Exegesis, Exegesis, and once more, Exegesis" (17).

No major theologian since *Calvin* has produced more biblical exegesis than Barth. In addition to that, in his commentaries, sermons, and other writings, there are more than two thousand examples of detailed exegesis in the *CD*, with almost twice as much exegesis in each volume produced after the war than in each written before or during the war. Yet Barth's exegesis was a source of conflict throughout his career. Critics attacked *Rom* I primarily because of its exegetical method, which is one reason Karl Adam called it a "bombshell that fell on the playing field of theologians." Barth had already drawn the battle lines between himself and "the dominant science of biblical exegesis" in his foreword drafts to *Rom* I, but he continued to defend his approach in forewords to subsequent editions of *Rom* II. The battle over "What is exegesis?" raged in the German-speaking theological world throughout the 1920s and early 1930s, particularly in the "pneumatic exegesis" movement. Barth admitted his work had "occasioned" this movement, but he repeatedly expressed ambivalence toward it primarily because: "There is no method by which *revelation* can be made revelation that is actually received, no method of scriptural exegesis which is truly pneumatic, i.e., which articulates the *witness* to revelation in the Bible and to that degree really introduces the Pneuma" (I/1:183).

Barth expressed similar ambivalence toward the discussions of hermeneutics that dominated the 1950s and 1960s. He refused repeatedly to enter into them because "the question of the right *hermeneutics* cannot be decided in a discussion of exegetical *method*, but only in exegesis itself" (Busch, 389). Barth's conviction that "*methodus est arbitraria*" was not based on any a priori epistemological commitments, but rather on God's self-revelation in *Jesus Christ*, which he discovered, a posteriori, while exegeting the *Bible*. Scripture's object, he learned, was "sovereignly free," and this had hermeneutical implications, for example, the object to be known should determine the way taken in knowing. This is partly why Hans-Georg Gadamer in *Truth and Method* (2nd ed.) deemed *Rom* I "a virtual hermeneutical manifesto."

Yet contrary to those who suggest Barth's priority of exegesis over hermeneutics reflects a pragmatist penchant or postmodern proclivity toward merely "ad hoc hermeneutical principles," Barth had specific hermeneutical principles and a definite exegetical method, which he describes in his *Römerbrief* period, the *Göttingen, Christian,* and *CD,* and in the last most extensively under the rubric, "Freedom under the Word" (I/2:§21.2). As "the focal point of the Church's action," Barth came to understand exegesis in light of **freedom** because exegesis is, after **prayer,** the "decisive activity" (I/2:695) through which Jesus Christ governs the **church** and thereby sets it free (e.g., from dialogue with itself). Indeed, the church is free only to the extent that it is bound to biblical exegesis. Yet biblical exegesis is free only to the extent that it is bound to the Bible's content and theme. This relation requires explanation.

According to Barth, "The universal rule of interpretation is that a text can be read and understood and expounded only with reference to and in the light of its theme" (493). Scripture's content and theme is "Jesus Christ as the name of the God who deals graciously with man the sinner. . . . To hear this is to hear the Bible—both as a whole and in each one of its separate parts. Not to hear this means *eo ipso* not to hear the Bible, neither as a whole, nor therefore in its parts. The Bible says all sorts of things, certainly: but in all this multiplicity and variety, it says in truth only [this] one thing" (720). To interpret Scripture apart from this content and theme, therefore, is no interpretation at all. No matter how many parts are "explained," such explanation does not yet qualify as interpretation apart from interpretation in light of this whole. And because

this "sovereign name" and content requires submission, Barth claims: "The necessary and fundamental form of all scriptural exegesis . . . must consist in all circumstances in the freely performed act of subordinating all human concepts, ideas and convictions to the witness of revelation supplied to us in Scripture" (715).

Why is subordination the "fundamental form of all scriptural exegesis"? Because "our own ideas, thoughts and convictions, as such, as ours, certainly do not run in the direction of the testimony which has this particular content" (721). On the contrary, "When the **Word of God** meets us, we are laden with the images, ideas and certainties which we ourselves have formed about God, the world and ourselves" (716–17). The Word of God is intrinsically clear, but because it meets us in the "fog of our own intellectual life," it "always becomes obscure." Moreover, "God's thoughts in His Word do not come to us *in abstracto* but *in concreto* in the form of the human word of prophets and apostles." Again, the Word of God needs no explanation "because like the light of the sun above our atmosphere, it is clear in itself. But as such it would not have come to us, and we could have nothing to do with it." Though "clear in itself (even in the form of the scriptural word)" (722), it still needs explanation because it "has assumed the mode of our intellectual world and is thus exposed to the risk of being understood, or rather not understood, by us according to the habits of our mentality" (717). Exegesis (*Auslegung*) is, "as the very word suggests, the unraveling or unfolding of the scriptural word which comes to us in a, so to speak, rolled-up form, thus concealing its meaning" (722).

Exegesis, in this narrower sense, is only one phase in a threefold "process of biblical exposition" (*Schrifterklärung*) that includes *explicatio, meditatio,* and *applicatio.* As the "first plainly distinguishable aspect of the process," *explicatio* "is the act of observation" or seeing what is there. Because the divine Word in the scriptural word has "adjusted itself to our human world of thought, thus exposing itself to the darkening prism of our human understanding," what is there is not obvious. "Yet even in this darkening, it still retains its power to explain itself, which means above all to present itself. And as it does this, there arises the corresponding human task: to follow this self-presentation." Exegetes may not always be able to follow Scripture's self-presentation, but their task is to present it as "intrinsically intelligible," and this "is the problem of scriptural interpretation" (723). To understand the prophets' and apostles' words, they must be understood in "their concrete historical situation." Here "literary-historical investigation" is the most important tool. Literary criticism seeks to determine "the most likely inner connection" of the words of a given text and questions of literary dependence using "the methods of source-criticism, lexicography, grammar, syntax and appreciation of style," and so on. *Historical criticism* seeks to determine "what has taken place on the spot to which the words of the author refer, and of what has occasioned the author to use these particular words" (724). Literary-historical examination presents pictures of what stands in and behind the text. Everything depends, however, on whether "we really form an accurate picture of the object mirrored in prophetic-apostolic word." This object may force us to "modify, shatter and remold" previous pictures and bring to "understanding possibilities which hitherto and in other circumstances we regarded as impossibilities" (725). In any case, exegesis demands fidelity to the prophetic-apostolic words and the object reflected in them. "This fidelity does not imply a necessary suspension of historical orientation and criticism," but neither does it "tolerate any restrictions" as to what is possible (726). Barth calls such fidelity "the freedom of loyalty."

The second moment in exegesis (in the broader sense) is reflection (*meditatio*). It does not follow *explicatio* in time, but indicates "the moment of the transition of what is said into the thinking of the reader or hearer" (727). Neither does *explicatio* occur independently of *meditation*, for no one observes what is there "without at the same time reflecting upon and interpreting what is there." Barth describes the modern "scientific" ideal of unbiased, presuppositionless exegesis as "comical" (469). The fact is that everyone approaches "the text from the standpoint of a particular epistemology, logic or ethics, of definite ideas and ideals concern the relations of God, the world and man. . . . Everyone has some sort of *philosophy*. . . . This is true even of the simplest Bible reader (and of him perhaps with particular force and tenacity)" (728). The question, therefore, is not *if* but *how* we bring philosophies to the task of exegesis. Barth gives five guidelines (730–35). To summarize: we must neither fear nor commit ourselves unreservedly to any philosophy. Some may prove fruitful if they elucidate or help us follow the text. But all must be crucified, dead, and buried before they can be raised again in service of "the freedom and sovereign power of [Scripture's] object." To the extent this happens, Barth claims, "Even from a human point of view, it is possible to regard scriptural exposition as the best and perhaps the only school of truly free human thinking—freed, that is, from all the conflicts and tyranny of systems in favor of this object" (735).

The third moment in exegesis is *applicatio*, that is, appropriation or assimilation. Like *explicatio* and *meditatio*, this act does not occur abstractly or independently. "No appropriation of the Word of God is possible without critical examination and reflection" (736). Yet neither do "valid and fruitful" examination and reflection occur without appropriation or assimilation. "Assimilation means assuming this witness into our own responsibility." It means "contemporaneity" and "indirect identification ... with the witness of the revelation." We do not merely reflect on it, but think it "from inner impulse and necessity ... because it has become a fundamental orientation of our whole existence." Contrary to the "unholy doctrine of 'theory and practice,'" exegesis has not properly occurred if "it stops short of assimilation" (737). In assimilation we stop "using" Scripture, but learn that it "uses us," that it "is not the object but subject, and the hearer and reader is not subject but object" (738). The reader and hearer is thus decentered, liberated "from the system of his own concerns and questions," to focus not on himself but on the scriptural word and to follow it (739). This is freedom under the Word.

Barth articulated these same exegetical principles in his *Römerbrief* period, but in the *CD* with three greater emphases: (1) Exegesis is incumbent upon "all members of the Church and not upon a specialized class of biblical scholars." "The congregation which is passive in the matter of biblical interpretation" is guilty of "renouncing" freedom under the Word and "is committed already to secret rebellion," which will be "one day open rebellion." If "the Church declines its responsibility for this task ... it is no longer a true congregation of Jesus Christ" (714–15). (2) Exegesis requires listening to the commentaries of the whole church, militant and triumphant, and especially the creeds, confessions, and fathers as formal but relative authorities (see §20, "Authority in the Church"). (3) Exegesis requires prayer, for "we cannot read and understand Holy Scripture without prayer.... It is only on the presupposition of prayer that all human effort in this matter, and penitence for human failure in this effort, will become serious and effective" (684, passim).

———
R. E. Burnett, *Karl Barth's Theological Exegesis* (2004); M. K. Cunningham, *What Is Theological Exegesis?* (1995); D. Ford, "Barth's Interpretation of the Bible," in *Karl Barth*, ed. S. W. Sykes (1979), 55–87; E. Jüngel, "Theology as Metacriticism," in *Karl Barth*, trans. G. E. Paul (1986), 70–104; P. McGlasson, *Jesus and Judas* (1991); R. Smend, "Nachkritische Schriftauslegung," in *Parrhesia*, ed. E. Busch, et al. (1966), 215–37.

RICHARD E. BURNETT

Faith No theological concept so clearly sets Barth apart from other theologians in the modern era as his understanding of faith. "It was never a desirable tendency," he warns, "to exalt faith into an ontic and central concept, displacing the real object of *theology*, as though faith were the theme and the true event of *salvation*" (*EvT*, 100). But that is precisely what so many theologians have done, especially in the modern liberal tradition that since Barth has been dubbed "Neo-Protestantism." The hallmark of such theology—Barth calls it "pisteology" (or "faith-ology")—is *Schleiermacher*'s magnum opus, *The Christian Faith*, known informally as the *Glaubenslehre*, or "doctrine of faith." And that is just the point for Barth. By turning theo-logy into faith-ology, modern theologians have neglected its true object—the *God* of the *gospel*—and replaced him with the all-too-human, and all-too-subjective, experience of "faith."

All of which is not to say that faith is a minor or an unimportant topic for Barth. Far from it: for faith—properly understood—is the key to genuine theology, its presupposition and one of its crucial concepts, though decidedly *not* its object. Rather, faith is the human *response* to the true object of theological *science*, the *grace* of God as revealed in *Jesus Christ*. Christians have faith in *God*, not in their own faith. "Faith," Barth writes, " is the ... indispensable condition of theological science, but not its object and theme" (100). Properly understood, faith has several specific characteristics that can be briefly enumerated as follows.

1. *Faith is an event.* Perhaps the most important characteristic of Barth's way of doing theology is his **actualism**, his insistence on understanding the object of theology, and therefore theology itself, in terms of *event*. This actualism is grounded in the perfection of God, who is *actus purus*, sheer actuality with no residue of passivity, contingency, or potentiality. The human response to this God thus always has the character of an event: it is something that *happens*, something that cannot be hoarded, saved up for another day, or treated as a possession by the recipient.

2. *Faith involves knowledge.* Barth stands in the mainstream of historical Christian thought in his refusal to polarize "faith and **reason**," as though one had to choose between them. Early in his career (1927) he published the first installment of what he intended would become a multivolume *CD*. Before he got to the second volume, however, he became so dissatisfied with his own approach to theology that he abandoned the project, claiming that his encounter with the thought of the medieval theologian Anselm of Canterbury had reoriented his thinking and finally put him on the right track, one that soon led him to begin the *CD*, the project that he pursued to the end of his career. He learned from Anselm that theology consists in "faith seeking understanding" (*fides quaerens intellectum*). The purpose of theology is not to prove faith, or even to strengthen it; rather, faith is its presupposition and point of departure. And when he embarks on the search that faith entails, he discovers that "it is my very faith itself that summons me to knowledge" (*Anselm*, 18). So the knowledge that is implicated in faith is not a product of the autonomous reason of secular modernity but rather the *fidei ratio*, faith's own reason, grounded in the revealed **Word of God**. "Certainly this is not only an intellectual knowledge," Barth writes, "but . . . it is *also* knowl-

edge executed in concepts and spoken in words. Faith is allowed to reoccur repeatedly when it is *fides quaerens intellectum*, faith laboring quite modestly, but not fruitlessly, in the quest for truth" (*EvT*, 102). Barth emphasizes that this rational faith, this faithful reasoning, also involves imagination, for the person of faith "believes, receives, and follows God and his Word as a man, by the enlistment and use of his normal human understanding (although not leaving out his human imagination [*Phantasie*]!), his human will, and no doubt also his human feeling" (*EvT*, 101) .

3. *Faith must not be confused with religion.* One of the characteristics of Neo-Protestant theology is its tendency to identify faith with **religion**. Barth inverts their relationship by formally defining religion as *Unglaube*, "un-faith" or faithlessness (see revised translation of *CD* I/2:§17; *OR*, 53–84). Nevertheless, God's **revelation**, according to Barth, "is God's *hiddenness* in the *world* of human *religion*" (*OR*, 35); therefore, to deny that Christianity is religious is to deny revelation itself. Faith has a similar structure at the individual level, for as a human capacity it can lead only to error and idolatry, but by **grace** God can transform it into true faith. "The man who really has faith," Barth claims, "will never consider his faith as a realization or manifestation of his religious life, but will on the contrary admit that his capacity for religion would in itself have led him to the gods and idols, but by no means to Jesus Christ" (*KGSG*, 106–7). Faith, like religion, must be sublimated (*aufgehoben*) by the power of the **Holy Spirit** if it is to escape the vicious circle of idolatry. "[Man] has not created his own faith; the Word has created it. He has not come to faith; faith has come to him through the Word. He has not adopted faith; faith has been granted to him through the Word" (*CD* I/1:244). Faith, in other words, is not religion; but like religion it can—by the grace of God—be transformed into the bearer of God's **truth**.

4. *Faith is a mystery.* That faith leads to rational knowledge should not mislead us into denying its ultimate mysteriousness. Barth calls faith "a void, a bowing down before that which we will never be, never have, can never do." The reason why faith is always mysterious, of course, is because it is grounded in the revelation of the God of **Israel** and Jesus—in other words, in the supreme mystery of the world. Because it has its origins beyond the world, faith "is therefore never finished, never a given, never secured; psychologically considered, it is always and ever again a leap into uncertainty, into the dark, into empty air" (*Rom* II, 73).

5. *Faith is not a possession.* Because it is an event and not a condition or an experience or an idea, because it is grounded in divine mystery, faith can never become the possession of the one who lives by faith. "Faith is a *history*, new every morning. It is no state or attribute. It should not be confused with mere capacity and willingness to believe" (*EvT*, 103). "Faith is not an art," he insists, "nor is it an achievement. Faith is not a good work of which some may boast, while the others with a shrug of their shoulders can excuse themselves by saying that they have no capacity for it. With faith itself comes the conclusive insight, that no one has the capacity for faith by his own effort, that is either the capacity to prepare for faith or to start it, or to persevere in it, or to perfect it" (*KGSG*, 106–7). Like the Israelites who were nourished by manna in the wilderness, people of faith must discover it every morning afresh, they must "daily activate it anew" (*EvT*, 105).

6. *Faith comes by grace.* All that Barth has said about faith can be understood as a gloss on the Reformers' motto that we have been justified by faith through grace. As such, faith is never a matter of necessity but is always grounded in *freedom*—both ours and God's. The act of faith "is not a necessity but a permission granted man by God, consisting in the natural sequence and response by which man returns a bit of human *gratitude* for the grace shown him by God" (*EvT*, 102–3).

No account of faith in Barth's theology would be complete without attending to his important and controversial notion of the *analogia fidei* (**analogy** of faith). The key to understanding this theme in Barth's theology is to recognize that he means it as an alternative to the venerable doctrine of the *analogia entis* (the analogy of being), which he once called "the invention of the Antichrist" (I/1:viii). Without entering into the ongoing controversy about whether Barth has rightly understood that notion, it is nevertheless possible to see why he opposes it and what he thinks is at stake. Barth believes that the *analogia entis* wrongly assumes a point of similarity between the human and the Divine insofar as both share the commonality of "being," though in very different ways. This mistaken notion, he believes, is the foundation for **natural theology**, that characteristically modern error shared ironically by both Roman Catholics and Neo-Protestants. The analogy of faith, by contrast, describes a correspondence between the human act of faith and the action of divine grace, an analogy that is not ontological but miraculous (see Hunsinger, 283 n. 2).

K. Barth, *OR*; G. Hunsinger, *How to Read Karl Barth* (1991); J. Mangina, *Karl Barth on the Christian Life* (2001); B. L. McCormack, *Karl Barth's Critically Realistic Dialectical Theology* (1995); J. Webster, *Barth* (2000).
GARRETT GREEN

Forgiveness of Sins *Theology,* insofar as it "believes in the forgiveness of sins," differs substantially from all other sciences because, unlike them, it cannot rely on a subtly differentiated concept of unified reality (*CD* I/1:11). It "believes," that is, it does not start with establishing an extensive conceptual system or with theories that would master reality. Instead, theology tries to think in and through God's story and trustingly follow it, that is, the account of God's doing and of the promises unfolded through the activity of God's everlasting faithfulness. Only if **God** opens up humans to this story and "drags" them into its ongoing reality will they be able to seek the **truth** about themselves and the **world**. Although this significant statement belongs to the opening remarks of Barth's *CD*, "forgiveness of sins" is not a dominant topic in Barth's theology; at least it is not a prominent or even fundamental theological term. Focusing theology completely on a comprehensive **Christology**, Barth thinks only soteriological themes can explain who **Jesus Christ** is and how God acts on, with, and through him.

Forgiveness of sins relates to **justification**. Here, **reconciliation** takes place. This is actually God's new **creation** of a totally destroyed relationship that was corrupted by humankind's enmity against God's creation, God's abiding **love**, and God's expressed will. The theological interpretation of this event is an integral part of the doctrine of reconciliation, the core of Barth's **dogmatics**. Reconciliation implies justification, and forgiveness of sins is related to it because God in Christ overcame the devastating power of **sin**. This ordering of topics avoids the traditional location of justification after the saving work of Christ, as an application of Jesus Christ's dying for us. Barth's doctrine of reconciliation is very subtly composed and full of dramatic events: Christ's humiliation and exaltation are interwoven with his "two natures," his deity and his **humanity**. When it comes to justification, Barth relates his doctrine of reconciliation to God's sovereign judgment that enacts his justice by doing away with human injustice and selfishness. God steps into human lives and makes human wrongdoing his own affair. A fortiori, as God substitutes Jesus Christ in our place and us in Christ's, we become righteous, even as we *are just in Christ* (cf. 2 Cor. 5:21; *CD* IV/1:75–77). Being in Christ is

our true reality. God keeps and proves his faithfulness by incorporating us in the reality of his justice and sustaining us in it.

Reconciliation, which may be partially explained as *forgiveness of sins*, must not be misunderstood as mere peacemaking, with the corollary of establishing mutual confidence and the goal of being in accord with one another. This would be a cheap reconciliation and a terrible oversimplification of God's sovereign initiative to create anew the relationship with and among creatures that have squandered what God has entrusted to them. Although Barth is reluctant to refer to the reconciliation as *atonement*, he emphasizes the immense weight of sin perceivable at the cross of Jesus (411–12), who "takes away the sin of the world" (John 1:29) that no human can bear. God's incomparable and inexhaustible forgiveness destroys every fiction of an ever-understanding and lenient God who overlooks human iniquities. On the contrary, God judges when he forgives. His justice and mercy are inseparably one; both reveal God's faithfulness to himself, to his majesty as the Lord.

Justification involves "the turn, the change, the *transition* of the existence of man without God and dead into the existence of man living for God, before Him, and with Him and for Him" (580). It is, with the forgiveness of sins, a radical and entirely new beginning, but not as such a starting point for a new effort to gain a successful life. Justification, as an integral part of reconciliation, points to *redemption* as the eschatological completion of God's work, the consummation of his promise, and the disclosure of everything he has accomplished (596–99). With this **hope**, people who are called to receive forgiveness of their sins are set on the way. They know about the crisis of the relationship "between the holy God and sinful man" and about God's judgment—his "decision"—regarding this relationship. This is the "red thread" that runs through the doctrine of reconciliation and even of dogmatics (580–81), and grounds theology and all theological reasoning.

Accordingly, Barth avoids any juridical, moralistic, and psychological allusions. When God justifies he does not temper justice with mercy; nor does the forgiveness of sins spring from the mere generosity of God. God's gracious love arises out of his pain concerning people who are alienated from him, a pain that is the divine negation of sin: a creative, saving act, not a mood or sentiment. God's judgment clarifies a person's real situation. Through this divine involvement and interconnection, the person is liberated to be and to remain God's creature, free to live within the realm of God's *covenant* and so to be faithful to God's promise and obedient to his outspoken will.

This focus on the forgiveness of sins emphasizes that *persons* addressed by God are responsible for their deeds and failures. They cannot excuse their guilt by accusing other people or by blaming it on their circumstances. On the other hand, although he does not discuss it extensively, Barth is aware that sin cannot be restricted to individual affairs. Sin is regarded as a contradiction of God's justice not only in human social relations and politics, but also in the destruction of other creatures. Yet all this does not allow us to conceive of sin in relative terms. Sin is personal rebellion against God. God alone makes the sinner aware of being both the perpetrator (*Täter*) and victim of his or her own wrongdoings. Whatever may have caused him or her to be misled, God asks a person: "Where are *you*? What have *you* done?" Bad structures may be corrected or even altered, but persons must be healed in body, soul, and spirit. This excludes self-righteousness as well as any attempt at self-salvation.

Only as God addresses the sinner and calls him or her to be reconciled with God in Christ can the addressed person recognize himself or herself as a sinner. *Recognition* of the whole reach of sin is interwoven with forgiveness because both arise from God's *prevenient grace*, his grace that precedes all human insight and action. This *pre-* is a theological, not a temporal, sequence; its priority marks the character of God's mercy that humans need every moment of their lives. Therefore, recognition of sin is simultaneous with the prayer, "Forgive us our debts" (Matt. 6:12). Even if the clarity that God creates through his reconciliation may often sharpen our eyes to discern hidden injustice and far-reaching damage, recognition of sin cannot be an independent insight into any deplorable state of affairs or offenses against moral values. But in incessantly praying for forgiveness we also perceive other people in the light of the promise of reconciliation, and in this expectation we are willing to share God's forgiveness of sins with others—we are prepared to forgive.

How can forgiveness be conceived as a new beginning? No one can appraise oneself as being a new human being. "His own being contradicts his being in Christ. Confronted with his being in Christ, and precisely in the clear light of Him, he finds in his own being that the old man is still by no means dead nor newly created" (IV/1:97, rev.). "Being in Christ" is the future that is no longer determined by sin repeated again and again.

Forgiveness of sins implies the contradiction of God's judgment and the human self-recognition that would lead to either self-justification or self-condemnation. If humans think that they have attained moral progress and that God's help is needed only to achieve a better way of life, then they are blind to the depths of their guilt.

Barth stresses that God's judging and saving action is manifold. He reminds us of *Calvin*, who distinguishes the twofold gift of grace (*duplex gratiae*) that shapes those who believe in Christ: justification as forgiveness of sins and sanctification as rebirth and renewal (524–25). Similarly, the later *Luther* travels a "two-lane way" when he speaks of the "double *sanatio* of the human." The forgiveness of sins is accompanied by "the gift of grace, of a holy life that purifies itself from sin" (525, rev.).

What is already completed because it "happens in Christ" and what is to be performed "daily in us" are combined in a complementary way. The distinction between the imputation of Christ's righteousness and the gift of the *Holy Spirit*, which sustains the characteristic style of the two lines of this event, corresponds to the "relationship between *eternity* and *time*, . . . between heaven and earth," and of the divine and human natures of Christ (526). In view of the multidimensionality of the saving event, Barth sees the article by which the church stands or falls as subsisting not in the doctrine of justification as such, including the forgiveness of sins, but exclusively and all-inclusively in the *confession* of Jesus Christ (527).

K. Barth, *CD* IV:1–3; idem., *DiO*, 149–52; E. Busch, *The Great Passion*, trans. G. W. Bromiley (2004), 213–14; T. Gorringe, "Crime, Punishment, and Atonement," in *Commanding Grace*, ed. D. L. Migliore (2010), 136–61; K. Sonderegger, "For Us and for Our Salvation," in *Commanding Grace*, ed. D. L. Migliore (2010), 162–75.
GERHARD SAUTER

Freedom For Barth, "freedom" is first and foremost a theological concept describing a fundamental attribute of *God*. The term operates for Barth much like "sovereignty" operates in the Calvinist tradition. *Human* freedom is not for Barth an attribute arising naturally in human existence, but is strictly derivative—a quality of life produced by the action of the freedom of God.

The Freedom of God: The tautology, "God is who He is" (*CD* II/1:297), is used by Barth to avoid the identification of God with any descriptive terms at our disposal. "Our words require a complete change of meaning . . . if in their application to God they are not to lead us astray" (307). Thus, "freedom," which can never be unconditionally applied to human existence, must be understood differently when applied to God. To get at this characteristic of God, Barth employs two classical theological terms: God is said to be *actus purus*, "pure actuality," which means that there are no potentialities or possibilities in the being of God which do not already belong to who God is—and what God does. Similarly, God is said to be *a se*, or "self-derived." There is nothing outside himself that determines who and what God is. "If, therefore, we say that God is *a se*, . . . we say that He is the one who already has and is in Himself everything that would have to be the object [or purpose] of His *creation* and causation if He were not He, God" (306).

Barth's understanding of the structure of divine freedom may be elucidated under four headings.

1. *God is free in himself.* The unimaginable internal freedom of God cannot, Barth insists, be derived from a vastly expanded idea of human freedom. When Barth says that God's own freedom is such that "He does not need His own being in order to be who He is," he means that God's "non-being, or His being other than He is, is ontologically and noetically excluded" (307) from theological consideration. In this sense, we cannot even say that God's freedom is restricted only in that he cannot be other than he is. For Barth, the terms *need* and *necessity* cannot be applied to God.

2. *God is free from all other being*: This dictum flows from the first, and is conditioned by it. If God "has and is in Himself being, ground and limit in the actuality of His existence, and in the freedom proper to Him, how can He possibly need any other being, or need to be grounded or limited by it?" (II/1:308). God did not and does not create out of himself, but out of "nothing," and thus his creation has its own being, a being other than God, but it does not

thereby pose any hindrance or limit to God's freedom. "God confronts all that is in supreme and utter independence, i.e., He would be no less and no different even if they all did not exist, or existed differently" (311)

3. *God is free for us*: The freedom of God in himself and from all other being would render him remote, unknown, and irrelevant were it not that God's absolute and unlimited freedom expresses itself in the *incarnation* of himself in *Jesus Christ*. "If He wished to reveal Himself, if He wished to be free for us, this very miracle had to take place, namely, that without ceasing to be Himself He entered our sphere, assumed our nature" (I/2:32). Since Barth's theology is from first to last a theology of *revelation*, of the *Word of God*, it begins and ends with *Christology*—so that all other ways in which God is free for us, in *creation*, providence, and redemption, devolve from that primary movement hidden in the eternal life of the *Trinity*. This form of God's freedom is in some sense paradoxical. In creating a reality other than his own, in granting it its own kind of freedom, and especially by reconciling it to himself on the cross, God appears to restrict and limit his freedom. "But in this His freedom, in which He spontaneously binds Himself in a certain way to the *world*, He remains unbound [in respect to] the world and its specific determinations" (II/1:314). This requires us to say, finally, that

4. *God, understood as Father, Son and Spirit, is free from any particular way he is free for us*. This form of God's freedom must be asserted (a) as a necessary correlate of the first two forms of God's freedom, and (b) as a logical extension of the actual outworking of his freedom for us. "God is free to be present with the creature by giving Himself and revealing Himself to it, or by concealing Himself and withdrawing Himself from it. . . . God is free to perform his work either within the framework of what we call the laws of *nature* or outside it in the form of miracle. . . . God is free to

be provoked and to be merciful, to bless and to punish, to kill and make alive" (II/1:314–15). In the incarnation, "God is free to rule over the world in supreme majesty and likewise to serve in the world as the humblest and meanest of servants . . . to be despised . . . and rejected by the world" (315).

The dialectical tension in which this form of God's freedom places theology is illustrated in Barth's doctrine of *election* (II/2). There the freedom of God for us is found in Christ, who, in himself, reveals the fact that God is a gracious, electing God in whom all find their identity as those called according to God's eternal decree. At the same time, however, Barth insists that we cannot reduce this single election of *grace* to a theory of universal *salvation*. "If we are to respect the freedom of divine grace, we cannot venture [such a claim]. . . . But, again, in grateful recognition of the grace of the divine freedom, we cannot venture the opposite statement that there cannot be . . . this final opening up . . . of election and calling" (II/2:417–18).

Perhaps the most remarkable and unexpected example of God's freedom *from* his freedom *for* is found in Barth's later thought, where he argues that, if Christ lives, "He exists in the manner of God" (IV/3.1:39). For Barth, this means that Jesus lives an "eternal life," overarching and uniting past, present, and future; and just as his freedom for us found expression in the *witness* of the prophets, later in that of the apostles, and now in the witness of the *church*, so Christ's being for us may take other forms of witness: "the capacity of Jesus to create these human witnesses is not restricted to His working on and in prophets and apostles and what is thus made possible and actual in His community. His capacity transcends the limits of this sphere . . . we cannot possibly think that He cannot speak, and His speech cannot be attested, outside this sphere." God's being for us in the life, death, and *resurrection of Jesus Christ* does not change, but "The eternal

Word of God . . . can change its form" (IV/3.1:117–18, 157).

Human Freedom: For Barth, the only real freedom available for human beings is brought about by the freedom of God. While liberty, independence, and even autonomy are universally desirable, for Barth these qualities, as products of human initiative, do not represent true freedom. Here Barth is simply being consistent with the New Testament: "So if the Son makes you free, you will be free indeed" (John 8:36). "For freedom Christ has set us free" (Gal. 5:1.) Barth insists, "Human freedom is the *gift* of God in the free outpouring of His grace" (*HG*, 75).

The dialectical radicality of Barth's thought is perhaps nowhere more apparent than in his claim that human freedom is not displayed in our capacity to choose. Although Augustine worried much over how human choice fits with divine **providence**, Barth writes: It would be a strange freedom that would leave man neutral, able equally to choose, decide, and act rightly or wrongly! . . . Human freedom as a gift of God does not allow for any vague choices between various possibilities" (*HG*, 76–77). Barth does not deny that we are endowed with a "natural freedom." "It is true that man's God-given freedom is choice, decision, act. But it is genuine choice; it is genuine decision and act in the *right* direction" (76, italics added). To refuse God's gift of freedom and choose instead self-interest, self-preservation, and self-justification is an expression not of freedom but of bondage. "*Sin* as an alternative is not anticipated or included in the freedom given to man by God" (77).

If true freedom is not personal choice, neither for Barth is it political. Barth was a Socialist. He wrote the **Barmen Declaration** against Nazi oppression, and supported revolutionary struggles against economic and racial injustice. He famously wrote: "God always takes his stand . . . on this side and this side alone: against the lofty and on

behalf of the lowly, against those who already enjoy right and privilege and on behalf of those who are denied it and deprived of it" (II/1:386). It is therefore the task of Christian obedience to take part in the struggle for human liberation. At the same time, however, Barth did not believe that we can achieve true freedom by such means. "The concept of freedom as man's rightful claim and due is equally contradictory and impossible. So is the thought of man's acquiring freedom by earning it or buying it at any price" (*HG*, 76). Barth thought that the revolutionary could be an agent of God, but revolutions cannot accomplish real freedom, for "even the most radical revolution can do no more than set what exists against what exists" (*ER*, 481), and what exists is *sin*. "Sinful man is not free, he is a captive, a slave" (*HG*, 77), because he exploits his natural freedom to serve himself.

Barth never tires of noting the inner contradiction of every attempt to maximize our own independence, autonomy, and "freedom." Barth objected to Kant's presupposition of man as a free moral agent, because such freedom is always and everywhere subverted by both the internal and external conditions of human life. Freedom, as a definition of *humanity*, is an ideal actually subverted by every attempt to realize it. The desire for personal autonomy is enslaving, because self-sufficiency amounts to self-idolatry, and "who," asks Barth, "can exercise a worse tyranny over us than the god in our own breast?" (I/2:668).

Is human "freedom" for Barth then impossible? To this question two answers are necessary. First, there is, even after the fall, a kind of freedom given to the human creature in respect to "choice," to those ordinary human functions of thinking, deciding, and acting. We experience freedom of will, even if we have to admit all sorts of physical and psychological restrictions in its exercise. While Barth's theology never denies the unlimited power and supervision of God over his creation, he does not follow Augustine and *Calvin* in a reductionist doctrine of providence that effectively eliminates the possibility of a secondary freedom available to the human creature. The creation and the human creature have their own proper independence and "freedom," but that freedom is not yet the "freedom [for which] Christ has set us free" (Gal. 5:1).

The second answer, however, is that, for Barth, there is also the possibility of human action, choice, and *determination made* free by the action of God. This movement of the human will as it is worked upon by the divine will has been called by George Hunsinger "double agency," in which a human action is accompanied, lifted up, and transformed by God, and which thereby actually participates in divine freedom. When discussing the activity that belongs to human *sanctification*, Barth described this reflexive, participatory freedom in the following way: "The lifting up of man effected by his sanctification is his own act, and it is similar to all his other acts. Yet it is different from all his other acts to the extent that the initiative on which he does it, the spontaneity with which he expresses himself in it, does not arise from his own heart or emotions or understanding or conscience, but has its origin in the power of the direction which has come to him in these spheres. It is necessary and indispensable that he should rouse himself and pull himself together and find courage and confidence and take and execute decisions, but this is only the spiritual and physical form of a happening which does not originate in himself and is not his own work, but the gift of God. It is not as his own lord, but as the recipient of this gift that he carries through the movement which we call the lifting up of himself. . . . No matter how similar this movement may be to those of all other men—for he has no other means at hand than those common to all men—it is absolutely dissimilar in the fact that it is his correspondence to the life-movement of

his Lord, as produced, not by own caprice, but by the will and touch and address and creation and gift of this Lord" (IV/2:528–29).

E. Busch, *The Great Passion*, trans. G. W. Bromiley (2004), 106–27; J. Couenhoven, "Karl Barth's Conception(s) of Human and Divine Freedom(s)," in *Commanding Grace*, ed. D. L. Migliore (2010), 239–55; C. Gunton, "The Triune God and the Freedom of the Creature," in *Karl Barth*, ed. S. W. Sykes (1989), 46–68; G. Hunsinger, *How to Read Karl Barth* (1991); A. J. McKelway, *The Freedom of God and Human Liberation* (1990).

ALEXANDER J. McKELWAY

God   Barth's initial revolutionary approach to *theology* exploded on the scene with *Rom* II, recognizably echoing Kierkegaard in a highly vigorous and lively rhetorical style. What he emphasizes here, however, is less the nature of God than the antithesis between God and everything else, the "infinite qualitative difference" between *time* and *eternity*, the transcendent otherness of God, and the eschatological quality of the divine Word. Barth's *Romans* reflects a vision of the contemporary immediacy of the biblical echo of that Word as it leaps across the centuries, sees itself in the context of Protestant theology as especially on the wavelength of *Luther* and *Calvin*, and does not have much positive to say about the theology produced in the centuries since them. "Letting God be God," however, to use a slogan of the *dialectical theology* that *Rom* I–II unleashed, ended less in a new or clearer conception, vision, or understanding of *God* that in a kind of *via negativa*, better able to emphasize what God is *not* than what God *is*.

That, however, was only the beginning. With his new responsibilities as a theological professor in the University of Göttingen, Barth took a new interest in *dogmatics*, reflected in several semesters of lectures that were published only after his death (ET: *Göttingen Dogmatics*). So began a journey that led through the well-known "false start" with volume 1 of the projected *CD* in 1927 to the newly conceived and executed *CD* from 1932 on. From the beginning, this study of dogmatics was marked by a double concern—to take up the questions and themes to which over the centuries dogmatics had given so much attention, but at the same time to rework them in the framework of a fresh understanding of what dogmatics and the task of dogmatics are.

In the *CD* the doctrine of God takes up volume II. *KD* II/1 was published in 1940 and II/2 in 1942 (ET of both volumes appeared in 1957). Barth expresses the significance of the theme and the inquiry at the beginning of *CD* II/1: "In the *Church* of Jesus Christ men speak about God and men have to hear about God. About God the Father, the Son and the *Holy Spirit*. . . . But always and in all circumstances about God Himself, who is the presupposition, meaning and power of everything that is to be said and heard in the Church, the Subject who absolutely, originally and finally moves, produces, establishes and realises in this matter. In dogmatics it is the doctrine of God which deals with this Subject as such. In the doctrine of God we have to learn what we are saying when we say 'God.' In the doctrine of God we have to learn to say 'God' in the correct sense. If we do not speak rightly about this Subject, how can we speak righty of His predicates?" (3).

Each part of volume II contains two chapters, though Barth's chapters in *CD* tend to be as long as or longer than many monographs: V. "The Knowledge of God"; VI. "The Reality of God"; VII. "The Election of God"; VIII. "The Command of God."

The choice of these specific themes and the way in which they are arranged is characteristic of Barth's understanding of the integrative task of dogmatics—treating topics not merely extensively and distinctly, as it were in

individual isolation, but in such a way as to bring out inner coherences and connections between them. Chapter V is not only (though it certainly is also) a recapitulating bridge back to volume I (*The Doctrine of the Word of God*); more fundamentally, it reflects Barth's conviction that the divine self-communication is inherently bound up with God's own being and nature, which enable and are reflected in the event and content of *revelation*. Chapter VIII deals with the theme of *gospel and law* and follows his related insight that dogmatics and *ethics*, cognition and action, are not two separate fields but belong together, so that each dogmatic locus must include an ethical dimension as integrally belonging to it.

In the narrower sense, however, it is chapter VI that deals with central traditional topics of the doctrine of God, while chapter VII is especially radical both in treating the theme of *election* (traditionally: predestination) as part of the doctrine of God and in the way election itself is handled—quite freshly and indeed surprisingly, though in the end thoroughly consistently with Barth's integrative method and what has been called his "christological concentration." The rest of this article therefore concentrates on these two themes.

Chapter VI, "The Reality of God," contains in turn four "sections": §28, "The Being of God as the One Who Loves in Freedom"; §29, "The Perfections of God"; §30, "The Perfections of the Divine Loving"; and §31, "The Perfections of the Divine Freedom." Each section, as throughout *CD*, is in turn prefaced by a proposition that summarizes quite precisely the argument it contains. So, for instance, §28: "God is who He is in the act of His revelation. God seeks and creates fellowship between Himself and us, and therefore He loves us. But He is this loving God without us as Father, Son and Holy Spirit, the *freedom* of the Lord, who has His life from Himself."

Following from this opening to the chapter, Barth offers a strikingly fresh and refreshing account of what dogmatics had traditionally termed "the attributes of God." In the older tradition of Protestant orthodoxy, various schemes were developed to distinguish and order the divine qualities, sometimes in a rather arbitrary way, for example by distinguishing the two categories of "communicable" and "incommunicable" attributes. Barth does not reject that tradition, but restates it in a new perspective. First, in §28, he offers one deceptively simple, dialectical definition: God's being is to be understood as that of the one who loves in freedom. *Love* represents God's commitment, self-binding; freedom stands for the fact that this commitment is spontaneous, unforced, and uncompelled. This dialectic of love and freedom is the key to the very nature of God. On that basis Barth goes on to develop his own classification of the divine attributes, for which he prefers the term *perfections* (§29), and lays these out in §§30–31 in the following pattern. In §30, under the heading "The Perfections of the Divine Loving": (1) "The Grace and Holiness of God"; (2) "The Mercy and Righteousness of God"; (3) "The Patience and Wisdom of God." In §31 under "The Perfections of the Divine Freedom": (1) "The Unity and Omnipresence of God"; (2) "The Constancy and Omnipotence of God"; (3) "The Eternity and Glory of God." (See *perfections of God*.)

It is central to this classification that God's *being* and God's *action* are held together: What God is and what God does belong together, for the divine being is expressed in the divine action. Similarly, God's being is eternally in itself (*ad intra*) what it then reveals itself to be in God's relations *ad extra*. That enables Barth to go on to include in the doctrine of God the two following chapters on the divine election and the divine command.

Four pointers offer decisive clues to the nature of Barth's handling of the doctrine of election in chapter VII. First of all, it is an integral part of the doctrine of God, and that is already a

significant shift from the pattern of the older Reformed dogmatics. Barth sees God's fundamental decision expressed in election and reprobation not simply as a determination of that which is *not* God but as a self-determination of *God's very being*. The fundamental choice to which the doctrine refers is a decision not merely about the destiny of creatures but about the nature and character of God as the one "who loves in freedom." That is Barth's reason for treating the doctrine of election as part of the doctrine of God and not merely as the opening of a new chapter dealing with the divine activity *ad extra*.

Second, it is characteristic that he insists here on talking primarily of the doctrine of *election*, specifically the election of **grace**—in German, *Gnadenwahl*. He does not begin by speaking of a symmetrical or quasi-symmetrical "double decree" of election and reprobation. It is of fundamental importance for Barth that God's primal decision is a **determination** of grace, a Yes! and not a No!

Third, however—and this is where Barth diverges from many other modern representatives of the **Reformed tradition** who have tended to want to put this entire doctrine somewhere on a high shelf, out of sight and out of mind—Barth insists on retaining the No, the note of reprobation, within the context of the Yes of the divine election. The Yes does include a No, though the negative is contained within the positive, and neither contradicts it nor carries equal weight to it. Barth does, in his own way, maintain a doctrine of double predestination in the sense that he speaks of both election and reprobation.

Fourth, however, the way in which Barth does this represents a radical *christological* refocusing both of election and of reprobation that totally changes the light in which the matter is seen.

It is helpful here to have in mind the earlier history of the treatment of the theme, particularly in Calvin and Reformed theology. The background is to be sought first of all in the long run of passages in the *Bible* that seem to speak of God's activity in terms of choosing and rejecting, in terms of mercy and of judgment, in terms of discrimination. The story of Jacob and Esau is one example, as is the mystery of the hardening of Pharaoh's heart. In the New Testament many other passages speak of a discriminating divine judgment and in some cases at least trace this back to a divine foreknowledge and even a divine predestination, or speak of vessels of honor and dishonor. In the New Testament of course there is no systematized doctrine of "double predestination," but there are thoughts that point in that direction—and all the more clearly when we take into account similar and more developed ideas in contemporary Jewish sources such as Qumran. Clearly, predestinarian ideas focusing on the idea of a minority chosen for *salvation* were current in Judaism and find resonance in the New Testament as well.

These pointers went on to make history particularly in the Western theological tradition rather than in the Eastern. A major turning point was the theology of Augustine with his radicalization of the doctrine of the corruption of human nature resulting from the fall and his insistence over against Pelagius and others that fallen *humanity* consist of nothing but a *massa perditionis* from which individuals can only be extricated by the saving election of divine grace. So too Aquinas (*Summa theologiae* I, q.23) offers a doctrine of predestination that in substance, argument, and biblical basis differs hardly at all from that defended later by Calvin. Aquinas insists that there is a divine election of grace that does not extend to all humans. There is also therefore a divine reprobation that consists in leaving sinners in their *sin* instead of saving them from it. In Aquinas (as in Augustine), however, there is a clear asymmetry between the divine decision to elect some—that is, as it were, a conscious and deliberate decision on the part of God—and the de facto consequence that the nonelect

fall into damnation because God has not chosen to elect them too. It is not so much that God has deliberately *chosen not to elect* them; rather he has simply as a matter of fact *not chosen to elect* them. That may seem a fine distinction, but it is the only difference between Aquinas and Calvin. For Calvin the reprobation of the nonelect cannot simply be an accidental accompaniment to the election of those who are to be saved: it too must be the consequence of an equally deliberate choice on God's part to elect some and to damn others. It is this sense that Calvin teaches "double predestination," holding to a twofold, symmetrical decree of election *and* reprobation; and in this the main lines of classical Reformed theology up to the eighteenth century followed him.

Barth's discussion in chapter VII is again divided into four sections: §32, "The Problem of a Correct Doctrine of the Election of Grace"; §33, "The Election of Jesus Christ"; §34, "The Election of the Community"; §35, "The Election of the Individual." Barth begins, as he frequently does, by trying to fix the "problem." This means more than simply "difficulty." It has the overtones of "the problem posed" or "the task to be resolved," very much in the original sense of the Greek *problēma*. In the same way Barth speaks at different places in *CD* of the "problems" of dogmatics, of *Christology*, of pure doctrine, of man as an object of dogmatics, of nothingness, of special ethics, of *justification*, of the doctrine of *reconciliation*.

This, then, is the subject of §32 with its three parts, considering in turn (1) what kind of doctrine we are dealing with and answering: *the sum of the Gospel*; (2) where is its basis, with the answer: *Jesus Christ*; (3) where does it belong in dogmatics, with the answer: *in the doctrine of God*. These preliminary sightings, each in its own way, show how radically different Barth's approach is from that of the older orthodoxy. Election is a doctrine of grace, not a doctrine of grace for some and retribution for others; Jesus Christ is not merely the instrument of the decree of election but is himself its content and fulfillment; its place is in the doctrine of God as the one who loves in freedom and whose ways and works begin in eternal grace.

Barth proceeds in §33 to follow through the implications. This means integrating the lines of thought associated with election and reprobation, mercy and judgment, salvation and damnation *christologically*. They are related to the person of Jesus Christ as being both the God who elects and the human who is elected. Election is to be understood first of all in terms of the action of God upon creaturely humanity in Jesus, who both represents God to humans and humans to God in such a way that his person with his *history* gathers up, grounds, and centers the whole history of the Creator with his creatures. There is more than an echo here of Irenaeus and his theme of *anakephalaiosis* or *recapitulatio*, of the summing up of all things, in particular the entire history of salvation, in the history of the incarnate Word. Jesus Christ is not only the *key* to election; he is the *reality* of election, decided in eternity and realized in time. This also means that in Jesus Christ we have both sides of the coin, so to speak, of the divine election. For God's Yes is a claim that implies a corresponding No—God's rejection and judgment of the sin of the creature that is at the same time the divine will to do away with that sin. When that No is finally spoken—as it is on the cross—it is not only spoken by God but also heard and accepted by God. So Barth can say that God chooses reprobation for himself in order to choose election for sinful humanity. The dialectic of election and reprobation is from the outset both christologically reconceived and radically reoriented by comparison with the old pattern, where election had to do with one group of human beings, reprobation with another, and Jesus Christ had to do only with the first group, not with the second. The reprobation he bears is the reprobation of all sinful humanity, just as his election is the election of all in him. It is hard to imagine a more radical reworking—yet what is remarkable is that virtually all the elements of the old pattern are preserved, yet recast by turning the whole inside out.

Barth then goes on to discuss the election *of the community* in §34 before coming finally to the election *of individuals* in §35. This again is a radical departure from the individualism of the older tradition that generally saw election and reprobation exclusively in terms of the salvation or damnation of individual persons. When Barth does finally come to the bearing of election and reprobation on individuals, he does so by stressing that reprobation is the shadow of election so that the elect always carries his own reprobation "not in him, not beside him, but with him." But it is his *election*, not his reprobation, that is the first and last word, at least so far as God is concerned. All human beings are elected by God in Jesus Christ, and the reprobation of all is borne by God in him.

This naturally raises the question: must not Barth, to be consistent, resurrect the doctrine of the *apokatastasis panton*? It might seem so, but he refuses to draw that conclusion. We cannot anticipate what the final outcome will be or whether God's grace will be resisted by any to the bitter end. But if they do so resist it will be by their own choice, not because God has either passed them by (as Aquinas has it) or deliberately predetermined them to everlasting death (as the old Reformed orthodoxy saw it).

Finally chapter VIII is also both new and radical in its handling of the classical Lutheran/Reformed issue of the relation between gospel and law. Typical here of Barth's integrative approach is his insistence that these two dimensions are not simply antitheses (any more than the Yes and No of election) but instead that the law is a form of the gospel—an identification that for some Lutherans even today is just as hard to take as it is for some Reformed to swallow Barth's reorientation of election. All of these themes, however, illustrate the characteristic features of Barth's doctrine of God as the one who loves in freedom.

K. Barth, *CD* II/1; II/2; E. Busch, *The Great Passion*, trans. G. W. Bromiley (2004), 57–127: O. Weber, *Karl Barth's Church's Dogmatics*, trans. A. C. Cochrane (1953), 73–116; J. Webster, *Barth* (2000), 75–93.

ALASDAIR I. C. HERON

Gospel and Law

Gospel and Law With the phrase "gospel and law" Barth deliberately reverses the traditional formula of "law and gospel." For *Luther*, and the Lutheran tradition in particular, law and gospel are essential building blocks for the Protestant doctrine of *justification* by *grace* through *faith* alone. The law shows us humans where and to what extent we are sinful. The gospel, centered in *Jesus Christ*, shows us where and to what extent God rescues us from our sinful condition. Reversing the phrase, Barth challenges that whole calculation of *sin* and *salvation*.

Barth's landmark essay "Gospel and Law" (1935) was his last lecture on German soil before World War II. He was prevented from giving the lecture himself. As Gestapo agents escorted Barth by train to the Swiss border, a stand-in speaker read his address to a packed church at Dahlem, Germany, on October 7, 1935. The essay was explosive in the context of pre-War European debates about natural *revelation* (largely Lutheran, but some Reformed) and political ideology (National Socialism, "German Christians"). These groups severed the law from the gospel by tying the law to the self-standing human conditions of *nature*, race, nation, *history*, *culture*, and experience. To the contrary, Barth insists, the law finds its true place and importance only in its inner, binding connection to Jesus Christ and the gospel in his name.

The *Word of God*, says Barth ("G&L," 71–84), contains both gospel and law in itself. As the Word made flesh, Jesus Christ manifests the decision of God to be with and for sinful *humanity*. Jesus Christ keeps the law at every point of his birth, life, teachings, death, and resurrection from the dead. In *content* the gospel of Jesus Christ is God's pure gift of grace. In *form*, the gospel of Jesus Christ is law, which conveys God's demand for faith, obedience, and discipleship. But grace brackets the law on both sides. By grace the law issues from the Word of God at the beginning, and by grace the Word of God fulfills the promise of the law at the end. As *content and form*, gospel and law differ from each other, yet each one requires the other. If either is separated from the other or one of them is deformed, the biblical *truth* is lost for both of them.

Late in his life Barth acknowledges how much gospel and law, as articulated in the 1935 essay, "belong to the basic substance of my dogmatics as hitherto presented" (*CD* IV/3.1:370). Gospel and law arise for him in three ways: (a) as poles of the dialectical framework that pervades his *theology* from beginning to end; (b) as emerging themes in his early theological work; and (c) as basic building blocks for his mature theology.

Barth's theology proceeds in a twofold movement or dialectic of gospel > law (Yes-No) and law > gospel (No-Yes). The dialectic traces God's activity from *creation* to *reconciliation* to redemption, as revealed in the *Bible*. Tied to the life, death, and *resurrection of Jesus Christ*, the dialectic becomes concrete in *time* and history. One early essay shows traces of Hegel's three-point dialectic, but Barth says there explicitly that God stands above any such dialectic ("Society," 305–26). Although gospel and law, Yes and No, set the poles of his dialectic, Barth does not reconcile these poles into a synthesis (vs. Hegel), nor alternate back-and-forth between them (vs. Lutherans). For Barth the process is one-directional, irreversible, and weighted toward its end ("G&L," 87; *CD* III/1:§42.3(3–4); *EvT*, 92–94). This article follows the 1935 essay closely, but the same pattern recurs in *CD* III/1:§42.3, and elsewhere.

Barth's dialectic first moves from gospel to law, from Yes to No. Gospel is the starting point marked by the gift of created life, which God makes in and through the Word (John 1:1ff.). In his birth and obedient life Jesus Christ represents humanity fully as God intended it to be. When humans act as if they are God instead of being merely God's image, however, creation is thrown into a crisis. The dilemma pertains to both the law and the gospel. In the hands of sinners the law becomes an avenue of self-righteousness, bringing only condemnation and punishment ("G&L," 85–89). In the hands of sinners the gospel becomes merely a way to bestow grace on themselves, and it cannot avert God's legitimate judgment on human sin ("G&L," 89–94). Representing this sinful humanity on the cross, Jesus Christ bears both the curse and the consequences of God's law against human sin.

The second movement of Barth's dialectic goes from law to gospel, No to Yes ("G&L," 94–100). To take this step, however, Barth has to restate the significance of Jesus' crucifixion. So, at the beginning of the second movement, the death of Jesus Christ is all at once God's act of forgiveness, the defeat of death, the justification of the sinner, and the starting point for a new creation. Only God acting out of unfathomable mercy and power can transform the death of Jesus from judgment and punishment of a fallen humanity into the supreme act of forgiveness and the beginning of a new creation out of nothing. That, says Barth, is precisely the claim of the gospel (96–97). The dialectic then moves from the crucifixion of Jesus Christ to his resurrection from the dead. Christ's resurrection re-creates humanity out of nothing . . . into the image of God, eter-

nal life with God, and the fulfillment of God's law. Now fulfilled by Jesus Christ, the law points to a humanity free from the bondage of sin, condemnation, fear, and punishment (97ff.). Now transformed by the gospel, the law marks the place where humanity lives joyfully in fellowship with the living God and with one another forever (99–100).

The early writings already reflect Barth's concern for the "dialectic of the subject matter" (*ER*, 5–10, passim), as outlined above. Barth saw dialectic as a way to keep theology in constant motion, like a bird in flight or a cat on a narrow wall constantly walking to keep from falling off. The dialectic moves with *what God is doing as God,* instead of hunkering down in fixed, *humanly grounded* positions ("Society," 282–83). The early essays emphasize the moment of crisis (the No), but both legs of the dialectic are clear in Barth's repeated concern for the resurrection of Jesus Christ.

The dynamics of gospel and law run throughout the *CD*. The dialectical movement of Yes-No is plain in I/2, where Barth portrays religion as unbelief, rooted in self-righteous works of the law. The dynamics of gospel and law also emerge in his treatment of *election* (II/2:§33) and *ethics* (II/2:§§36–39). As the Elect One of God, Jesus Christ manifests in his death *both* the judgment *and* the forgiveness of God upon human sinners. *The focal point of election for Barth thus marks the crucial step from one movement of his dialectic (Yes-No) to the other (No-Yes).* Furthermore, as a command that God utters and also keeps, the law cannot be separated from either God or the gospel. In the context of God's electing grace, the law is a gift that, like Calvin's third use of the law, describes who and where God is, paving the way for human participation in what God is doing at any given moment. Theological ethics thus finds its roots in Barth's dialectic of gospel and law.

Gospel and law also inform Barth's doctrine of creation (III/1–4). *Covenant* is to creation as content (grace) is to form (law), says Barth. As such, creation is the external basis of the covenant (§41.2), and covenant is the internal basis of creation (§41.3). Barth then centers the doctrine of creation in Jesus Christ: the Word of God become creature. He traces the entire dialectical movement of gospel and law succinctly in III/1:§42, "The Yes of God the Creator," and especially III/2:§42.3, "Creation As Justification."

Gospel and law come into play explicitly in the doctrine of reconciliation (IV:1–4) at every point where Barth deals with the knowledge of human sin (IV/1:§60.1; IV/2:§65.1; IV/3.1:§70.1). Following *Calvin*, Barth insists that we humans recognize the depth and extent of our sin only *after* we know of God's redeeming grace in Jesus Christ. Gospel here precedes law in a familiar pattern. Barth's doctrine of reconciliation brings to a true climax his earlier formulations about Jesus Christ, election, covenant, and the dynamics of gospel and law that inform them.

Barth, *CD* IV/1–3; idem, *ER*; idem, *EvT*; idem, "G&L"; idem, *WGWM*; E. Busch, *The Great Passion,* trans. G. W. Bromiley (2004), 152–75; J. Couenhoven, "Law and Gospel, or the Law of the Gospel," *JREth* 30 (2002): 181–205; S. Rae, "Gospel, Law and Freedom in the Theological Ethics of Karl Barth," *SJT* 25 (1972): 412–22.
MERWYN S. JOHNSON

Grace A stoutly Reformed theologian, Barth adopted the "cause of grace" as a hallmark of his dogmatic *theology*. From his earliest writings until his last, Barth insisted that the *God* and Father of the Lord *Jesus Christ* was a God of grace, and could be known and obeyed only in grace. Indeed, the central reality of the Christian *faith*, Jesus Christ, is at heart a living grace, the righteous Judge who has not forgotten how to be gracious. The *Holy Spirit* is the Lord of grace, who erupts into the *world* to conform human words—including Holy Scripture—to the true *Word of God*, and to conform human lives—sinful and needy—to the Savior. Nothing creaturely makes a person or a word or an object worthy and capable of divine favor; it is grace alone that takes the wayward and powerless creature into the Divine Presence, and sets it right. Grace marks the path the Christian takes to proper *knowledge of God*: grace, for Barth, is an epistemological term. But grace also characterizes the nature, identity, and sovereignty of the triune God and the incarnate Word, Jesus Christ, so grace is a key metaphysical term as well. From beginning to end, the gospel of Jesus Christ is a word of grace, the great good news of deliverance from "real *sin*, real death, real *evil*," to a life of true *freedom*, won not by works, but granted purely and only by grace alone. The Reformation cry—*sola gratia*—was heard, defended, and celebrated by Barth as by few theologians since the sixteenth century.

Little wonder, then, that G. C. Berkouwer, the distinguished twentieth-century professor of dogmatic theology at the Free University in Amsterdam, titles his influential study *The Triumph of Grace in the Theology of Karl Barth.* Berkouwer does not mistake the central place of grace in Barth's dogmatic work; indeed, he magnifies it. "Barth wishes to emphasize above all the triumph of God's grace," Berkouwer writes. "From countless explicit statements as also from the whole structure of his *dogmatics*, it appears that this theme has become the dominant motif in the theology of Barth" (Berkouwer, 19). Startling to read, however, is the conclusion Berkouwer draws from his extensive study of Barth's doctrine of grace: it is, he argues, a dangerous and mistaken innovation, contrary to Scripture, and undermining of the core doctrines of Reformed theology. Since the publication of *Triumph of Grace*, Berkouwer's criticism has set the terms of the debate for any examination and assessment of Barth's doctrine of grace; and we will follow his lead here.

Barth's "triumph of grace," Berkouwer charges, eviscerates the doctrines of sin and evil, and empties the doctrine of *election* of content and authority. Traditional in Reformed theology is the teaching that God in his sovereignty and *eternity* chooses some sinners to eternal life and reprobates others to eternal death. In this election or predestination, God is entirely just—"all have sinned and fall short of the glory of God"—and the justice of *creation* is preserved against evil and sin. The ground and goal of God's electing work is God's own glory alone, traditional Reformed dogmaticians say; there is nothing in the human creature to merit this supreme act of grace. To realize the sovereign work of election, God makes use of Christ's own sacrificial death, so that Christ's cross is the means or instrument by which sinners are saved.

In *CD* II/2, *The Doctrine of God*, Barth famously rejects this traditional Reformed doctrine of election. The object or *scopus*—to use the technical term of Reformed theology—cannot be, Barth reasons, the individual person and her destiny, whether to life or to eternal death. Through a long and masterful reading of Old and New Testament texts, Barth argues that Scripture teaches a wholly different *scopus* for election: Jesus Christ himself is the proper object of God's election. The twofold predestinating will of God—*predestinatio gemina*—must apply, Barth insists, to Christ, first and properly. He is the one predestined to be elected for rejection. The aim of God's election, then, cannot be simply to exhibit his own glory or justice. Rather, God's election exhibits *grace*, the grace of Jesus Christ, the "Judge, judged in our place."

More controversial still is Barth's insistence that Christ is both the elected and the electing God. Readers familiar with Barth's rejection—or radical attenuation—of the *logos asarkos* (the unembodied Word) will recognize the dogmatic pattern here: the eternal Son cannot be other than Jesus Christ, the incarnate Word. From the "beginning

of all God's ways and works," Barth writes, the Son of God elects himself to be the Savior of fallen *humanity*. The Son takes for his own the rejection of the creature, and elects to be gracious to it. Just this is what it means, Barth says, for God to be the one who loves in *freedom*. The doctrine of election, if it be true to Scripture, then, must be a doctrine of grace—the grace of a God who in his own inner life determines to be the great good news of his creature, taking reprobation for his own, and giving life and *salvation* in exchange.

Two dangers threaten here: Barth's reworking of the doctrine of election as a doctrine of grace appears to make grace a *necessary* attribute of God, a position that threatens the independence and sovereignty of God over his creation. Barth's emphasis, further, on grace as a synonym or "Name" for Jesus Christ appears to undermine a traditional element of Latin theology, that grace for sinners is "created," a gift, that is, given to a creature that is distinct from the Giver. These two worries in the doctrine of grace bring Barth close to his Roman Catholic contemporary, Karl Rahner. Rahner has left a twofold legacy to modern Thomism: that the God of the Immanent Trinity must be one with the God of the Economy (the "Rahner maxim"); and that God's gift of grace must be "Uncreated," the "inexpressible nearness" of the Creator himself to the creature. As in Rahner, so in Barth: the doctrine of grace and the doctrine of God appear to be two expressions of the one Reality, that God himself is Grace.

Now Berkouwer does not express his quarrel with Barth in quite these terms; yet they are not far from them, all the same. Consider, Berkouwer says, Barth's doctrine of sin and evil. Here we have a notion of evil that once again transforms the object or *scopus* of the doctrine: the object of evil's destruction is not the creature, first and properly, but rather the Creator. God himself is the target of evil, and its principal enemy. In a massive reworking of the Augustinian legacy, Barth termed evil "nothingness" (*das Nichtige*). It is not a creature, nor does it have the dignity of creaturely reality. Rather it possesses its own form of reality as that which is prohibited. Evil by its very nature is deceptive and imperceptible—it does not possess the creaturely dignity of visibility—so it can be spotted only indirectly in Holy Scripture. Evil can be seen behind the rejection of chaos, for example, in the creation narrative in Genesis, or the apocalyptic undoing of creation, threatened in the prophet Isaiah. Evil, then, cannot be an element of creaturely life: the suffering, and disease, and sorrow of human *history*, Barth underscores, cannot be nothingness, but is rather the "shadow side" of the good creation. Creation itself is gracious: human history in its poverty and in its wealth is under the lordship of Christ, so good, full of hope, and a sign of grace. True evil, nothingness, can be seen only in the light of Christ, the electing God. At the cross, Barth writes, Christ at once reveals the true character of sin and evil, and defeats it. Sin is shown in its futility as the "impossible possibility." Grace triumphs over evil at Golgotha; only its husk remains.

Berkouwer fastens his criticism of Barth exactly here. Can sin be a serious and real struggle for the creature if Christ assumes and defeats it decisively on the cross? Can evil genuinely oppose and threaten the creature if Christ triumphs over death and destruction in his own death? Can the doctrine of election be anything more than playacting if Christ himself is the true, elected reprobate, and dies in just this way for every sinner? Berkouwer considers Barth an unacknowledged universalist: the call to faith and the weight of that decision is reduced to a mere recognition of what Christ has always and already done for his creatures—deliver them, apart from faith or from merit, from the reprobation Christ alone bears as Lord of grace. To sum up: Grace, Berkouwer charges, is the "dominant motif" of the *CD*, and an abstract idea now governs theology and dictates what it may say.

Assessment of Berkouwer's criticism will turn on the room readers make for *actualism* in theology. Barth insists that Christ and his redeeming work is an *event*, a living relation between the electing God and his creatures. Grace simply is the name of this life, this exchange between Christ and sinners. It cannot be a "motif" or "abstract concept"; there is none such in proper dogmatics, Barth says. What might be taken in other theologies as deductions from an original premise cannot be assumed to be such for Barth. A living relation cannot be reduced to a system: that is Barth's central dogmatic method. Grace is the event of Christ's victorious death for the unworthy, and in just this way is the true, inner life of the triune God himself.

———

K. Barth, *CD* II/1:§30; II/2:§§32–35; III/3:§50; IV/1:§60; G. C. Berkouwer, *The Triumph of Grace in the Theology of Karl Barth*, trans. H. R. Boer (1956); M. K. Cunningham, *What Is Theological Exegesis?* (1995), 78–85; G. Hunsinger, *How to Read Karl Barth* (1991), 76–102, 185–224; B. L. McCormack, "Grace and Being," in *Cambridge Companion to Karl Barth*, ed. J. Webster (2000), 92–110.

KATHERINE SONDEREGGER

Gratitude "Thankfulness is the first, not merely the last, word in the *Christian life*." It is "the first and decisive word by which we must describe our *sanctification* and therefore all good action and Christian living. To be sanctified, good, Christian, means to be thankful" (*KGSG*, 123). In fact, "it is legitimate to put thankfulness before repentance, because we thereby make clear what true repentance is" (122). Participation in God's *revelation* "can consist only in the offering of our thanks" (*CD* II/1:216).

"To believe in *Jesus Christ* means to become thankful." Barth says this cannot be understood radically enough. "It is not merely a change of temper or sentiment or conduct and action. It is the change of the being of man before *God* brought about by the fact that God has altered His attitude to man." Gratitude becomes not merely a quality but the very essence of the creature's being. "It is not merely grateful. It is itself gratitude. It can see itself only as gratitude because in fact it can only exist as this, as pure gratitude towards God. What the creature does in its new creatureliness, which in Jesus Christ has become gratitude to God, is to glorify God" (II/1:669), and it is in gratitude to God that our genuine *humanity* is realized (IV/1:15).

In unfailing dialectical connection, Barth insists: "Χάρις [*grace*] calls for εὐχαριστία [thanksgiving]. But εὐχαριστία is itself the substance of the creature's participation in the divine χάρις" (II/1:670). In other words, "Grace and gratitude belong together like heaven and earth. Grace evokes gratitude like the voice of an echo. Gratitude follows grace like thunder lightning." Barth underscores that this occurs "not by virtue of any necessity of the concepts as such," but only because of the grace of God in Jesus Christ. Here, Barth says, "only gratitude can correspond to grace, and this correspondence cannot fail" (IV/1·41). The only circumstance in which it fails is *sin*. "Radically and basically all sin is simply ingratitude—man's refusal of the one but necessary thing which is proper to and is required of him with whom God has graciously entered into *covenant*. As far as man is concerned there can be no question of anything but gratitude; but gratitude is the complement which man must necessarily fulfill" (41–42).

It might appear that Barth agrees with Cicero: "Gratitude is not only the greatest of virtues, but the parent of all the others." But as response to the Word and Spirit of God (grace), Barth distinguishes gratitude from more common conceptions in six ways.

First, gratitude "does not have its necessity in itself; it does not happen on its own account: but it is evoked by an object. Nor does it have its necessity in us who do this work; we do it, not because we are forced by an inner compulsion or enabled by an inner desire, but because the demand for us to do it is imposed upon us from without, because God is God in His revelation, because it is His true revelation and because we are truly claimed by it" (II/1:216); "In the abstract, it is a complete untruth to say that we have the power to thank and serve the glory of God" (671).

Second, gratitude as "simply a response to God's revelation . . . takes its place with other—and in their own way good—works of man, [but] it cannot try to commend itself as compared with them" (216). "It will have only its hidden excellence in its character as response to the Word" and, as an act of *witness*, will point away from itself to God's grace. "It will be a *witness*, question and summons to all other works. But it will not enter into competition and strife with them" (217).

Third, gratitude "can consist only in an acknowledgment of the revelation of God. It cannot consist, then, in a requital, in a work which is comparable in nature with the work of God, in an adequate reply to what has been said to us by God about God. . . . Where man repays like with like, there is no question of thanksgiving but only of a transaction: we are at the market which is ruled by the mutual adjustment of supply and demand, value and price." Genuine thanksgiving, by contrast, "can only be acknowledgment, and the one who acknowledges places himself and his action consciously and expressly under the giver and his gift." It is an act of subordination, not of commerce (217).

Fourth, gratitude "is put under the measure, order and rule of His revelation. It takes place in the sphere of our humanity and claims our very best—

and therefore our best thinking and speaking to this end. But this does not mean that it is abandoned to our arbitrary selection of this best according to our own choice and pleasure" (218). Such gratitude may not be expressed any way we please. "Purposeless or arbitrary thanksgiving, the thanksgiving in which the giver is guided either by chance or by his own humor, fancy or obstinacy, is not thanksgiving at all." "True gratitude enquires—and it does not enquire in a soliloquy, but it enquires after Him to whom it wants to show gratitude." It acts "not arbitrarily, not according to its own discovery of gratitude, but in such a way that the One to whom it would be grateful is the law of its action. This means . . . we are not left to ourselves, whether in the form of chance or of the willfulness of our general or individual nature, thinking and speaking. It is always a question of acknowledging God's revelation. This definite object rules our thinking and speaking" (218).

Fifth, "*Joy* is the simplest form of gratitude" (III/4:376). Indeed, gratitude "cannot take place except in joyfulness. . . . A gratitude that consists in an involuntary, mutinous and therefore forced and unjoyful action is not thanksgiving. A tribute to tyranny, however paid, is not thanks" (II/1:219). Rather, through Jesus Christ, ours is "a joyful deliverance from the godless fetters of this world for a free, grateful service to his creatures" (Barmen Declaration, article 2).

Finally, and fundamentally, gratitude is an act of "amazement" and "wondering awe" that arises ineluctably in human consciousness when the distance and incongruity between God as the known and the human knower—in all the latter's inadequacy and lowliness—is recognized as having been overcome from God's side, and not our own, in revelation (*CD* II/1:220–23).

K. Barth, *CD* II/1:216–23, 668–73; III/2:175–76; IV/1:41–42; idem, *KGSG*,

122ff.; M. Boulton, "'We Pray by His Mouth,'" *MTh* 17, no. 1 (2001): 67–83; J. Mangina, *Karl Barth on the Christian Life* (2001), 132ff.

RICHARD E. BURNETT

Harnack When Barth wanted to begin theological studies, the one teacher with whom to start was Adolf Harnack (1851–1930). After spending two semesters in Berne, he arrived in Berlin in the autumn of 1906. His enthusiasm for Harnack knew no bounds, to the detriment of Berlin's cultural riches. But this changed radically: Harnack and Barth met at a conference in Switzerland in 1920 where both presented an address, Harnack on "What Has *History* to Offer as Certain Knowledge Concerning the Meaning of *World* Events?" and Barth on "Biblical Questions, Insights, and Vistas." Near the end of his presentation, and in Harnack's hearing, Barth said this: "Religion's blind and vicious habit of asserting eternally that it possesses something, feasts upon it, and distributes it, must sometime cease, if we are ever to have an honest, a fierce seeking, asking and knocking" ("Vistas," 86–87). Harnack told a friend: "the effect of Barth's lecture was just staggering. . . . I saw the sincerity of Barth's speech, but its *theology* frightened me. . . . Instead of losing any of its force, it appears to me more and more hazardous, yes, in a way even scandalous" (von Zahn-Harnack, 415). The two met again in 1926; Barth was writing a *dogmatics* and Harnack said that if he ever were to write one he would entitle it "The Life of the Children of God." Barth acknowledged that such a topic had a place in the doctrine of the *Holy Spirit* and so entitled a chapter in his magnum opus (*CD* I/2:362ff.), thereby paying homage to his former teacher.

Harnack was born in Dorpat, now Tartu, Estonia, the second child of Theodosius Harnack, professor of theology, and Anna Ewers. He studied theology at the universities of Dorpat and Leipzig, completing his doctoral and habilitation dissertations at the latter. Both faculties were shaped by Lutheran orthodoxy but also open to the methods of textual and *historical criticism*. In Leipzig his insistence on the *primacy of scholarly method* was strengthened and guided him to the end. His teaching career began at Leipzig in 1875, continued in Giessen (1878–1886), where he began to write his monumental *History of Dogma* and assumed the editor-in-chief position of the prestigious *Theologische Literaturzeitung*. He gained international recognition: in 1885 and again 1898 Harvard University offered him a position; Harnack declined both offers. In 1886 he followed a call to Marburg but left after two years to join the faculty at the University of Berlin; the German emperor had personally signed the call, adding that he wanted no bigots in his university (von Zahn-Harnack, 127). A member of the Prussian Academy of Sciences and of eleven other academies in eight other countries, Harnack served as a full professor in Berlin until age 72.

His service to the academy is amazing: a literary legacy of sixteen hundred titles; multiterm presidencies of distinguished national and international congresses; general director of the Royal Library, Berlin; first president, by imperial decree, of the Kaiser Wilhelm Society for the Advancement of the Sciences; principal editor of the fifty-volume critical edition of the Greek church fathers; author of the four-volume history of the Prussian Academy of Sciences. In addition to all this, he served the German government by taking on extensive administrative responsibilities, which in 1914 prompted the Kaiser to confer knighthood on Harnack: Adolf *von* Harnack! The relationship between the Kaiser and Harnack was so close that the Kaiser asked Harnack to write his speech to the German nation after the outbreak of World War I. And when critics declared that the war had made plain the bankruptcy of *religion*, Harnack countered that instead the war

had unearthed deep, hidden sources of religion. That was the issue over which Barth broke radically with Harnack's liberal theology.

To call Harnack's theology "liberal" and "liberal theology at its height" is, above all, to identify its overriding commitment to the *freedom* of theology. "Harnack's work manifests a powerful conviction in relation to the imperative of freedom: the freedom of thought, of pursuing *truth* on every path, the freedom from interference by those who have been given authority in human institutions, from human declarations and rules so that conscience may develop as fully as possible." Harnack's "*liberalism*" also included the sense of responsibility toward the object and subject of what humans do and say; he knew that there are limits to what we see and declare. "But they were not limits set . . . by dogmas, affirmations defined by duly authorized people, to be affirmed and held as true for the sake of *salvation*; such limits were seen to be antithetical to other highly characteristic features of the 'liberal' position. Among those were the confidence in the human, finite, spirit, the reverence for the dignity, competence and authority of the power of human thought and the ability to transcend one's subjectivity in the endeavor to attain to genuine objectivity" (Rumscheidt, 33). The religious *faith* of such *theology* is one that, because it is "methodological," not only knows God, but also *how* it knows. The liberal theology Harnack represents has at its fingertips the methods that yield what is said to be "assured" knowledge or, in more technical terminology, affirms that "the *noetic* ratio of the mind's comprehension is univocally expressive of the *ontic* ratio of what is being comprehended." This method, developed by Descartes and other epistemologists, "in the final analysis reduces the distance between the knower and the known to such an extent that the known can no longer appear to be a limit on the knower. The limit-free knower is, therefore, radically free from, but also radically free for, reality" (Rumscheidt, 34–35). Barth presented at length his critique of Harnack's theological methodology and what that method declared to be the substance of Christian faith in the open correspondence of 1923 where he called for that honest, fierce seeking, asking, and knocking. Harnack opened the exchange with a letter raising "Fifteen Questions to the Despisers of Scientific Theology," to which Barth gave succinct answers (the second open letter of the correspondence.) Harnack replied, rejecting some points and raising critical questions to others. Barth's reply (the fourth letter) was quite lengthy, expanding what he had said in the first reply. Harnack ended the exchange with a regretful note, saying that he was not able to understand much of Barth's theological position and felt that further correspondence could not help (see *Beginnings*, 163–87).

In Harnack's "liberal" theology, incorruptible reasonableness and unshakable religious faith go hand in hand; his sense of giving all for the freedom of theology is embedded in his deep awareness that he was dependent on the Creator Spirit whom to pray for is the task of believing Christians. On his tombstone in Berlin are the words that he had chosen for family coat of arms: *Veni Creator Spiritus.*

H.-A. Drewes, "Auseinandersetzung mit Adolf von Harnack," in *Karl Barth in Deutschland (1921–1935),* ed. M. Beintker, C. Link, and M. Trowitzsch (2005), 190–203; H. M. Rumscheidt, *Revelation and Theology* (1972); H. M Rumscheidt, ed., *Adolf von Harnack* (1989); A. von Zahn-Harnack, ed., *Adolf von Harnack* (1951).

H. MARTIN RUMSCHEIDT

Hell

The reality of hell, according to Barth, is revealed in the cross. Hell is known only by reflecting on the unique death of *Jesus Christ,* who bears the sins of the whole *world* and, as a result, dies

as the one who was made a curse for *humanity* (Gal. 3:13). Jesus Christ suffers *eternal* corruption in his death. In other words, Jesus Christ enters hell in his death. It is at this point that the New Testament portrayal of human death, based on the death of Jesus Christ, differs from that of the Old Testament. While the Old Testament presents the picture of dead souls dwelling in the comfortless yet tolerable wasteland of Sheol, the New Testament presents the vivid picture of flames, outer darkness, unquenchable fire and torment that leads to weeping and gnashing of teeth. Hell is God's decisive and positive punishment of sinful humanity (see *CD* III/2:602ff.).

Barth explains this difference by pointing to the centrality of the cross to the New Testament *witness.* Hell is not introduced because of a pessimistic anthropology or abstract speculation regarding life beyond the grave; rather, hell is an actual threat to sinful humanity because it is the only way of accounting for the torment that Jesus Christ endured in the face of his imminent death—the cup from which he prayed to be spared and the *baptism* that caused him distress. The death that Jesus Christ faced, the prospect of which caused him great anguish, was not mere physical death as fate or chance; rather, it was the full weight of the judgment of *God.* Consequently, hell is the annihilatingly painful existence that results from alienating opposition to God. Hell is what sinful humanity deserves and that which Jesus Christ receives from the wrathful hand of God.

At no point does Barth underplay the severe reality of hell as God's wrathful judgment of sin and human sinners. Yet he refuses to address the reality of hell apart from the actuality of God's victory over hell in the triumphant death and *resurrection of Jesus Christ.* Barth insists that hell is a real and deserving threat that hangs over humanity, who as sinners must be rejected by God. However, he also insists that Jesus Christ gave himself up to the depths of

94   Heresy

hell on behalf of and in the place of sinful humanity. Furthermore, since Jesus Christ is *the* Rejected of God, Barth can assert that "God makes Himself rejected in [Jesus Christ], and has Himself alone tasted to the depths all that rejection means and necessarily involves" (II/2:496). Moreover, according to Barth, Jesus Christ's suffering of eternal punishment—his descent into hell—is the precise means of God's reconciling the world to himself.

Even though Barth emphasizes the triumphant and saving power of Jesus Christ's tasting the depths of hell for all of sinful humanity, this does not remove the threat and danger of damnation that hangs over the head of sinful humanity like a sword (IV/3.1:465). In short, Barth does not assert an empty hell. Judgment, condemnation, damnation, and hell are real eschatological possibilities that threaten sinful humanity. However, Barth contends that there is genuine *hope* that is based on the knowledge of the gracious God who does not inflict wrathful punishment on sinful humanity that he has not already inflicted upon himself by handing over Jesus Christ to the depths of hell (II/2:496; see also 92).

O. Crisp, "Karl Barth and Jonathan Edwards on Reprobation (and Hell)," in *Engaging with Barth*, ed. D. Gibson and D. Strange (2009), 300–322; G. Hunsinger, "Hellfire and Damnation," in *Disruptive Grace* (2000), 226–49; D. Lauber, *Barth on the Descent into Hell* (2004); A. E. Lewis, *Between Cross and Resurrection* (2001).
DAVID LAUBER

Heresy Faith's most serious conflict is not with unbelief as such (which *apologetics* often assumes) but with unbelief that comes in the form of *faith*. Heresy is "a form of Christian faith which we cannot deny to be a form of Christian faith from the formal standpoint" but which we cannot understand as Christian faith in terms of its content. We "can only understand this faith as another

faith" (*CD* I/1:31–32). Thus, unlike apostates or unbelievers, heretics must get some things right in order to qualify as such. Though on opposing sides, they are "pieces on the same chessboard" (*ThC*, 17–18). Hence in the conflict between the *church* and heresy there is, at least at the beginning, agreement about the point of disagreement: "This is why there can be strife. We have to do with differing interpretations of the same theme" (I/1:33).

However, the interpretations are so different that "the menacing question arises whether they are not really dealing with different themes, and therefore whether the opposing and different faith is not really to be understood as unbelief. The conversation between the church and heretics would not be so serious if it were conducted elsewhere than under the shadow of this menacing question," that is, if in the voice of heresy one heard not only unbelief but also "a possibility of faith. To be sure, it will see it as a profoundly incomprehensible one, which can be regarded only as a possibility of the disruption and destruction of faith, as a possibility against which it must be on guard. Yet it must still understand it as a possibility of faith . . . hard though it may be to think of it as such" (33–34). This is why the conflict is so serious.

Evangelical faith stands in such conflict with **Roman Catholicism** ("in the form which it gave itself in the 16th century") and Protestant *liberalism*. If we do not evade "the formal justice of their claim," both encounter us not as "irrelevant paganisms" but as "possibilities of faith within and not without the Church." As such they serve an important purpose. They "force us to see clearly to what extent, in what sense and with what inner foundation we stand on the one side and not the other" when it comes to our knowledge of *Jesus Christ*, *revelation*, the church, and so on. Such "purification" of our knowledge is necessary (34). Had he known more about it in 1932, Barth later said he would have included fundamentalism as a heresy (*TT*, 41).

Without embracing its abuses, Barth generally accepts Protestant orthodoxy's "stringent way" of interpreting heresy (e.g., Polan) but also its "warning against a careless use or arbitrary application of the term." It applies only where it is authorized by a decision of the church, is held consciously and incorrigibly, and directly affects the substance of the faith (I/2:812). Heresies are usually more than "onesidedness" or "a truncated version of the *truth*" (808), but they often begin as such.

The church must constantly battle heresy because of self-will among its members (807–8). Yet in light of the parable of the Talents (Matt. 25:14–15) and, specifically, the servant who buried his talent, Barth claims that worse than a "heresy-propagating Church" is "the Church which, despite the purity of its doctrine, does not make proper use of it" (847). Heresy is the result of failure to hear the voice of Jesus Christ. What safeguards against it, at least formally, is the teaching church that is alert to "preheretical deviations" and is served by good *dogmatics* that not only reminds the church of the voice of its Master in the past, but calls the church to a fresh hearing of his voice in the present.

K. Barth, *CD* I/1:31ff.; I/2:807ff.; T. F. Torrance, "Karl Barth and the Latin Heresy," in *Karl Barth* (1990), 213–40; M. Welker, "From Fighter Against the 'Roman Heresy' to Leading Thinker for the Ecumenical Movement," *SJT* 57, no. 4 (2004): 434–50.

RICHARD E. BURNETT

Hermeneutics In *Wahrheit und Methode* ([2nd ed., 1965], 481), Hans-Georg Gadamer described *Rom* I (1919) as "a virtual hermeneutical manifesto." This is ironic because the word *hermeneutics* does not appear in *Rom* I or II and because Barth's theological revolution represents a protest against

modern theology's preoccupation with method and, therefore, hermeneutics. Barth's revolution was in part an effort to overcome the hegemony of "general hermeneutics" and the tradition of its most influential and sophisticated formulation through *Schleiermacher*. Preoccupation with hermeneutics or "understanding in general" is what Barth thought he and his fellow travelers in the 1920s had agreed was a false path (see *dialectical theology*), which is why he saw his contemporaries' return to it in the 1950s and 1960s as a return to "Egyptian bondage" ("RB—AUH," 127). Barth's repeated refusal to enter into their discussions over the "New Hermeneutic" led some to conclude that Barth "very unjustly trivialized the hermeneutical problem" (Ernst Fuchs and Gerhard Ebeling), that he had nothing to contribute to the topic, and therefore that the fruitful limits of his *theology* had been reached (James M. Robinson).

Actually, Barth's refusal was based on his conviction that "the question of the right hermeneutics cannot be decided in a discussion of exegetical *method*, but only in *exegesis* itself" (Busch, *Karl Barth*, 390). Yet this too was misunderstood. Barth's commitment to the priority of exegesis over hermeneutics was not based on any pragmatist penchant or postmodern proclivity toward merely "ad hoc hermeneutical principles" (contra M. Cunningham) anymore than it was on a priori epistemological commitments or presuppositions based on general hermeneutics. Rather it was based on what he discovered through biblical exegesis—the sovereign *freedom* of Scripture's object, the *revelation* of *God* in *Jesus Christ*. And this discovery and subsequent reckoning with the freedom of Scripture's object had hermeneutical implications. If, for example, as Barth posited, "The universal rule of interpretation is that a text can be read and understood and expounded only with reference to and in the light of its theme" (*CD* I/2:493), then not only should the freedom of Scripture's object and theme be respected and recognized as such throughout, but why not the object and theme of other books as well? Indeed, it is from the freedom of Scripture's object that we learn to respect the freedom of and maintain loyalty and openness to other objects of investigation and their manner of self-presentation.

Thus, on the one hand, Barth could say *"methodus est arbitraria"* because the object to be known should determine the way taken in knowing. Yet, on the other hand, Barth did not discover this *in abstracto* but from reading the *Bible*. And because he believed he had not gone to its school in vain and was never so naive to think he had no method or that presuppositionless exegesis was possible, Barth articulated specific hermeneutical principles and a definite exegetical method. In fact, when Jülicher charged that he was a "pneumatic" and had only offered an arbitrary and idiosyncratic interpretation of Paul's Romans when he should have acted as a "scientific exegete" and dealt with the Bible like any other book, Barth responded that he would have tried to approach the task of interpreting Goethe or Lao-Tzu in the same way had it been his task to interpret Goethe or Lao-Tzu (*Rom* II, xv–xvi). Barth's response to Jülicher is a denial that his interpretation was arbitrary or privileged, but it is not as such an admission that he had interpreted the Bible "like any other book," that is, according to the standards of general hermeneutics. And herein lies an important implication of the so-called scandal of particularity.

Barth's move from the particular to the general is exemplified in his move from special hermeneutics (i.e., biblical or theological hermeneutics) to general hermeneutics. In other words, instead of reading the Bible "like any other book," Barth tried to read other books like he read the Bible, that is, with the same respect for and openness to the freedom of the various objects represented relative to the freedom of Scripture's object. Barth never denied the basic concern

that gave rise to general hermeneutics, namely, arbitrary, idiosyncratic, and privileged interpretations of the Bible and other books as well. On the contrary, he affirmed general hermeneutics' goal of avoiding arbitrary, idiosyncratic, and privileged interpretation by including all "the methods of observation used in general hermeneutics" and considering "all the questions, without exception, which arise from that point of view in forming its general picture of the text" (I/2:726), including the grammatical, psychological, historical, and divinatory aspects of interpretation that Schleiermacher and his followers had so carefully developed.

However, Barth refused to "tolerate any restrictions" and insisted that genuine interpretation "will allow the text to speak for itself in the sense that it will give full scope to its controlling object. It will not seek to conceal its ultimate determination for the sake of any preconceived notion of what is possible. It will not distort the text by trying to obscure and level down and render innocuous its real object." This was Barth's problem with general hermeneutics: it is not "accustomed to take seriously the idea that what is said in a text, that is, the object which we have to reproduce, might bring into play other possibilities than those known to the interpreter. . . . It thinks it has a basic knowledge of what is generally possible" (725).

Of course, biblical hermeneutics has "its own definite presupposition": the sovereign freedom of Scripture's object that "prescribes its own law for our activity" (726). But by refusing to limit the scope of interpretation and make "absolutely no prejudgment" and no "arbitrary exception" as to what is possible, biblical hermeneutics is not "claiming for itself a mysterious special privilege" but is "consistent as hermeneutics" (725), unlike "general hermeneutics which has not yet been better informed in this regard." If it were better informed, "biblical hermeneutics might then be only a special case of general hermeneutics"

(727). But until then "Biblical hermeneutics must be guarded against the totalitarian claim of a general hermeneutics" and remain "a special hermeneutics only because general hermeneutics has been so mortally sick for so long that it has not let the special problem of biblical hermeneutics force its attention upon its own problem. For the sake of better general hermeneutics it must therefore dare to be this special hermeneutics" (472).

N. T. Bakker, *In der Krisis der Offenbarung* (1974); R. E. Burnett, *Karl Barth's Theological Exegesis* (2004); M. K. Cunningham, *What Is Theological Exegesis?* (1995); H.-G. Gadamer, *Wahrheit und Methode* (2nd ed., 1965), trans. J. Weinsheimer and D. Marshall (1989) (ET: *Truth and Method*); E. Jüngel, "Theology as Metacriticism," in *Karl Barth*, trans. G. E. Paul (1986), 70–82; H. Kirschstein, *Der souveräne Gott und die heilige Schrift* (1998).

RICHARD E. BURNETT

Herrmann   After studying *theology* at the University of Halle, where he was influenced by August Tholuck, a pietist thinker, Wilhelm Herrmann taught dogmatic theology at the University of Marburg from 1879 until his retirement in 1917. His most famous book, besides his *Ethics* (1901), is *The Communion of the Christian with God: Described on the Basis of Luther's Statements* (1886). As a Lutheran theologian affiliated since 1875 with the Ritschlian school, he greatly contributed to the renown of the University of Marburg, attracting many students from Europe and beyond. The young Barth was one of them: Marburg became his theological Zion. He arrived there in 1908 as a "convinced Marburger," and later he wrote: Herrmann "was *the* theological teacher of my student years" ("Herrmann," 238).

What first attracted Barth was Herrmann's way of combining Kant and *Schleiermacher*. As a Kantian, Herrmann saw a close link between *religion* and morality. The quest for one's

personal truthfulness is "the way to religion," that is, the way to *faith* and to *God*. But morality, for all its importance with regard to religion, is not yet religion. In his *On Religion: Speeches to Its Cultured Despisers*, Schleiermacher correctly preserved the autonomy of religion against those who threatened to dissolve religion either into metaphysics (the rationalists) or morality (Kant and his followers). In his mature years, Herrmann could not praise Schleiermacher's *Speeches* too highly. Schleiermacher showed in his Second Speech how "religion's essence is neither thinking nor acting," neither scientific, theoretical knowledge nor morality, for religion has essentially to do with a longing "to be grasped and filled by the universe's immediate influences in childlike passivity." Herrmann believed that the answer to our moral concerns lies beyond our capacities and moral tasks, in the historical event of God's *revelation* in the person of *Jesus Christ*. His theology is rooted not just in *ethics* but also in *history* in the sense of *Geschichte* rather than *Historie*, that is, in a fact of history that still has an impact on our lives. This fact is God's revelation in Jesus Christ. In it we discover a reality that *transcends* what our *world* can give us (otherwise God would be an idol). But one has to be careful not to misconstrue this event. Christian faith does not consist merely in giving one's assent to miraculous deeds witnessed not by us but only by contemporaries of Jesus. Rather, faith consists in the experience of the power of Jesus' personality or "inner life." Christian faith is a surrender, a complete trust in a revelation that authenticates itself and cannot be verified by external criteria (e.g., historical or psychological criteria). Any pretension at mastering revelation leads to idolatry: God is always beyond our attempts at proving his existence. This clear demarcation between what is experienced in revelation and what can be demonstrated objectively and scientifically remained a deep point of disagreement between

Herrmann and another towering figure of Protestant theology at the time, Ernst Troeltsch.

Like Schleiermacher, Herrmann argued that an actual encounter lies at the basis of the Christian faith. Christian theology is secondary and seeks to express adequately what this encounter means. To confuse the original existential moment and the doctrinal aspect that derives from it is a dangerous mistake, according to Herrmann, who never tired of criticizing the various "orthodox" theologians who presented faith essentially as an assent to doctrinal propositions. Doctrinal propositions are important, but the Christian should never confuse surrender to them with surrender to God. Unfortunately, in Herrmann's opinion, both orthodox and liberal theologians were leading Christians to confuse the two. This meant that the good news was becoming a command, a law. As a Lutheran theologian using the distinction between law and gospel (see *gospel and law*), between a task and a gift, Herrmann felt compelled to counter this interpretation of the Christian faith by focusing on the experience of trust. Trust alone makes a Christian. Revelation is not a task but a gift. To transform it into a task is to distort the good news.

This, in short, is the theology that Barth made his own as a student and minister. It is only after he experienced his own "twilight of the gods" in the fall of 1914, when he was utterly shocked to see some of his former professors, including Herrmann and *Harnack*, using theological discourse to support Germany's war effort, that Barth reoriented his entire theology. He was looking for a different ground than the individual experience of revelation. Indeed, on such subjective ground one could claim that Germans alone "experienced" the war as a sacred calling. Barth's theological objectivism or realism, centered not on individual experience but on the objective reality of the *Word of God*, was a consequence of his disillusion in 1914.

Ironically, Herrmann's sense of God's "otherness" and transcendence led Barth to react against him.

After 1914, Barth retrieved various aspects of Christian theology that were not central in Herrmann's thought, including the cross and the resurrection (see *resurrection of Jesus Christ*), the authority of the *Bible* and *dogma* in their relation to revelation, the doctrines of the *Trinity* and *election*. Barth rejected Herrmann's "reduction" of Christian theology and embraced the vast horizon of Scripture. He remained aware of Herrmann's overarching concern to eliminate all intellectualist interpretations of faith as assent, but he could not take this concern too seriously (see *CD* III/2:446–47 and IV/1:761). Besides his major assessment of Herrmann's theology in 1925, which represents a formidable attempt at turning Herrmann's own theology upside down in order to make it resemble his own theology at the time, one finds only sparse comments on Herrmann's theology in Barth's mature works.

The obvious elements of discontinuity between Barth's theology after World War I and Herrmann's theology should not obfuscate the elements of continuity that remained. One could point to their shared "Christocentrism," even if it took different shapes and had different contents (indeed, Herrmann was no longer a "christocentric" theologian around World War I), or to their common rejection of Troeltsch's objective, "scientific" approach for the sake of an understanding of theology as faith seeking understanding on its own terms, unapologetically and independently from *science* and philosophy.

But another significant lesson learned by Barth, one that had important consequences for his entire theological career, was Herrmann's willingness to allow paradoxes to be present in Christian theology. Theologians need not be afraid of seeming contradictions: they are an inherent part of theology. One who has no sense for God's judgment will not understand God's *love*. God's action in the world is not simply a worldly action, it is also super- and counternatural. God's very being is not either absolute or personal, but both at the same time, even if our intellect cannot reconcile these attributes. In 1913, after reading an article by Barth, Herrmann wrote to him: "You have not silenced the strength which is embedded in the paradox, precisely when it is openly admitted and when, far from being an arbitrary construction, it is rooted in the subject matter (*Sache*) itself" (Chalamet, 74). If Barth became a dialectical theologian and never ceased to be one, acknowledging a dialectical tension in the subject matter of theology itself (*ER*, 10), it is quite possible to trace the roots of Barth's use of the "paradox" back to the theology of Herrmann. In this sense, Herrmann's theology never disappeared from Barth's theology. As Barth wrote in 1957: "I repeat: the 19th century is not to be dismissed, nor is its theology. . . . They [the nineteenth-century theologians] live, excitingly enough, also for us. They will not cease to speak to us. And we cannot cease to listen to them" (*HG*, 32–33).

K. Barth, "Herrmann"; C. Chalamet, *Dialectical Theologians* (2005); W. Herrmann, *The Communion of the Christian with God* (1892), trans. J. S. Stanyon (1971); B. L. McCormack, *Karl Barth's Critically Realistic Dialectical Theology* (1995), 49–68.
CHRISTOPHE CHALAMET

Historical Criticism   In his foreword to *Rom* I (1919), Barth asserted: "The critical historical method of biblical research has its place; it points to a preparation for understanding that is never superfluous. But if I had to choose between it and the old doctrine of *inspiration*, I would resolutely choose the latter. It has a greater, deeper, more important place because it points directly to the task of understanding, without which all preparation is worthless. I am happy that I do not have to choose be-

tween the two" (*Beginnings*, 61). Compared to earlier, more combative claims in his foreword drafts, Barth thought this was an irenic way of stating his position. Yet these words drew intense fire from biblical scholars. They charged that indeed he had chosen *against* historical criticism, that he was a "gnostic," "pneumatic," and "Biblicist," that his so-called commentary said more about him than it did about Paul, that it was the product of sheer "dogmatism," "eisegesis," and "enthusiasm," that he was "contemptuous of scientific exegesis," "despised the past," and cared nothing about the real "historical" Paul but instead had done "violence" against him. In short, they pronounced Barth a "declared enemy of historical criticism."

Barth was thoroughly inculcated into historical criticism by his first teachers at Bern, some of whom were direct pupils of Wellhausen and F. C. Baur. For example, the notoriously critical Rudolf Steck, Barth's first New Testament teacher, did not think that even Galatians was authentically Pauline! Barth was grateful for what he learned from these teachers. He later reflected: "What I owe despite everything to those Bern masters is that I learned to forget any fears I might have had. They gave me such a thorough grounding in the earlier form of the 'historical-critical' school that the remarks of their later and contemporary successors could no longer get under my skin or even touch my heart—they could only get on my nerves, as is only too well known" ("Postscript," 261–62).

However, such teaching may have gone deeper than he remembered. At Berlin his favorite teachers were **Harnack** and Gunkel, two of the day's greatest historical critics. Under Harnack he wrote a 156-page historical-critical examination of Paul's missionary journeys in which he concluded: "Acts is and remains a secondary source for Pauline doctrine" (Busch, *Karl Barth*, 39). "It was thanks to Gunkel," Barth later acknowledged, "that it first began to dawn on me that the Old Testament might be a real option." Barth was never attracted to Troeltsch's historicism. But as an avowed proponent of modern theology, and notwithstanding his subsequent discovery of *Schleiermacher* and *Her-* *rmann*, he was as committed to historical criticism as any student of his day.

However, Barth's perspective changed in the pastorate. The most serious crisis he eventually faced: "The textual basis of my sermons, the *Bible*, which hitherto I had taken for granted, became more and more of a problem" (*LKB–RB*, 154). He wrote scornfully in the foreword to *Rom* II, near the end of his Safenwil *ministry*: "I know what it means to have to go into the pulpit year in and year out, obliged to understand and explain, and wishing to do so, yet being unable to do it because we were given almost nothing at the university except the famous 'respect for history,' which despite the beautiful expression means simply the renunciation of earnest, respectful understanding and explanation" (*Beginnings*, 93–94). It was in the aftermath of his discovery of "the new world of the Bible" that Barth began to express frustration over his contemporaries' preoccupation with the Bible as *history*: "The Bible is the literary monument of an ancient racial *religion* and of a Hellenistic cultus religion of the Near East. A human document like any other, it can lay no *a priori* dogmatic claim to special attention and consideration. This judgment, being announced by every tongue and believed in every territory, we may take for granted today. . . . For it is too clear that intelligent and fruitful discussion of the Bible begins when the judgment as to its human, its historical and psychological character has been made and *put behind* us" ("Vistas," 60–61).

Attacked by critics of his first *Römerbrief*, Barth pulled no punches in his foreword to *Rom* II (1922). He gratefully acknowledged his indebtedness to "historians" for their efforts at a first "primitive attempt at explanation" and said he

"never dreamed of doing anything else in the field of establishing 'what is there' than to sit attentively at [their] feet" (*Beginnings*, 91–92). But what he found astonishing was "the modesty of their claims." For example, "how quickly" a scholar such as Jülicher could, instead of wrestling with what Paul actually says, explain Paul "by means of a few rather banal categories of [Jülicher's] own religious thought" or attribute "the meaning of the text to the 'personality' of Paul, to the 'Damascus experience' (which evidently can explain the most incredible things), to Late Judaism, to Hellenism, to the ancient world in general, and to some other demigods." Barth felt that by reducing Paul to his psychological parts or the meaning of his words to various sociohistorical antecedents, that it was "the dominant science of biblical exegesis" that was "doing violence to Paul." Historicism and psychologism, the two main tools used in modernity to reduce theological claims to matters of mere history or psychology, had exercised such influence over biblical scholars that they had produced "pictures of Paul," Barth said, that "are for me and a number of others no longer at all believable even historically" (95).

Moreover, beyond their atomistic preoccupation with historical-psychological circumstances *behind* the text, Barth objected to historical critics' pretense of unbiased objectivity. In Godlike fashion, many presumed a position of unprejudiced, nonparticipatory observation outside or above history, though their claims were often as prejudiced, speculative, and dogmatic as those they were seeking to overcome. Because they seemed blind to the relativity of their own judgments and prejudices, Barth exclaimed, "The historical critics must be *more critical* to suit me!" (93). Not content with an explanation of the text which he could not "regard as any explanation at all, but only as the first primitive attempt at one," nor with a bifurcated, two-stage, "double-entry book-keeping" approach whereby historical-critical "results" stand on one side of the ledger and theological truths on the other, Barth insisted on *theological exegesis*, that is, an approach that incorporated historical criticism, "using all the crowbars and wrecking tools needed to achieve relevant treatment of the text," including source criticism (CD I/2:723), yet without losing sight of Scripture's central subject matter, content, and theme. Indeed, Barth later claimed: "The demand that the Bible should be read and understood and expounded historically is, therefore, obviously justified and can never be taken too seriously. The Bible itself posits this demand" by the fact that "in its actual composition it is everywhere a human word, and this human word is obviously intended to be taken seriously and read and understood and expounded as such" (464).

Yet if Scripture's central subject matter, content, and theme is not a historical fact like others that can be "dug up" (683), if it is not something a historian qua historian can find behind the biblical *witness*, what is historical criticism's role? Despite its potential for abuse, Barth insists it can provide indispensable service. By determining, even if only provisionally, "what has taken place on the spot to which the words of the author refer, and of what has occasioned the author to use these particular words" (724), it can provide a modest check on those who would treat Scripture as a wax nose. It can provide an initial preparation for understanding, a disciplined rather than arbitrary process for determining "what is there." Because what is there is often not only propositional claims or expressions of piety but words that point to actual events and circumstances, historical criticism can be useful in reconstructing pictures of such events and circumstances. However, three qualifications must be made.

First, the reconstruction of such pictures is not only necessary, it is inevitable. The prophetic-apostolic witness does indeed have to do with historical

situations. Interpreters ineluctably reconstruct these situations in their minds, with or without the help of historical criticism. The question, therefore, is not whether interpreters should reconstruct what lies behind the text, but the appropriateness of the pictures they reconstruct. Obviously, some are "better," that is, less anachronistic, than others. This does not mean that precritical interpreters are precluded from truthful readings of the Bible, only that an understanding of the *truth* of the Bible is no substitute for historical study any more than historical study of the Bible can substitute for an understanding of its truth. All the historical facts that can be established about the Bible do not *necessarily* equal one ounce of actual knowledge of its truth because the truth at issue in the Bible, Barth insists, is "etwas Ganzes" (something whole). It is one and cannot be divided up, parceled out, tacked on, distributed, applied, or treated as some sort of aggregate. It is whole, complete in itself, self-determining and self-actualizing, or it is something else altogether ("Society," 277).

Second, historical criticism is a theoretical enterprise. The pictures it reconstructs are provisional, based on probability, the product of an intellectual exercise and not to be identified with the actual events themselves or "the object mirrored in the prophetic-apostolic word," namely, *Jesus Christ*, *revelation*, truth (I/2:724–25). Thus historical critics should be wary of making idols of such pictures (GD, 257). Because of the *freedom* of Scripture's subject matter, they should not be bound by the strictures typically imposed by general *hermeneutics* as to what is possible, but continuously, in fidelity to the text's object (and perhaps better historical information), allow the picture rendered by it to "modify, shatter, and remold" their own previous pictures (I/2:724).

Third, Barth warned: "neither too little nor too much should be expected" from historical criticism. "One is entitled to expect from it that it will clarify the whole human form of the witness to Christ in the Old and New Testaments, throwing light on its linguistic, literary, historical and religious-historical aspects. But we should not expect it to set before us the object of this testimony, which is God's revelation and therefore Jesus Christ as the Messiah of *Israel* and the Lord of His *Church*" (*KGSG*, 66–67). This occurs only through revelation. Thus, if historical criticism fails to reckon with *this content*, how, Barth asks, "can it rightly clarify even its human form? It is to be feared that the scientific study of the Bible practiced by superstition, error or unbelief will perform its task poorly in its own sphere also. How can it see the form when it does not see the content?"

Barth once asked Ernst Käsemann if the hyphen often inserted today between the words "historical" and "criticism" was there only to emphasize power and importance (Busch, *Karl Barth*, 448). Barth had little sympathy with old or new quests for the so-called historical Jesus. He shared Martin Kähler's concerns about treating the prophets and apostles primarily as sources instead of witnesses, pressing the evidential quality of their testimony and interrogating them, as it were, under their hot lights. Nevertheless, Barth frequently claimed that he was interested in the results of historical-critical investigation. Some assume he was bluffing. Others claim he was much more aware of critical scholarship than he has been given credit.

Historical criticism, in Barth's view, can help to free readers from layers of false presuppositions and conceptions laid upon the text by the history of interpretation or tradition. It can serve to shatter false images, inappropriate conjectures, and unwarranted constructions that interpreters bring. It can serve to alert readers to the foreign nature of the Bible and its world. By disabusing presumptions of familiarity, it can reinforce, even if only at a human level, both the otherness of the text and its object. It can neither undermine nor establish

faith, but it can assist interpreters in being self-critical (I/2:734). Because the Bible is, notwithstanding its divine content, a truly human document, historical criticism is an invaluable observational tool for analyzing its concrete *humanity*. Written in human speech by specific individuals at specific times in specific places, in specific languages and with specific motives and intentions, the Bible itself requires historical analysis. Unless one embraces a docetic understanding of the Bible, Barth claims we can no more ignore its historical-critical investigation than we can ignore the humanity of Jesus Christ.

R. E. Burnett, *Karl Barth's Theological Exegesis* (2004); M. Gignilliat, *Karl Barth and the Fifth Gospel* (2009); E. Jüngel, "Theology as Metacriticism," in *Karl Barth*, trans. G. E. Paul (1986), 70–82; W. Lindemann, *Karl Barth und die kritische Schriftauslegung* (1973).

RICHARD E. BURNETT

History   *Der Römerbrief* (1919) "fell like a bombshell on the playing field of theologians" in part because theologians, in Barth's view, had misunderstood the nature of *revelation* and history, subordinated the former to the latter, and made revelation a predicate of history. Barth claimed that apart from revelation, history is "nonsense" (*Rom* I, 142), "a confused chaos of meaningless relations and events" (143) that reflects God's wrath (501). He scorned historians' pretense of unbiased objectivity and insisted that beyond their "interest" or "empathy," history could not be understood truly apart from participation in a "living context" established by *Jesus Christ*, who is the "beginning" and "end of history." When critics complained he had not done justice to history and was an "enemy of *historical criticism*," Barth raised the stakes in *Rom* II (1922) by including a polemical foreword and a new chapter on "The Voices of History" in which he stated the "crisis" of revelation even more sharply.

Barth claimed that Jesus Christ is not an object of historical investigation that historians qua historians can understand apart from revelation. Although revelation occurs *in* history, it is not *of* history ("Vistas," 90). Yet having identified revelation with "salvation history" at one point in *Rom* I (222), he left open the possibility that revelation might still be derived or deduced *from* history as such. Thus in *Rom* II Barth emphasized the "infinite qualitative distinction" between revelation and history, that revelation "intersects vertically, from above," that in Christ's resurrection two worlds meet (see **resurrection of Jesus Christ**). "The new world of the **Holy Spirit** touches the old world of the flesh, but touches it as a tangent touches a circle, that is, without touching it" (*ER*, 29–30). He continued to emphasize Jesus Christ as the "single and unified theme" of history and that apart from revelation history remains "deaf" and "mute" (145–46), but now he identified revelation as "the Unhistorical" and claimed "the action of God cannot occur in *time*; it can occur only . . . in *eternity*" (435). "Within history, Jesus as the Christ can be understood only as Problem or Myth" (30). Barth had not wished to deny that God acted in history, but such statements left him open to misunderstanding. Later he issued "an express warning" against such passages in his *Römerbrief*, where revelation was depicted as "permanently transcending time, merely bounding time and determining it from without." He acknowledged, "Then, in face of the prevailing historicism and psychologism which had ceased to be aware at all of any revelation other than an inner mundane one within common time, the book had a definite antiseptic task and significance. Readers of it today will not fail to appreciate that in it Jn. 1:14 does not have justice done to it" (*CD* I/2:50).

In *CD* I/2:§14, "The Time of Revelation," Barth deepened his critique of modern theology's "portentous failure" (56) to understand revelation and history by clarifying the relationship: *"Revelation is not a predicate of history, but history is a predicate of revelation"* (58). In other words, history as such cannot disclose the meaning of revelation, but revelation discloses the meaning of history. Having propounded the first part of this equation throughout his *Römerbrief* period, Barth elaborates the second by delineating three kinds of time disclosed by revelation: (1) "created time" or time as originally created, which, since the fall, we do not know and ought not speculate about; (2) "our" time, "lost, fallen, or condemned time," that "some day will cease to be," which is always more or less subjectively conceived yet in Promethean fashion we sometimes call "world history," but which is often only mythology; and (3) "fulfilled" or "revelation time," which historians often call mythology but which is the only real time or history because here God is the primary subject who acts. Barth makes clear that the time revelation creates does not remain transcendent over "our" time but enters it, as Scripture makes clear that revelation is not timeless but eternal and temporal, hence the significance of "passus sub Pontio Pilatus." Indeed, "fulfilled time is the time of the years 1–30." This means "revelation becomes history, but not that history becomes revelation" (58). Revelation does not pass over into or become a product of history, but rather "assumes" history. How? "Just as man's existence became something new and different altogether, because God's Son assumed it . . . , so time, by becoming the time of Jesus Christ, although it belonged to our time, the lost time, became a different, a new time" (51). In assuming "our" time, Christ "mastered" it and reveals what real history is. Thus we do not understand revelation "if we do not state unreservedly that it took place in 'our' time. But, conversely, if we understand it as God's revelation, we have to say that this event had its own time" or history (49).

In §41, under the rubric "Creation, History, and Creation History," Barth defines this history as "the *covenant* of grace . . . the sequence of events in which God concludes and executes this covenant with man, carrying it to its goal, and thus validating in the sphere of the creature that which from all eternity He has determined in Himself" (III/1:59). He calls this history "*the* history" and reintroduces it as "salvation history." However, we must not understand salvation history within world history or any other history, as if it were one among others. Rather, salvation history is "the true history which encloses all other history and to which in some way all other history belongs" (60–61). *Creation* belongs to, aims at, and provides the context for this history. Barth insists while the biblical creation narratives depict "pre-history" in the form of saga, they nevertheless reflect unique but "genuine history" (76–81), not as "*Historie* . . . something that can be proved by general historical science," but as "*Geschichte* . . . something that really took place in time and space, but may or may not be proved" (*TT*, 45). To dismiss this history as somehow inferior is "only a ridiculous and middle-class habit of the modern Western mind which is supremely fantastic in its chronic lack of imaginative fantasy" (III/1:81).

In short, for Barth, we have no warrant for understanding anything in light of a "general concept of history," which, as typically conceived, Barth calls "a hard surface of secularity, smooth as a mirror" (I/2:62). Rather, we are to understand everything in light of salvation history, the history of the covenant. Revelation not only *has* a history but also *is* a history. Barth claims: "the being of man is a history" (III/2:157), which he elaborates in §44. But where we come to understand this history definitively is in the saving history that *is* Jesus Christ, which Barth meticulously unfolds throughout IV/1–3. This history,

to be sure, is real history. Barth begins §59: "The atonement is history. To know it, we must know it as such. To think of it, we must think of it as such. To speak of it, we must tell it as history. To try to grasp it as supra-historical or non-historical truth is not to grasp it at all. It is indeed truth, but truth actualized in a history and revealed in this history as such—revealed, therefore, as history" (IV/I: 157). However, Jesus Christ is not only the living, active center of this history, unlike so much that is called "history," but also and always its sovereign Lord. Christology, therefore, is key to understanding history for Barth. But some christologies are more helpful than others.

Interpreting the *unio hypostatica* in terms of two "successive states" with "the great calm of a timeless and non-actual being" at the center, older *Christology* risked positing "a kind of great phenomenology of the relationship between the Logos and its two natures, or between the two natures themselves," which implied the being of Jesus Christ was "itself static, immobile and at rest." By reinterpreting concepts such as *unio*, *communio*, and *communicatio* from the static ontological categories of older *dogmatics* to the actualistic categories of continuous "actions, *operationes*, events," Barth "re-translated that whole phenomenology into the sphere of a history." This, he said, "is the new form we have given to Christology." Barth claimed this was necessary because the being of Jesus Christ "is not a phenomenon, or a complex of phenomena, but a history. It is the history of God in His mode of existence as the Son," which consists of the continuous twofold movement and mutually interpreting moments of humiliation and exaltation. This history "took place once and for all in the birth and life and death of Jesus Christ and was revealed for a first time in His resurrection." But this history "is not enclosed or confined to that given time." Because "Jesus Christ lives" and "is the same yesterday, today, and for ever" (Heb. 13:8), "His history takes place in every age." It is not only "the most up-to-date history" and "world history" (IV/2:105–8, 269). Rather, "His history is as such our history" (IV/1:548), not primarily in the sense that he is a fact in *our* history, but that we are fact in *his*.

K. Barth, "Vistas"; idem, *CD* I/2:§14; III/1:§41; IV/1–3; H. W. Frei, *The Eclipse of Biblical Narrative* (1974); H.-J. Kraus, "Das Problem der Heilsgeschichte in der 'Kirchlichen Dogmatik,'" in *Antwort*, ed. E. Wolf, et al. (1956), 69–83; T. Ogletree, *Christian Faith and History* (1965).

RICHARD E. BURNETT

Holy Spirit In Barth's voluminous writings many references to the nature and work of the Holy Spirit can be found, but his key treatment of central pneumatological issues is in the *CD*. Its four volumes do not include a volume devoted to pneumatology, unlike volumes I to IV with the doctrines of *revelation*, of *God*, of *creation*, and of *reconciliation*. In I/1, chapter II, "The Revelation of God," part I, "The Triune God," §§10–12 associate God the Father with creation, God the Son with reconciliation, and God the Holy Spirit with redemption, which indicates that the projected volume V on the doctrine of redemption was intended to have a pneumatological focus, but it was never composed.

However, we do have in I/1, the beginning of chapter II, "The Revelation of God." Its first part, "The Triune God," includes §12, "God the Holy Spirit," with its two sections, "God as Redeemer" and "The Eternal Spirit." Later, in I/2, the third part of the same chapter on revelation, "The Outpouring of the Holy Spirit," contains three sections: §16, "The Freedom of Man for God"; §17, "The Revelation of God as the Abolition of Religion"; §18, "The Life of the Children of God." In particular, §§12 and 16 are keys to Barth's understand-

ing of the Holy Spirit in its connection with revelation, the *Trinity* and *Christian life*.

Much later, within the complex architecture of Barth's doctrine of reconciliation in IV/1–3, each of these part-volumes has at the same place within the general pattern they share (which is explained in detail in IV/1:§58) two more sections specifically on the action of the Spirit in the *church* and the classical Christian virtues: in IV/1, chapter XIV, "Jesus Christ, the Lord as Servant": §62, "The Holy Spirit and the Gathering of the Christian Community," and §63, "The Holy Spirit and Christian Faith"; in IV/2, chapter XV, "Jesus Christ, the Servant as Lord": §67, "The Holy Spirit and the Upbuilding of the Christian Community," and §68, "The Holy Spirit and Christian Love"; in IV/3, chapter XVI, "Jesus Christ, the True Witness": §72, "The Holy Spirit and the Sending of the Christian Community"; §73, "The Holy Spirit and Christian Hope." The pneumatology unfolded in the *CD* is thus also linked in closely with the church and Christian life. Also important, if tantalizingly fragmentary, is IV/4, *The Christian Life: Fragment*, with its thematic contrast of *baptism* with the Holy Spirit (as a divine act) and baptism with water (as a human act).

Three characteristic (and by no means uncontroversial) aspects of Barth's discussion of the Trinity in I/1 relate directly or indirectly to the Holy Spirit. The first has to do with the venerable tradition in Christian theology of seeking *vestigia trinitatis*, "traces" or "footprints" of the Trinity, in the natural order, in human relations, or in the human person. This began as early as Tertullian in his *Adversus Praxean* early in the third century and attained full bloom in Augustine's *De Trinitate* two hundred years later. Barth addresses the notion of the *vestigia trinitatis* only to dismiss it. There is and can be no natural *analogy* for the triune being of God. He is prepared to admit one and only one analogy—and it is to be found not in "*nature*," but in the threefold form of the *Word of God*, which itself reflects the threefold pattern of God's communicative action. That apart, the search for traces of the Trinity can only be a snare and a delusion—which ties in, of course, with Barth's radical rejection of *natural theology* and of the *analogia entis*.

Even more controversial is the line Barth takes on the ancient use of the term *person* to label the Father, Son, and Spirit, the three divine *personae* within the one undivided *substantia*. From Tertullian the term has been used among others for the distinct members or *hypostases* within the Godhead. In the early period that was not problematic, as "person" then did not have the individual, subjective character it has since acquired. But at the latest from the beginning of the sixth century, Boethius's definition of *persona* as *individua substantia rationabilis naturae* has focused the word to mean what it does today: a thinking, acting, sentient subject, an *individual* in the psychological sense. *This* sense, Barth argues, is utterly inappropriate for the "modes of being" of the one God; it can only issue in a tritheistic polytheism.

Barth's position here was disputed when he presented it and has remained debatable ever since. His preferred alternative, *Seinsweise* or "mode of being," is in fact equally traditional, rendering the Greek *tropos tēs hyparxeōs*. But to choose it in preference to "person" does seem to suggest "modalism," another name for Sabellianism. This does at least raise the question whether there may not be a tendency toward Sabellianism in Barth's Trinitarian theology. Other indications in the area of pneumatology could seem to support such a suspicion, particularly Barth's apparent tendency to see in the Holy Spirit nothing other than the presence and action of the risen Christ—which brings us on to the third aspect.

This is Barth's massive assertion and defence of the *filioque*, of the doctrine maintained in the West and rejected in

the East that the Holy Spirit "proceeds from the Father *and the Son*." Barth defends the *filioque* particularly in the face of the *Sophia* speculation developed by some Eastern Orthodox thinkers—a theology of the divine Wisdom, identified with the Holy Spirit as a distinct source of divine revelation alongside the Son or Word. This highly speculative theology seemed to Barth just another version of natural theology, and the *filioque* the necessary and appropriate bulwark against it. He is very adamant about this; in *Dogmatics in Outline* he remarks almost patronizingly that "the poor folk in the Eastern Church have never quite understood, that the Begetter and the Begotten are together the origin of the Holy Spirit, and so the origin of their unity" (*DiO*, 44). But he himself was scarcely in much significant conversation with serious representatives of Orthodox theology. Recent decades have brought an intensification of dialogue on the matter, and not many representatives of Western thinking today would feel quite so confident that the *filioque* can deliver what Barth expects—not least in view of the fact that the kind of natural theology he is attacking has generally been more a Western than an Eastern phenomenon.

The close connection between *Christology* and pneumatology is equally emphasized in *CD* IV and is reflected in the leading propositions of §§62, 67, and 72 on the Spirit and the church. So §62 runs: "The Holy Spirit is the awakening power in which Jesus Christ has formed and continually renews His body, i.e., His own earthly-historical form of existence, the one holy catholic and apostolic Church. This is Christendom, i.e., the gathering of the community of those whom already before all others He has made willing and ready for life under the divine verdict executed in His death and revealed in His resurrection from the dead. It is therefore the provisional representation of the whole world of humanity justified in Him."

The same pattern is reflected in §67 and §72 as well: the Spirit is "the quickening power with which Jesus the Lord builds up Christianity in the world as His body" (§67) and "the enlightening power of the living Lord Jesus Christ in which He confesses the community called by Him as His body" (§72). The language used in all three propositions might indeed seem to suggest that *Jesus Christ* is envisaged as the active subject, the Holy Spirit merely as energy or power by which he acts. But while a kind of "merely" is certainly involved here, to express it like this would risk putting a false color on Barth's meaning, which is anchored in the very foundations of his theology and is indicated, for example, in IV/1:§62.1, "The Work of the Holy Spirit." What concerns him—apart from the significant fact that he has no interest in exploring the dimensions of the idea of "spirit" as such, but only in its meaning in this specific theological setting—are three connections vital to his understanding of the Spirit's activity. First, the "subjectivity" of the Spirit is the subjectivity of *God*: when the Spirit acts, it is God who is acting as the Spirit. Second, this action is the "subjective" side, the "in us" of the divine revelation and reconciliation, and as such is most closely integrated with and reflective of the "objective" side, the activity of God in Jesus Christ. It is in no way another separate or independent divine activity. Third, as is made especially clear in IV/4, there is a subtle interplay between divine action and the free human response. Without that response the action of God does not find its fulfillment, but the human answer is itself only possible through the divine initiative, not by any human power or will. (This connection between the Holy Spirit and free human response is also more briefly emphasized in chap. 21 of *DiO*.)

So Barth comes in §62 to say: "It is strange but true that fundamentally and in general practice we cannot say more of the Holy Spirit and His work than that He is the power in which Jesus Christ attests Himself, attests Himself effectively, creating in man response and

obedience.... He is the power of Jesus Christ in which it takes place that there are men who can and must find and see that He is theirs and they are His, that their history is genuinely enclosed in His and His history is genuinely enclosed in theirs. Anything beyond this description of fact is either a report of His history as such ... or it is an account of its significance and relevance and effect in the life of the community.... The confession: *credo in Spiritum Sanctum* ... occupies in the creed a strangely isolated position—almost, we might say, as though it were naked and empty.... How gladly we would hear and know and say something more, something more precise, something more palpable concerning the way in which the work of the Holy Spirit is done! ... The confession *credo in Spiritum Sanctum* does not tell us anything concerning this How" (IV/1:648–49).

The question of how the Spirit works can be answered only by reference to the work of God in Jesus Christ or to the outworking of that action in individual believers or the church, that is, by reference either to its *source* or to its *impact*. The working itself remains hidden. Similarly Barth's account of the being of the Holy Spirit in I/2 limits itself to an exposition of the relevant clause of the Nicene Creed in the Western form including the *filioque*, the whole interpreted in a way that owes more to Augustine than anyone else and understands the consubstantiality of the Spirit as *communio quaedam consubstantialis* (I/1:420): the Spirit is the relation of *love* and communion between the Father and the Son, and this is the key both to the distinctive identity of the Spirit's particular "mode of being" as contrasted with the "modes" of Father and Son and to the Spirit's equal dignity and divinity with them as a "mode of being" of the one God.

It can be observed that this thoroughly Augustinian approach does not only exclude much sympathy or understanding for the Eastern rejection of the *filioque*, as was noted above. It also scarcely opens the road to any serious exchange with Pentecostal theology. That was in any case hardly a realistic option in Barth's lifetime, but the situation was to change in the decades after his death through the rise of neo-charismatic movements in mainline Western churches. Barth's thought in the area, though it is indeed profoundly linked to and integrated with his radical new approach to *dogmatics*, remains a classic statement of Western, Augustinian theology—one that still demands to be considered in future theological work but that also may require modification or further development.

D. Guretzki, *Karl Barth on the Filioque* (2009); G. Hunsinger, "The Mediator of Communion," in *Disruptive Grace* (2000), 148–85; C. Link, "'Leben um der Gerechtigkeit willen,'" in *Komm, Heiliger Geist*, ed. P. Eicher (1990), 49–67; T. Smail, "The Doctrine of the Holy Spirit," in *Theology beyond Christendom*, ed. J. Thompson (1986), 87–110; J. Thompson, *The Holy Spirit in the Theology of Karl Barth* (1991).
ALASDAIR I. C. HERON

Hope   Frequently Christians think of hope in terms of *things* hoped for. Perhaps these could be eternal life, the *kingdom of God*, the millennium, the beatific vision, heaven, and the like. For Barth, however, such items must be put into their proper perspective. *Eschatology* cannot be simply the study of the *eschata* (the "last things") as such, but rather the *eschatos*, he who is our End. Barth, in the context of a discussion of hope, was able to echo Kohlbrügge's claim that "he was converted on Golgotha" (*CD* IV/3.2:500). Barth was engaged in developing, defining, and applying such a theological hermeneutic from the mid-1920s in Göttingen, culminating in his treatment of *Jesus Christ* as "Electing God" and "Elect Man" in *CD* II/2.

Eschatology, Barth had determined, is about Jesus Christ in his threefold Parousia ("effective presence") of resurrected life, presence in the Spirit, and consummating coming. Therefore the hope that takes its rise from this perspective is that which hopes in (i.e., from his resurrection; see *resurrection of Jesus Christ*), through, and with, and for his coming. That is why Barth emphasizes that "Jesus Christ is our hope" (*Credo*, 120). In his obedient life and death, Jesus fulfilled that which *humanity* had not done, the *covenant* fellowship ("you will be my people") with the electing *God* ("I will be your God"). As the true human being (and true God), indeed the prototypical human being, Christ is the eschatological one raised to eschatological/new life for the *world*. "As the Subject of the faith and love of the Christian, Jesus Christ is also the Subject of his hope" (IV/3.2:915). From this basis, Christian *faith*, *love*, and hope spring and take shape. Hence hope's "final and decisive basis lies in the fact that the prophetic action of Jesus Christ, and therefore . . . the kingdom of God come and the will of God done in Him, . . . while it is complete in itself, is only moving towards its fulfilment, i.e., not to an amplification or transcending of its content or declaration . . . but to a supremely radical alteration and extension of the mode and manner and form of its occurrence" (903).

Barth later complained about Jürgen Moltmann's "theology of hope," and in particular its "open future." Any sense of "mere futurity" "announces *nothing new*" (*Credo*, 118). Eschatology, as the ground of hope, cannot be an abstract principle, or a concept that is arbitrarily fillable, or a future we can shape. In contrast, hope is determined by an eschatology that is a repetition "from the standpoint of the future all that has been said from the standpoint of the present" (*Credo*, 163). There can be no "amplification or transcending of its [viz., revelation's] content or declaration" (IV/3.2:903). Consequently, "what it [the *church*] looks forward to cannot be any sort of neutral future," among other things (*Credo*, 118).

Essential to this account of hope is that the future casts its shadow over all contemporary contexts. Karl Marx had recognized that hope has a regulative function. His own hope for the communist society played an important part in determining the nature of his critique of modern capitalist societies, and he had noted how Christian belief/hope operated in performing the task of redirecting the vision of those alienated from the products of their labor, one another, and themselves.

Mentioning Marx here is highly appropriate when one remembers that Barth, when pastor in Safenwil (1911–1921), became actively involved in the social and political affairs of his parish, and had joined the Social Democratic Party in 1915. Barth, the "red" pastor crusading for justice, was to "mature" into the theologian of *freedom*—divine freedom, a freedom that is to be mirrored in and through (or witnessed to by) social, political, and personal affairs. As a consequence of these practical engagements, and his developing theological perspective, Barth learned that hope cannot legitimately be that which Marx and others claimed it to be if it is "Christian"—a shying away from the practical processes of engaging with the world's injustices.

Barth insists that eschatology, and the fragile hope (since it is a human act of response to *grace*) that it inspires, cannot be motivated by idle curiosity or speculative knowledge. In applying these themes to a nonescapist ethic, he claims that the hope for Christ's coming (for God's being all in all, redemption of the world in Christ, and sin's destruction), necessarily determines the shape of hope's active expression in "our whole life" (*DiO*, 154). In the lecture fragments of *CD* IV/4 published under the title *The Christian Life*, Barth develops this hopeful ethic in the context of sustained reflections on the Lord's Prayer.

Eschatology, then, "the rude incursion of God's kingdom" in Christ, provides an image (or rather a "Reality") that shows the present to be corrupted by *sin*, and yet (more fundamentally, ontologically speaking) to be that which is created, sustained, and reconciled by God's love in Christ. Consequently, Christians have no "freedom" (in the sense of *right*) to become pessimistic or hopeless about this world "in face of the existing world of appearances" (IV/3.2:935). In this sense, Christian hope is expressed as ethically regulative, taking a form that is both interrogative/critical and creative/liberating for the sake of "all humanity and the whole cosmic order" (932). In other words, hope seeks to liberate humanity from all things that dehumanize it, act against needless suffering, and participate in God's "dedemonizing" of the world (on saying that, however, guidelines for human acting depend on actual concrete circumstances).

K. Barth, *EvT*, chap. 13; J. C. McDowell, *Hope in Barth's Eschatology* (2000), chaps. 6–7; G. Sauter, "Why Is Karl Barth's Church Dogmatics Not a 'Theology of Hope'?" *SJT* 52 (1999): 407–29; J. Webster, *Barth's Moral Theology* (1998), chap. 5.
JOHN C. McDOWELL

Humanity Unlike many of his predecessors, Barth develops his anthropology from a christologically determined doctrine of **creation**. Barth dialogues with many philosophies and worldviews, including those of Aristotle, Descartes, Kant, Schopenhauer, Darwin, Nietzsche, and Sartre. *Theology* can learn from all of these but they are all bracketed by **revelation**. Theological anthropology is concerned with human beings in the light of the **Word of God**, which shows humans in their perversion and corruption but does not reveal *sin* as their essence. The *grace* of *God*, disclosed in *Jesus Christ*, is primary. Following his foundational method of the *analogy* of *faith*, Barth develops four fundamental analogies between the being of Jesus and human being in general that he elaborates in *CD* III/2.

Jesus is, first, the Man for God. In the New Testament Jesus is understood only as the bearer of an office. His work is to do the work of God, and in this *history* he is one with God. We learn from this that to live for God is what makes us truly human. Humans have to be understood as coming from and moving to God. Like Jesus, we are summoned because chosen. We live in a history with God characterized by *gratitude*, responsibility, and obedience. Only thus do we transcend ourselves.

Jesus is, second, the Man for others. The glory of Christ's humanity is to let himself be claimed by his fellows. His being is wholly with a view to this alien being. Jesus is a supreme "I" wholly determined by and to a Thou, first divine but then human. We learn from this that humanity is not seen truly when there is ascribed to a person an existence that is abstract—abstracted from the coexistence of his or her fellows. If we see humans without their fellows we do not see them at all. Every supposed humanity that is not radically and from the very first fellow humanity is inhumanity (cf. Nietzsche). Being in encounter: (1) is being in which humans look each other in the eye; (2) consists of the fact that there is mutual speech and hearing, (3) means that we render mutual assistance in the act of being; (4) and also means that all these occurrences are done on both sides with gladness. Barth argues famously that the gender encounter is the most fundamental form of meeting, where difference makes colonization impossible.

Third, Jesus is whole Man, a union of soul and body. Christ is embodied soul and besouled body. Everything is the revelation of an inner, invisible, spiritual plane of life and everything has an outer, visible, bodily form. There is an irreversible order: Jesus' body is the body of his soul and not vice versa. Jesus is true man in the sense that he is whole man—a meaningfully ordered unity of soul and body. Jesus' existence derives from the movement of God to humanity that is the *Holy Spirit*. Humans exist as they have spirit. That they have spirit means they are grounded, constituted, and maintained by God as the soul of their body. It is human essence both not to be God and not to be without God. Humans cannot escape God because they always derive from him. They are as they have spirit. We cannot say that they are spirit because in Scripture spirit denotes what God himself is and does for creation. Spirit is the operation of God on creation, the movement of God toward humans. It is not a third thing alongside soul and body. It belongs to our constitution in that it is its superior, determining, and limiting basis. It is as the principle of the soul that the Spirit is the principle of the whole person.

In being a soul it is not without a body. It is, only as it is a soul of a body. Hence every trivialization of the body, every removal of the body from the soul, and every abstraction between the two, immediately jeopardizes the soul. To be human is to be wholly and simultaneously soul and body. Therefore there can be: (1) no dualism, (2) no materialistic monism, and (3) no monistic spiritualism. We are a union of body and soul. Soul is life, self-conscious life—capacity for action, self-movement, self-activity, but only as a corporeal moment. Body is the openness of soul. Body is the capacity in humans in virtue of which another can come to them and be for them. Humans have awareness insofar as they are soul of their body. They desire as the soul of their *body* and will as the *soul* of their body. When we think and will as humans we stand at a distance from our sensing and desiring. We pass ourselves under review. We become an object for ourselves. In this freedom to stand at a distance, pass under review, and become object, we conduct ourselves as soul of our body. As they are grounded, constituted, and maintained by God as soul of their body, and thus receive and have the Spirit, there occurs the rule of the soul and the service of the body. In this occurrence humans are rational beings.

Finally, Jesus is also Lord of *time*. The eternal God is not without time. *Eternity* is authentic temporality. The burden of the resurrection stories was that the limitations of the past had been broken, and that the past of Jesus had become a present reality (see *resurrection of Jesus Christ*). Time as the form of human existence is always in itself and as such a silent but persistent song of praise to God. In all its hiddenness it is the rustling of the Spirit. If we are to speak of prevenient grace it is in the simple fact that time is given to us humans. Living in awareness of time means that we live without escapism, resignation, or crippling guilt. Recognition that Christ is the Lord of time frees us from fear of death. That we are time limited means that our lives are marked by an urgency that would be lacking if we set our hopes on deliverance from the limitation of our time, and therefore on a beyond, instead of on the eternal God himself. Human life, in this perspective, is fundamentally characterized by *hope*.

K. Barth, *C&A*; T. Gorringe, *Furthering Humanity* (2004); E. Jüngel, "The Royal Man," in *Karl Barth*, trans. G. E. Paul (1986), 127–38; W. Krötke, "The Humanity of the Human Person in Karl Barth's Anthropology," in *Cambridge Companion to Karl Barth*, ed. J. Webster (2000), 159–76; S. McLean, *Humanity in the Thought of Karl Barth* (1981); H. V. Mikkelsen, *Reconciled Humanity* (2010); D. J. Price, *Karl Barth's Anthropology in Light of Modern Thought* (2002).

T. J. GORRINGE

Incarnation   For Barth, "If *God* had not become man, as is recognized and confessed in the second Article [of the Apostles' Creed], then everything we could conceive and say to ourselves about God *over* man and about God *with* man, would hang in the air as arbitrarily, as mistakenly and as misleadingly, as the corresponding ideas which, in the long run, have been fashioned about God and man in all religions and cosmic speculations" (*Credo*, 40).

Since God became incarnate in *Jesus Christ*, it is from him alone that we know God in *truth*, and it is in him alone, and not from some prior analysis of the human condition, that we recognize both the seriousness of our *sin*, wickedness, and despair and the solution to these evils (*CD* IV/1:128ff.; IV/2:26); therefore it is also from him alone that we learn to know the truth about our own human nature (III/2:54). Accordingly, "We cannot go back on it [the incarnation], or abstract from it, or act as though it had not happened: *et homo factus est*. This is the beginning of all beginnings in Christian thinking and speaking" (IV/2:45–46). That is why, for Barth, incarnation means *reconciliation*. "'Incarnation of the Word' asserts the presence of God in our world and as a member of this world, as a Man among men. It is thus God's revelation to us, and our reconciliation with Him" (I/2:172–73; cf. I/1:409; IV/1:90ff.). In spite of our sin, God has befriended us by becoming a human, this particular human, Jesus of Nazareth, an Israelite in whom the *covenant* was fulfilled (IV/1:170); he experienced God's wrath and judgment in our place and on our behalf (175). "When God was in Christ He reconciled the world to Himself (2 Cor. 5:19), and therefore us, each one of us. In this One *humanity* itself, our human essence, was and is elevated and exalted" (IV/2:269). Incarnation, reconciliation, and *revelation* cannot be separated even momentarily in Barth's thinking, since Jesus' person and work are inseparable. The one who is the eternal Son of the Father is indeed "God for us" precisely as the reconciler and revealer. He is God's *grace* to us and for us.

For Barth, the incarnation is the hermeneutical key, so to speak, for interpreting correctly the first and third articles of the creed; "God is unknown as our Father, as the Creator, to the degree that He is not made known by Jesus" (I/1:390). Indeed, "Jesus Christ is the Word by which the knowledge of *creation* is mediated to us because He is the Word by which God has fulfilled creation and continually maintains and rules it" (III/1:28). Nonetheless, Barth had no interest in the "incarnation" as a principle or as a general idea through which we might interpret other theological categories, including Jesus Christ himself as the incarnate Word; he even stressed that in spite of its importance, "we ought not to say that the incarnation is the proper content of the New Testament" because as a principle, idea, or truth abstracted "from the name of Jesus Christ . . . even the incarnation is admittedly not peculiar to the New Testament" and since the idea may be found in various religions and myths. What makes the incarnation centrally important is simply the fact, established by God himself, that "the Son of God is called Jesus of Nazareth, and Jesus of Nazareth the Son of God" (I/2:14). Therefore one truly knows the Father and Spirit only through the incarnate Word and by the Spirit. In light of these statements it is perhaps easier to see why Barth insisted on understanding the incarnation as a mystery and miracle.

As a mystery, the incarnation is an inconceivable but not absurd act of God's *love* for us; it can only be acknowledged and confessed and then understood precisely as a mystery in its inconceivability (173). The preeminent sign of this is the virgin birth, that is, the fact that Jesus' origin simply cannot be explained from anything within *history* but must be understood as grounded exclusively in an act of God the Son (I/2:185ff.; IV/1:207). That God and humanity really can be one in spite of human sin therefore is a miracle, that is, a special new direct act of God that includes us in relation to

God and restores our fellowship with God. But it cannot be explained at all from our side.

Barth stresses two important facts concerning the incarnation: (1) Jesus is truly God, the Son of the Father, begotten before all worlds; and (2) he is truly human so that "he not only resembles us men; He is the same as us" and indeed he is "a man who is in action" and is thus no "marionette" (*DiO*, 97); but, with God as the Subject, this particular human being acts precisely as and because he himself is the incarnate **Word of God** (IV/1:179; IV/2:30). There is no conflict in Barth's thought concerning Jesus' acting humanly as the divine Word so that one might, for instance, wonder how Jesus could act as a fully human being if he were simultaneously divine. For Barth it is precisely as the Word that Jesus acts humanly; thus his humanity has no independent existence and our humanity finds its meaning only in him: "Man never at all exists in himself . . . [but] in Jesus Christ and in Him alone; as he also finds God in Jesus Christ and in Him alone" (II/1:149; IV/1:90–92; III/2:132). The crucial point of Jesus' human activity as the activity of the incarnate Son of God is that, "faced with God, Jesus did not run away from the state and situation of fallen man, but took it upon Himself, lived it and bore it Himself as the eternal Son of God." Barth affirmed that humanly Jesus had a will of his own "different from the will of God although never independent of it" (I/2:158) and rejected any quest for the "historical Jesus," any notion that Jesus is the revealer in his humanity as such (I/1:323; II/1:56), any idea that Jesus' humanity was "divinized" (IV/2:72, 87), or any attempt to focus on his humanity that circumvented his deity (I/2:136ff.). For Barth, "The revealing power of the predicate 'flesh' stands or falls with the free action of the Subject Logos. The Word is Jesus Christ" (I/2:137). Following the Council of Ephesus, Barth believed that Mary is the "mother of God," but he rejected any independent Mariology because it focused on humanity as though it had a meaning independent of the incarnation (I/2:138ff.). Barth's *Christology* was deeply Chalcedonian in character since his thinking about divine and human agency implicitly and explicitly was patterned on the union and distinction without separation or confusion advanced at Chalcedon with regard to the hypostatic union. Barth avoided stressing Christ's divinity at the expense of his humanity or his humanity at the expense of his divinity by understanding them as dialectically united without confusion or separation.

In full accord with early church *theology*, Barth embraced the doctrines of *anhypostasis*, namely, that Jesus' human existence has no reality apart from "the mode of being (*hypostasis*, 'person') of the Word": "He exists as Man so far and only so far as He exists as God" (I/2:163); and *enhypostasis*, namely, that it has genuine human reality in and by the Word so that one cannot under any circumstances separate or confuse his divine and human reality; such confusion or separation would always issue in what Barth categorized as some form of ebionite or docetic misunderstanding of the person and work of Jesus himself (I/2:12–25; IV/1:136). The former would consider Jesus an extraordinary human being who was thought of as the Son of God based on the impression he made on his followers. The latter would deem Jesus one of a number of historical manifestations of God so that God could be understood without and apart from Jesus. Barth rejected both approaches to understanding Jesus Christ because he took the incarnation seriously—there was a real hypostatic union of the true God with a truly human being in Jesus of Nazareth: "The Word or Son of God became a Man and was called Jesus of Nazareth; therefore this Man Jesus of Nazareth was God's Word or God's Son" (I/2:13; IV/2:51ff.). For Barth, neither the Father nor the Spirit became incarnate; only the Son actually became incarnate. While it is by the Spirit that Jesus was conceived of the Virgin Mary, "The result, however, is the incarnate Logos, not the incarnate *Trinity*" (GD, 154; CD IV/2:43–44).

Barth spoke of a real becoming of the Word since the Word assumed human nature into unity with his divine being without in the least surrendering his divinity and without becoming some intermediate being between God and creatures (IV/1:127–28, 136). No human becoming can explain this unique becoming. That Jesus is "God and Man" (I/2:161) is the inconceivable act of becoming on the part of the Word. Paraphrasing the statement that the "Word became flesh" (John 1:14) with the words the "Word assumed flesh," Barth stressed that the incarnation was not an act that befell the Word or that determined him from without. "Nothing befalls Him; but in the becoming asserted of Him He acts" (I/2:134; IV/1:179–80). It was an act of suffering, veiling, and humiliation that was his own will and work: "He did not become humbled, but He humbled Himself" (I/2:160; IV/1:180; IV/2:42, 47). That is how Barth understood *kenosis*. Being in the form of God, the Word did not grasp at equality with God, but without ceasing to be equal to God and entirely himself as the Word through whom God created all things, this Word existed among us as revealer and reconciler, as Jesus of Nazareth (IV/1:180).

For Barth, "the Word's becoming flesh is not a movement of the creature's own . . . it is a sovereign divine act, and it is an act of lordship different from creation" (I/2:134). The incarnation is a free act of God grounded in the "eternal relation of God, Father and Son" (135), but it cannot be explained "in terms of the world-process," and it does not "rest upon any necessity in the divine nature or upon the relation between the Father, Son and Spirit, that God becomes man. . . . God acts with inward freedom and not in fulfilment of a law to which He is supposedly subject. His Word will still be His Word apart from this becoming, just as Father, Son and Holy Spirit would be nonetheless eternal God, if no world had been created. The miracle of this becoming does not follow of necessity from this or that attribute of God" (135).

Later on, Barth deliberately sought to present an understanding of Jesus' humanity and divinity in actualistic and historical categories that faithfully portrayed the mystery of Jesus as *vere Deus* and *vere homo*. Far from abandoning his earlier view of God's freedom, Barth declared: "In the inner life of God, as the eternal essence of Father, Son and Holy Ghost, the divine essence does not, of course, need any actualisation. . . . Even as the divine essence of the Son it did not need His incarnation, His existence as man and His action in unity with the man Jesus of Nazareth, to become actual" (IV/2:113).

What needed to become actual in the incarnation was not the triunity of God but the unity of "the Son of God with the Son of Man" (113). In this union God's action is directed toward the goal of reconciliation. This is the "divine essence of the Son in the act of condescension . . . characterised by His act, by His existence not only in itself but also in human essence" (114). In IV/2 Barth preferred to avoid the expression "God-Man," which he used occasionally in I/2 to speak of the incarnation as a completed event and a completed *event* (I/2:165–70) to emphasize that the incarnation was an "accomplished fact" and an act of God that is not limited by the human existence of Jesus. Later, Barth believed the expression could obscure the fact that "He acts as God when He acts as man, and as man when He acts as God, not in the state but the event of the co-ordination of the two predicates" (IV/2:115). Nonetheless, Barth always stressed that the hypostatic union "is a union in which there can be neither mixture nor change, division nor separation" of Jesus' divine and human ac-

tivity (109) so that "in their common working they [the human and divine] are not interchangeable. The divine is still above and the human below. Their relationship is one of genuine action" (116). He also had no qualms using the expression "God-Man" in IV/1 and elsewhere as long as it was not statically understood.

Because the incarnation involved a veiling of Jesus' divinity that was unveiled in his resurrection and **ascension**, it is important to realize that for Barth the resurrection is the fulfillment of the incarnation as it is the power in and through which Jesus made himself known as the one he was before Easter; Jesus' bodily resurrection means that reconciliation is an eternally valid living reality for us in him (IV/1:158; see **resurrection of Jesus Christ**). For Barth, however, the resurrection does not constitute Jesus' divine sonship nor does his human history constitute his divine being; his resurrection discloses who he was and is and what he did and does for us. But he "was no less true God in the manger than on the cross" (I/2:38). "The resurrection is the event of the revelation of the Incarnate, the Humiliated, the Crucified. . . . The resurrection can give nothing new to Him who is the eternal Word of the Father; but it makes visible what is proper to Him, His glory" (I/2:111; III/2:448). Barth's theology of the incarnation is a benchmark in contemporary theology by which he could demonstrate how and why every aspect of Christian theology finds its peculiar strength and meaning only in and through the man Jesus and no one and nothing else.

G. Hunsinger, "Karl Barth's Christology," in *Cambridge Companion to Karl Barth*, ed. J. Webster (2000), 127–42; P. D. Jones, *The Humanity of Christ* (2008); B. Marshall, *Christology in Conflict* (1987); P. D. Molnar, *Incarnation and Resurrection* (2007); J. Thompson, *Christ in Perspective* (1978).

PAUL D. MOLNAR

Inspiration   When Barth wrote in his foreword to *Rom* I (1919) that if forced to choose between *historical criticism* "and the old doctrine of inspiration, I would resolutely choose the latter" (*Beginnings*, 61), he was not kidding. Before breaking with *liberalism* he called the latter "untenable" (*Konf* 68–69), a "product of the post-Reformation" (*VkA* I, 113). He never denied that the *Bible* was inspired, but he scorned verbal inspiration as demeaning of human *freedom*, individuality, and creativity. It reduced biblical authors to passive instruments of the *Holy Spirit*, as "only tools, slate pencils" (*Konf* 68–69), which, like *Schleiermacher*, he saw as dehumanizing. But while serving as an assistant pastor in Geneva (1910–1912) Barth began to study *Calvin* and wrote an essay in which he praised Calvin's doctrine of inspiration and said that if it had been taken seriously it would have "had the effect of dynamite, blowing up the entire house of orthodoxy," and "Protestant theology would have saved itself the embarrassment of having to be awakened from its dogmatic slumbers by Enlightenment criticism" (*VkA* II, 206–7).

Even so, Barth had not fully grasped Calvin's notion of "the internal testimony of the *Holy Spirit*." He denied it had anything to do with *verbal* inspiration, associated it with romantic concepts (*Einfühlung*), and saw no reason why inspiration as such "should be limited to biblical authors" (208–9). But what he found so compelling was that it seemed to take seriously the *humanity* of authors then and there, but also the Spirit's role in communicating to readers here and now. In stating, "The same Spirit, therefore, who has spoken through the mouths of the prophets must penetrate into our hearts to persuade us that they faithfully proclaimed what had been divinely commanded" (*Institutes* 1.7.4), Calvin recognized the link between inspiration and illumination, which Barth saw as vital.

However, around 1915, when the Scriptures "began to speak to us very differently than we had supposed we were obliged to hear them speak in the school of what was then called 'modern' theology" ("Postscript," 264), Barth not only embraced the doctrine of inspiration but *verbal* inspiration, and not merely as tenable but helpful and, eventually, even necessary. Compared to the "scientific principle" of mistrust, the nonparticipatory distancing of oneself required by the dominant *science* of biblical *exegesis*, Barth wrote in a foreword draft to *Rom* I that he found "the doctrine of verbal inspiration more fruitful. It at least contains the wise challenge of stubbornly occupying readers with a biblical text until it is brought forth to significant speech" (Burnett, 288). In subsequent forewords to *Rom* II, Barth illustrated its superiority over Jülicher's approach and defended it against *Bultmann*, who charged that Barth had intended "to establish a modern dogma of inspiration."

Elaborating his doctrine of inspiration in succeeding cycles of his *dogmatics*, Barth still insists on the inseparability of inspiration and illumination. But now, wary of temptations on the theological left to highlight the latter at the expense of the former and on the right to highlight the former at the expense of the latter, he sees inspiration and illumination as points in a circle that must not be confused, isolated, or granted independent actuality in the event of *revelation*, much less apart from it. The latter temptation arose, Barth claims, in the early *church*, which "soon displayed a striking inclination to concentrate interest in the inspiration of Scripture upon one particular point in that circle, and to limit it to it: namely, to the work of the Spirit in the emergence of the spoken or written prophetic or apostolic word as such" (*CD* I/2:517).

Contrary to 2 Timothy 3:14–17, which represents Scripture as an "object of expectation," "as a gift [that] now acquires the character of a task which has still to be taken up and executed" by the Spirit (504), there was an attempt among second-century apologists to freeze revelation and turn it into a "datum" (517), a static object, as if God's Spirit were an "attribute inhering once for all in this book as such" (530). Contrary to 2 Peter 1:19–21, which represents the Holy Spirit as the primary author of Scripture and the prophets and apostles as genuine though "secondary authors" without "any ignoring or violating of their *auctoritas* and therefore of their humanity" (505), there was an attempt to downplay their concrete humanity and consider it "real only in appearance" (518). Hence the emergence of docetic dictation theories that turned biblical authors into passive instruments, for example, "flutes," according to the "heathen model [of] a mantically-mechanical operation." Contrary to 2 Corinthians 3:4–18, where "everything depends on the fact that without this work of the Spirit Scripture is veiled, however great its glory may be and whatever its origin" (515), Barth claims a "secularization" of revelation occurred and the inspiration of the Bible was turned into its "*inspiredness*" (518–19). No longer dependent upon "a free act of the grace of *God*" (514), "a divine disposing, action, and decision" (502), the Bible gained independent actuality. No longer having the character of a promise but of a secured possession, the mystery of inspiration turned into magic (529), the miracle (*Wunder*) became a marvel (*Mirakel*) (520 [*KD* I/2:578]).

The "obvious aim" for "the secular compression of inspiration to an objective inspiredness," Barth suggests, "was a stabilizing of the word of man as the *Word of God*" (518–19) against real threats (e.g., Montanism). Hence the early church's desire for assurance was not "wrong" (534). But the price was high, as developments in the Catholic tradition demonstrate. Moreover, such efforts, Barth says, gave only "false as-

surance" and betrayed "a secret desire to evade the mystery of this matter: that here a real human word is the real Word of God." The Reformers, by contrast, developed "a new doctrine of Scripture, and especially the inspiration of Scripture, corresponding to Scripture itself." "For them the literally inspired Bible was not at all a revealed book of oracles, but a witness to revelation, to be interpreted [according] to its theme" (521). They "restored the context in which the inspiration of the Bible must be understood," namely, in light of the revelation of God in *Jesus Christ* and the work of the Holy Spirit in both inspiration and illumination in "exact correspondence." But this context was gradually eclipsed in the post-Reformation. In late Protestant orthodoxy's polemics against Enlightenment critics and Rome, a secularization of inspiration reemerged. The Bible was transformed into "a highly relevant historical record" (523), "a *divina et infallibilis historia*" (525). "What was wanted was a tangible certainty, not one that is given and has constantly to be given again" (524). Calvin's emphasis on the internal testimony of the Spirit "became one ground with others and the other grounds gained an interest and acquired an importance as though they were, after all, autonomous" (536). Thus the historicizing of the Bible against which it sought to defend was prepared for.

Neo-orthodoxy emphasized Barth's opposition to such false objectivism, to the Bible as a "paper Pope" (525), and so on. Yet Barth equally opposes the "danger" of a false subjectivism that implies "our faith makes the Bible into the *Word of God*, that its inspiration is ultimately a matter of our own estimation or mood or feeling" (534), that is, the illuminist fallacy. He also rejects the notion that inspiration has merely to do with the Bible's content or the thoughts and experiences of the prophets and apostles and not with their words (517–18). Inspiration has to do with "an attitude of obedience in virtue of its direct relationship to divine revelation" (505). Still, a definite promise goes with the prophets' and apostles' words (516–17), yet not because their words as such are superior or special. Like the children of *Israel*, they are special only because they are "chosen" as the rule and norm of our knowledge and speech about God. Like "the pillar of cloud by day and the pillar of fire by night," the promise made on their behalf, Barth says, is "the promise which is the traveling portion given to our undertaking to know God if it is an obedient undertaking" (II/1:236). "Verbal inspiration does not mean the infallibility of the biblical word in its linguistic, historical and theological character as a human word. It means that the fallible and faulty human word is as such used by God and has to be received and heard in spite of its human fallibility" (I/2:533). Thus, Barth insists, "If inspiration is coordinated into that circle of God's manifestation by the Spirit only for our illumination by the same Spirit, the inspiration of the biblical witnesses which is the link between the two, between God and us, can and must be regarded quite definitely not merely as real but as verbal inspiration" (518).

If, therefore, inspiration can only be understood in light of this circle as "a divine decision continually made" (contrary to the occasionalist fallacy popularized by neo-orthodoxy that says the Bible "becomes" the Word of God only occasionally) (535); and if, as Calvin says, "God alone is a fit witness of himself in his Word" (*Institutes* 1.8.4); and if, as Barth says, "The Bible must be known as the Word of *God* if it is to be *known* as the Word of God," then it may appear this circle is vicious and that D. F. Strauss was right when he called the doctrine of inspiration "the Achilles' heel of the Protestant system." Yet if, as Barth says, "The doctrine of Holy Scripture in the Evangelical Church is that this logical circle is the circle of self-asserting, self-attesting truth" (535),

then here "at its weakest point, where it can only acknowledge and confess, it has all its indestructible strength" (537).

———

D. Bloesch, *Holy Scripture* (1994); R. E. Burnett, *Karl Barth's Theological Exegesis* (2004); B. L. McCormack, "The Being of Holy Scripture Is in Becoming," in *Evangelicals and Scripture*, ed. V. Bacote, et al. (2004), 55–75; T. F. Torrance, "Karl Barth, Theologian of the Word," in *Karl Barth* (1990), 82–120; T. Ward, *Word and Supplement* (2002).

RICHARD E. BURNETT

Israel   In a path-breaking work on Barth's treatment of Israel, Friedrich-Wilhelm Marquardt described the *CD* as the "discovery of Judaism for Christian *theology*." Whether that discovery conveys a blessing upon Jews and Judaism or instead something far more sinister is the open question, a somber one, in Barth's doctrine of Israel.

The blessing is not hard to spot. It emerges quickly from a survey of Barth's writings in the decades between the world wars. Barth cut his teeth as a theologian commenting on Paul's letter to the Romans—a commentary famously described as the "bombshell in the playground of the theologians." In *Rom* II (1922), Barth devoted several long chapters to Romans 9–11, Paul's agonized reflection on Jew and Gentile in the emerging *church*. In those years Barth was content to read those chapters as a kind of structural pattern or "code" for the Christian's relation to the *world*: for "Jew," in Paul's lexicon, Barth read "Christian"; for "Gentile," he read "secular world." Such a reading runs the danger of emptying Paul's *language* of concrete, historical reality. Not real, historical Jews concern the apostle Paul, but rather an abstraction, "religious believers," filled out in Barth's interpretation by Christians. That is an early danger Barth would later overcome through a fresh discovery of the "plain" or realist sense of Scripture. But the blessing in this early, more abstract commentary is striking. Even in *Rom* II we can detect Barth's strong instinct to join together Christians and Jews, his conviction that they are one before *God*, even assimilating one to the other.

So strong is Barth's instinct of Christian solidarity with Jews that he opposed Nazi ideology from its earliest days, rebuking its anti-Semitism through pamphlets and lectures, and repudiating its claim to total obedience by drafting the **Barmen Declaration**, a key document of the German Confessing Church movement, and refusing to sign the Hitler Loyalty Oath, a decision that cost him both his home and his work. From Basel, where he found refuge after his expulsion and his lifelong work, Barth supported and directed the Confessing Church, calling for Swiss involvement in the war against Nazism. Barth was courageous and farsighted, certainly; but not perfect. Barth himself found reason after the war to fault his leadership in the Resisting Church and, critics say, not without cause. He later realized that he had not condemned explicitly and unmistakably the Nuremberg laws, nor named directly anti-Semitism as a *sin* the church must confess and reject. Barth mentioned neither in his refusal to sign the Loyalty Oath; instead his reluctance was entirely doctrinal—a Christian, he said, could give total allegiance only to God, not to any human leader. So conscientious was Barth in his postwar reflections that he accused himself, in a private letter to Marquardt, of an "allergic reaction to Jews," a sin, he said, he could not extirpate in himself but was relieved to see completely absent in his sons. Whatever Barth or we might say about his inner response to Jews, Barth remained in his actions and public statements a courageous and firm supporter of the state of Israel, even when his natural allies—the German-speaking left—repudiated Zionism and embraced the Palestinian cause. Throughout his life,

Barth exemplified his earliest exegetical insight: that Christians and Jews belong together, a *covenant* people in two forms, Israel and the church.

In the *CD*, the major work of Barth's inter- and postwar life, Barth developed, with systematic rigor, the unity of Christians and Jews. Central to this development was Barth's massive reworking of the doctrine of *election* in II/2. Like his Reformed ancestors—but unlike **Calvin**—Barth located the doctrine of election in the doctrine of God: election was a matter of the divine nature and will. But unlike those ancestors, Barth did not *ground* election in the divine sovereignty and glory alone, his absolute right over his creatures to determine eternal life or death. Rather, the divine election finds its ground in God's free self-determination to be *gracious*: **Jesus Christ** is the proper and principal ground of election.

Barth could be daring in theology, and this is a central example. The Son of God, Barth said, was both the Elected and the Electing God. More daring still, that Son must be *identified* with Jesus Christ, the incarnate Lord. "At the beginning of all God's ways and works," Barth would repeatedly affirm, God elected for himself to be gracious in Jesus Christ, to be the earthly, crucified, and risen Savior of his people. This position, associated with the medieval scholastic Duns Scotus, has the effect of making the *incarnation*—in a sense difficult to determine—eternal, and conceptually free of and prior to human *sin*. In more modern idiom, we might say that Barth denied—or severely qualified—the doctrine of the preexistent Son, or, in Barth's terms, the *logos asarkos* (the unembodied Word). (Among contemporary theologians we might identify Wolfhart Pannenberg and Robert Jenson as two disciples of this position.) The election of God, Barth concluded, was always and principally the free act of the triune God to be Savior of his creatures through the "one man, Jesus Christ."

God determined himself for "Jewish flesh," Barth wrote; not for any other, nor even less for flesh-in-general. God is eternally a Jew; this one Jew, a son of David, a son of the covenant. Any disciple of Jesus Christ who rejects "Jewish flesh," or seeks to distance the church from Israel, cannot receive Jesus Christ himself: Barth is quite firm on this point. Even more, any Christian who does not recognize that Israel is the eternal and irreplaceable elect of God—the "environment" and people of Jesus Christ—does not belong to the one community God has determined for himself, the one covenant declared to Abraham and sealed by the Jew Jesus. The "mission to the Jews," a strong evangelical movement of nineteenth-century German Protestants, could not receive Barth's blessing. Jews were already and always the elect of God, already known of God and confessing him. Barth, then, is clearly and strongly antisupersessionist: God has not and will not "cast off his people." Jesus Christ is Israel's Messiah, and nothing—neither Christian nor Jewish disobedience—can alter this divine decree and grace. Both **Harnack** and Marcion are wrong: the church itself can only be the community called from Jew and Gentile. An anti-Semitic or supersessionist or "Marcionite" church is for Barth a contradiction in terms. These are clearly blessings for Israel and Judaism within Barth's dogmatic theology, a discovery of Israel in the heart of the doctrine of election.

But a dark shadow gathers in the light of this blessing. All Israel, all Jews *ante- and post-natum Christi*, are elect in Christ; but they—like him, their Messiah—are elected for rejection. In this post-Holocaust world, Barth's doctrine of rejection makes for somber reading indeed. The intense light cast on Israel by Barth's christocentric election—the discovery of "Jewish flesh" in God's inner determination and nature—brings into high relief the gospel narrative of Christ's rejection as Israel's king. The passion, Barth said, tells the story of Christ's being "handed over," betrayed by his own flesh, and in this way handed

over to Gentiles for a suffering death. Israel rejects its Messiah, with, as the Evangelist Luke puts it, the "complete foreknowledge and will of God"; the elect of God must be, then, the people God elected for rejection. Jews must become the people who "pass away," who "have no future," who must represent, in the divine economy, the death of the sinner, the "crowding out" of the betrayers by the one who bears this scorn and rejection for his very own. Through the cauterizing, burning, and holy judgment of God—through the Lord's annihilating *love*—Jews are brought into the passion of the elect Son and are to rise to life in his church. Apart from this life wholly dependent on Christ's *grace*, Jews can live only an empty life, an illusion built up on the "gruesome" synagogue and its "cheerless" life. There is no "eternal Jew," Barth can write, even less an "eternal Judaism," because the eternal will for all Israel is to become "obedient to its election," to "rise up to life in the Church." Barth is no supersessionist, certainly; but he *is* anti-Judaic, and strongly so.

This somber theme of Israel's election for rejection reaches its dark magnificence in Barth's remarkable reading of the figure of Judas, the one of the Twelve "elected for rejection." He is the center point of the gospel story of betrayal—of handing over—and the sum, under the shadow of rejection, of Israel's long history of covenant and of covenant breaking. Barth's doctrine of Israel is principally collective, as is his doctrine of election; he resolutely displaces and undermines a doctrine of **faith** or of **salvation** that centers on the individual, first and only. Yet because Jesus Christ lived an individual life, a "man among men," the doctrine of election must finally concern itself with each human life, just as Israel itself must finally be typified and summed up in the distinctive life of its representatives. After a remarkable and influential reading of Old Testament figures, including a moving *exegesis* of King Saul, Barth completes his commentary on Israel's elect individuals with a sustained exploration of Judas, the betrayer.

Judas sums up Israel's history just because he stands within the inner courtyard of the covenant—an apostle in closest contact with the Messiah—and from that intimacy and calling manifests that he understands nothing of his Lord's *mission*, and refuses the grace and judgment it represents. Barth places Judas next to Mary, the woman, tradition says, who anoints Jesus' feet with oil and prepares him for his burial. Mary is prodigal with her grief and her *love*, Judas controlling and indifferent; Mary devoted to no one and nothing but her Lord, Judas with his own piety and religious duty; Mary, the penitent, consumed with *grace*, Judas, the proud, consumed with a "righteousness of his own." Such a man can only be a thief, Barth writes, a man who steals from God the love and self-giving that is his due. Judas can be only a betrayer, an intimate who shows with his kiss in Gethsemane that he stands immediately next to his Messiah, yet still at the farthest remove from him. His election, his destiny, is to imitate his Lord through his very betrayal: this is his election to rejection. Like Christ, he will die a terrible death; like him, he will be rejected by the high priests and elders of his people; like him, he will be scorned and mocked; like him, he will be "handed over" for sinners' sake. In the end, Judas and his office must die. His place will be assumed, taken over, by the Jew Saul, who dies to his disobedience and rises to life as Paul, the apostle to the Gentiles. Paul will complete Judas's work: he will "hand over" Christ to the Gentiles, so that Christ may be Lord of both Jew and Gentile, the Savior of the world.

In the end, Barth's doctrine of Israel finds its richness and depth, its light and its shadow, in this typological reading of Judas. Judas stands at once as the "greatest apostle," the clearest servant of God's saving decree for his lost creatures, and as the very model of rejection,

the proud and disobedient Israelite who will not answer the grace of the Lord with repentance and conversion. Barth's extended and searching reflection on the ultimate destiny of Judas—can this one be saved?—may serve as *locum tenens* for the whole of Israel. Can Israel, the one, true, irreplaceable covenant people of God, be converted to its own election in Christ? That question—and not the more benign question about the enduring validity of Judaism—haunts Barth's theology of Israel, and his exegesis of Romans 9–11. Christians who search the tradition for an answer to the covenant purposes of God will find in Barth a theologian passionate about and passionately committed to Israel, a theologian who can never forget that Jesus and his community are Jews, a theologian keen to find the gospel in the Old Testament, the Word of saving grace extended to every sinner, typified and summed up in the history of ancient, disobedient Israel. That is the discovery of Israel for Christian theology. But to discover *Judaism* for Christian theology is a task left for other theologians to complete. It remains a high and urgent calling.

K. Barth, *CD* II/2:§§34, 35; III/3:§§49, 50; IV/1:§59; IV/3.2:§72; R. Jenson, *Systematic Theology* (1997), 1:42–60, 125–45; F.-W. Marquardt, *Die Entdeckung des Judentums für die christliche Theologie* (1967); K. Sonderegger, *That Jesus Christ Was Born a Jew* (1992); R. K. Soulen, *The God of Israel and Christian Theology* (1996), 81–106; M. Wyschogrod, "Why Was and Is the Theology of Karl Barth of Interest to a Jewish Theologian?" in *Abraham's Promise*, ed. R. K. Soulen (2004), 211–25.
KATHERINE SONDEREGGER

Jesus Christ   Barth observes that it is in the New Testament that Jesus Christ is to be found. Not that he exists only there. "But He exists only there for our knowledge. . . . Wherever the *Church* has been alive, it has lived by and with the Jesus Christ of the New Testament" (*CD* IV/2:155–56). It is not the case, however, that the New Testament Gospels present us with a biographical portrait of Jesus Christ. A real human being is depicted by them, but everything about him is so singular, so unique, so out of scale in comparison with other human beings, that he can not be grasped by any historical category at hand. In sum, the Gospels attest Jesus Christ as a man, but as a man in his identity with the one Son of the heavenly Father (165).

Barth detects three stages in the Gospels' description of Jesus' identity. In the first stage we have an account "of the sayings and acts of Jesus Christ in His entry into and life in Galilee within the wider and narrower circle of His disciples, the multitudes, and the spiritual and (on the margin) the political leaders of the people. Jesus over against and in the midst of His disciples stands out in marked contrast to this whole *world* of men. He belongs to it, and He intensively addresses Himself to it, but He is a stranger within it" (IV/1:224). His activity is that of a judge, but "judge" in a singular sense. His encounter with his fellow human beings brings to light what was in those he encountered, who and what they were. It divides them one from another and within themselves. Where it divides them one from another it has nothing to do with other differences among them, but runs across them, even across the closest of common ties. Jesus Christ is present and decides as the judge in the sense that he brings about and brings to light the final divisions within and among human beings. "Do you think I have come to give peace to the earth? No, I tell you, but rather division!" (Luke 12:51; cf. Matt. 10:34; Heb. 4:12–13; Matt. 3:12; Eph. 5:13). His coming means the coming of the **kingdom of God** in threatening proximity to every sphere of human power and lordship. Jesus Christ comes as one who has already made *his* decision: "I must work the works of him who sent me" (John 9:4). It is because of his own definite de-

cision that those whom he encounters must choose between him and all the things that seem necessary and important to them (wealth or plentiful food or pleasure or reputation, Luke 6:24–26) and even between him and those closest to them (Matt. 10:37). "Whatever separates, or even restrains, a man from Jesus is [an offense]. . . . In relation to Him there can be no serving of two masters" (Matt. 6:24; cf. 13:47). The antithesis is absolute: one hears his words and does them or does not hear or do them (cf. Matt. 7:24ff.; 7:13ff.). In sum, Jesus separates human beings to the right or to the left according to his own criterion. "Whoever is not with me is against me" (Matt. 12:30); "Whoever is not against us is for us" (Mark 9:40) (IV/2:157–59).

Jesus divides between humans and *within* humans. What is the result? At the end of the first and second stages of the gospel history (the second stage will be presented next), who is with him? The publicans and sinners and crowds, all of whom seemed to receive him gladly and willingly? Peter? Judas? The rest of the disciples? The chief priests? Herod? "According to [the gospel history] there has passed through the midst of all these men One who is absolutely superior to them. . . . He is finally gone from them after . . . revealing their corruption, after . . . revealing them to be, in His light and confronted by Him, blind and deaf and lame, driven and controlled by all kinds of demons, even dead. The Lord has been among them. And in the course, and as a result of His being among them, in fulfilment of His proclamation and work, and as its consequence, the Lord has shown Himself their Judge, the One . . . on whom they all were broken to pieces, in face of whom they all showed themselves . . . to be sinful and lost *Israel*, sinful and lost humanity . . . a sinful and lost band of disciples." (There are a couple of strands in the recounting of the first stage that soften this picture and enable us to understand that this is the first word about Jesus Christ, but not the final word. Yet these strands can only be understood as prophecies in light of what Jesus accomplishes according to the history attested in the second and third stages of the Gospel accounts, during which the prophecies are fulfilled; see IV/1:225.)

Barth reckons that the second stage of the gospel history commences either with Jesus' entry into Jerusalem or with the events in the Garden of Gethsemane and ends with Jesus' burial. The second stage is the end to which the first stage hastens. Barth takes careful note of the diction of the second stage. After the events of the Garden of Gethsemane are recounted, there is an unbroken sequence of events, in which there are very few sayings of Jesus and no actions at all. "Jesus no longer seems to be the subject, but the object of what happens." What is depicted is "an arrest, a hearing and prosecution in various courts [a verdict], a torturing, and then an execution and burial" (IV/1:226).

Barth thinks that what might well be expected in the second stage of the gospel history is that Jesus Christ, attested as judge in the first stage, will try the world and Israel and the band of disciples, all of which have rejected him. Instead, the one tried and judged is the one divinely appointed to judge. There occurs a complete reversal of roles. "Those who are to be judged are given space and freedom and power to judge. The Judge allows Himself to be judged. This is why He came to Jerusalem. . . . accusation, condemnation and punishment . . . all fall on the very One on whom they ought to fall least of all, and not at all on those on whom they ought to fall." The contrast is made vivid by the acquittal of the murderer Barabbas and the condemnation of Jesus to be crucified in his place. Also made vivid is that he dies the death of a criminal, for it is recounted that he was crucified between two thieves ("He was numbered with the transgressors"; IV/1:226–27).

If Jesus the Judge in the first stage revealed the unrighteous, he now enacts right by choosing to let himself be judged in their place. "He speaks for Himself by being silent. He conquers by suffering. Without ceasing to be action, . . . His action becomes passion" (238).

Ingredient in the gospel history is its account of the great and well-founded astonishment at the inconceivable character of this reversal of roles. It is not at all evident that Jesus should be given the cup and drink it (Mark 14:36). His cry, "My **God**, my God, why have you forsaken me?" (15:34) attests his wonderment. The shrinking of Pilate as he makes his decision indicates that the scandal of this situation is not concealed from him. The cosmos itself announces the inconceivable character of the event: darkness descends at the hour of Jesus' death (15:33); the veil in the temple is rent (15:38); the earthquake shakes the rocks and opens graves (Matt. 27:51–52) These witnesses express at different levels the great astonishment at the inconceivable reversal in which the Judge is judged, in which the Holy One is mocked and regarded as one who is godless.

Barth reads the narrative of the second stage as emphasizing that not only did this reversal in fact take place, but it had to take place. It was necessary that Jesus Christ should "suffer these things" (Luke 24:26). "In that strange and scandalous reversal we have a necessary fulfilment of the divine purpose which the Son accepts in fear and trembling as the will of His Father, and which the participants in what is done to Jesus must serve *nolentes volentes* [whether they like it or not]. They thought to do Him evil, . . . 'But God meant it unto good, to bring to pass, as it is this day, to save [many] people alive'" (Gen. 50:20). The divine good that God wills for all humans means for Jesus the ordeal in which he "must and will allow Himself to be the one great sinner among all other men . . . to be declared to be such by the mouth of every man, . . . yet not apart from the will of God, not in abrogation of it, but according to its eternal and wise and righteous direction, in fulfilment of the divine judgment on all men." Jesus allows himself, as he must, to take the place that is not his, but theirs—for their sake and for the sake of divine righteousness. Its accomplishment took place "when Jesus was sought out and arrested as a malefactor, when He was accused as a blasphemer before the Sanhedrin and as an agitator against Caesar before Pilate, in both cases being prosecuted and found guilty. It took place when He refrained from saving Himself, from proving His innocence, from defending and justifying Himself, from making even the slightest move to evade this prosecution and verdict. It took place when by means of His great silence He confessed eloquently . . . that this had to happen, that He must and will allow it to do so." Why did He allow it to happen? "He saw the triumph of His honour as the One sent by God in what happened to Him, in what He had to suffer when He was set in antithesis to all other men as the one great sinner, because He fulfilled the will of God in so doing, because He did what had to be done for them and the world, taking upon Him[self] their sin and in that way taking it away from them." The gospel story declares this as the meaning of his passion simply by recounting the sequence of events of the second stage without adding theological explanation (IV/1:238–39).

Barth gives special emphasis to the Garden of Gethsemane episode in this second stage, identifying it as the turning point of the gospel history. He detects three points that emerge from this passage that singularly elucidate the passion and its centrality in the Gospels. (1) Despite the fact that Jesus asks the disciples to pray with him, to call upon God with him, he alone makes the *prayer*. There is no one to share his burden with him. Jesus alone prays and in the place of the disciples. (2) Jesus did not receive any answer or sign from the Father. The only sign will be the actual event of his death. The frightful thing that Jesus faced was that the an-

swer of God was identical with the will and action of Satan. (3) Thus the content of Jesus' prayer is that God's will and its enactment do not coincide with Satan's will and its enactment. Jesus clearly wished that this could be so. But he would only let this wish determine his activity if God were "willing" (Luke 22:42). "He does not advance any claims. . . . He does not cease to allow that God is in the right, even against Himself" (270). He never expressed an intention that was opposed to the will of God. If the triumph of Satan could be avoided, he wanted it to be avoided. But if God, whose will he did not question, willed the coming event, he would willingly obey that will. "He was ready to pronounce this sentence Himself and therefore on Himself; indeed, He was ready to fulfil the sentence by accepting His suffering and dying at the hands of [sinners]" (271).

"In the power of this prayer Jesus received, i.e., . . . put into effect, His freedom to finish His work, to execute the divine judgment by undergoing it Himself, to punish the sin of the world by bearing it Himself, by taking it away from the world in His own person, in His death. . . . In this prayer we can see [in a nutshell] the positive content of the suffering and dying of Jesus—the act of righteousness . . . and obedience . . . of the one man, in the power of which the vindication of all men was accomplished as the promise of life," to be fulfilled in the final coming of Jesus Christ (272). But the knowledge of this positive content awaits the events of the third stage.

Why is there a third stage in the gospel history? Or, as Barth puts it, after Jesus had completed the span from birth to death, why had he the subsequent time of the forty days? Because, Barth answers, "in this time the *man* Jesus was manifested [to the apostles] in the mode of *God*" (III/2:448), and thus in this time it was manifested to them that the judgment Jesus rendered against them and Israel and the world (during the first stage) was the judgment of God; and the judgment Jesus bore for them and Israel and the world (during the second stage) was God's own self-humbling and sacrifice for their sake and for the sake of Israel and the world.

It is of prime importance to note the fact that Jesus appeared to the apostles during the forty days as a *man*. "'Look at my hands and my feet; see that it is I myself. Touch me and see; for a ghost does not have flesh and bones as you see that I have.' . . . They [then] gave him a piece of broiled fish, and he took it and ate in their presence" (Luke 24:39–43). That the risen Christ can be touched puts beyond all doubt that he is the selfsame man Jesus whom the disciples had earlier accompanied. "To be an apostle of Jesus Christ means not only to have seen [the resurrected One] with one's eyes and to have heard Him with one's ears, but also to have touched Him [with one's hands]" (448). The appearances were not a vision of the apostles. Jesus had actually come again. While the disciples rejoiced in Jesus' coming again in the flesh to them, this alone did not prompt them to believe (Luke 24:41).

It is of equally prime importance to note that Jesus appeared to the disciples during the forty days in the mode of *God*. "During this period, [the disciples] came to see that He had always been present among them in His deity, though hitherto this deity had been veiled. They now recalled these preliminary manifestations of [his] glory [e.g., the miracles] which they had already witnessed during His earthly life, but with unseeing eyes, and which now, [during the time of the forty days,] acquired for them the particular import which they had always had in themselves, though hidden from them" (448–49). Now they came to behold his glory. Now they recognized Jesus' judgment as the judgment of God on them and all flesh and his sacrifice as the sacrifice of God for them and all flesh. This was the truth that shone upon the apostles and effectively convicted them during the forty days. Jesus

Christ was no longer both veiled and manifest, manifest and veiled, but he was now unequivocally manifest. "For the disciples [the manifestation of Jesus as God] was not a self-evident truth, nor a discovery of their own, but a conviction that went utterly against the grain. This is made abundantly clear in the resurrection narratives, where the disciples begin by doubting and even disbelieving" (449; see, e.g., Luke 24:41). But the resurrected Jesus Christ manifested in the mode of God overcomes their doubts and disbelief, indeed definitively. "Then [Jesus] said to Thomas: 'Put your finger here and see my hands. Reach out your hand and put it in my side. Do not doubt but believe.' Thomas answered him, 'My Lord and my God!'" (John 20:27–28). There took place for the disciples the total, final, irrevocable and eternal revelation of God; the resurrection appearance of Jesus Christ to the apostles during the forty days is the revelation to them that Jesus is God himself. Thus he speaks with binding authority. "All authority in heaven and on earth has been given to me" (Matt. 28:18). He also speaks effectively. In the course of the forty days Jesus' declarations overcame the fears, the griefs, bewilderments, doubts, and disbeliefs of his disciples. The direction he gives them constitutes their commission for the task he now gives them. Their task will neither depend on the resources they bring nor on what they are able to achieve nor will it be thwarted by their inadequacy, for "I am with you always, to the end of the age" (Matt. 28:20).

It is Jesus' presence in the mode of God to the apostles during the forty days that leads them to speak of Jesus as Lord, signifying absolute deity. After the forty days the apostles know Jesus only as the Lord. And while the New Testament, which arises from their witness, can and must recount the first and second stages of the gospel history as times when Jesus' lordship was veiled from the apostles, the gospel history in its unity and totality presents the words and acts of his judgeship as the words and acts of the Lord, and his passion and death as the passion and death of the Lord (448–50).

The identification of Jesus Christ as Lord means that his judgment and his bearing of it are the effective and decisive determination of the apostles, but also of all humans and of the cosmos. Jesus' history brings the genuine histories of all humans into being and maintains and completes them. Our histories are to be interpreted by his history and not vice versa. For Jesus Christ himself in his history, which took place there and then, is the Lord, the Lord over the here and now and over all times and places. And risen in his flesh to eternal life with the Father, he promises to and will effect eternal life for all those who abide in him (cf. IV/1:227–28).

K. Barth, *CD* IV/1–3; idem, *FCh*, 53–119; idem, *HC*, 40–54, 63–83; D. E. Demson, *Hans Frei and Karl Barth* (1997), 1–23, 69–110; G. Hunsinger, "Karl Barth's Christology," in *Cambridge Companion to Karl Barth*, ed. J. Webster (2000), 127–42.

DAVID E. DEMSON

Joy We meet the theme of joy at virtually every point in Barth's *theology*. It is one of the signature motifs of his reflection on the Christian gospel. Even his famous *Rom* II—mistakenly read by many readers as relentlessly critical and purely negative in its effect—in fact bears eloquent witness to the *God* who is *wholly other* than the gods of our own making and who alone can bring life out of death and create new *hope* and true joy in the midst of hopelessness and despair.

If in his earliest cycle of dogmatic lectures in Göttingen, Barth could describe the dogmatic task in the modern period as "burdensome," the Barth of the *CD* views the work of theology as a joyful enterprise. He agrees both with Anselm's description of theology as *faith* seeking understanding and with his claim that

understanding is sought not simply for its own sake but also for the joy that accompanies it. According to Barth, somber faces and dour ways of thinking have no place in theology. Indeed, "the theologian who has no joy in his work is not a theologian at all" (*CD* II/1:656). As his thought increasingly centers on the good news of God's sovereign *grace* in *Jesus Christ*, Barth speaks of theology as "a singularly beautiful and joyful *science*" (IV/3.2:881).

The source of true joy for Barth is, of course, the good news of God's decision and action to be with and for us and our *salvation* in Jesus Christ. In the *history* of the Son of God attested in Scripture, God takes on the burden of our *sin* and death and at the same time declares us righteous and gives us new life in Christ. This "merciful exchange" (IV/2:32) of divine self-humbling and human exaltation calls forth our thanksgiving and joy.

The joyful message of the gospel requires a radical rethinking of the triune reality, singular perfections, and electing grace of God. As triune, God lives in joyful communion and wills to share that communion with *humanity*. According to Barth, there is both an indwelling joy of God and a joy that God's glory awakens in us. The glorious life of the triune God is supremely beautiful and radiates joy. When the doctrine of the *Trinity* is denied, the result is "a God without radiance and without joy" (II/1:661). As for the *perfections of God*, they are descriptions of the richness of the life of God make known to us above all by the *incarnation* and atoning work of Jesus Christ. When properly understood, the perfections of the God who freely loves and loves in *freedom* are expressions of the glory or beauty of God that awakens our joy. In a striking exposition of the glory of God, Barth describes God as "beautiful in God's own way," an incomparable beauty that gives pleasure and elicits joy (II/1:650–51). To an extent unprecedented in the history of Christian theology, the joy of the gospel also marks Barth's christocentric reconstruction of the doctrine of **election**. Far from being "a mixed message of joy and terror," the doctrine of election is "the sum of the gospel," an unambiguous "proclamation of joy" (II/2:13).

The motif of joy is also pervasive in Barth's doctrine of humanity. For Barth, the God who abides in joyful relationship has created humankind in and for relationship with God and one another. Life in glad relationship with others constitutes the image of God in human life. Such life in relationship involves not only seeing and being seen by another, speaking and listening to the other, receiving and offering assistance to the other, but also doing all this gladly (*gern*). Being with and for the other gladly is the "small secret" of humanity that corresponds to the "great mystery" of God, who has freely determined to be with and for us in Jesus Christ. "In his essence, his innermost being, his heart, he [the human being] is only what he is gladly" (III/2:267). Just as God has freely and graciously determined to be God for us, so humans are truly free, truly what God intends humanity to be, only as they freely offer joyful thanksgiving to God and exist gladly with and for others.

The theme of joy is pervasive in Barth's **ethics** as well as his theology. Barth's ethics is not an ethics of solemn duty or of anxious striving toward some self-appointed goal, however noble such portrayals of the ethical life might appear. For Barth, Christian ethics is an ethics of freedom, and in particular, an ethics of free, glad, and thankful response to the grace of God. Sacrifice and thanksgiving are true marks of Christian discipleship only as they are "offered gladly" (II/1:219). This is why Barth can describe the command of God as permission. That is, the command of God is enfolded in the gracious activity of God. The gospel always precedes the law and includes it as the fitting response of the recipient of God's grace. The command of God is to be and act as who we truly

are by the grace of God in Jesus Christ, not grudgingly or in resignation but "freely and cheerfully" (III/4:4).

Not surprisingly, the theme of joy is prominent in Barth's theology of **culture**. According to Barth, culture is the human effort "to hold the good gift of his humanity in honor and put it to work" (HG, 54). More precisely, culture is human activity that is both creative and playful. It is activity that, for all the seriousness of life under the conditions of the fall, is done "gladly, voluntarily, and cheerfully" (Eth, 506). While culture can also display the evil of humanity, God can and does work through it to produce parables of the divine goodness, and with regard to these secular parables of God's grace, "no proud abstention but only reverence, joy, and **gratitude** are appropriate" (HG, 55). The music of Mozart was for Barth a special exemplar of human culture displaying freedom and joy. In Mozart's music "joy overtakes sorrow without extinguishing it. . . . the Yea rings louder than the ever-present Nay" (Moz, 55).

Finally, for Barth the **church** in both its **worship** and **mission** acts in joyfulness or it is not the church. The spirit with which the church is called to speak and act on behalf of the **world** should not be one of chiding the world for its secularity and ungodliness. The mission that the church has received from its Lord is far greater than exposing the superficialities and failures of an unbelieving world. Critical psychological and sociological analyses of the world are unable to reach those who do not yet know the joy of the gospel. Only the radiance of God in Jesus Christ can give the gift of "joy in the **knowledge of God**" that effectively and victoriously attracts the children of the world (CL, 127).

Even though Barth did not live to write the final volume of the CD that would have dealt with the doctrine and ethics of redemption and that would have pointed to the consummation of all of God's purposes, we can be certain that joy would have been a dominant, possibly even the central, theme. To say that the joy of the Christian is "anticipatory" and has an "eschatological character" (III/4:377) is simply to say that, while it looks to the final *revelation* of Jesus Christ and his kingdom, it is nevertheless based on what God has already accomplished for our salvation and is thus an unmistakable mark of Christian life here and now. No doubt already contemplating the shape of the unwritten final volume of his magnum opus, Barth declares that by the grace of God human beings are "free supremely to rejoice. [They are] also free to become finally serious and thankful, to obey, to think and speak and act responsibly, to believe and *love* and hope, to serve God and man. But above all, in a way which is basic, decisive and normative for everything else, [they are] free to rejoice" (IV/3.1:247).

K. Barth, *CD* II/1:640–77; III/2:265–85; III/4:374–85; idem, *HG*, 37–65; J. Capper, "Joy in the Church Dogmatics?" in *Karl Barth,* ed. G. Thompson and C. Mostert (2000), 98–121; D. L. Migliore, "Editorial," *ThT* 43, no. 3 (1986): 309–14.

DANIEL L. MIGLIORE

Justification   In his doctrine of justification Barth follows the main outlines of Reformation **theology**. In particular he affirms the three *solas*: *sola fidei, sola gratia,* and *solus Christus*. Justification takes place through **faith** alone (apart from works of the law), by **grace** alone (apart from merit), and most especially in Christ alone (apart from any contribution by those who are justified). "Christ alone" is the hinge that holds "faith alone" and "grace alone" together.

A major alternative is thereby ruled out. *Jesus Christ* is not seen as the source of a saving grace through which the believer is justified by cooperating with it. On the contrary, he is not the source of anything other than himself in his finished and perfect work. As the object of faith, he himself is the gift of justification in its full reality and content. As *Luther* never tired of stating, and Barth agreed, Christ alone is our righteousness and our life.

In Barth we find a combination of various Lutheran and Reformed themes. At the same time he went beyond them in notable ways. For example, Barth retrieved the formula *simul iustus et peccator* from Luther and made it central to his account. This is a phrase that does not appear as such in **Calvin** (although its various elements can be found dispersed throughout the 1559 *Institutes*). Barth took over Luther's formula in its strongest, most paradoxical sense. In this life believers were at once totally (not partially) righteous in Christ while yet also totally (not partially) sinful in themselves (*totus/totus,* not *partim/partim*).

Like Calvin, however, in contrast to the general line found in Melanchthon and the Lutheran confessions, Barth stressed that justification took place "in Christ" rather than merely "on account of Christ." Union with Christ was as indispensable for Barth as it was for both Calvin and Luther. More than either of them, however, and especially more than Luther, Barth thought mainly in terms of the believer as being "in Christ" (a ubiquitous phrase for him) as opposed to Christ being "in us." Although the two were not contrary (and were indeed inseparable), Barth laid his emphasis almost entirely on Christ as the one who united us to himself rather than on the believer in whom Christ was pleased to dwell. It was by virtue of being in Christ that the believer was righteous before **God**.

The centrality of the phrase "in Christ" points to ways in which Barth could affirm justification as a forensic event that was nevertheless more than forensic. By definition, the very idea of "justification" finds its home in a courtroom metaphor. The scene is one of judgment. The terrified sinner is hauled before the tribunal of a righteous God. Through a complex transaction between the sinner and Christ, the sinner (who in some sense remains a sinner) is not condemned but "justified" or acquitted because of having been wonderfully made righteous by Christ. Much depends on how much the complexities of this transaction are thought to be explicable in merely judicial terms. Without losing sight of the forensic elements, Barth draws upon a wide range of other ideas and metaphors as well, including those that are substitutionary, participationist, and, not least, apocalyptic.

The following account traces Barth's doctrine of justification in *CD* IV/1:514–642.

1. *The Problem of the Doctrine of Justification* (*CD* IV/1:514–28). In Barth's doctrine everything centers on the death and *resurrection of Jesus Christ*. The human predicament is described only in relation to this center, and not apart from it.

Forensic terminology is used to set the scene: the divine "judgment" by which the sinner is pronounced guilty is followed by the divine "sentence" in which the sinner is condemned to death. This outcome is inevitable once the accused party is summoned before God. The terrifying human predicament is one of guilt, condemnation, and death.

It is in Christ, however, that God's judgment and sentence are executed. It is in his death that the divine judgment upon us is carried out, even as the depth of its meaning is not disclosed until his resurrection. Not only does this judgment involve the agony of abandonment by God, but it is unexpectedly reversed and overcome precisely in being carried out.

The problem of justification is fraught with tensions that seem impossible to resolve. How, from God's side, can divine mercy coexist with divine justice so that neither one is compromised? How, from the human side, can the sinner, who is truly a sinner, be at the same time truly righteous, and again both without compromise?

The doctrine of justification, according to Barth, "not only narrates but also explains" the history in which the problem is solved (516). The importance of regarding justification as a *"history"* cannot be overestimated. It is a history centered in Christ, and yet whose scope finally involves the whole *world*. The problem of justification is solved not so much by a doctrine as by a history.

Standard Lutheran accounts insist that justification is the doctrine by which the *church* "stands or falls." Barth gives this idea only qualified support. The reasons for his reservations have not been well understood by his critics (e.g., E. Wolf, A. McGrath, E. Jüngel). The pivotal doctrine, for Barth, is not justification but *reconciliation*. Reconciliation involves more than simply justification. It also involves *sanctification* and *vocation*. As three distinct forms of a single, indivisible whole (each of which represents the whole from a distinctive vantage point), justification, sanctification, and vocation correspond to the threefold office of Christ—Priest, King, and Prophet—in his one saving, reconciling work. To single out justification at the expense of the other two main elements in reconciliation would be an example of misplaced concreteness.

2. *The Judgment of God* (IV/1:528–68). How can a positive relationship between God and humankind be restored despite the abyss of *sin* and guilt? Three conditions must be met.

a. A right must exist that is "absolutely superior" to human wrong. The right of God cannot be appreciated except in his judgment. It is God who defines what is right, not the reverse. God's right means that God is and must be true to himself. Righteousness is an intrinsic divine property. God would not be righteous if he did not condemn sin and abolish it. He abhors sin and treats it accordingly.

Human wrong, however, remains subordinate to the right of God. The superiority of God means that God can encounter human wrong in his own person. Human wrong cannot alter God's original relation to the creature as the gracious Creator and Lord of the *covenant*. God is true to himself by upholding this covenantal relation even as he judges its perversion.

It is not sin's punishment but its removal that satisfies God's righteousness (a point of great importance). God cannot merely hate the sin but *love* the sinner, because the sin and the sinner are inseparable. Order is restored only when the disorder is removed. The removal takes place in a way that is harsh and apocalyptic. In the death of Christ the sinner is annihilated and destroyed. God would neither be righteous nor gracious if the sinner qua sinner were permitted to exist.

b. This transcendent right must also be worked out from the human side. What happened in Christ will never cease to be true—for him as well as for us. His one saving work there and then, as a finished and perfect work, is henceforth a perpetual operation. "His history is as such our history" (548)—in two ways. Objectively and *de iure*, we were included by grace in his history as it took place. When he died, we died with him; when he rose, we also were raised. We were there through a real and objective, though vicarious, participation.

Subjectively and *de facto*, on the other hand, Christ comes to us here and now as the one he was for us there and then. He discloses himself to us in the present as the one who embraced us in his person by his death, suffering judgment for our sakes and in our place. His objective work apart from us is not fulfilled until we subjectively acknowledge and partake of it by faith. The objective and subjective aspects are inseparable elements of a single divine saving work.

Our new reality before God—our righteousness and justification—is thus real, hidden, and yet to come. It is not any the less real for being hidden, nor for being something that is also yet to come. It is already real and true in one form (definitively) while also yet to come in a final and glorious form (unsurpassably). For the time being we do not see it in ourselves, but only by faith as we look to Christ, with whom we are one. Our righteousness, in the time between the times, is hidden with Christ in God (cf. Col. 3:3).

Christ gives us his righteousness by giving us himself. We will never have any other righteousness than the righteousness we have in him. This righteousness is "alien" because it will never be ours except as it is his, and as it was accomplished by his obedience in our place. It is "passive," because we can never receive it except by receiving it as his gift, whole and entire. We do not, and could not possibly, add anything to it.

c. As this higher right is worked out, the human wrong must be set aside and a new human right established. In the history of Jesus Christ, God identifies with humankind by entering into its plight. The plight is therefore overcome from within. Human wrong is destroyed and a new human right is established.

God incarnate destroys both the wrong and the wrongdoer by taking them to himself on the cross. This drastic removal is necessary to satisfy the righteousness of God. At the same time, a new and higher righteousness is established. The perfect obedience of Christ establishes a new righteousness for those who were guilty. It is given to them when they repent of their wrong and receive Christ by faith. The gift of righteousness is grounded in God's mercy as revealed in Christ's resurrection.

The mystery of this transaction cannot be understood apart from the themes of participation (objective and subjective), substitution, and exchange. These themes, which are essentially priestly and cultic, serve to supplement the forensic metaphor without replacing it.

In and through his life history, Christ takes our place and puts us in his place.

A double transfer occurs. The guilt of the guilty is transferred to the one who is righteous so that the guilty are made righteous by a righteousness not their own. It is the mystery of this transaction that the doctrine of justification narrates and explains by the term *imputation*. Our sin and death are imputed to Christ, even as his righteousness and life are imputed to us (e.g., Isa. 53:5, 11; Rom. 5:15–18; 2 Cor. 5:21; Gal. 3:13–14). In this history the forensic transition from condemnation to acquittal takes place by means of a great exchange (*admirabile commercium*) whose logic is not forensic but essentially cultic (innocence ⇆ guilt), participatory (Christ ⊃ us), and apocalyptic (death/resurrection). The doctrine of justification can be understood only as a commentary on the irreducible mystery of this history.

3. *The Pardon of Man* (IV/1:568–608). Justification is a history with two poles, inseparable but distinct. On the one hand, it involves the history of Jesus Christ for our sakes, such that our history is included in his. In that history we have died and risen with him, been accused and pardoned through him, and transformed from sin to righteousness because of him. Our relationship to his history there and then is one of objective and passive participation, because Christ by grace has made us his own.

On the other hand, justificaton also involves our personal life history as individuals, in which the history of Jesus Christ and its significance for us are apprehended by faith here and now. This apprehension is both noetic and ontic. It is at once a matter of acknowledgment and perception (noetic), while also of real reception and participation (ontic). From this vantage point, our relationship to Jesus Christ and his saving history is one of subjective and active participation, as by grace though faith we make him and his righteousness our own.

What takes place in justification is a transition from the objective to the subjective. Just as our history was included

in his there and then, so his comes to be included in ours, and ours in his, here and now. What is already real about us in Christ comes to be apprehended and received in the present, that is, in the course of our existence. However, this present acknowledgment and participation—this coordination of the subjective with the objective—involves a complex *eschatology*. In it we are already justified, we are not yet justified, and we are justified instantaneously by faith and then each day anew. The transition from the objective to the subjective involves a transition from the past to the future, which takes the form of a pilgrimage.

a. We are already justified. What Christ has done for us is real and irrevocable. It does not need to be, and cannot possibly be, done again. By virtue of our objective participation in Christ, we have been made righteous with a righteousness not our own. This righteousness is perfect, whole, and entire. It already belongs to us as a gift. It clothes us despite all our sins, past, present, and future. It does not come to us in bits and pieces, or in any partial form, nor does it need to be supplemented by anything we might do. It either comes to us as an indivisible whole, or not at all. It comes to us in and with the self-giving presence of Christ here and now, with whom we are one. Nevertheless, this righteousness remains hidden. It cannot be apprehended except by faith, and except as we look away from ourselves to him. We do not see it, in its fullness and perfection, in ourselves. For now it remains hidden but real and all-sufficient. That is its mysterious status for the time being, in the *time* between the times.

b. We are not yet justified. The justification that has already been accomplished is not yet fully manifest in our lives. Although our old, sinful *humanity* has been put to death with Christ, it still paradoxically clings to us as that from which we are not yet wholly free. Sin is the past that has no future and yet it remains a presence in our lives. The justification that is fully real for us in one form is not yet real in another. It remains hidden with Christ in God (the present-tense form) until that day when we shall be perfectly righteous like him, because we shall see him as he is, and ourselves as we are in him (the future-tense form). It is one indivisible justification in three different temporal forms: the form in which it has been accomplished apart from us in Christ (past or perfect tense); the form in which it is real, hidden, and yet to come (present tense); and the form in which it will be revealed and actualized in glory for what it is and has been all along (future tense). This multi-faceted reality is apprehended by faith and eagerly anticipated in *hope*.

c. We are justified each day anew. We live as justified sinners in the tension between the past and the future. We live in the presence of a past that has been put to death and is passing away; but all the more, in the presence of a triumphant future that breaks into the present here and now in ways that are ever new. The *Christian life* is a pilgrimage from this past to this future. It is a constant turning from the one to the other. It turns from the sin that is seen to the justification that is real though not yet seen. In this pilgrimage we are *simul peccator et iustus* (at once sinful and justified), "yet not half *peccator* and half *iustus* but both altogether" (596); because sin and righteousness are, by definition, not essentially matters of degree but indivisible and categorical wholes. Justification on the subjective side begins with the apprehension of being condemned and ends with the apprehension of being pardoned. Our being pardoned as sinful human beings does not merely match but exceeds our condemnation, because our pardon is "no less than this: *totus iustus*" (596), in a way that brings us eternal life. It encounters us here and now through a daily *"baptism,"* a daily dying and rising with Christ anew.

4. *Justification by Faith Alone* (IV/1:608–40). Justifying faith is the

faith that apprehends our justification. It apprehends it in Christ as something achieved by Christ alone. It therefore has two aspects. On the one hand, it is the obedience of humility, while on the other hand, it excludes all works and therefore all merit that may derive from works.

a. Justifying faith is the obedience of humility. Humility is not just a part of faith but a determination of faith as a whole, so that from one vantage point faith is "wholly and utterly humility" (618). Negatively, faith means the destructon of our pride. Although the sin of pride still remains, the faithful have acquired a radical distaste for it. They admit that they are proud and are ashamed of it. While their pride would lead them to despair, it is transformed by grace into a comforted despair, a *desperatio fiducialis* (confident desperation; Luther). The faithful adopt this humble attitude in a free decision of obedience.

b. Justifying faith excludes all works and therefore all merit that derives from works. Justification is the work of God alone. It is therefore a sheer gift apprehended by faith in the mode of pure reception. Although good works follow from faith, they are a consequence, not a cause, of justification. Justification is not a gradual process in the believer that begins with faith but needs to be completed by the infused grace of love. It does not arise as the faithful cooperate with grace on the basis of grace. It arises as they cling to Christ alone so that in union with him they are clothed in his perfect righteousness despite their ongoing sin.

Justifying faith does not need to be "formed by love" in order to be what it is because it is already formed by Christ. He and he alone is the true and only righteousness of the faithful. The righteousness he gives them is truly theirs, but only as they receive it from him ever anew. As they find "their being in Him and His being in them" (642), they surrender all self-assertion. They bring no dignity or merit to God, but constantly turn to God with empty hands, pleading only the merits of Christ.

G. Hunsinger, "Justification and Justice," in *What Is Justification About?* ed. J. Burgess and M. Weinrich (2009), 207–30; idem, "A Tale of Two Simultaneities," in *Conversing with Barth*, ed. J. C. McDowell and M. Higton (2004), 68–89; E. Jüngel, *Justification*, trans. J. F. Cayzer (2001), 18–24; H. Küng, *Justification* (1964); A. E. McGrath, *Iustitia Dei*, 2 (1986), 174–82; M. A. Seifrid, "The Subject of Rom. 7:14–25," *Novum Testamentum* 34 (1992): 313–33; T. F. Torrance, "Justification," *SJT* 13 (1960): 225–46; E. Wolf, "Die Rechtfertigungslehre als Mitte und Grenze reformatorischer Theologie," *EvTh* 9 (1949–1950): 298–333.

GEORGE HUNSINGER

Kingdom of God   The term *kingdom of God* ("Reich Gottes," "Gottesreich," "Reich Christi," or "Herrschaft Gottes") sheds light on fundamental ideas in Barth's early **theology** as well as on significant developments exemplifying its challenging open-endedness.

In his Safenwil period, Barth refers to the kingdom of God as the central idea of the religious socialist movement. Though he sympathizes with the political aims of Leonhard Ragaz, he rejects Ragaz's central assumption that God's kingdom and the struggle for justice and equality are related phenomena. One cannot see the kingdom in everyday life or act as the kingdom's agent, as Ragaz claims, because the kingdom is not a human product (*B-Th Br* I, 29, 69–70; e.g., "We must think of the kingdom of God as otherworldly as possible," 299). This fundamental assumption shapes the *eschatological* understanding of the kingdom.

In sermons of this period Barth points out that the kingdom opposes false gods (e.g., mammon) and is at the same time not visible as a worldly fact (*P–1915*, 47–48). The kingdom, though at hand, is an inward reality in humans

and something for which one must deliberately decide (67). Barth rejects such ideas of inwardness and decision in his later work, but there are at least two basic and persistent ideas that he clearly points out as early as 1915 and 1916: (1) God's kingdom is hidden and mysterious and at the same time the most precious good; (2) God's kingdom and the coming of Jesus are two sides of the same fact (*P–1916*, 447; for further details see 29–44).

Both aspects dominate Barth's use of the term in *Rom* II. Now the kingdom of God is a wholly eschatological term, and Barth emphasizes that the kingdom must not be understood as a worldly fact (*Rom* II, 77). Thus the kingdom of God is also in strict opposition to *religion*, as Barth points out in anticipation of his later idea of religion as opposed to *faith* (350). Barth holds that the kingdom is the reality of **God** himself. This is also at the core of Barth's position in various publications after 1920 (e.g., *RD*, 111ff.). His early idea that the kingdom is opposed to false gods is reflected in article 5 of the **Barmen Declaration** (1934) and plays a prominent role throughout Barth's work even where he does not speak of the kingdom. The "kingdom of God" is among the most important concepts used by Barth to articulate his theology of crisis. However, he states that although this crisis was needed, theology has to go on to explain how the holy God comes to save humankind (*KD* II/1:717). This is the main task of the *CD*, where the term plays a significant role.

Barth demonstrates continuity with his earlier claims when he states that the kingdom is not an independent entity but "entirely connected to the coming Messiah" (*KD* II/1:310). He himself is "the essence of the kingdom" (684). But Barth now stresses that in the coming of Jesus, God himself enters the human realm. This has far-reaching consequences: (1) The powers that stand against God are already broken and must serve him (II/2:768–69). (2) Nobody's life is by itself a life in the kingdom, but God enters humankind and even enters "into man" (774) and thus makes himself man's Lord. As Barth puts it, the life of the new man is his life understood as and lived by *Jesus Christ* (770; cf. III/3:176–77), that is, the kingdom dwells among humans insofar as their personality is found within God's acting.

In his unfinished manuscripts for *CD* §78, Barth returns to the theme by reflecting on the words of the Lord's Prayer, "Thy kingdom come!" Again, he stresses that God's kingdom is hidden to us and cannot otherwise be thought of properly because it is the reality of the living God himself. The kingdom becomes a reality among humans when God comes as Lord and King. Those who pray, "Thy kingdom come," ask for something that only God can do and be. In doing so, they perform what humans can do at that point and they are within the reality of the kingdom. Consequently, their life goals and choices are kept within that kingdom: they are fascinated by and moved toward the kingdom and simply have "no other choice but to look ahead and also to live and think and speak and act ahead, to run . . . to the goal, its final manifestation" (*CL*, 262). It is the miraculous work of God the *Holy Spirit* who moves and directs us toward the kingdom (256). Consequently, Barth, in one of his last essays, outlines the future task of a detailed theology of the Holy Spirit that has still not yet been fulfilled ("Postscript").

K. Barth, *CL*; E. Busch, *The Great Passion*, trans. G. W. Bromiley (2004), 280ff.; H. Gollwitzer, *Reich Gottes und Sozialismus bei Karl Barth* (1972); M. Hailer, *Die Unbegreiflichkeit des Reiches Gottes* (2004).

MARTIN HAILER

Knowledge of God   The development of a strictly theological account of the knowledge of *God* absorbed Barth's attention throughout his career, and his distinctive insights here are as significant for subsequent Christian *theology* as any of his material contributions to other doctrines. Addressing himself to the problem of the possibility of theological knowledge, which so dominated nineteenth-century Protestant thought, Barth set for himself the task of articulating a nonspeculative aposteriori account of theological knowledge, wholly grounded in God's own speech, and judged by its conformity to *Jesus Christ* as attested by Holy Scripture. In this essay, I will present a few of the central themes of Barth's view as they appear in the *CD*.

Conventionally modern in that it begins with a lengthy prolegomenal discussion, the *CD* cuts against the grain of post-Kantian theology by conducting these investigations from a starting point in *revelation*. Rather than moving from the possibility of theological knowledge to its reality, Barth insists that God can be known, and is known, simply and strictly because he graciously reveals himself as Lord. God makes himself the object of human knowledge without thereby ceasing to be its subject—in other words, he does not merely initiate and make this knowledge possible, but energizes and sustains it from beginning to end. The Father knows the Son and the Son knows the Father in the unity of the Spirit (Barth calls this immediate divine knowledge "primary objectivity"), and God then shares this knowledge with human beings in a way appropriate to creatures distinct from him (Barth calls this mediated knowledge "secondary objectivity"). The latter occurs as God miraculously "unveils" himself through creaturely media intrinsically unfit for this event, yet in such a way that he remains "veiled" within them. This is so first and foremost in the man Jesus. The resulting knowledge is not esoteric, since it occurs through our ordinary cognitive faculties as the illumination of human *reason*; it is truly objective, since it has a definite content (as Barth puts it, *pistis* says more than *gnosis*, but in all circumstances it says *gnosis* too); and it is distinct from all other knowing in that it originates exclusively in divine action and occurs as the conformity or correspondence of human knowledge with God's self-knowledge (this is Barth's famous *analogia fidei*). Moreover, and crucially, knowledge of God cannot be reduced to mere apprehension or cognitive awareness. To know God is to acknowledge him, to submit to his lordship, and thus is not a matter of detached and supposedly neutral speculation, but is rather the total self-offering of the total person to God, and therefore occurs as a conflict resulting in the death and resurrection of the knower.

Thus Barth holds revelation, *reconciliation*, and *election* in the closest possible connection. In election, God freely determines both divine and human being for existence within the *covenant*, and his being in *time* corresponds with this eternal decision. As *vere deus Jesus Christ* is God's self-revelation, and as *vere homo* he establishes and reveals true *humanity*. Analogously, those whom Jesus Christ represents and reconciles to God realize their true identities through obedience, which corresponds to, coheres with, and shares in Jesus Christ's divine-human obedience. Disobedience, the foolish decision to live against the *truth* established in Christ, is thus a contradiction not only of God but also of one's own true self. This thought sheds light on the common charge that Barth supposedly overemphasizes the objective reality of Jesus Christ such that genuine human agency is eliminated and Christian *faith* is reduced to bare intellectual awareness of a completed event. This criticism is wrong for a number of reasons. Chief among them, and one that has largely been overlooked, is that the universal objective (*de jure*)—participation of humanity in Jesus Christ—is itself a teleological reality oriented toward subjective (*de facto*) realization within the lives of individuals. The *Holy Spirit*, in the power of *resurrection of Jesus Christ*, effects this transition

through the creation of Christian faith. Thus rather than eclipsing genuine human agency, Jesus Christ's life, death, and resurrection establish it. Where and when such faith occurs, it is, and always remains, a gift of sheer *grace*; and thus the human knower, set free by the Spirit, remains ever-dependent upon God. *Prayer*, then, is a *conditio sine qua non* of Christian faith. And the goal of knowledge of God is ever-greater conformity to the will of God, which is to say ever-greater conformity to Jesus Christ, whose whole existence, both divine and human, is one of total obedience to the Father.

With these observations in mind, one can appreciate Barth's famous rejection of *natural theology* as not simply an endorsement of Kant's critique of metaphysics, but rather as an attempt to underscore a series of crucial affirmations: that knowledge of God is a divine possibility and only for that reason a human one; that God's being and act are one; and that the god that natural theology is capable of producing is in fact an illusion. There is only one God—the triune God, attested in Holy Scripture, who acts with and for humanity in the covenant, whose act is essential to his being, and who is the Lord of his act of revelation. And there is no compelling reason to think that this God can be conveniently coordinated with the *rerum omnium principium et finis* (beginning and end of all things) or, simply, the *creator* of natural theology, since the latter presents itself as the result of human reason operating independently and without reference to the covenant *that is essential to God's being*. Such a god exists, of course, but only as a projection of human pride, which willfully seeks to know God on its own apart from grace, and thus as an idol that blocks rather than leads to the true and living God.

Yet this does not mean that God is incapable or unwilling to reveal himself beyond the sphere of the *church*. Rather, where and when he does so, and through whatever media he chooses to do so, this occurs as participation in Jesus Christ's *history*, which is the center and criterion of all theological knowledge. Barth makes this point in the first volume of the *CD* and develops it in the *Lichterlehre* of IV/3, where he argues that Jesus Christ, the light of the world, bears *witness* to himself by the power of the Spirit through a multiplicity of lesser lights. His rejection of an independent pneumatology disconnected from *Christology* does not constitute a restriction of the universal scope of the Spirit's work in and through *creation*; God is free to bear witness to himself through any form of creaturely reality he chooses. Thus, rather than being hostile to *philosophy*, Barth draws freely and eclectically from Plato, Kant, and the Neo-Kantians, Hegel, and others for insights which he can put to use in service of the gospel, and nothing would in principle prevent him from treating non-Christian religions similarly.

K. Barth, *CD* II/1:3–254; C. Chalamet, *Dialectical Theologians* (2005); G. Hunsinger, *How to Read Karl Barth* (1991); C. Kooi, *As in a Mirror*, trans. D. Mader (2005); B. L. McCormack, *Karl Barth's Critically Realistic Dialectical Theology* (1995).

ADAM NEDER

Language   (Theological)

However true it is that language is God's *creation* (*CD* II/1:228), that "Our words are not our property, but His" (229), or that "God is the first and last *truth* of all our words" (233), Barth demonstrated no interest in, nor does his *theology* depend upon, a general theory of language. Like *time*, there is a difference for Barth between the ways *God* created and possesses language and the way we experience it (Isa. 55:8–9). Since Scripture says little about the content of the former, Barth sees little warrant in speculating about it. Yet with the *hermeneutics* of suspicion that entered the garden via the serpent's words, "Did God say?" (Gen. 3:1), and the judgment

"by which human language is confused and sundered" ever since the tower of Babel (Gen. 11), Barth says "there can be no doubt" that the problem of human language "is a severe one" (III/4:316). Indeed, he acknowledges its severity as drastically as any postmodernist or Romantic poet, for example, the disillusionment expressed in the sentiment, "Words are 'sound and fury,'" is justified given our "constant deflation of the word." However, Barth says, "It is not the words that are really empty," but the speakers and hearers. In other words, human language is as such weak, corrupt, impotent, ambiguous, and vacillating as any creaturely reality subject to the fall. But the deeper problem is that we are sinners and as such make "inhuman and barbaric" use of language (III/2:260).

Though Barth shows concern for the ethical use of language (III/4:287ff.), he asserts that Scripture's primary concern is not the problem of language generally, that is, for ordinary human discourse. Rather its concern is "the problem of theological language" (I/1:344), that is, talking about God truthfully. With Moses, Isaiah, Ezekiel, Jeremiah, Daniel, and others, as well as various New Testament passages, Scripture gives ample testimony that talking about God truthfully is a problem not merely because of our sin, but because of "the inadequacy of all human language." It is "not simply a question of technical imperfections and their removal" but the very "impossibility" that humans can apply language to God properly apart from a miracle of *grace*. Barth claims: "the mouth of Balaam's ass is opened . . . to show that the divine possibility involved does not have a limit, let alone a condition, in humanity" (II/1:220–23).

Barth famously described the predicament this presents to both academic theologians and preachers in 1922: "As ministers we ought to speak of God. We are human, however, and so cannot speak of God. We ought therefore to recognize both our obligation and our

136 Language (Theological)

inability and by that very recognition give God the glory" ("Task," 186). Given the basic difference between God and *humanity*, the majesty of theology's object and human language, Barth says this problem cannot be resolved. But it is "overcome" from God's side through *revelation* (II/1:220ff.) since God has spoken and continues to speak through the human language of Scripture (see *inspiration*).

How does this happen? It happens not because of any capacity, possibility, or potential within language itself to "claim," "comprehend," or "correspond" to God. Rather, it happens by means of "conscription" (I/1:340). God "commandeers" (334) our fallible words, which are "doubly hidden from ourselves (by our creatureliness and our sin)," to speak "His infallible truth" (II/1:228–29). By employing the military metaphors of "conscription" and "commandeered" (also "commissioned" [I/2:533], "requisitioned" [II/1:219], "enlisted" [231], and so forth) to describe what happens to human language and its speakers and hearers in the event of revelation, Barth was asserting that human words do not have any innate or "secret affinity or fitness" for such service. "The truth is rather that their original character as alien elements has first to be removed, that they have first to receive a new nature, and be awakened and newly created for this service" (I/2:682).

Yet Barth qualifies this claim (countering his military metaphors) when he says that our words "are not, so to speak, put into uniform," that is, "their particular character" as human words "is not effaced or suppressed" any more than the speakers and hearers are made passive or inhuman in the event of revelation. "They are genuinely affirmed" (683). God does not do something "inappropriate" with human language in the event of revelation nor are human words "alienated from their proper and original sense and usage." Rather, as belonging "originally and properly to

Him," they are "restored" (II/1:228–29). This does not mean their "divinization" (I/2:683) or that they undergo a "magical transformation" whereby they cease to be human words. "He does not perform a violent miracle, but exercises a lawful claim and makes a restitution, when, in His omnipotence, He causes the miracle to happen by which we come to participate in the veracity of His revelation, and by which our words become true descriptions of Himself" (II/1:229).

None of our words are true in any original, primary, or proper sense apart from God as "their first and last and proper subject" (II/1:228–29). But in "elevating our words to their proper use, giving Himself to be their proper object, and therefore giving them truth," Barth says, "they are in a sense raised from the dead," and "He gives to them the thing which by nature they cannot have," namely, a proper relationship to the truth (230–31). However, the means by which our words and knowledge come to participate in the truth is by way of *analogy*, which "means similarity, i.e., a partial correspondence and agreement (and, therefore, one which limits both parity and disparity between two or more different entities)" (225). Barth elaborates the critical distinction between an analogy of being and an analogy of *faith*, but the upshot is that even when taken into the service of revelation our words refer neither univocally nor equivocally to God or his truth. This means not that we are left with a "double truth" or a merely metaphorical, "pictorial," or "as if" truth. "On the contrary, He establishes one truth, His own, as the truth of our views, concepts, and words." This means "the unity of truth in Him who is the truth" has an order: we come to know our truth by way of his truth, not his truth by way of ours (228–29).

This order has implications for our understanding of theological language. "For example," Barth says, "the words 'father' and 'son' do not first and properly have their truth at the point of reference to the underlying views and concepts in our thought and language, i.e., in their application to the two nearest male members in the succession of physical generation of man or of animal creation generally." Rather, by the grace of revelation they can refer, "in a way which is incomprehensible and concealed from us," originally and properly "to God, in the doctrine of the *Trinity*" (229). The same applies to words such as *lordship, patience, love*, and others that God applies to himself in revelation. We too, "looking back from God's revelation," may use such words properly "when we apply them to God" in contrast to "when we apply them within the confines of what is appropriate to us as creatures." Yet it "does not lie in our power to return our words to their proper use" (229–30). Everything "stands or falls," Barth claims, on "the decision made in His revelation." "Everything depends on our actually appropriating His promise and therefore not using our human words without the permission and command of His revelation" (231).

To be sure, the words God applies to himself in revelation, namely biblical words, have no intrinsic or "metaphorical aptitude" for such service (I/1:436). "It is not, therefore, a question of the character native to them, but of the choice which comes upon them" (I/2:682). Nor, unlike the freedom granted Adam to name the animals, does God leave it to us to choose arbitrarily the words from which we draw analogies about him: "one analogy here today and another there tomorrow." Rather, God makes a "selection" from among an infinite number of words and not only grants us permission to use them but also commands that we bind ourselves to them (II/1:232–33). Thus, like the children of *Israel*, what makes the words of the *Bible* special is not any intrinsic capacity but simply that God chooses them and promises to go with them. Like "the pillar of cloud by day

and the pillar of fire by night," Barth refers to this as "the promise which is the traveling portion given to our undertaking to know God if it is an obedient undertaking" (236).

By frequently referring to biblical language as "the language of Canaan" (Isa. 19:18–19), Barth sought to emphasize that the Bible's entire vocabulary derives from an ethnic ("secular") language shaped and conditioned by a particular history (IV/3.2:735–38), with particular characteristics and limitations, like any other human language; and, notwithstanding its appropriation by revelation, it could and should be studied as such.

Yet given its especially concrete character, Barth was aware of the tendency, from the patristic era to our own, "to overemphasize the impropriety" of its anthropomorphic language (talk of God's mouth, arms, hands, remembering, forgetting, pity, wrath, repentance, and so forth) and to ascribe "in contrast a kind of moderate impropriety to abstract concepts like the being, wisdom, goodness and righteousness of God, and a genuine propriety only to negative concepts like incomprehensibility, immutability, infinity, etc." Barth objected that the latter terms did not provide "safety" or "surer ground" for theology, but rather the "occasion for the pitiful transition from theology to *philosophy*, or from the theology of revelation to *natural theology*" and that such terms, though supposedly more "spiritual," were "just as anthropomorphic as those which indicate concrete perception." Moreover, Barth claimed that the Bible's "crass anthropomorphisms" were more adequate than the vague, abstract generalities of philosophical language because they are less misleading about their concrete humanity and creatureliness and therefore the necessity of a miracle in order for them to refer to God. Thus, so long as "it lets itself be guided by its object, theology ought to try to evade these anthropomorphisms least of all" (222–23).

Barth celebrated occasions when the Bible's language of Canaan still seemed to speak clearly to modern people in a world supposedly "come of age," when many theologians, preoccupied with the problems of hermeneutics, translation, and language-events (CL, 139), thought such clarity impossible (III/3:213; HG, 59–60). He also defended the church's right to insist at times on using its liturgical language, "the language of Zion" (III/4:86). Nevertheless, he contended that the church's language is not an "end in itself." It cannot simply parrot the language of Canaan. "There must be translation, for example, into the language of the newspaper," especially if it fulfills its task of confession. Otherwise its language outside the church "is as effectual as Chinese" (DiO, 33). However, translation depends on interpretation. "Human words need interpretation because as such they are ambiguous" (I/2:712) and not least of all biblical words. But Barth draws an important distinction between interpretation and illustration: "Interpretation means saying the same thing in other words. Illustration means saying the same thing in other words." And he adds: "Where the line is to be drawn between the two cannot be stated generally. But there is a line, for revelation will submit only to interpretation and not to illustration" (I/1:345).

Certainly even the best interpretation of revelation will "contain elements of illustration," and in order to describe its various relations, theological language will utilize the conceptual language of philosophy. But therein is always the danger that theological language will be co-opted by philosophy. Uncommissioned or unbaptized terms or concepts can enter in like a "Trojan horse" and "suddenly a μετάβασις εἰς ἄλλο γένος" or change of categories, can occur, and we are then talking about something totally different from revelation. Such has occurred throughout the history of the church, under the auspices of "vestigia trinitatis in creatura," for example. There-

fore, if our interpretation of revelation is serious, Barth insists, we will remember that: "Theological language is not free to venture anything and everything." And if theological language is to maintain fidelity to its object we will remember Hilary of Poitiers' words, "Non sermoni res, sed rei sermo subjectus est," that is, "The word serves the content, not the content the word" (I/1:333–54, 367).

In sum, all our words must be crucified, dead, and buried before they can be properly applied to the subject matter of theology. Indeed, "our words require a complete change of meaning, even to the extent of becoming the very opposite in sense, if in their application to God they are not to lead us astray" (II/1:307). But if, as Barth claims, "The goal of language must be determined by the unique object in question" (I/2:125), then theological language can serve to indicate that the fulfillment and "future of every human word" is not as a captive to "the totalitarian claim of a general hermeneutics" (472), but as a free witness to Jesus Christ (Phil. 2:11).

K. Barth, CD I/1:333–47; II/1:204ff.; G. Hunsinger, "Beyond Literalism and Expressivism," in Disruptive Grace (2000), 210–25; E. Jüngel, God's Being Is in Becoming, trans. J. Webster (2001), 17–27; B. L. McCormack, "Graham Ward's Barth, Derrida and the Language of Theology," SJT 49, no. 1 (1996): 97–109; G. Ward, Barth, Derrida and the Language of Theology (1995).

RICHARD F. BURNETT

Liberalism "When we established Zwischen den Zeiten in the fall of 1922," Barth wrote in 1933, "we were, so we thought, in reasonable agreement with respect to what we wanted: in contrast to the positive-liberal or liberal-positive theology of Neo-Protestantism at the beginning of the century with its human-god, which we came to recognize as its holy shrine, we wanted a theology of the **Word of God** as it had imposed itself upon us young pastors more and more through the Bible and the Reformers' exemplary attention to it" (ZZ 11 [1933]: 536). The turn against liberalism and liberal theology as such characterizes Barth's theology and **dialectical theology** in general. Since *Rom* II (1922), Barth became one of the most famous spokesmen of theological antiliberalism.

"Liberalism," for Barth, did not refer to a particular trend in modern, "Neo-Protestant" Christianity, but to a constellation of ideas that connected various groups (liberals, conservatives, and pietists). Barth took up Ernst Troeltsch's concept of Neo-Protestantism as a category of historical description and also as a legitimate systematic theological program. He then turned the latter upside down. Throughout Barth's work, terms such as *liberalism, Neo-Protestantism,* and *modern theology* are used polemically to delegitimize its representatives as nothing less than proponents of "a **heresy** which destroys" the **church** (CD 1/2:291). He did not hesitate to use such terms even against "dissident" dialectical theologians such as Gogarten, **Brunner**, or **Bultmann**.

In the 1920s, *anti*liberalism was a de facto consensus uniting very different, if not antagonistic, Protestant groups; for example, the "Luther Renaissance" from the far right wing to the "religious socialists" from the left wing. Most members of both groups were members of the post–World War I generation born around 1880. It was the same in theology as it was in many other intellectual realms: the "parallels between criticisms of the right and left [were] surprising" (Bracher, 78). Most of them shared the conviction that the war had revealed the crisis of modern, civil society whose basic values derived from the concept of a rational, individual, self-confident subject. Such values as individual liberty, humanism, tolerance, privacy, and so on were considered as either intrinsically wrong or too abstract, having derived from a Western (and not German) or Catholic (and not Protestant) concept

of natural law. For this and other reasons such values were regarded as too weak to build a coherent society upon, that is, a society that would be more than merely a loose "aggregate" of "atomistic" individuals, a *Gemeinschaft* (community) rather than merely a *Gesellschaft* (society).

Using the semantics of the "conservative revolution," Barth spoke of "authority" instead of "autonomy," "obedience" instead of "individual rights," "community" instead of "individuality," "decision" and "venture" instead of "rational agreement," "charismatic leadership" instead of "compromise" and "parliamentarianism," and so on. In doing so, Barth, like many other theologians, contributed to "the crisis of liberalism between the World Wars" (see von Thadden) and perhaps also to the congenital defect of the Weimar Republic, namely, it was a "democracy without democrats."

However, Barth's antiliberalism and antimodernism played a key role in his fight against National Socialism and its theological devotees. In Barth's eyes, National Socialism was a modern secular **religion** and "German Christians" were a completely legitimate offspring of modernist theology. Even when noting that liberal theologians were vastly different from one another and divided over their political attitudes toward fascism (e.g., Gottfried Traub and Georg Wobbermin on the one hand and Martin Rade and Hermann Mulert on the other), Barth tended to interpret such political pluralism as a consequence of antifoundational inconsequence and as a principle of arbitrariness that, from his perspective, was typical of theological as well as political liberalism.

In essence, Barth's theological antiliberalism is really a kind of theological antipluralism. More precisely, it is a basic protest against any element of arbitrariness in the foundation of belief and theological knowledge. For Barth, religious or theological liberalism means: "Choosing one's own **God**." That God has chosen and elected humankind (and every human being) in *Jesus Christ* means that all human efforts to choose and elect God are heretical.

In spite of his rigorous opposition, one should not overlook that throughout his life Barth considered himself in fundamental agreement with theological (and political) liberalism at one point: he was concerned about the *freedom* of every individual human being. Ultimately, and paradoxically, it is this common concern that motivated his nearly lifelong battle *against* theological liberalism.

Indeed, Barth said in 1968: "I am liberal as well—and perhaps even more of a liberal than those who call themselves liberals in this area [of theology]" (*FT*, 33). Barth's late summary of his liberal antiliberalism is appropriate, at least with regard to his self-assessment of his motives.

His effort to overcome theological liberalism by deepening its foundations can be traced back to the very beginnings of his independent theological thinking. In 1910 Barth, as a student of Adolf von *Harnack*, Martin Rade, and the Neo-Kantian thinkers Wilhelm *Herrmann* and Hermann Cohen, sketched an ambitious, foundational theory of a religious-philosophical system that sought to be both theocentric and practical. Specifically, he sought to relate "the idea" (in the Platonic sense) of God or the Absolute to actual religious practice. Such a system should entail the concepts of true individuality (in Herrmann's sense), and of a transindividual and genuine historical (Troeltsch), "cultural consciousness" (Cohen). True human freedom, he was convinced, cannot be safeguarded by human rights conferred from outside. On the contrary, its realization must be understood as the decisive ethical goal of individual, communal, and political development. A strong collective agent for this process would be needed.

Terrified by the depersonalizing effects of contemporary industrial capitalism, the young pastor from Safenwil became a religious socialist in 1911 (following Kutter and Ragaz). He worked toward a synthesis of liberal Christianity and the Socialist movement, inspired by the socialistic *eschatology* of Christoph Blumhardt. When in late 1914 both of these groups compromised themselves in Barth's eyes by supporting the immoral enterprise of a nationalistic war, Barth turned again. But this time it was a turn to a strictly theocentric theology based on the idea of the "radical autonomy of God" as the one and only subject in whom human freedom could be realized, thus "recapitulating the process of enlightenment once again . . . but in a radical and systematic perspective" (Rendtorff, 164). Even the radically negative dialectical theology of *Rom* II can be read as a constructive theory of true individual freedom by setting up the agent of theological knowledge in the form of an ongoing process of deconstructing religion (Pfleiderer, 337–75).

In a public controversy with his former teacher Harnack in 1923, Barth particularly demonstrated the antihistoricist elements of his new theocentric theology. In his lectures on the theology of Reformed confessions, *Calvin*, Zwingli, and *Schleiermacher* (1922–1924), the Göttingen professor of Reformed theology emphasized the highly ambivalent aspects of the relationship of Reformed theology to the modernization of Christianity (Troeltsch!). In his dogmatic lectures from 1924 to 1925, Barth refers to the dogmatics of old Protestant and especially Reformed Orthodoxy, organizing all dogmatic contents as the unfolding of structural elements of God's self-revelation as the absolutely free subject. As in his *Römerbrief*, the point of this new ("unsystematic") theological system is to unfold the gnoseological structure of belief, grounded in God's Word as the principle of individual freedom. In his lectures on *Ethics* given in Münster and Bonn between 1928 and 1931, Barth opposed an understanding of individual "conscience"—the key classical term of Protestant ethics—as a self-evident anthropological foundation of religious ethics. He rather reconstructed it as the leading concept of the final (pneumatological) aspect ("redemption") of the Trinitarian structure of Christian *ethics*.

In the *CD*, the ambivalence of his theological theory of individual freedom appears particularly as follows: (1) negatively, in his sharp methodological distinction between a theology of *revelation* versus all "*natural theology*," leading to a fundamental denegation of religion (I/2:§17), which applies to the criticism of Ludwig Feuerbach and Franz Overbeck, Neo-Protestantism, and liberal theology *in toto*; (2) positively, in his christocentric conception of the Reformed doctrine of God's absolute election (II/2); in his ethics of *creation* (III/4), which is not only conceived as an ethics of "freedom" in general, but also presents a differentiated and sensitive concept of the individual, its bodily existence (§55) and personal conduct in life (§56), including even positive references to a modern concept of human dignity.

Finally, in *Rechtfertigung und Recht* (1938), Barth acknowledges modern constitutional law as the decisive positive accomplishment of politics. During the last decade of his life, more conciliatory sounds concerning central requests of modern theological liberalism can be heard in Barth's work: he now emphasizes "the *humanity* of God," has friendly words for Schleiermacher (see "Postscript"), and praises the missionary and social activities of the modern age church, based on an at least relative willingness to accept the secular world as such (IV/3.1:18–38). The ugly, broad ditch between revelation and *nature* is now (even though still one-sided) bridged by a "comprehensive" understanding of "the one light of God and the many lights of his creation" (152).

K. D. Bracher, *The Age of Ideologies*, trans. E. Osers (1984); G. Pfleiderer, *Karl Barths*

praktische Theologie (2000); T. Rendtorff, "Radikale Autonomie Gottes," in *Theorie des Christentums* (1972), 161–81; R. Thadden, *Die Krise des Liberalismus zwischen den Weltkriegen* (1978).

GEORG PFLEIDERER

Lord's Supper Barth never lived to present his doctrine of the Lord's Supper, which was originally planned as part of the doctrine of *reconciliation* (*CL*, ix; cf. *CD* IV/2:xi–xii). But he did write his "radically new view" of the sacrament concerning *baptism* and noted that from this, "intelligent readers may deduce . . . how I would finally have presented the doctrine of the Lord's Supper" (*CD* IV/4:ix). After expounding his view of Spirit and water baptism as the foundation of the *Christian life*, Barth intended to develop a section on the *ethics* of reconciliation, guided by the Lord's Prayer followed by his "doctrine of the Lord's Supper (as the thanksgiving which responds to the presence of *Jesus Christ* in His self-sacrifice and which looks forward to His future)" (ix). The Lord's Supper would be understood as that human work which corresponds to the divine work in the history of Jesus Christ made present now in the power of his Spirit and above all as giving thanks to *God* for his benefits without focusing on the benefits but as "an honoring of God for his own sake" (*CL*, 87). Thanksgiving corresponds to the nature of God's *grace* in *revelation* as the one who freely reveals and reconciles us to himself—it accepts God's free and unmerited miraculous acts of love for us that come to determine our existence (*CD* II/1:197). Barth had a very lively sense of the fact that the risen, ascended, and coming Lord, who is hidden from us now until he returns, is present in the power of his Spirit freeing people to gather in his name and to exist as "an earthly-historical event" and thus as "the earthy-historical form of His existence" (IV/2:695–710).

He thus saw the Lord's Supper as an aspect of divine service with a liturgical root so that the community gathers neither arbitrarily nor on its own, but "their King and Lord Himself gives them direction and orders and commands, and consolation and promises. It is He who gives the *freedom* for what takes place" (699). They give thanks, pray, and confess in *faith, hope*, and *love* through the *Holy Spirit* in correspondence to who Jesus was and is as the reconciler of *humanity* to God (699ff.), namely as "a fellowship of baptism" (701). In this context the Lord's Supper looks forward, in hope, to the eternal life toward which all are ordained (702–3). Thus the community lives by the promise that the risen Lord "will give them food and drink, that in the life in which they too are surrounded by death He will provide, and will Himself be, their wayside sustenance. And so they go and come to the gathering of the community to seat themselves, and to eat and drink, as brothers and sisters at the table where He Himself presides as Lord and Host, and they are His invited and welcome guests. They go and come to the Lord's Supper" (703).

In these acts they are strengthened by eating one bread and drinking the common cup precisely "because it is He, Jesus Christ, who brings them to it, who invites them . . . who is Himself, indeed, their food and drink. It is thus a question of their nourishment by Him" (703). While this *worship* is always problematical from a human standpoint, the community nonetheless is "a fellowship of the Lord's Supper, united by Him both with Him and also, because with Him, in itself; *communio sanctorum* as a fellowship of the sure and certain hope of eternal life" (704). It is in this basic sense that the community exists in communion.

This explains why Barth opposed what he called sacramentalism and moralism. The former focused on the action of the *church* as the factor by which someone either becomes a Christian

(baptism) or is renewed in the Christian life (Lord's Supper). The latter sees Christians' attitudes or actions as factors that distinguish them from others and that sanctify them. Barth stressed that God himself, present in his incarnate Son and empowering our corresponding thanksgiving through the actions of the risen Lord in his real presence to us through the Holy Spirit, is the sole basis, meaning, and goal of the church's sacramental actions.

He also opposed "secularization" and "sacralization" as forms of self-justification to stress that the sole criterion of the church's being and action is Christ himself prophetically present, enabling his kingdom to be built on earth through the church's obedient actions (667–68). In this he was entirely consistent with an emphasis that was already evident early in the *CD* when he asserted: "The criterion of . . . Christian utterance [God-talk] is thus the being of the Church, namely, Jesus Christ, God in His gracious revealing and reconciling address to man" (I/1:4). This means that since the church is the earthly-historical form of Christ's bodily presence on earth between his first and second coming, it cannot arrogate to itself the power to make Christ present or bring in the **kingdom of God** here and now; nor can it orient its life by its liturgy or sacramental action as such without risking some sort of self-glorification.

In a very similar way Barth rejected such notions as *ex opere operato* and *ex opere operantis* as explanations of how God's grace works in the church's sacramental actions. Such attempts to maintain the objective validity of the sacraments independent of the minister's personal activity and holiness were problematic for Barth because each, in its own way, ascribed that objective validity either to the human action as such or to the disposition of the recipient, thus making the sovereignty of grace and the presence of Christ in some sense dependent upon and even indistinguishable from the community's human actions as such.

Becoming more suspicious of the traditional Reformed understanding of sacraments that he once embraced before calling for their "cautious and respectful 'demythologising'" (IV/2:xi), Barth held there was only one sacramental mystery, namely, Jesus Christ himself (IV/2:54; Molnar, 227ff.), which could not be confused in any way with the human activities of the church, even in its sacramental actions. Barth no longer accepted the idea of sacraments as means of grace because he believed this tended to confuse Christ's unique mediation with the actions of the church, which can be no more than witnessing actions to Christ's actions here and now; he thus moved toward a more Zwinglian interpretation of sacraments, with certain reservations, as signs that neither save nor give "assurance or confirmation to faith" as *Calvin* believed (IV/4:129; Molnar, 299).

Barth's new view of the sacrament was thus christologically determined. And this led to his quite powerful understanding of real presence that he articulated in a manner that followed his view of the *analogia fidei*. As he rejected the idea that Jesus is the revealer in his humanity as such, so in his view of *analogy* Barth held that there were no concepts that were true in themselves and therefore that no church actions (including sacraments) were valid in themselves. Hence the signs could never be confused with the reality signified. Barth rejected the Roman Catholic doctrine of transubstantiation on christological grounds, insisting that just because Jesus' humanity is the humanity of the Son of God, it would be wrong to suppose that "Godhead has taken the place of His manhood, that His manhood is ... swallowed up or extinguished by Godhead, that His human form is a mere appearance, as the Roman Catholic doctrine of transubstantiation maintains of the host supposedly changed into the body of Christ. That he is true

God and also in full differentiation true man is the mystery of Jesus Christ" (III/2:207–8).

For Barth, Christ's real presence is his real spiritual presence that includes *nature* (bread and wine) and does not change them into mere appearances. Hence "Bread remains bread and wine wine.... The realism of sacramental consecration does not imply destruction of the signs' own existence" (I/1:94). The focus is not on the elements or even on the human actions of eating and drinking; rather it is on the communion effected between the community and its heavenly head through the Holy Spirit. While eucharistic references to Christ's body and blood referred to "the life of Jesus offered in His death," for Barth "the decisive event in the Supper is not the recollection as such, but present participation in the fruit of this sacrifice" (214). Consequently, "as you eat this bread My life is given to you as yours, and ... as you drink of this cup you may live with joy and not with sorrow, as innocent and not condemned" (214). This is done in remembrance of Christ "until His presence, already experienced here and now with this eating and drinking, is revealed to all eyes" (214). Barth opposed any docetic understanding of the church's action and being in *history,* and so he saw the Lord's Supper as a joyous celebration of and renewal of our communion with Christ through the Spirit and in faith (IV/1:152, 666). All of this of course presupposes Christ's bodily resurrection (see *resurrection of Jesus Christ*) and *ascension.*

Despite his positive intentions expressed above in rejecting the term *sacrament* with regard to the church's actions in baptism and the Lord's Supper, Barth's later view of the sacrament has been forcefully criticized for: separating divine and human being and action too sharply; rejecting infant baptism; departing from his earlier view that sacraments are means of grace; rejecting even his earlier sacramental views espoused in I/2 and II/1; and subtly redefining sacraments as human ethical responses to God's actions within history instead of noticing that they represent our human inclusion in the life of the *Trinity* through Christ's own continuing high-priestly mediation as the ascended and advent Lord.

J. J. Buckley, "Christian Community, Baptism and Lord's Supper," in *Cambridge Companion to Karl Barth*, ed. J. Webster (2000), 195–211; T. George, "Running Like a Herald to Deliver the Message" in *Karl Barth and Evangelical Theology*, ed. S. W. Chung (2006), 191–208; P. D. Molnar, *Karl Barth and the Theology of the Lord's Supper* (1996); J. Webster, *Barth's Ethics of Reconciliation* (1995); J. Yocum, *Ecclesial Mediation in Karl Barth* (2004).

PAUL D. MOLNAR

Love "To know what love is," Barth wrote, "we have first to ask concerning the unique love of *God* for us" (*CD* I/2:376). His account of love is therefore deeply rooted in the basis of his theological work: we learn what love is from God's act of graciousness toward us in *Jesus Christ*; we understand human love as our response to the love that God has shown to us. Barth considered this theocentric mode of answering the question the only way of avoiding completely arbitrary accounts of the concept of love. How, then, does God love? Barth's summary answer is to identify God as "the One who loves in *freedom*" (II/1:257), willing fellowship with God's creatures for its own sake as a necessity of God's own being, without regard to their readiness or suitability and without being conditioned by anything beyond Godself. Barth explains that God's loving is gracious in seeking fellowship but also holy, excluding any softness or sentimentality. God's loving is merciful in sharing the distress of another, but is also conditioned by God's righteousness. It is patient in allowing space for development to others, but is also

wise in its intelligence and reliability (II/1:351–439).

In response to this love shown by God, those beloved of God are called to love God and their neighbor (Mark 12:28–31). Early in his career, Barth's account of this human response was threatened by his emphasis on the divine initiative in all human action. This led him to say that "love towards God is an occurrence . . . which has its origin at every moment in God Himself, and which must therefore be sought and found only in Him" (*ER*, 324). Barth later regretted having given the impression that humans could not show love for God (IV/2:795) and insisted that, despite what *Luther* and Nygren say, Christians cannot be seen merely as pipes or channels for God's love. Human love is a gift of God, but it is nonetheless a creaturely reality, "a spontaneous and responsible human action" (IV/2:752).

The question then arises of how the commands to love God and to love one's neighbor are related to one another. Again, Barth's thought develops in this area. In Rom II he says that love of God is demonstrated primarily in *worship* and secondarily in love of the neighbor, apparently subsuming the second love commandment under the first (*ER*, 452). In the *CD*, however, he recognizes that such a move fails to do justice to the way the commands are recorded in the *Bible*. The commands are closely related, but should be seen as applying to the believer in different spaces and worlds (I/2:409), in two different spheres of activity (III/4:49), or in two different dimensions (IV/1:105–6).

In relation to the controversial topic of how love represented as *eros* is related to love as *agape*, Barth is hard to fathom. He variously represents *eros* as a power of human creativity (I/2:192), sexual desire (III/1:312–13), the *eros* of Greek *philosophy* (III/2:379), sanctified *eros* between husband and wife (III/4:319–20), and self-love (IV/2:734–35). At times, Barth depicts self-giving *agape* and self-seeking *eros* as opposites (*ER*, 320, 451, 467, 496; *CD* IV/2:736); at others, he defends the positive elements of *eros* against its Christian critics (III/1:279–85; III/4:126). His final discussion of the two kinds of love in the *CD* recognizes that both coexist conflictually in the life of the Christian, who has to choose whether to love in one way or the other, and in fact "loves in both ways at the same time." The resulting conflict leads to a "falling out" similar to that caused by the believer being simultaneously sinful and justified (IV/2:736).

A final interpretive question concerns whom the Christian is to love. Barth states that the biblical command to love one's neighbor is not a universal command to love **humanity**, but a command to love those who "stand in a certain proximity to the one who loves" (IV/2:803). He interprets the parable of the Good Samaritan as identifying the neighbor as the one who shows compassion and therefore becomes the bearer and representative of the divine compassion (I/2:416–20). Not everyone stands in this relationship to the one who loves, Barth comments, though he is clear here that the boundaries of the visible church do not coincide with this definition of the neighbor (I/2:422). Later in the *CD*, however, he does state that the proper objects of Christian love are "those with which we find ourselves in this context of this **history** of salvation," that is, other members of the **church** (IV/2:806–8). One useful section of the *CD* that aids interpretation of Barth's thought in this area is the third section of III/4:§54. The German section title is "Die Nahen und die Fernen," literally, "The Near and the Far." The English translation is headed "Near and Distant Neighbours." "Distant neighbours" may sound like an oxymoron, but in this section Barth insists that we are called beyond the exclusivity of church, family, or nation to be on our way toward those who are distant from us. This dynamic may indicate a way of reconciling Barth's insight that Christian love must be more than an abstract universal, while always reaching out toward neighbors that are distant, as well as those we find nearby.

D. Clough, *Ethics in Crisis* (2005), chaps. 2, 6; P. D. Molnar, "Love of God and Love of Neighbor in the Theology of Karl Rahner and Karl Barth," *MTh* 20, no. 4 (2004): 567–99; G. Outka, *Agape* (1972), chap. 7; C. J. Simon, "What Wondrous Love Is This?" in *For the Sake of the World*, ed. G. Hunsinger (2004), 143–58; and J. Webster's response, 159–64.

DAVID CLOUGH

Luther   The figure of Martin Luther exerted a complex and profound influence on Barth. In the *CD*, references to Luther's works surpass those of **Schleiermacher** and even **Calvin**. Barth often drew from the works in the Weimar edition, especially the Small and Large Catechisms and *The Bondage of the Will*, as well as Luther's scriptural commentaries and his sermons. The two thinkers share a fundamental commitment to the active nature of the **Word of God**, the cross, Jesus Christ's complete and perfect work of **salvation**, and the shape of the **Christian life** as *simul iustus et peccator*. But Barth is uncompromising in his criticism of Luther's doctrine on law and gospel, and he operates with a different understanding of human agency than Luther.

Luther and Barth share an unwavering focus on the person and work of **Jesus Christ**. Both reject any notion of **salvation** as a gradual process to which the human contributes, insisting that the complete salvation of **humanity** happened *extra nos* in the perfect Savior, Jesus Christ. This fully completed saving act presents the believer with scandal and mystery. Whereas the scandal of the cross suggests a conflict within God's own being in Luther's **theology**, Barth sees the cross as tied to the **revelation** of God's deepest and inmost nature. He roots his theology of the cross in the doctrine of *election*, namely, in God's eternal and gracious decision not to be *God* without the *world*. This gives election a central role in Barth's theology (*CD* II/2), in contrast to that of Luther.

The two thinkers also share a commitment to the primacy of the Word of God. Barth works in the vein of Luther when he describes the Word of God as a divine initiative that acts upon the human hearer (I/1:§§3–6), and when he insists on proclamation as a foundation for dogmatic reflection (I/1:70, 90, 95). Drawing from Luther's theology of the Word in his dispute with Neo-Protestantism, Barth argues that faith is grounded solely in the Word itself and never in any human faculty. While both thinkers share a low opinion of human *reason*, Luther focuses on the human *will* as being bound to *sin*, death, and the devil, whereas Barth sees human *reason* as bound to sin and its own creaturely limitations.

Both Luther and Barth are unyielding in their shared view that *grace* and *faith* are never qualities inhering in the human, but rather the initiative of God alone. Grace and faith come to the human anew every day, forming the Christian into a *simul iustus et peccator*. Although Barth shares Luther's eschatological view of the Christian life, he does not express the movement of the *simul* in Luther's terms of a "daily *confession*." Instead, in his mature works, Barth speaks in terms of a turning back to Christ (IV/3.1:197ff.). The Christian's participation in God's grace through faith consists of the human saying again and again a particularly creaturely yes to the divine Yes, which God says in Christ to humanity.

Barth holds that the famed Lutheran doctrine of *justification* by faith is indeed the *truth* upon which the church stands (IV/1:523). But more importantly, the *articulus stantis et cadentis ecclesiae* is its confession that Christ himself is Lord of the universe. Confessing Christ means

that theology must go farther than the doctrine of justification and give due regard to the "moment" beyond justification and *sanctification*, namely, to *vocation*, the sending of the Christian into the world as a function of the prophetic office of Christ (IV/3.1:7ff.). Although Luther has a doctrine of vocation that is deeply rooted in the work of Christ on the cross and in *baptism*, it is not as closely tied to Christ's prophetic office as it is in Barth's thought.

Two aspects of Luther's theology that Barth clearly rejects are the doctrines of the law and gospel, and Luther's notion of the hiddenness of God. Although the two thinkers share the understanding that the one Word of God can be expressed as either law or gospel in our lives through faith and the *Holy Spirit*, Barth does not accept Luther's teaching that the law is an unambiguous word of God alongside of and differentiated from the word of the gospel. According to Barth, if knowledge of sin comes primarily through the law and not first through the reconciling word of the gospel, it becomes severed from the *knowledge of God* in Jesus Christ (IV/1:369). Consequently, the knowledge of sin then relies on a revelation of God's wrath, which can be traced back to a hidden God who is free *from* God's revelation in Christ (II/2:63–64). Such a differentiation between God's words of judgment and salvation undermines Luther's insistence that faith can rest assured in Christ's saving work as God's final word about the fate of humanity. To be sure, Barth upholds the distinction between *gospel and law*, or *love* and fear, as he stated on occasion, but the two must be bound up in a unity that begins with God's election of humanity in Jesus Christ.

Another factor that affects the way Barth views Luther's theology of law and gospel is a particularly modern notion of human agency that stands in contrast to the medieval notions of human passivity pervading Luther's thought. For Luther, hearing the gospel requires that the human move through a moment in which one is fully and utterly passive, in which the law falls upon the head of the sinner. This kind of passivity stands in stark contrast to Barth's anthropology. To a modern theologian like Barth, the human being is constituted by agency and action. When the law and gospel are heard and believed, the human acts in a way that corresponds to the divine act. In contrast to Luther's interior, subjective concept of faith, Barth insists on the human's own outward act in faith. This modern ontology of external act allows Barth to integrate *ethics* into theology in a very different way than Luther and Lutheranism.

Barth's engagement with Luther's theology waxed and waned. From the late 1920s into the 1930s, Barth discovered anew the theology of the Reformation. But these years also plunged the Swiss thinker into the German Church struggle, compelling Barth to reject both a form of *natural theology* that he saw as an outgrowth of Luther's thought ("No!" in *NTh*, 67–128), as well as Luther's doctrine of the two kingdoms. Despite this rejection, however, Barth also argued that the Reformation understanding of the God's righteousness leads directly to particular political tasks and ethical action in the world ("C&S").

In the decades following the Second World War, Barth seemed to be seeking an authentic Luther who would rise above the contradictions within Lutheran theology. Uncertain that he could find such a figure in the "Pandora's box" of the Weimar edition, Barth continued to use Luther in his later years but avoided Lutheran theological categories.

K. Barth, *CSC*; idem, "Luther's Doctrine"; idem, *Lutherfeier*; G. Ebeling, "Karl Barths Ringen mit Luther," in *Lutherstudien* III (1985), 428–573; G. Hunsinger, "What Karl Barth Learned from Martin Luther," in *Disruptive Grace* (2000), 279–304.

AMY MARGA

Ministry Barth's most thorough discussion of "ministry" comes under *CD* IV/3.2:§72, "The *Holy Spirit* and the Sending of the Christian Community." Having elaborated that the *church* does not exist for its own sake but for the sake of the *world* by praising *God* and living in solidarity with but not in conformity to the world, Barth discusses "*Der Dienst der Gemeinde*" (§72.4), which is rendered in the *CD*, "The Ministry of the Community" but should rather be translated, "The Service of the Community." Indeed, the word "ministry" should be translated throughout this section as "service," which provides a different connotation (see *mission*). Nevertheless, Barth defines the "ministry" or "service" of the community as "very definite, and therefore limited, but also full of promise" (830).

It is *definite* because it is *Jesus Christ*'s ministry. He is "the great, primary and true Minister" [Servant] whose ministry of *reconciliation* has already been accomplished yet continues because many do not yet know it. As the one "Mediator between God and man" and "Executor of the divine work of grace," he is "its one Hearer, Witness and Guarantor in advance of all others." Therefore, we do not bring Jesus into "our" ministry. He brings us into his. He is not part of our ministry nor its presupposition or goal. He "is the content of the *witness* which is alone at issue," and in him "it has already reached its goal and is already valid." Ministry is, therefore, not an ideal to be striven for but a reality in which the community participates. The community truly ministers therefore only to the extent that it does so "in His school and discipleship" and is "oriented by His ministry." Such orientation occurs by "constant listening to the prophets and apostles called by Him, and therefore its constant investigation of Scripture" (831–32).

This ministry is *limited* in two ways. First, as "active subordination to God from whom it derives and therefore to man to whom it turns," it is ministry to

God and humanity and not one without the other. The church is not "called to do anything and everything." "Where it is not clear in a given case that it has to render service to both God and man in the strict connection," Barth warns, "it is well advised to leave [such service] alone." Second, the ministry of the community is limited to witness. We "can neither carry through God's work to its goal nor lead men to the point of accepting it." Our "task" or rather "commission" (*Auftrag*) "consists in causing the divine Word of this divine work to be heard in the world." No more, no less, no other than this is demanded. The community may be tempted to perform other tasks and confess other realities, yet if it did "it would squander the time and energy which are demanded by its own task with its call for the strictest concentration" (833–37).

The ministry of the community is also *full of promise*. Given its isolation in the world, its many past defeats and failures and present weaknesses, it needs assurance. Faced with so many anxieties, pressures, and insecurities, it is tempted to think all its efforts are in vain. Yet the promise serves as "a superior counter-pressure" to sustain, protect, and renew the ministry. As a "free promise" the community "does not have it institutionally" or "even in the power of its own faith and knowledge," but only as "the subject of its prayer and thanksgiving," which it must always reach out for "with empty hands." Nevertheless, the promise "does not stand like a closed and brazen heaven above it, but can always demonstrate and confirm itself in specific fulfilments," that is, with more or less clear signs that the *Holy Spirit* is at work. "Never and nowhere, or at least never for long" has the community been left without such fulfillments. The community should receive them with *gratitude*, but not live for them or gauge its faithfulness or authenticity by them. However helpful and encouraging, they are only signs, which the community must be prepared to live without. The content of the promise is "the *Word of God* concerning reconciliation, the *covenant*, the kingdom and the new reality of the world as spoken to it in and by *Jesus Christ*." Already fulfilled in him the promise "is unshakeable and infallible." As the "glory in the gloom of its service," it gives the community "unparalleled assurance" and makes it "more sure of its cause and more cheerful than any other people" (838–43).

The *nature* of such ministry is that of witness, which consists inseparably in all its forms as "declaration, exposition and address, or the proclamation, explication and application of the Gospel." *Declaration* means to introduce to the world "what God says in the Gospel concerning what He has done and does and is for man." At all costs, with all means at its disposal and without anxiety about its success, the community causes the gospel to be heard. It raises a banner. "It may be that with its declaration it simply sets the world an annoying riddle, or leaves it indifferent." But without the "naïve force" of its simple proclamation (e.g., "Jesus Christ is risen, He is risen indeed"), the ministry would be totally lacking (843–46).

Yet the gospel is not content with "unfruitful acquaintance" or undeveloped declaration that is "loud and clear" but "mere assertion." *Exposition* is required, that is, explanation. The gospel "explains itself" and is "intrinsically clear" but "wills to be understood." Because Christian *faith* is faith that seeks understanding, the community cannot neglect the human service of explication. It cannot create the knowledge of faith, but can and should take "from man the illusion that [this] knowledge is possible only in the form of a *sacrificium intellectus*" and show "that even from the human standpoint this knowledge is quite as much in order as any other human knowledge." It will not overestimate what it can do or "regard its little explanation as divine revelation," but it will not "bury its talent" in this "modest but definite task." It will follow the "lines and contours" of the gospel's own "self-explanation" and avoid "alien principles of explanation in the form of metaphysical, anthropological, epistemological or religio-philosophical presuppositions" as to what is possible (846–50).

The community's declaration and explanation, however, do not occur in a vacuum but "in definite relations" to non-Christians, who like its own members have "gone astray" and are "under assault." It can declare and explain but still speak past or over them. In order to speak to them, in order to communicate with them, it must not merely "know them" but "really know them" as those whom God loves and for whom Jesus Christ has died and risen again. Its address, therefore, must be *evangelical address*. Not with threats and accusations but "inviting them to the feast," "summoning them to *joy*," its appeal must be "a dynamic, if only a humanly dynamic, invitation and wooing." It strides toward them in *love* and addresses "them on the assumption that [the gospel] is valid and effective for them too" and challenges "as strongly as possible their illusion that this . . . applies only to special individuals." "With great humility but also with great resolution," it lays the gospel message "right in front of them" (850–54).

Consistent in its nature as declaration, exposition, and evangelical address, the ministry is one. Yet its *forms* are diverse. Why? First, because it reflects "the being and life" of the Lord of the community who "is absolutely one God as Father, Son and Holy Spirit, yet not with an undifferentiated, lifeless and motionless unity, but as the eternally rich God who is the basis, source and Lord of an infinitude of different divine possibilities." Second, because it enlists the "special callings and endowments of individuals." It is not the calling of diverse individuals that makes ministry diverse. It is diverse callings to ministry that individuates. Though a strength to ministry, this sometimes

threatens its unity. Still, its activity is not that of an "ant-heap or beehive" or soldiers performing a "well-drilled maneuver." "The Holy Spirit does not enforce a flat uniformity" (854–59).

Yet, according to Scripture, and notwithstanding variations throughout history and perhaps in the future, there are "basic forms" of ministry. How are they determined? Following the example of Jesus Christ and his disciples, the "two great and distinctive elements" of ministry are word and deed, speech and action, in an inseparable "twofold form" of witness. Speech is not more important than action, though normatively "the Word precedes and the act follows," which means the latter interprets the former and the former holds the latter to account. But they belong together, and if there is "a form of the Church's ministry in which there is neither speech on the one side nor action on the other, it may be affirmed with certainty that at least this is not a basic form." Barth elaborates twelve basic forms. The first six are especially *speaking* acts. The latter six are forms of especially *active* speech. But they intersect and "cannot possibly be separated from one another." They are: (1) Praise (**Worship**); (2) **Preaching**; (3) Teaching; (4) Evangelism; (5) Mission; (6) **Theology**; (7) **Prayer**; (8) Care of souls (**Pastoral Care**); (9) Special Representatives (e.g., Mentoring); (10) Diaconal Service; (11) Prophecy; and (12) Fellowship (which includes, as "actions which establish fellowship," **Baptism** and the **Lord's Supper**) (859–901).

Barth served twelve years as a "working pastor," longer than any other major theologian of the twentieth century, and was a regular visiting preacher and pastor in his latter years to Basel Prison. At great length and in practical detail, Barth discusses ministry with an intimacy, passion, and sobriety that is unparalleled in modern dogmatic or systematic theology.

R. Anderson, *The Shape of Practical Theology* (2001); K. Barth, *CD* IV/3.2:830–901;

idem, "Task"; G. Pfleiderer, *Karl Barths praktische Theologie* (2000).

RICHARD E. BURNETT

Mission According to missiologist David Bosch, the late-twentieth-century consensus that "the *church* is missionary by its very nature" (Vatican II) profoundly shaped Barth's entire ecclesiology (Bosch, 373). Johannes Aagard described Barth as "the decisive Protestant missiologist in this generation" (Aagard, 238). As early as 1928, a leading German missiologist, Karl Hartenstein, challenged his guild to consider "what Karl Barth's *theology* has to say to mission" (see Hartenstein). Barth's biblically grounded gospel of unconditional *grace* and total dependence on God's action in *Jesus Christ* on behalf of sinful *humanity* confronted the realities of declining Christendom in post–World War I Europe. "The Church in the modern period has slowly but relentlessly lost its position in the world in the form in which it could previously enjoy it" (*CD* III/4:19). This was to be hailed, however, as the church undergoes a "spontaneous reorientation . . . outwards instead of inwards, to the world instead of to itself" (IV/3.1:35). For Barth, mission was about the church's turning outward to the *world*.

By the time Barth reinitiated his theological project with the first volumes of the *CD* in the mid 1930s, the fundamental importance of the sending of the church ("sending" = mission!) had become a guiding assumption in his thought. In his controversial lecture on "Theology and Mission in the Present Situation" (1932), Barth claimed that "all activity of the church is mission," whether it is gospel *witness* to the pagans in the church who continue to need to hear it or to those pagans outside the church who are hearing the gospel for the first time (*ThF&A*, 100ff.). Though Barth did not coin or ever use the phrase *missio Dei*, as claimed by some,

he anticipated the central missional thrust of his doctrine of **reconciliation** in a lecture given to students in Switzerland on August 7, 1934, on the theme, "The Christian as Witness," in which he expounded in six theses the meaning and action of the **Christian life** as witness, understood both individually and as the central purpose of the church as community: "Witness is a human word to which *God* gives the power to remind other people about the lordship, the **grace** and the judgment of God. Wherever the human word has this power, there is the church" (*ThF&A*, 185).

The fundamentally missionary *vocation* of the church is a pervasive theme in the *CD*. This emphasis reaches its full development in the later volumes of the project, in the doctrine of the church that is embedded in Barth's exposition of the gospel of reconciliation. But its force as a formative presupposition is constantly attested. The apostolic vocation defines the church's vocation. "What it means to be in the Church, and even what the Church itself truly is, may be seen typically in what is described in the New Testament as the reality of the apostolate. . . . In and with the grace which comes to it, the Church . . . has its essential direction outwards to mission, to the world, because it is not merely based upon the apostolate but is identical with it. . . . The apostolate consists of this sharing in Jesus' own mission" (II/2:430–32). The same emphasis is made with regard to "the **election** of the individual"; Barth expounds this election with the term *witness*, which for him is always linked with the calling and sending of the church: "The promise of his election determines that as a member of the community he himself shall be a bearer of its witness to the whole world" (306). "If God elects a man, it is that he may be a witness to Jesus Christ, and therefore a proclaimer of His own glory" (449). The community of witnesses exists for one purpose: to carry out their corporate mission. The "active life" of the Christian, which is always understood within the context of the community, is defined by "the task of mission committed to the community. . . . The community is as such a missionary community or it is not the Christian community" (III/4:504–5). "The Being of the Community" is essentially its mission: "Its mission is not additional to its being. It is, as it is sent and active in its mission. It builds up itself for the sake of its mission and in relation to it. It does it seriously and actively as it is aware of its mission and in the *freedom* from itself which this gives" (IV/1:725).

In the final book of volume IV, Barth draws the missional thrust of his ecclesiology together in three major steps. He expands the classic interpretation of the doctrine of reconciliation by adding "vocation" as the indispensible third dimension, together with *"justification"* and *"sanctification"* ("The Event of Vocation" and "The Goal of Vocation"; IV/3.2:497–554). He then defines the Christian's identity as witness, linking that definition with a critique of the classic understanding of what it means to be a Christian as one who enjoys the benefits of the gospel. To counter that inward focus, he argues that calling, throughout the *Bible*, is always linked to God's salvific purposes for all *creation*, and never to the benefit that accrues to the one called (554–614). Finally, in §72, he expounds the "sending [mission!] of the community of the *Holy Spirit*," with particular focus on the "commission" (not "task"!) (705–830) and the "service" of the community (not "ministry"!) (830–901). Among the concrete forms of service (both "speech" and "action"), the exposition of "praise," "Gospel proclamation," and "instruction" stresses in diverse ways that the purpose is continuing formation of "a people of God capable of bearing witness to the world and actually bearing it by its very existence" (871). In the discussion of "evangelization" and

"mission" (872–78), the priority of mission throughout the dogmatic project is underlined again when Barth speaks of the "true and original sense" of mission "in which sending or sending out to the nations to attest the Gospel is the very root of the existence and therefore of the whole [service] of the community. In mission the Church sets off and goes . . . taking the essentially and most profoundly necessary step beyond itself. . . . The vocation which constitutes the community is directly the command to take this message to this world, to the nations or the 'heathen'" (874). In doing this, the full vocation of mission is not only to call people to the enjoyment of their *salvation*, but into God's service as members of Christ's missionary people: "When God does convert a man by His call, then he does, of course, come to personal salvation, but supremely and decisively he becomes a witness in the world. Hence the goal of the missionary work of the community must be to attest to the heathen the work and *Word of God* who, as He has created them by His call, wills to make them, too, His witnesses, and to equip them as such" (876).

Mission is thus for Barth the necessary corollary to the integrative emphasis upon the person and work of Jesus Christ as God's self-disclosure for the healing of creation. "Mission is objectively the expansion of the reality and truth of Jesus Christ. . . . mission is concretely the going forth of salvation and its manifestation beyond the confines of *Israel* to the nations; the step in which the Messiah of Israel shows Himself to be the Saviour of the world" (*CL*, 97).

J. Aagard, "Some Main Trends in Modern Protestant Missiology," *Studia theologica* 19 (1965): 238–59; D. Bosch, *Transforming Mission* (1991); J. G. Flett, *The Witness of God* (2010); K. Hartenstein, "Was hat die Theologie Karl Barths der Mission zu sagen?" *ZZ* 6 (1928): 59–83.

DARRELL L. GUDER

Natural Theology "Natural theology is the doctrine of a union of *humanity* with God existing outside God's *revelation* in *Jesus Christ*" (*CD* II/1:168). It is "a *theology* which grounds itself on a knowability of *God* distinct from the *grace* of God, i.e. , on a knowability of another God than Him knowable only in His grace" (143). It is "a *science* of God . . . constructed independently of all historical religions and religious bodies as a strict natural science like chemistry and astronomy 'without reference to or reliance upon any supposed special exceptional or so-called miraculous *revelation*'" (*KGSG*, 3). Barth argued in his famous debate with Emil **Brunner** (1934) that, strictly speaking, it is "every (positive *or* negative) *formulation of a system* which claims to be theological, *i.e.* to interpret divine revelation, whose *subject*, however, differs fundamentally from the revelation in Jesus Christ and whose *method* therefore differs equally from the exposition of Holy Scripture" (*NTh*, 74–75).

Barth's debate with Brunner over natural theology can hardly be understood apart from the issues surrounding its immediate context: *der Kirchenkampf*, the **Barmen Declaration**, the nazification of the Christian faith, the rise of "German Christianity," *orders of creation*, and so on. Yet Barth insisted its significance was far wider and its roots went far deeper. Indeed, he marks his own theological conversion from the time, "since about 1916," when he and others began to learn "to understand revelation as *grace* and grace as *revelation* and therefore turn away from all 'true' or 'false' *theologia naturalis*" (71). Brunner was not sympathetic to the "blood, race, and soil" theology of "German Christians" (who deemed his pamphlet *Nature and Grace* "a veritable gold-mine"), but it was for his statement, "It is the task of our theological generation to find the way back to a true *theologia naturalis*," that Barth claimed Brunner had aided and abetted them (70, 72–73) and betrayed the theology of the Reformation,

that is, a theology of the Word for this "other task of theology."

An "avowed opponent of natural theology" (*KGSG*, 6) throughout his career, Barth's most sustained critique of natural theology is in *CD* II/1:63–178, under the title, §26, "The Knowability of God," which he divides in two sections, "The Readiness of God" and "The Readiness of Man." His thesis is: true *knowledge of God* depends on the former, not the latter. In the former section, Barth defines his terms, provides an overview of natural theology, surveys its history, and analyzes all the major biblical passages cited as a basis for it. He concludes: "Holy Scripture neither imposes the necessity nor even offers the possibility of reckoning with a knowability of the God of the prophets and apostles which is not given in and with His revelation, or bound to it. . . . [It] does not present us with 'another' task of theology, nor are we allowed to impose it upon ourselves. . . . it is from Scripture that we now hear the very definite command not to" (125–26). "What amputations (open or secret) have to be undertaken to make the biblical text really say what has to be said to find a biblical basis for natural theology" (107).

Natural theology, Barth claims, is based on an illusion: "the presupposed independent existence of man as such," and that as such (i.e., fallen) humanity is not truly an enemy of grace but a friend. "It is a powerful, illuminating and (if we want to leave out Jesus Christ) unconquerable illusion" (165), but one that contradicts the fact that the *truth* about humanity is in Jesus Christ for whom "there is no independent man as such. Man as such is in Jesus Christ the man taken up and accepted by God in the war of grace against [man's] enmity against grace" (166). If natural theology is valid and its pursuit justified, then, "What the **Bible** calls death is only sickness. What it calls darkness is simply twilight. What it calls incapability is merely weakness. What it calls ignorance is only confusion. The grace which comes to man . . .

does not really come to lost sinners. . . .
a certain uprightness still persists in
corruption" (105). For all its "respect-
ability" and "naturalness," its "very
unassuming and modest entrance"
(137–38), its deference and humility before "special" revelation, and its claims
to be merely subordinate, preparatory,
or supplemental, natural theology is a
"Trojan horse" (173) that will sooner or
later seek to conquer revelation by "ab-
sorbing" and "domesticating" it. It "re-
casts revelation into a new form of its
own devising . . . making revelation into
non-revelation," and thereby "masters"
it (139–40). It tempts man as such to
"play the rich man" (130–31) and think
that he can discover his own need for
God or grace abstractly and can choose
revelation as his own possibility, which
is "the ecstasy of the Pharisee pretend-
ing to be a publican." But "the grace for
which we think we ourselves can decide
is not the grace of God in Jesus Christ.
The illusion that we can disillusion ourselves is the greatest of all illusions"
(169).

Barth sought to understand nature
in light of God instead of God in light
of nature, that is, a theology of nature
instead of natural theology, which his
four volumes on *The Doctrine of Creation*
exemplify. However, Barth never denied the existence of natural theology
or its vitality: it is the inevitable sphere
and necessary undertaking of human
"self-exposition and self-justification"
in which "Naturally man will attempt
to understand and confirm and defend
himself." Though false, "natural theology is the only comfort of the natural
man in life and death" (168–69). We
cannot deny him this comfort, but we
cannot confirm him in it either. Indeed,
"it cannot really be the business of a Reformed theologian to raise so much as
his little finger to support this undertaking in any positive way" (*KGSG*, 6).

Despite its one "advantage over the
teaching of the Reformation," namely,
"it has no need of prayer" [*sic*!] (*KGSG*,
244), natural theology "must be excised

without mercy" in the sphere of the
church (II/1:170). Yet the only way to
oppose it is to refrain from "wrestling
with it" directly or on its own grounds
(164–65), to treat it as something "already destroyed," and to give it only
"incidental and supplementary attention" as "a side issue" (otherwise we
would still participate in natural theology even if against it). With the time left
to us, which is the time of grace, we are
not to presume upon God's patience and
forbearance (Rom. 2:4; Acts 17:30) and
play around with *apologetics, vestigia
trinitatis*, arguments for God's existence,
and so on, or try to establish a theological *point of contact*. Rather, with "strict
realism," we are to give our undivided
attention to the one task of proclamation and theology of the *Word of God*
and thereby serve not two masters but
the only "one real Master," Jesus Christ.

K. Barth, *CD* II/1:§26; idem, *KGSG*, 3–12;
E. Brunner and K. Barth, *NTh*; G. S. Hendry, *Theology of Nature* (1980); T. F. Torrance, "Natural Theology in the Thought
of Karl Barth," in *Karl Barth* (1990), 136–59.
RICHARD E. BURNETT

Nature Nature is a distinct and separate reality that is posited, willed, and
preserved by *God* for the purpose of *covenant* relationship. It is the outward and
external expression of God's own inner
being and goodness (*CD* III/1:331) and
therefore reflects the goodness of God
in its created being. Nature has no independent existence apart from the covenant of *grace* that is its internal basis,
but exists in itself for the sake of becoming "the theatre of grace" (II/1:509; cf.
III/3:47–48) without itself becoming or
being commingled with grace. Yet since
there is no inherent capacity on the part
of human beings to understand the essence of nature as such, we cannot learn
the *truth* about nature from nature itself
(*natura docet*) as modern thought since
Descartes has maintained, but only from
God in the covenant of grace (III/1:356).

Hence, the ground of nature and of our ability to understand it derives from the being of God himself as made known in *Jesus Christ*. "Nature in itself and as such is able to convey this truth [of its reality] to us only because it is created by God and because the God who is its Creator Himself bears witness to us that this is so" (III/1:362). Only in the light of grace can nature be seen for what it really is in the goodness of its own relative *freedom* and autonomy and in absolute dependence on its Creator.

Human nature, too, cannot be understood according to a general cosmology or anthropology, but only in light of Jesus Christ, who in his divine-human unity reveals God's innermost essence as Father, Son, and *Holy Spirit* in the *humanity* in Jesus Christ who takes up the cause of human misery and suffering as God's very own (III/2:211). Human nature, therefore, must be understood essentially in terms of coexistence, coinherence, and reciprocity with God and others just as the being of God himself is a being for others (III/2:218). Human nature thus retains its essential relation to God and others that, even in the corruption of *sin*, cannot be destroyed (IV/1:492) or opposed to grace (III/2:224), though it remains incapable on its own of entering into or maintaining covenant relationship.

Properly conceived, nature as such does not have grace as a predicate or property of its existence. In itself and as such the activity of nature is its own, but nature is able to cooperate with grace to the extent that God authorizes and qualifies it to do so (III/3:110–11). For Barth, therefore, grace does not perfect nature by elevating or divinizing it nor does grace simply destroy nature or override its created capacities. Rather, grace works in, with, through, and over nature according to the supremacy of God's freedom and *love* that maintains the ontological distinction between nature and grace as God condescends to take on human nature in order to enable it to participate in God and cooperate with God's work of *salvation* according to its own created capacities (133).

H. Urs von Balthasar, *The Theology of Karl Barth*, trans. E. T. Oakes (1992), 267–325, 334–57, 381–85; E. Brunner and K. Barth, *NTh*; H. P. Santmire, *The Travail of Nature* (1985), 143–56.

MICHAEL T. DEMPSEY

Orders of Creation

As a type of theological *ethics*, the doctrine of "orders of *creation*" (*Schöpfungsordnungen*) holds that such basic structures of human life as the family and the *state* derive from the creative will of *God* and are therefore bearers of God's command. These essential forms of community constitute the "reality" (a favorite term) that Christian ethics must take into account.

Barth made use of a version of this concept in his 1928 lectures on *Ethics*. In these lectures Barth identifies four orders of creation in the context of which we seek to know and do God's will: work (or *culture*), marriage, the family, and our life with others as characterized by both equality and leadership. (State and *church* are also acknowledged as orders of God, but not orders of creation; they belong rather to the sphere of *reconciliation*.)

Later, Barth's antipathy toward *natural theology* led him to distance himself from this approach. In his treatment of "The Command of God the Creator" (*CD* III/4), Barth takes issue with Emil *Brunner*, whom he regards as the chief representative of the appeal to "orders of creation" in Christian ethics. In *Das Gebot und die Ordnungen* (1932; lit., "The Command and the Orders," which assumed the English title, *The Divine Imperative*), Brunner defines the orders as "those existing facts of human corporate life which lie at the root of all historical life as unalterable presuppositions, which, although their historical forms may vary, are unalterable in their fundamental structure, and, at the same time, relate and unite men to one another in a definite way" (Brunner, 210). These social structures—marriage and the family, the economic order, the state, and (in a sense) the empirical church—are the framework within which our life is lived. According to Brunner, we can infer the will of the Creator from these forms of social organization. An example of moral reasoning on this basis is Brunner's defense of monogamy on the grounds that "every human being is irrevocably the child of one man and one woman" and that genuine natural *love* is essentially monistic. Thus the "indissoluble trinity of husband, wife, and child" and the monistic character of love provide the objective basis of monogamous marriage (Brunner, 345, 347).

Barth finds Brunner's approach wanting. For one thing, "reality" is too complex and its meaning too obscure to serve as a reliable guide for ethics. More importantly, he challenges the legitimacy of proclaiming any such orders as *divine* commands. How can we make the leap from sociological indicative to divine imperative? The attempt to do so is a piece of natural theology, which does not lead to genuine *knowledge of God*. We cannot speak reliably and legitimately about God's command "when we lay aside His Word revealed in Jesus Christ and seek information on the subject from other sources" (III/4:21). Barth's third objection is that Brunner's approach is dualistic. It sets the will of God the Creator over against the will of God the Reconciler, and thus creates a "split in the one command of God" (37).

If orders of creation do not provide a basis for ethics, what is Barth's alternative? In addition to the uniqueness of each instance of God's commanding, there is also a *horizontal* or contextual element that persists from one ethical encounter to another. But where do we learn about this continuity? Barth insists: "We have reliable and legitimate information about this horizontal either by God's Word or not at all" (III/4:19). By this he means not a legalistic reading

of particular biblical texts but the basic structure of God's *revelation* in Christ.

The God who commands is the one who is revealed as Creator, Reconciler, and Redeemer. "Wherever and whenever the command of God encounters a man, it is always determined by the fact that He is this God" (III/4:25). Likewise, the hearer of the command is the human being who corresponds to this threefold divine work—God's *creature*, created to be God's *covenant* partner; the *sinner* to whom God is gracious; and the *child* of God who awaits the fulfillment of the promise as the heir of the *kingdom of God*. So creation, reconciliation, and redemption are the spheres to which theological ethics must look for guidance in preparing to hear God's command. This history discloses the fundamental situation in which human beings act.

In the sphere of creation, we take our bearings from the relationship between God the Creator and the human creature as known to us in the *incarnation*. Based on the christological understanding of human nature set forth in III/2, Barth lays out four lines of inquiry for the ethics of creation: *freedom* for God, freedom in fellowship, freedom for life, and freedom within limitations.

In spite of his insistence that ethics must be based solely on the *Word of God* in Jesus Christ, Barth's discussion of the ethics of creation still exhibits traces of "orders" thinking, as when he classifies the man-woman and parent-child relationships as two "circles of natural fellow-humanity" in contrast to one's relation to one's people or nation, which is too fluid to be considered "natural and necessary" (III/4:299).

Perhaps the most dubious aspect of Barth's attempt to derive ethics from theology is his use of analogies, as when he argues for monogamy because God's *election* of *Israel* is a covenant of one God with one people, or when he states that procreation is no longer a requirement in marriage because Christ has come. Such biblical analogies seem too arbitrary to give solid ethical guidance.

Most of the time, however, Barth combines his biblical-theological insights with broadly pragmatic appeals to human experience. His case against capital punishment, for example, cites the crucifixion but also argues that the death penalty is not necessary for protecting society and that it makes rehabilitation impossible. He claims that such secondary considerations are theologically legitimate because they are backed up by God's command. Just how that is the case is not made clear.

E. Brunner, *The Divine Imperative*, trans. O. Wyon (1937); C. Link, *Schöpfung* (1991); P. T. Nimmo, "The Orders of Creation in the Theological Ethics of Karl Barth," *SJT* 60, no. 1 (2007): 24–35; R. Palmer, "Karl Barth and the Orders of Creation" (PhD diss., University of Iowa, 1966).

RUSSELL W. PALMER

Pastoral Care Barth sets his discussion of pastoral care, or as he prefers to call it, "the cure of souls," within the larger framework of the doctrine of *reconciliation* at the point where he reflects on *Jesus Christ*, the true *witness* (*CD* IV/3.2). The immediate context of the discussion on pastoral care is the section on the *ministry* of the community as a consequence of the *Holy Spirit* and the sending of the community into the *world* (§72).

This immediate context for Barth's discussion of pastoral care has a threefold structure: the theological boundaries within which the ministry of the community is rightly understood, the characteristics or nature of ministry in general terms, and finally the multiple forms in which this ministry is acted out in the world. Pastoral care, as a specific form of ministry, one among twelve that Barth discusses, is set within this threefold structure.

First, Barth discusses the theological boundaries of the ministry of the community, identifying a threefold structure: the ministry of the community is

definite, limited, but also full of promise. The ministry of the community is definite because as the community of Jesus Christ it exists for the world. The task is to witness to Jesus Christ, the *Word of God*, to the world. He is its content. As such, the ministry of the community is a *witness* to *God* and a witness to humankind. Further, the ministry of the community is limited because its task is to bear witness, trusting in God to bring forth the fruit. The great acts of redemption are not its task, and the community must at all points avoid taking on for itself the place of Jesus Christ. The reconciliation of the world to God, the *covenant*, the *kingdom of God*, and the new life for the world are not the work of the community. Its work is no more than but no less than witness to Jesus Christ. Finally, this ministry stands under the free promise of God, fulfilled in Jesus Christ, which can only be received as gift. Pastoral care, then, is set within these boundaries.

Second, Barth discusses the nature or the elements of the ministry of the community. He suggests three: declaration or proclamation, exposition or explication, and address or application. To begin with, the ministry of witness is a declaration of the gospel. As such, the community has the responsibility, no more but also no less, than to utter the gospel in the world. Further, this entails explaining and unfolding the gospel so that it is intelligible. The gospel gives itself to be known. The community cannot create this knowledge for others, but it offers its articulation of the gospel, leaving it to God whether, or how far, it is known by the world. Finally, Barth notes that in all its forms the ministry of the community is evangelical address by which people are claimed for the gospel. An appeal is made, a summons is announced.

It is now in this twofold context of theological boundaries and an awareness of the elements of ministry in general that Barth turns to the various tasks of ministry. These various tasks involve both speech and action. Barth identifies twelve ministries: praise of God, *preaching*, instruction, evangelism, *mission*, *theology*, *prayer*, cure of souls, *Christian life*, the rendering of service, social witness, and fellowship.

As a general point, pastoral care is a ministry of the community that is definite insofar as it exists to bear witness to the world concerning Jesus Christ, it has no other task alongside that, and it goes about its work trusting in the promise of God as a *hope* in which the community has trust. Further, pastoral care as a ministry of the community is characterized by kerygmatic, interpretive, and evangelical elements.

In particular, pastoral care is a ministry of the community to individuals by which it bears witness to Jesus Christ both within itself and to the wider world. As cure of souls it is concern for the individual in his or her wholeness in the light of God's purpose for him or her (Barth interpreting the soul as the person in his or her individual existence), of the divine promise and act on his or her behalf, and of the witness to the gospel that is demanded of everyone. It is a ministry person to person. While this is a ministry of the whole community, some are specifically gifted and called to this work. The focus of pastoral care in particular is to show people that the kingdom has drawn near for them. This is a concrete actualization whereby the person ministering holds the gospel of Jesus before another with his or her particular burdens and afflictions in view. This ministry may announce the promise of remission of sins, issue the call to amendment of life, and summon the person to be a hearer of the Word of God in order to fulfill the purpose of life as a witness to Jesus Christ.

Clearly, for Barth, the goal of pastoral care is not mental health as such, but the ministry of the community at this point is encouraged to use various forms of psychology and psychotherapy, though in such a way that pastoral care proper begins where psychology and its healings cease.

In summary, Barth understands pastoral care, as also every form of ministry, to be a modest and restricted function, in which the community is clear about what its task is, aware that everything depends upon God. In this way there is no fear that over and against the healing arts it might become a superfluous religious duplication. In closing, Barth notes that the sketch of the cure of souls properly leads into reflection on the Christian life and action for the reason that the goal of pastoral care is the summons to a person to bear witness to the gospel of Jesus Christ.

———

D. Hunsinger, "Becoming Bilingual" (PhD diss., Union Theological Seminary, 1993); idem, *Theology and Pastoral Counseling* (1995); A. Purves, *Reconstructing Pastoral Theology* (2004); E. Thurneysen, *A Theology of Pastoral Care*, trans. J. Worthington and T. Wieser (1962).

ANDREW PURVES

Perfections of God   To know *God*, for Barth, is to know his perfections: "there is no possibility of knowing the perfect God without knowing his perfections" (CD II/1:322). The doctrine of the divine perfections plays not only a crucial role in Barth's doctrine of God but also in his *theology* as a whole, for to speak of who and what God is, is to speak with reference to God's perfections. Ascertaining the character and shape of God's perfections is, of course, a task that must be undertaken in closest connection to *revelation*. Indeed, it is because of revelation's claims that Barth is compelled to describe God's attributes as perfections, precisely because the term *perfections* "points at once to the thing itself," namely, that the perfections are indeed ingredient in God himself (322). Thus an account of the perfections of God is not a gloss upon the character of human knowledge of a supreme being, or, of human religious experience, but rather, a series of identity descriptions that indicate who God is.

Right from the start, then, Barth emphasizes that the perfections of God belong to the one God: God "is who He is and what He is in both unity and multiplicity" (323). This is Barth's way of *resolving* the historical shape of the problem—that is, nominalism and expressivism—as it pertains to the classical doctrine of the divine attributes. The pitfall of the former—and this is a shortcoming that Barth attributes to both Thomistic and Protestant Orthodox treatments of the divine attributes—is that it suggests that human ideas and descriptions have no corresponding reality in God. Hence the many attributes that one ascribes to God on the basis of revelation are best described as accommodations to the limited and finite character of human knowing, precisely because the simple God cannot also be many. Barth's criticism of such an understanding is that it determines in advance—apart from revelation—that God's oneness excludes multiplicity. By contrast, Barth describes God as both simple *and* multiple. The one God is his many perfections because who he is—his being—includes a multiplicity of perfections. The historical shape of the problem is also found in the so-called expressivist approach, an approach that Barth attributes to *Schleiermacher*. Expressivism treats the divine attributes as "an objectification of the individual aspects of the religious self-consciousness," with the result that the attributes function as delineations of one's religious consciousness as it intuits the divine (338). Quite the opposite for Barth: the attributes are proper to the God who makes himself known as he is and, in turn, makes it possible for the human to participate in his self-knowledge.

The dogmatic home for Barth's doctrine of the divine perfections is his doctrine of God's being. Because the perfections as perfections are proper to God's being, there is an appropriate order to the treatment of the perfections in terms of perfections of *love* and perfections of *freedom*. That is, the divine reality itself evokes an ordering to which the account of the perfections must correspond. The perfections that are within the sphere of the divine love—the doctrine of the perfections first concern—bespeak the communicative reality of the divine being: that God, in the love that God is, wills to be himself for us; whereas the perfections of the divine freedom witness to the fact that God in his self-giving remains himself. Thus Barth's treatment of the perfections adheres to the sequence unfolded in revelation, and thus to the necessity of a duality in the distribution of the perfections along the lines of love and freedom. In so doing, Barth overturns the shape of the distinctions prevalent in classical treatments by ruling out the idea that metaphysical perfections, such as *eternity* or omnipotence, are more real to the life of God than those perfections that indicate God's relation to humankind in the economy of *grace*, perfections such as grace and patience.

Among the perfections of the divine love, Barth treats six in particular: grace and holiness, mercy and righteousness, patience and wisdom. Throughout his treatment, Barth is at pains to discount any notion that these perfections could somehow be isolated from God's being. For example, in describing grace and holiness, Barth is describing the grace and holiness of the being of God—grace and holiness as determinants of God's being. "Grace denotes, comprehensively, the manner in which God, in His essential being, turns toward us" (353). And only because God is grace *in se*, God is free to turn toward the creature, to overcome her resistance. For this reason, holiness, which stands opposite to God's grace in Barth's treatment, is not itself a new theme. Holiness is the condemnation, exclusion, and annihilation of all contradiction and resistance to God's will that his turning—his grace—effects. Holiness, understood as God's salutary turn to the creature, reflects a turn in which God remains true to himself and makes his own will prevail. "God is holy because His grace judges and His judgment is gracious" (363).

Mercy attests God to be one who espouses the creature's cause and thereby relieves her distress. But God does not act in such a way because God is compelled to do so by the creature: God is self-moved. God in his mercy freely accepts our distress and takes our place. Indeed, the effectual compassion displayed in the economy of grace is the very revelation of God's disposition and heart. Commensurate with God's mercy is God's righteousness. God's righteousness attests that God wills and establishes what corresponds to his own worth, that God does what befits himself and is worthy of himself. For this reason, God judges, condemns, and punishes *sin*, for God's judgment and pardon of sin are the very operation of his mercy.

God's patience and wisdom are further denominators of God's love, the love that is the very content of God's being. For Barth, God's love bears, in an essential sense, the character of patience: patience because God maintains what God has created in order that it may continue to live. Holy Scripture testifies to God's patience as the Word of his power by which he upholds all things. And to uphold the creature is to be jealous for the creature; God's patience cannot be said to leave the creature to its own devices. Such patience bespeaks God's wisdom: God's whole being and all God's doings have *truth*, order, beauty, meaning, purpose, and *reason*, grounding the sphere in which the human can live.

Following Barth's treatment of the perfections of God's love is his treatment of the perfections of God's freedom. The six perfections of God's freedom, as is the case with the perfections of his love, are paired with one another so that one perfection cannot be said to exist without another: unity *and* omnipresence,

constancy *and* omnipotence, eternity *and* glory. It is important to note that Barth does not suggest that these descriptions—or any other descriptions, for that matter—are exhaustive. Rather, they can claim only the character "of an attempt or suggestion" (442). This is because Barth's account of the perfections of God's freedom, like those of his love, is an attempt to follow after the object—the triune God—in his self-manifestation. The perfections of the divine freedom attend to the God who is himself in his work: "He is constant and eternal in Himself and in all His works. This is His freedom" (440).

The perfection of God's unity simply affirms that there is no God beside God: that in all God is and does, God is wholly and undividedly himself. If such is the case, God's omnipresence is not to be equated with a general understanding of presence. God is present everywhere (secondarily) because and as he is present (primarily) in Jesus; God's primary presence in Jesus is the starting point for an account of his secondary presence in the Word. The human nature of Christ, in its unity with the deity of the Son, is the reality of the divine space by which all other spaces are created, preserved, and encompassed. Barth's christologically informed account of omnipresence is indicative of how he handles the so-called metaphysical attributes in general. God's omnipresence is not that of a supreme being, but rather that of one whose general presence in *creation* in its totality is determined by his special presence in his work of revelation and *reconciliation* in *Jesus Christ*.

God is constant and omnipotent: constant because God is not subject to alteration; constant because God cannot turn against himself or contradict himself. That is not to say, however, that God is immobile. God is so very free in relation to the *world* that he allows himself to be conditioned and limited by the world. Even when God becomes and is one with the creature in Jesus Christ, God is constant. God's constancy coexists with his omnipotence—God's "power to be himself" (522). Such power is real power because it is God's power. God, as a person, is both knowledge and will and is as such free, superior in relation to all the objects distinct from himself. God is omnipotent, in turn, because he is not conditioned by the creature's freedom or misuse of her freedom: the creator/creature relationship, for Barth, cannot be inverted. Rather, God establishes the creature, even in the misuse of her freedom, by grace. This is God's active omnipotence that meets us as decision "in his omnipotent Word by which he created, governs and upholds the world" (605). Hence knowledge of the omnipotent knowing and willing of God is always normed by *Christology*, by the knowledge of the crucified one, for Barth.

The last set of perfections treated under the auspices of God's freedom is that of God's eternity and glory. This last section is arguably the most important in Barth's treatment in *CD* II/1, in that Barth delineates the content of the perfection that is, for him, the chief perfection and the perfection that sums up all others—the divine glory. But before Barth expounds God's glory he offers a brief treatment of the perfection of God's eternity. Eternity, as with the other perfections of God's love and freedom, denotes the extent to which God gives his very own self to the creature, the extent to which God exists in an act of self-giving that encompasses the creature. More specifically, eternity, as a description of the being of God, attests that God is eternal in the manner that God has his being. In this sense, then, eternity is not, in contradistinction to the metaphysical tradition, the infinite duration of *time* or the absence of time. Eternity, rather, is "the unique time of the triune God. It is the time of God's self-identity, self-differentiation, and self-unification, . . . the time of the divine life in freedom" (199). Eternity describes the manner in which God has time for us, the manner in which God's *perichoresis* includes time

and temporality within itself as the basis for the fellowship of eternity and time with one another in Jesus Christ.

God's glory, as "the self-revealing sum of all divine perfections," attests God's freedom to love the lost creature as God is in himself; glory is the particular freedom of the triune God to be related in love—to coexist—with creaturely reality (644, 645). The perfection of God's glory, at its most basic, is reiterative of God's divinity: God maintains his identity as the glorious one in his self-declaration. God's glory, in turn, is not his distance, but rather that God comes low as the very one he is. What Barth does, then, in his treatment of the "sum" of the perfections, is to redescribe the central theme that God does not keep the fellowship in which he exists to himself. What Barth also does in his treatment of the sum of the perfections is to account for the mode of human action effected by the revelation of God's own perfections. The disclosure of God's glory, as with the other perfections, involves the human *covenant* partner. That is, God draws the human up into his self-glorification. More specifically, God draws the human to himself by virtue of his beauty, beauty that invites and engenders a response. God's beauty accounts for what makes God an object worthy to be loved. In fact, Barth also incorporates the notion of beauty to indicate the efficacy of the divine glory: the divine glory "is effective because and as it is beautiful" (652). Beauty, then, as an identity description, simply points to God as one who does not overwhelm the creature with power, but rather attracts the creature to himself and convinces the creature of the veracity of his self-revelation by virtue of the splendor that he is. Barth's treatment of beauty, as a further specification of God's glory, also shows how deeply invested Barth is in providing an account of the affective response that arises from God's self-declaration. Because revelation concerns *God*, it concerns the creature too.

God wills that the human participate in his self-glorification, the glorification of the Father through the Son by the power of the Spirit: "It belongs to the essence of the glory of God not to be *gloria* alone but to become glorification" (661). To correspond to God's glory is to glorify God. This is the form of existence appropriate to the covenant partner as the beloved child of God; for the disclosure of God's glory generates human subjects who correspond to it, subjects who glorify God. Thus Barth's account of glory commends a way of creaturely existence commensurate with the object itself, namely the praise of God through the exaltation of *humanity* that has taken place in his only begotten Son.

In sum: Barth's account of the perfections forms a critical part of his doctrine of God and of his theology as a whole, because it is an account that concerns one with God, with the God who does not hold anything back, but rather encounters the human in the economy of grace as he is, making her into a fit *witness* and correspondent to what has been revealed. The perfections, for Barth, are indeed perfections of *God*. They are ingredient in God's being, and thus serve as descriptions which undertake the particular theological work of telling one what God is like, and who God declares himself to be.

C. R. J. Holmes, *Revisiting the Doctrine of the Divine Attributes* (2007); idem, "The Theological Function of the Doctrine of the Divine Attributes and the Divine Glory, with Special Reference to Karl Barth and His Reading of the Protestant Orthodox," *SJT* 61 (May 2008): 206–23; E. Jüngel, "Theses on the Existence, Essence, and Attributes of God," trans. P. G. Ziegler, *TJT* 17 (Summer 2001): 55–74; R. B. Price, *Letters of the Divine Word* (2011).

CHRISTOPHER R. J. HOLMES

Philosophy   Among twentieth-century theologians, Barth stands out

for his opposition to mixing *theology* and philosophy. During a symposium at the University of Chicago in 1962, for example, Barth responded to an inquiry from Schubert Ogden about whether theologians might depend on philosophy by emphasizing its distinctiveness. "The work of a theologian is of necessity and by nature independent from that of a philosopher. I wonder, Mr. Ogden, how you came to ask that question, because from the very beginning of my theological work it was my primary intention, or one of my primary intentions, to procure *freedom* and independence for theology over against philosophy" (*G-1959–1962*, 460–61). What Barth intended to separate, scholars of Barth have brought back together again. Since the 1980s monographs have appeared on the relation between Barth and a host of philosophers, including Derrida, Heidegger, Husserl, James, Kierkegaard, Wittgenstein, to name a few. Barth himself penned independent studies on the philosophy of Rousseau, Lessing, Kant, and Hegel and discoursed about philosophers from Descartes to Sartre in the *CD*. Obviously, there is more to Barth's position than a theological declaration of independence from philosophy—as he admitted in that Chicago symposium.

Barth came of age during an intellectual period in which theologians and philosophers regularly engaged in dialogue. The stringent philosophical judgments against the sense (or senselessness) of theological propositions put forward by the Vienna Circle and later by analytical philosophers such as A. J. Ayer had not yet strained the relation between philosophers and theologians. Barth developed his ideas during the age of philosophical systems, which flowered before the First World War. For philosophers of this period, being systematic required finding a suitable place for **God** and *religion* within one's philosophical system. Theologians, while appropriating aspects of philosophical systems, sought to distinguish theological knowledge from philosophical speculation. In his emphasis on the independence of theology and philosophy, Barth could look back to his liberal teachers, including Friedrich *Schleiermacher* and Wilhelm *Herrmann*. From the beginning, Barth refused to make theology into a structural component of a philosophical worldview.

The most significant philosophical influence on Barth during his formative years was a school of Neo-Kantians associated with the University of Marburg, where Barth himself studied from 1908 to 1909. The major philosophers of the Marburg School were Hermann Cohen and Paul Natorp; Barth's younger brother, the philosopher Heinrich Barth, also adhered to this school. In his earliest work, Barth attempted to put theology into dialogue with the philosophy of this school, seeking a way to incorporate a realistic *revelation* into their idealistic scheme. In *Rom* II (1922) Barth made more direct use of philosophical elements from the Marburg School. Strikingly, he appealed to Cohen's idea of the *Ursprung*, or originary source, as a philosophical synonym for God. More lastingly, he embraced the Marburg School's rejection of historicism and psychologism—the objective *truth* about God and *humanity* cannot be discerned by the study of historical or psychological processes. In subsequent work, Barth distanced himself from Neo-Kantianism, though opponents like Cornelius Van Til charged that his mature work continued to be founded on the "Critical" philosophy of Kant.

In 1929 Barth argued in "Fate and Idea in Theology" that a structural parallelism exists between philosophy and theology. Philosophical schools, he contended, may be classified by their tendency toward realism (i.e., "fate") or idealism (i.e., "idea"). In like manner, this "basic problem of all philosophy" ("F&I," 32) also shapes theology. Theologians either begin with the givenness of God, that is, God's presence in the created universe, or with the nongivenness of God, that is, God's critical distance from the *creation*. The primary difference between the disciplines is that philosophy strives to overcome the dialectic between realism and idealism by seeking an encompassing synthesis whereas theology foregoes any reconciliation of opposites by confessing the *freedom* of God's Word. Barth's theology has been described as "critically realistic" (see McCormack) because of his insistence on the dialectic between the givenness and nongivenness of God's Word.

Barth faced new philosophical challenges in the period between the wars. On the one hand, he engaged in debate with the philosopher Heinrich Scholz, who mediated to him a form of the linguistic philosophy developed by the Vienna Circle and other scientifically minded philosophers. Scholz criticized Barth's use of the dialectic, arguing that putting forward two contradictory propositions is equivalent to failing to assert anything. Scholz also challenged him to demonstrate the empirical "controllability" of theological propositions. Barth responded negatively to these challenges in the first volume of the *CD*, declaring these demands "unacceptable" (I/1:9). Wolfhart Pannenberg, Harry Kuitert, and Wentzel van Huyssteen have subsequently explored the debate between Barth and Scholz.

On the other hand, Barth resisted the influence of existentialism on theology. He himself explored the nascent possibilities of existentialism in the *Epistle to the Romans* and participated in the Kierkegaard renaissance of the 1920s. By the 1940s, however, Barth emerged as a primary opponent of the movement to combine existentialism and theology. In particular, Barth repudiated Rudolf Bultmann's project of basing theology on Martin Heidegger's "fundamental ontology." He regarded *Bultmann* as returning to the philosophical anthropology that was the hallmark of nineteenth-century *liberalism*.

In a Festschrift published in 1960 for his brother Heinrich, Barth wrote a valedictory essay on the topic of philosophy and theology ("Philosophy"). The philosopher and the theologian both confront the same *truth*, though from different perspectives and with distinct methods and orders of priority. Barth denied that philosophy and theology could be unified as a *philosophia christiana*—the disciplines must always remain opposed—but not that theologians could learn from philosophers and vice versa.

Barth presupposed that philosophy was systematic and system building. His reputation for disregarding philosophy came from his refusal to adopt philosophical underpinnings or to subscribe to a worldview. However, Barth was not against logical reasoning or conceptual clarification; his Anselmian project of "*faith* seeking understanding" invites the analysis of *reason* in theology and leaves the door open for fruitful dialogue between philosophers and theologians, especially in the present climate of wariness toward philosophical systems.

K. Barth, *F&I*; idem, *G-1959–1962*, 231–79; idem, "Philosophy"; B. L. McCormack, *Karl Barth's Critically Realistic Dialectical Theology* (1995).

CLIFFORD B. ANDERSON

Pietism

Throughout his long life as a theologian, Barth dealt often with pietism. At times he did so critically, but he was also open to its actions and intentions. The concept of pietism refers to the varied movement in the eighteenth century, the revival movement in the nineteenth century, and the community movement of the twentieth century that took place mainly in the German-speaking areas of Europe. When Barth summarized these manifestations of "pietism," it was based on his conviction that in spite of all their differences a common bond united them.

It is interesting to see how much Barth dealt with pietism in his later years. In those years he acknowledged that pietism claims a legitimate concern, which needs to be taken up by *theology* if it seeks to think ecclesiologically. This concern has to do with the acknowledgment of the very important concepts of *sanctification*, revival, conversion, rebirth, and discipleship. Barth's positive reception of pietism's concern is expressed in his explanation of the sanctifying work of *Jesus Christ* found within the framework of his doctrine of *reconciliation* (CD IV/2). The move in this direction came about because of Barth's increased focus on the figure of Jesus Christ. He thus moved closer to the theology of Zinzendorf, whom he now called the most "genuine Christocentric man of the modern age" (IV/1:683). This was indeed true, though other pietists rejected Zinzendorf.

Even stronger than Zinzendorf, Barth emphasized that when we say Jesus Christ, we say true *God and* true man. In him does God not only make himself available to *humanity*, but humans are set free to rise up in fellowship with him. In Christ God not only justifies the sinner, but also sanctifies him and awakens him to repentance in order to follow Christ, to do good works, and to bear the cross. This is what Barth presents in IV/2:511–613 as he now shows his agreement with the pietists' concern (IV/2:x). The following quotations clearly show the extent of this agreement: "If we believe in God in the sense of the Church we believe in an awakening of man to conversion. We count on the fact that there is such a thing. No, we count on the fact that God Himself gives and creates and actualizes it" (558). This is not "a question of improvement, but . . . about a new life. The change therefore is called turning around—we cannot avoid the loaded word: *conversion*" (560, rev.). Sanctified by Christ, the sanctification of Christians is a "real alteration of their being" (529), so that by it they *are* indeed "differentiated from the world" (524).

Barth also remarks however that this did not make him a pietist (x). He is critical of pietists and says that it is possible to speak in a biblical way about repentance, sanctification, and revival without becoming a pietist. Taking up the pietists' concern, he still talks about it in a *different* way. I mention two points.

First, the new humanity is clearly nothing within us but is given to us in Christ and his work, which he has done "in our place, for us" (516, rev.). To say it with Paul: "Christ Jesus, who became for us . . . sanctification" (1 Cor. 1:30), and we "are sanctified in Christ Jesus" (1 Cor. 1:2; cf. John 17:19; Phil. 1:1; Heb. 10:10). Our sanctification *consists* solely in our participation by *faith* in our already real sanctification in Christ. As street reflectors light up at night when they are struck by light, so we are new people as we are focused on Christ by faith. The reality of our sanctification is outside of us (*extra nos*) and the more decisively we focus on Jesus Christ by faith, the more clearly we participate in it. As we participate in Christ's sanctification we merely acknowledge again that which in him is already true for all humankind.

Second, God's holiness is determined by his *covenant* will: "I will be your God, and you shall be my people" (499; see Jer. 7:23; 31:33; Ezek. 36:28). The understanding of holiness as separation from others is thereby destroyed. God's holiness includes the *freedom* to "go beyond" itself in order to be united with those who are unholy. This is God's holiness that he, "although being so different (from the world), is turned toward it" (511, rev.). Therefore our participation in the sanctification completed in Christ will consist in no longer belonging and listening to the world but in being turned toward it.

At the end of his life, Barth took a further step toward pietism. He was hoping for an emerging "theology of the *Holy Spirit*," which would confess Christ through the awakening and all-renewing power of the Holy Spirit. He held on to this *hope* "for the benefit of the pietists" so that their old concern in its fullness would illuminate the *church* in a new way, not as the truths about humanity circling around itself but as the truths about the Holy Spirit who takes hold of us ("Postscript," rev., 278–79). At the end of 1967, he said: "What we really need today is a new kind of pietism," which emerges in an inwardly renewed form, but in such a way that it asserts itself as the concern of a new Pentecost (B-1961–1968, 488).

Barth had this expectation just as old Moses did when he looked for the promised land. But he did not see it fulfilled in the appearing of the fundamentalist "confessing movement." This he saw as a reactionary relapse into the nineteenth century because he saw it sharing the same presuppositions of thought that it accused its "enemies" of having (G-1964–1968, 212–15). In both cases the same alarming presupposition is made that the reality confessed in the gospel is put into the hands of Christians. At this point the old pietistic opinion takes revenge when it implies that the reality of Jesus Christ will become valid only as we apply it to our lives. The validity of this reality then becomes dependent upon how we deal with it. The confessing movement is the offspring of the *very* spirit against which it wanted to fight.

But consideration must be given to the pietistic language by which Barth shared his concern regarding these issues: "We do not have to take care of God but he takes care of us. In every respect, we must rely on this and calmly live our lives in this assurance: . . . He takes care that his truth will not fall underneath the table but will remain on the table." Much rather we should "put our trust in the Holy Spirit, who has always seen to it that the truth remains the truth, regardless of what humans might say against it." "Nothing can prevail against the Holy Spirit. . . . What I said against the confessing movement I would like to . . . paraphrase with the [sentence]: A servant does not make noise. The confessing movement is a noisy movement. . . . But nothing can be done here with noise. . . . The Holy Spirit does not blow in mass meetings but . . . it blows in a quiet, I almost said, in a humble but very sure way. Whoever knows a little bit about rebirth and the new life . . . will be sure about this matter." And one therefore does not have to argue and continually emphasize to others that *he* is the one who has the correct confession, but he will, in the Spirit and power, demonstrate that the confession has him (423–26). Basically, Barth does not speak against pietism here, but he is thinking from the foundation he is standing on, which is the Holy Spirit and rebirth. It is from this perspective that he expects pietism to be able to live out its faith more convincingly. This would then be "a kind of new pietism."

E. Busch, *Karl Barth and the Pietists*, trans. D. Bloesch (2004); idem, *Karl Barth und der Pietismus* (1987); W. Knappe, "Karl Barth und der Pietismus," *Licht und Leben* 39 (1927): 499–501, 515–18; C. T. G. Winn, *"Jesus Is Victor!"*(2009).

EBERHARD BUSCH

Point of Contact As a natural capacity for **God, revelation**, or **faith** inherent in fallen **humanity**, Barth rejected the notion of a point of contact (*Anküpfungspunkt*) as inimical to the **gospel**. In his debate over **natural theology** with Barth (1934), Emil **Brunner** claimed there is "in man a point of contact for the divine message which is not disturbed by **sin**." Brunner did not identify it with an *analogia entis*, which Barth deemed an "invention of the Antichrist" (*CD* I/1:xiii) nor with human rationality as such, neither with certain "*orders of creation*" with the racial implications extrapolated by "German Christians" whom Barth accused Brunner of aiding and abetting. Rather Brunner identified it with a merely "formal" likeness to God, which because of "preserving

grace" remained "undestroyed" by the fall: "the fact that man is man" and as such is responsible, has a conscience, a "capacity for words" (*Wortmächtigkeit*), and thus the "possibility of being addressed." Barth agreed, "man is man and not a cat" even after the fall and is not as bad off as he could be, but is this all Brunner meant by "general" or "preserving grace"? And, "If a man had just been saved from drowning by a competent swimmer, would it not be very unsuitable if he proclaimed the fact that he was a man and not a lump of lead as his 'capacity for being saved'?" What would be the point of asserting such a capacity "unless he could claim to have helped the man who saved him by a few strokes?"

Brunner's merely "formal" point of contact, Barth claimed, had significant material (positive) content. However "confused and distorted," Brunner asserted that "what the natural man knows of God, of the law, and of his own dependence on God" is "the necessary, indispensable point of contact for divine **grace**." "Perhaps," Barth asked, despite all his denials, Brunner's drowning man "can swim a little, after all?" Barth insisted such a point of contact contradicts evangelical faith, which depends on grace alone (*sola gratia*) through **Jesus Christ** alone (*solus Christus*) as attested by Scripture alone (*sola scriptura*). The **Bible** speaks of no such point of contact or "capacity for revelation." "Where in Galatians 2 or I Corinthians 2 has Brunner found anything of the sort?" Rather the Bible speaks not of any human "capacity for revelation," but of "incapacity," not of "contact," but of "repulsion," not of "repair" of the old nature but of "rebirth" based on the miracle of a "new **creation**." Barth affirmed John **Calvin**'s claim that Romans 1 speaks not of a natural capacity or **knowledge of God** that humans have retained after the fall; and such natural knowledge they now have, unless idolatry serves as preparation for the gospel, certainly does not serve as a point of contact for true knowledge of God. For Calvin, "real knowledge by natural man of the true God, derived from creation, is," because of the fall, "a possibility in principle, not in fact." Nor does Acts 17 warrant appeal to any theological point of contact, as Barth later elaborated (II/1:122–23). In short, revelation, like faith, is a divine, not a human, possibility. It is a gift not dependent on any human capacity, potential, or aptitude. Brunner's rejection of the virgin birth, Barth said, betrayed Brunner's need of a point of contact and his misunderstanding of revelation, which is always a miracle, a matter of grace not to be confused with *nature* (I/2:180ff.).

Brunner stated, "It is the task of our theological generation to find the way back to a true *theologia naturalis*" (*NTh*, 59). Barth responded: "Ever since about 1916," he had thought it was his generation's task to "learn again to understand revelation as *grace* and grace as *revelation*" (71). Still, Barth acknowledged he too had been tempted by natural theology in the more "dangerous form" of a negative point of contact and had, in certain passages of his *Römerbrief*, perhaps succumbed to it: knowledge of God based on rational self-examination of one's existential condition apart from God, that is, grief or despair identified as God's wrath. Brunner had earlier articulated such a negative point of contact, as had Kierkegaard and Heidegger (114). But Barth rejected it because it still portrayed revelation as a human possibility. Only grace can teach us that we are sinners, not nature. Only "godly grief produces a repentance," whereas "worldly grief produces death" (2 Cor. 7:10); and God's wrath can be truly understood only as *God's* wrath. Moreover, "to sit in judgment on human existence, to inform oneself concerning oneself, to know oneself to be punished with despair" (121) from oneself, Barth said, is still to be, "even all the more, my own lord and master" (119). This is why such a point of contact is so dangerous. The *"truth"* I discover about myself independently,

the "throne" I mount in the *freedom* and power of my own will "to see through all gods and to unmask them as idols," is "the worst of all idols." "Has there ever been a more explicit Prometheanism than that of the *philosophy* of an existence despairing of itself?" Barth said: "According to Calvin, true knowledge of the self in real humility cannot precede the knowledge of God, it must follow the latter" (119–20).

Barth rejected the notion of a theological point of contact as "incompatible with the third article of the creed. The *Holy Spirit*," he said, "does not stand in need of any point of contact but that which he himself creates" (121). The *Word of God* or "revelation itself creates of itself the necessary point of contact in man" (I/1:29). Barth affirmed "common ground" between believers and unbelievers (IV/3.2:681–762), and the necessity of translating the gospel, so long as the What (the content) determines the How (the method), not vice versa. But, however well intended the missionary (875) or "pedagogic and pastoral" concern "to reach people where they are" (*CL*, 139), Barth opposed the establishment of a theological point of contact as injurious to both truth and love (II/1:88ff.). Besides, he said, "I have the impression that my sermons reach and 'interest' my audience most when I least rely on anything to 'correspond' to the Word of God already 'being there'" or "on my ability to 'reach' people," but *"allow* my *language* to be formed . . . as much as possible by what the text seems to be saying" (*NTh*, 127).

Brunner claimed Barth later changed his mind on the issue, but Barth concluded a letter of August 6, 1966, to Ingeborg Heitmann, who had inquired about it: "[God] posits the necessary point of contact . . . making the deaf to hear and the blind to see. That's the way it is" (*L61–68*, 217).

K. Barth, *CD* I/1:27–30, 236–39; I/2:263–64; II/1:§26; IV/3.2:494–96; E. Brunner, "The New Barth" (trans. J. C. Campbell),

SJT 4 (1951): 123–35; E. Brunner and K. Barth, *NTh*; K. Johnson, *Karl Barth and the Analogia Entis* (2010).

RICHARD E. BURNETT

Prayer   Barth has written much about prayer—almost six hundred pages—and this doctrine plays a pivotal role in his *theology*. "No other theologian of the twentieth century took prayer more seriously or developed a more extensive theology of prayer than did Barth" (Migliore, 95). Yet no major study has been made of his doctrine of prayer.

Moreover, for Barth prayer is not only a subject about which one writes but one cannot do theology well apart from the act of prayer. In his swan song, *Evangelical Theology*, Barth writes, "The first and basic act of theological work is *prayer* . . . without prayer there can be no theological work" (*EvT*, 160). Since the task of theology is a reflection on the *revelation* of *God* in *Jesus Christ*, theology is not only a rational inquiry but also an activity of wonder, *love*, and praise. Hence all true theology will begin and end with prayer and be pervaded by prayer.

In contrast to most treatments of prayer, Barth discusses prayer primarily in the context of *ethics*, which, for him, is an integral element of *dogmatics*. The exception is the treatment of prayer in *CD* III/3. In §49.4, "The Christian under the Universal Lordship of God the Father" (264–88), Barth discusses prayer in the context of the *providence* of God. Even here, however, prayer is defined as "the most intimate and effective form of Christian action" (264). This theme is carried out in the ethics of *The Doctrine of Creation*, III/4:87–115, and in the unfinished ethics of *The Doctrine of Reconciliation*, IV/4: *Lecture Fragments*, published as *The Christian Life*. This volume is devoted almost entirely to a discussion of the first two petitions of the Lord's Prayer.

Discussing prayer in the context of ethics suggests that prayer is not to be thought of as primarily quiescent meditation that fosters passivity. To the contrary, *ora et labora*—prayer and work! (III/4:534; *EvT*, 160). In prayer we become partners with God in the *covenant* he has established (IV/3.2:883).

A common perception of prayer is that it is something we initiate, but Barth maintains that prayer is only possible because God in his *freedom* invites us to pray. God's action precedes ours. "When the Christian prays," he does so "in answer to the Word and work of the Son of God." We can draw near to God because he has drawn near to us in his Son (III/3:269).

For Barth, prayer is above all petition, which is "the basic form of Christian obedience." A key text for Barth in this connection is the command in Ps. 50:15: "Call upon me," although he cites several other texts that contain a similar imperative (III/4:93; *CL*, xi, 44). But in our asking, seeking, desiring, and making requests of God, we are at the same time making "the most genuine act of praise and thanksgiving, and therefore *worship*" (III/3:269, 270).

Barth has been criticized for so strongly emphasizing prayer as basically petition, but he had a polemic reason for this emphasis, one that is especially relevant today in the light of new age spiritualities. He warns against thinking of prayer as basically meditation that has no concrete substance. There are, he says, "certain theories of prayer which finally amount to little more than an understanding of prayer as the highest form of religious or Christian self-edification, a living and fruitful dialogue between the Christian and himself" (284).

In regard to the difficult question as to what extent God is moved and changed by our prayers (see Jesus' parables in Luke 11:5–13 and 18:1–8), Barth affirms that God "does not act in the same way whether we pray or not." Indeed, "prayer exerts an influence upon God's action, even upon his existence" (*Pr*, 13). Our feeble, flawed prayers notwithstanding, God "lets himself be touched and moved" by our prayers (*CL*, 106).

God in his free *grace* even makes believers his "partners" and allows them to "collaborate with him" (*CL*, 105; *Pr*, 20). Such statements might be interpreted as if this undercuts God's sovereignty, but Barth insists that in this "reciprocity" between God's freedom and the freedom he has granted believers by his grace, their "codetermination of the divine action . . . implies no limitation of the divine sovereignty. It means that God's sovereignty is not like that of a tyrant" (*CL*, 105). "There is no creaturely freedom which can limit or compete with the sole sovereignty and efficacy of God" (III/3:285).

This type of paradoxical reasoning may appear to some people as incoherence, but George Hunsinger refers to this kind of dialectic as a "double agency" that must be seen in the light of the Chalcedonian treatment of the natures of Christ (222; cf. *Pr*, 88, 139 n. 69).

Despite its many strengths, even some sympathetic interpreters have pointed to what they regard as deficiencies in Barth's treatment of prayer: his emphasis on prayer as petition (Shapiro, 31; Migliore, 111); his minimizing the prayer of lament (Migliore, 110); and that there is more *Vertrauen* (trust) than *Zweifel* (doubt) in Barth's doctrine of prayer (Schultze, 140 n. 13). Perhaps such criticisms reflect the optimistic tenor of Barth's theology. He might well respond to these criticisms with the words that conclude the last regular volume of the *CD*. After citing Rom. 12:11–12, he adds, "The Christian will stride out of the present into the future if he is and remains 'persistent in prayer'" (IV/3.2:942, rev.).

K. Barth, *CD* III/3:264–88; III/4:87–115; idem, *Pr*; idem, *SPr*; G. Hunsinger, *How to Read Karl Barth* (1991); D. Migliore, "Freedom to Pray," in K. Barth, *Prayer* (2002), 95–113; H. Schultze, "Gebet zwischen Zweifel und Vertrauen," *Evangelische Theologie* 30, no. 3 (1970): 133–49; L. Shapiro, "Karl Barth's Understanding of Prayer," *Crux* 24, no. 1 (1988): 26–33.

I. JOHN HESSELINK

Preaching   In 1922 Barth told a group of pastors that what had begun to receive attention as his *theology* began with "the minister's problem, the sermon" ("Need and Promise," 100). In preparing a sermon, a preacher must find a way "between the problem of human life on the one hand, and the content of the *Bible* on the other." The real problem in preaching is not how it is done, but how it is possible (103). The preacher is confronted with a congregation, perhaps reduced to a mere handful, coming to *worship* and asking a crucial question: "Is it true" (that *God* is present and active in the *world*)?

Two years later, in the *Göttingen Dogmatics*, preaching appears as a form of the *Word of God* in the Trinitarian analogy Barth would employ from then on: "The Word of God on which dogmatics reflects . . . is one in three and three in one: *revelation*, scripture, and preaching . . . neither to be confused nor separated" (*GD*, 14). Preaching is the one form of the Word of God that continues in our time, proceeding from revelation and Scripture, "as the *Holy Spirit* proceeds from the Father and the Son." Preaching is "the Word of God today" (15–16). As such, preaching is the form of the Word of God that gives occasion and urgency to *dogmatics* as a living discipline.

Barth always acknowledged that the Word of God might be preached outside the *church*. The Word of God could conceivably be proclaimed in *nature*, *history*, art, or, "who knows, even in my own heart and conscience" (34). If such were to happen, we must hear it, even though it is unexpected and not the norm. In addition, it is possible to hear the Word of God preached in other churches than one's own, or addressed to the church by voices outside it. None of these possibilities is normative, however, and each must be weighed individually. Every Christian ordinarily hears the Word of God in a particular church. That we do not claim to hear it spoken there alone does not mean preaching in "my church" is not "the center of my attention" for each Christian (35).

Moreover, congregations need not accept as the Word of God without question whatever their ministers say from the pulpit. The minister, together with the gathered congregation, is "an unworthy servant," judged by the Word of God, which must be preached all the same. On the other hand, it is useless for the minister to complain, "I have nothing to say," and for the congregation to complain, "It has nothing to offer me." Such criticism is the work of dogmatics, which is therefore of interest to every Christian (35–36).

Barth regarded preaching as broader than the pastor's deliverance from the pulpit, including in this concept "whatever we all 'preach' to ourselves in the quiet of our own rooms" (16). Later, he came to speak of this broader category as "proclamation" (*Verkündigung*).

In 1932–1933, while teaching at Bonn, Barth taught a course on homiletical theory and practice. He proposed two dialectically related theses about preaching. On the one hand, "*Preaching is the Word of God which he himself speaks.*" On the other, it is "*the attempt enjoined upon the church to serve God's own Word.*" In a sermon, these related events come together around a text of Scripture that God claims for the purpose of relevant exposition, and that the preacher expounds in relevant human words. "The totality forms a closed circle which begins with God and ends with him" (*Hom*, 44). Preaching is a dually caused event in which God speaks his Word in the speaking of a preacher who uses freely chosen human words.

Barth explicates his twofold definition in terms of nine factors he takes over from Leonhard Fendt: (1) Christian preaching conforms to revelation, as "a message that a herald is commissioned to deliver." (2) It takes place in the church. (3) It is "a function of worship" (64), commanded and commissioned by God. (4) It is the task of a minister called by God and the congregation, a task no one may "arrogantly . . . take up" (71). (5) It is provisional, relying on *sanctification*. (6) A sermon is an exposition of Scripture, modestly paying and calling attention to the text. (7) It is the proclamation of particular, unique individuals who "do not have to play a role" (82). (8) Preaching takes place in a particular congregation that the preacher knows, loves, and respects. (9) It takes place in the midst of *prayer* because for the sermon to be God's own Word, God must act, and this cannot be taken for granted.

Because preaching begins and ends with God, every attempt on the part of the preacher to have a preconceived effect on the sermon's hearers is excluded. The sermon must not reduce its text to a theme or a proposition, nor may it require certain conduct in the name of relevancy (49). Both because the sermon is an act of worship (127) and because the time available for preaching is limited (122), it is important to dispense with special introductions and conclusions. While introductions "offer many opportunities for much wit and cleverness," they create distractions and other psychological barriers (122). Moreover, they are often "plain *heresy*" in that they suggest "that this little door to the inner self must first be found and opened before it is worthwhile to bring the message" (124). Instead, "we have simply to adopt the attitude of the messenger who does not have to create a mood for the message" (125). The situation is similar with conclusions: "If a summary is needed, it is already too late to give it; the mischief has been done. A theoretical sermon cannot be made more practical by a concluding application" (127).

In the *CD*, preaching accompanies the sacraments as an element of the church's proclamation. In theory, proclamation could occur in other dimensions of cultural and congregational existence. It is impossible with God to limit proclamation to these two elements of Christian worship. In a sentence widely quoted and sometimes misunderstood, Barth acknowledges: "God may speak to us through Russian Communism, a flute concerto, a blossoming shrub, or a dead dog." Yet this does not mean ordinary ministers (who are not "prophets and founders of a new church") are called to include what they think they hear from such sources in the church's proclamation (*CD* I/1:55). *Jesus Christ* has commissioned "proclamation by preaching and sacrament" (I/1:57). The proclamation God has commissioned is performed by a person who has been set apart with "a special, imperious calling." This person, the preacher, receives Christ's promise, "And remember, I am with you always" (Matt. 28:20). With this promise the preacher undertakes, not "arbitrary religious discourse," but "discourse which as the exposition of Scripture is controlled and guided." When these elements come together, there is (as an act of the Holy Spirit) an actual encounter between God and the congregation (I/1:58–59).

K. Barth, *DiO*; idem, *Hom*; idem, *PGos*; idem, *WWorld*; W. Willimon, *Conversations with Barth on Preaching* (2006); idem, *The Early Preaching of Karl Barth* (2009).
MICHAEL D. BUSH

Providence   Located in the third part-volume of the doctrine of *creation*, Barth defines providence as the "superior dealings of the Creator with His creation, the wisdom, omnipotence and goodness with which He maintains and governs in time this distinct reality according to the counsel of His own will" (*CD* III/3:3). With this Barth follows the tradition of his Reformed forebears and rejects the scholastic placement of the doctrine in the being of *God*. By doing so, Barth underscores the notion

that providence does not simply belong to God's general foreknowledge abstracted from the *covenant* of *grace*, but refers to the dynamic knowing, willing, and acting of God in the *history* of creation and in creaturely action. The doctrine of providence thus affirms that the entire created order stands under God's immediate and direct care, yet in such a way that the creature's own agency is allowed and enabled to serve the glory of God's own history as it fulfills its own meaning, purpose, and *joy*.

Throughout his treatise on providence, Barth is at pains to distinguish the biblical concept of providence from any theory of divine-human relations, *philosophy* of history, cosmology, opinion, or worldview. As a matter of *faith* in *Jesus Christ*, providence cannot be perceived from *nature* or history, but can only be received by hearing the *Word of God*. While it is possible to acquire some genuine skill in recognizing the work of God in history, the individual perception of providence remains subject to human distortion, which sees the *world* "divinely ordered" in one's favor (III/3:18), and thus requires faith in Jesus Christ to be constantly given anew by the *Holy Spirit*.

The Christian doctrine of providence refers to the positive, material, and inner coordination of creaturely history with *salvation* history, as God himself orders and arranges all things according to God's eternal decision (*prothesis*) in Christ (Eph. 1:11). Christians may believe in providence not because they stand under a predetermined divine plan that demands blind submission and may elicit bitter resignation to an all-powerful fate, but because God himself creates in them genuine *freedom* and autonomy and moves them to trust in God and provide (*prostithesthai*) for others in strict accordance with the gospel. Only in this way may Christians confidently cast all their suffering onto God (1 Pet. 5:6), seek first God's kingdom (Matt. 6:33), and trust that all things work together (*synergei*) for the good

(Rom. 8:28) because God himself orders all creation according to Jesus Christ.

Barth follows the **Reformed tradition** and divides his treatise into the doctrines of divine *conservatio, concursus,* and *gubernatio.* The divine preservation is the action whereby God upholds and sustains all things in space and *time* for the sake of covenant fellowship. In every moment of its individual and social existence, the creature is preserved in its being from nothingness by God's direct and immediate activity, yet in a way that also includes the work of creatures. "It is God alone who does everything according to His own free good-pleasure . . . by maintaining the creature, by means of the creature" (III/3:65). The divine preservation remains wholly a spiritual act that operates through creatures who, by no power of their own, are allowed to share in God's preservation by guarding, strengthening, and preserving one another in their being and faith for fellowship with God in time and *eternity*.

The divine *concursus* describes the mystery of God's eternal lordship in, with, and over the autonomous activity of the creature, such that the creature's own acts take place simultaneously with those of God. As God accompanies the creature, the entire history of created being takes place in God's active presence, which goes before (*praecursus*), with (*concursus*), and after (*succursus*) the creature. God is able to act within creaturely agency because God's causality is radically unlike anything in creation and cannot be compared with the creature in any way. As long as the divine *causa* is not understood mechanistically or as belonging to the same genus or order as that of creatures, God may operate within the world of natural causes without necessity or coercion because God is "absolutely above" the world of natural causes. "As Father, Son, and Holy Ghost, God is *love* in and of Himself, and in the overflowing of this love He loves the creature" (III/3:107). God is thus free to create within creatures a corresponding and analogous love and

freedom that neither overrides their natural capacities nor assimilates them into God through synergistic infusions of grace. Yet the basic condition for perceiving God's work within creaturely agency is not intellectual, but spiritual. It consists in overcoming the fear complex that suggests that God is a tyrant who begrudges the freedom of the creature. Only when Christians are purged of this fear and acknowledge that the *maior Dei gloria* cannot be affirmed without the *minor gloria creaturae* will the arguments for the divine *concursus* gain force and validity (III/3:97, 147–48).

The divine government refers to God's active determination and coordination of all things according to God's wisdom and goodness as God orders them to himself as the final goal of history. As God rules all things, God grants each and every thing a time, place, and purpose in the **kingdom of God**. The divine rule thus becomes an event in history as creaturely action itself is brought into a formative economy and disposition. The normative image used to understand the transcendent rule of God within history is found in 1 Corinthians 12, where greater dignity and honor goes to those parts that are least in the body of Christ. As creaturely action is formed in this specific way, the divine government becomes actualized in time through creatures who are lifted up to share in God's sovereign rule as God cooperates with them. "The glory of God is the salvation and glorification of the creature" (III/3:159).

After establishing the doctrine of providence in God's action in history, Barth examines some objective reminders of providence in the history of Holy Scripture, the church, the Jews, and the limitation of human life, concluding with an extended reflection on the **Christian life** in the unity of faith, obedience, and **prayer** under the universal lordship of God.

————

G. Hunsinger, *How to Read Karl Barth* (1991), 185–224; C. Schröder, "'I See

Something You Don't See,'" in *For the Sake of the World*, ed. G. Hunsinger (2004), 115–35; K. Tanner, "Creation and Providence," in *Cambridge Companion to Karl Barth*, ed. J. Webster (2000), 111–27; idem, *God and Creation in Christian Theology* (1988), 77–88; J. Webster, *Karl Barth* (2000), 105–10.

MICHAEL T. DEMPSEY

Reason   Barth rejected the philosophical project of providing a rational basis for theological truth claims. More precisely, he rejected what he termed a *theologia rationalis*. This rejection has led many to classify him as a fideist, that is, one who founds truth claims on **faith** rather than reason. This charge, though not wholly unwarranted, misunderstands Barth's mature theological project of "faith seeking understanding."

A look back at the liberal theological tradition in Germany provides perspective on the distinctiveness of Barth's approach to rationality. The liberal tradition was shaped by Immanuel Kant's distinction between theoretical and practical reason. In his *Critique of Pure Reason*, Kant contended that the application of theoretical reason to theological ideas, as exemplified by the traditional proofs of **God**, winds up in antinomies and false inferences. However, Kant also claimed that key theological ideas could be shown to be presuppositions of practical reason, that is, of rational ethical principles. As Kant famously summarized his views, "I have . . . found it necessary to deny knowledge, in order to make room for faith" (Kant, 29). Theologians in the liberal tradition generally accepted Kant's demolition of the theoretical proofs of God, but chafed at his basing **theology** on practical reason. Friedrich **Schleiermacher**, for instance, joined Kant in rejecting the theoretical proofs of God but also rejected the grounding of theology on practical reason. At a high level of conceptuality, one might feasibly interpret the project of liberal theology in the nineteenth century as the search for a rational basis for theology in light of Kant's criticisms of its relation to theoretical reason and Schleiermacher's criticisms of its purported relation to practical reason.

Barth developed his understanding of the relation between reason and theology within the liberal tradition. In an early essay on the cosmological proof (1909), Barth affirmed the limitations that Kant placed on theoretical reason, arguing that Christians can know God only through lived experience. By *Rom II* (1922) Barth ascribed a wholly negative function to reason. Reason leads to its own crisis, raising questions it cannot answer and pointing to limits beyond which it cannot see.

In *Anselm: Fides Quarens Intellectum*, Barth broke with the liberal conceptuality and articulated his mature understanding of the function of reason within theology. In that work, he rejected any theological appeal to "universal human reason" as a capitulation to unbelief (*Anselm*, 67). However, he also rejected the notion that faith was "illogical, irrational" (22). Against the options of rationalism or irrationalism, Barth contended that **revelation** had an objective or ontic rationality to which the subjective or noetic rationality of the believing mind (graciously) conforms. "The element of reason in the knowledge of the object of faith consists in recognition of the rationality that is peculiar to the object of faith itself" (50). The possibility of raising questions and putting forward arguments in theology depends on this distinction, which allows for rational debate of theological doctrine without suspending the authority of revelation.

Barth's mature understanding of the function of reason within theology broke with the Kantian "Copernican" revolution. Whereas Kant asserted that "objects must conform to our knowledge" (22), Barth held that, at least in theology, reason must be conformed to revelation.

K. Barth, *Anselm*; idem, "Der kosmologische Beweis für das Dasein Gottes," in *VkA 1905–1909*, 373–419; I. Kant. *Critique of Pure Reason*, trans. N. K. Smith (1929); D. P. La Montagne, *Barth and Rationality* (2012); S. G. Smith "Karl Barth and Fideism: A Reconsideration," *AThR* 66 (1984): 64–78.

CLIFFORD B. ANDERSON

Reconciliation

In various ways, Barth critically advocates the unity of "objective" and "subjective" reconciliation between the *world* and *God* (cf. 2 Cor. 5:19ff.) already in *Rom* I (1919). He sees it specifically as a process that aims at redeeming the world and is grounded in Christ, the eternal *Urbild* of Adam. Barth develops an almost Hegelian "logic of *reconciliation*" (the "negation of the negation"). In *Rom* II (1922) *Jesus Christ* is the place of reconciliation for all, to which he has been destined eternally by God's decree as the first and last word of God's faithfulness to humankind. In Barth's *Göttingen Dogmatics* (1924–1926), reconciliation is distinct from redemption (the latter belongs to *eschatology*) and depends on God's faithfulness (§27), which refers back to God's gracious *election*, discussed in the doctrine of God (§18) and presented again, with modications, in its sharp, Reformed form as double predestination.

Leaping forward to the *CD*, especially IV/1–3 (1953–1959) and in accord with Barth's specific Christocentrism, we see the topic of reconciliation present throughout. Since reconciliation is "the heart of the message received by and laid upon the Christian community and therefore . . . of the Church's *dogmatics*," it also illumines the doctrines of *creation* and of the "last things" (redemption and completion) (IV/1:3). The christologically transformed doctrine of double predestination implies that dogmatics essentially "has no more exalted or profound word—essentially, indeed, it has no other word—than this: that God was in Christ reconciling the world [with] Himself" (II/2:88). Reconciliation, therefore, adds depth to our understanding of reality (cf. II/2:§33, "The Election of Jesus Christ"). At the same time, one can read his doctrine of reconciliation as a dogmatics within the dogmatics. In the midst of continuities and new recapitulations, it offers surprises. This can be expounded here only in brush strokes. Since the English translation of even basic terms is sometimes problematic (especially the concept of "substitution" for *Stellvertretung*), I will occasionally modify it.

A first cross-section of the doctrine of reconciliation is IV/1. It is a mostly "quiet debate with Rudolf **Bultmann**" (ix). Later, Barth adds that it relates to the historical context of the East-West conflict, just as I/1 (1932) refers to German politics. As a dogmatic theologian and ethicist, Barth is a critical observer of contemporary events.

The first section (§57, "The Work of God the Reconciler") already transcends the classic doctrinal division of Jesus Christ's person and work, or *Christology* and soteriology, in order to preserve their christological base. This is consistent with the fundamental thesis of God's being and life in act (II/1:§28.1). Barth emphasizes "the free act of the faithfulness of God in which He takes the lost cause of man, who has denied Him as Creator and in so doing ruined himself as [His] creature, and makes it His own in Jesus Christ, carrying it through to its goal and in that way maintaining and manifesting His own glory in the world" (IV/1:3). Here we already see, in contrast to what Barth occasionally criticizes as the "nostrification" of God, that God is concerned with God's self and God's own honor—exactly at the point when and where God is engaged, in a self-determining way, on behalf of his sinful creature. The concept of "honor" may sound close to Anselm. Yet when Barth explains how reconciliation in Jesus Christ is the work of *God*, the Son, he is not thinking of the satisfactory deed of a *human being* with meritorious value for all human beings, achieved through the divine being of Jesus.

Moreover, God's work as reconciler, developed as the framework for the entire doctrine of reconciliation, is presented as a theology of the *covenant*. God's work in Jesus Christ is the fulfillment of the single (!) gracious covenant, which concerns both divine and human justice and righteousness. It is the eternal *precondition* for the reconciliation between humankind and God and constitutes, in its fullfilment, a radical transformation of the covenant with *Israel*. Through this transformation, the purpose of creation, the eschaton of God's kingdom, becomes objectively, universally, once for all, a present reality on earth, complete in the person and *history* of Jesus Christ. It is the most exclusive and also the most inclusive history, with far-reaching consequences. For "God with us" in this person, the "Immanuel," also means "we with God," in the sense of an asymmetrical partnership that was already the goal of the covenant with Israel. More precisely, it means that *we participate in God's being, life, and acting* (but not as the divinization of human beings!), because *God participates in our being, life, and acting*, in an explicitly nonsynergistic way. In the work of reconciliation, the human being is not merely a passive object of the reconciling *grace* that triumphs over covenant breaking. Rather, the human being becomes supremely liberated and energized, and is objectively and also subjectively reconciled, converted to God by God. Barth's theology of the covenant, which undergirds his doctrine of reconciliation, continues his doctrine of Israel (II/2:§34), albeit in a modified way. It explains his claim of a divine neccessity

that the *incarnation* happened in *Jewish* flesh (IV/1:167ff.).

On the one hand, the "we with God" is soon related to the *congregation*, as a sign that Jesus Christ and his congregation belong together in a special way. But the congregation only receives and carries the message that the world is reconciled with God in Jesus Christ, once and for all, in an eschatological sense. Therefore, on the other hand, the specific christological section (IV/2:§64, "The Exaltation of the Son of Man") goes even further, explaining that the expression "we with God" refers primarily to the incarnate, unique, newly created human being Jesus. And as Barth already emphasizes in the covenant theology of §57, the Christian congregation with its *witness* in word and deed does not constitute a prolongation of the reconciliation of the world, which God the reconciler, standing in the place of us all, has fully accomplished in Jesus Christ (IV/1:12–13), with the corresponding reconciling process that would refer only to the congregation. Here one should also consider the ecclesiological sections of IV/1–3 (§§62, 67, and 72), since the congregation of Jesus Christ is the provisional representation of the whole of humankind that has been reconciled with God in Jesus Christ, that is, all who have been justified, sanctified, and called.

Even though Barth principally rejects the idea that God needs to be reconciled (which is not Anselmian), he prefers a *costly grace* over against a cheap grace, out of respect for humankind's covenant breaking. The strange shape of God's solemn and bitter protest against the senseless rebellion of humankind who breaks the covenant (thereby destroying itself and forfeiting its destination to eternal *salvation*) is due to God's holiness and righteousness. God's protest is the result (but not the goal!) of the "nevertheless" aspect of reconciliation grace—in contrast to creation grace—which, in accordance with the asymmetrical reciprocal participation of God and *humanity*, is more than a restitution of original righteousness. God's No! is an integral part of God's Yes! the incomprehensible overflowing and triumph of grace. This triumph occurs as the radical exchange of places, that is, the substitutionary suffering of God's (the Father's) wrath, punishment, and judgment by God the reconciler. Thus God's being *for* and *with* us in Jesus Christ includes a being *against* us. God himself does enough, for himself and at the same time for humankind (IV/1:13). This has two implications.

First, in Jesus Christ the terrible rift between us and God is thus overcome by being revealed, in spite of its veiling through our self-justification. The result of presenting **knowledge of God** and self-knowledge in a christological unity is that Barth does not preface his doctrine of reconciliation with a doctrine of *sin*. Rather, he includes the latter in the former, locating it like a negative mirror image immediately after the fundamental christological sections on reconciliation (cf. §58, which outlines the structure of IV/1–3).

Second, it means that in Jesus Christ, sin, and even the sinner himself or herself as the root of sin, is removed, once for all and, again, objectively. Such a claim contradicts the prevalent and christologically often uprooted differentiation between person and work, as far as human beings are concerned. Yet it corresponds to Barth's (problematical) anthropological thesis of being and life in doing and certainly to what recently has been called *Existenzstellvertretung*. It also fits his understanding of the (sinful) world's reconciliation with God as its conversion to God, in the sense of a radical, creative new beginning, as far as the latter presupposes an end that has begun with the incarnation.

The recognition of Jesus Christ and, therefore, of the work of God the reconciler, has three aspects that are asymmetrically bound together: Jesus

is "(1) very God, that is, the God who humbles Himself, . . . (2) very man, that is, man exalted and therefore reconciled by God, and (3) in the unity of the two the guarantor and witness of our atonement" (§58, superscription). In this way, the doctrine of the two states, humiliation and exaltation, as well as the distinctly Reformed doctrine of Jesus Christ's three offices (the prophetic, high-priestly, and royal), are taken up *and radically transformed*. This has consequences for understanding the incarnation and the doctrine of two natures, which Barth affirms but modifies (IV/1:133ff.; IV/2:26ff., 37ff., 89ff.). The self-humiliation of God the Son occurs in and through the incarnation, seen primarily as *unio personalis hypostatica*, by taking on (*assumptio*) humanity with its openness to temptation. It is concluded on the cross. Asymmetrically and simultaneously, it is also the elevation of humanity to its true being, elevated by and reconciled with God. The obedient self-humiliation of the eternal Son, his "way . . . into the far country" (IV/1:§59.1), proves his true divinity. Likewise, the "homecoming" of the Son of Man (IV/2:§64.2), occurring asymmetrically yet simultaneously, indicates and represents (with clear ethical consequences!) the new, true human being who participates in the being, life, and acting of the self-humiliating God (§64, superscription). Only if one tries to know the true being of God and humankind apart from Christ does the person and work, or history, of Jesus Christ present a blind and absolute paradox.

The asymmetrical simultaneity of God and humankind in Jesus Christ, which includes the asymmetrical reciprocity and unity of God's and humankind's being and life in acting, is developed in three parts: "Jesus Christ, the Lord as Servant" (IV/1), "Jesus Christ, the Servant as Lord" (IV/2), and "Jesus Christ, the True Witness" (IV/3). Each of them begins with a basic christological section (§§59, 64, 69). The first of them, "The Obedience of the [Eternal] Son of God," is of fundamental importance for all parts and contains again the whole in a nutshell. It presents incisive insights as well as difficulties and sharp edges, which warrant a few comments.

The first section is titled "The Way of the Son of God [the subject of reconciliation] into the Far Country" (§59.1). The Son's noble humility suits the historical enactment of his unreserved solidarity with humankind as sinful flesh. God appears in the form of the sinner, standing under God's (the Father's) judgment and verdict but without actually sinning as a human being, since the personal relational unity with the obedient Son of God uplifts him. He acts in exemplary as well as perfect obedience. In his self-humiliation, the Son compromises himself with and delivers himself to humankind's satanic opposition to God as well as to the judgment of God the Father, which is carried out in and through this opposition, in the execution of the eternal divine decree (cf. II/2).

In the second section, the high-priestly office is explained in juridical terminology: "The Judge Judged in Our Place" (§59.2). It especially recalls question 52 of the Heidelberg Catechism, although the juridical model is not regarded as absolute (cf. IV/1:211ff.). Barth says: "He took our place as Judge. He took our place as the judged. He was judged in our place. And He acted justly in our place" (273). As the *judge*: the human being, who is sinful exactly because he or she wishes to be judge and thus replace God, becomes a "displaced person," in order to reestablish God's function as judge and for the sake of being liberated to his or her true being (232ff.). As the *judged*: Jesus Christ positions himself both as subject and object under the indictment and sentence, which should apply to us. Right from the moment of incarnation, he thus takes the world's sin upon himself as the one rejected and condemned person, so that our sin is no longer ours, and we are acquitted once for all. As *being judged*: the

passion of Jesus Christ, even to the cross, is, in an absolute and exclusive sense, God's own passion. Hence we as sinners and also sin itself, including its consequences (e.g., eternal death), have come to an end and are dismantled (245ff.). As the *just one*: he positively fulfills all of God's justice in the course of events. The factual, concrete, but not automatic sinlessness of the Incarnate One occurs when God's justice is acknowledged through wholehearted penance, instead of seeking self-justification. Hence the removal of injustice and its perpetrator is not achieved simply through their negation (257ff.). This theme is developed further in IV/2, with consequences for understanding the exaltation.

Barth's edgy idea of *Stellvertretung* (as distinct from mere representation) is softened by the priority of God's mercy and grace. Yet the primacy of juridical terminology remains odd, in view of the New Testament Gospels. Similarly, the conceptual duality of judge and judged cannot do justice to the idea of *Stellvertretung* even in juridical terms. Moreover, Barth occasionally says that judgment results in grace, anger in *love* (IV/1:222). And how can Jesus Christ in *time* have suffered the *eternal* death, deserved by the sinner, if it should mean (but here Barth is ambiguous) something other than complete "nothingness," that is, eternal anguish, and if Barth demythologizes, with both **Luther** and **Calvin**, the classic idea of Christ's *descensus ad inferos* from the perspective of a theology of the cross? Does that not presuppose speculations about the divinity of the "Son of God" (e.g., that only God could have suffered such a death), as they are known from seventeenth-century Protestant orthodoxy? Finally, apart from the problem that the people who condemn and kill Jesus are merely God's instruments (cf. 240), can one say that it is God (the Father) himself who removes, destroys, and kills Jesus (222, 255, 346)?

"The Verdict of the Father" (§59.3), who is now the second judge (!), is carried out in the *resurrection of Jesus Christ*, as a new, relatively independent act by God the Father (through the *Holy Spirit*, though this is rather an after-thought for Barth). It is enacted also on the Son of God, and humankind has no part in it, as at creation. It adds nothing new to the reconciliation achieved once for all in the history of Jesus Christ leading up to the crucifixion. Noetically it reveals the reconciliation as an *unmerited act of grace*. Here Barth contradicts the classic doctrine of Jesus Christ's substitionary merit as well as the pre-Hegelian immanent dialectic of cross and resurrection as a one-sided theology of the cross. In order to emphasize that the new life from death is not natural or self-evident, Barth goes so far as to claim (against his own theo-logic) that the reconciliation of the world might have consisted merely in the removal of the sinner, the killing of the patient (295ff.). That would imply the reconciliation of God by God or a nihilistic salvation of the world from is self-contradiction. On the other hand, the act of grace is a juridical act qualifying the substitution that has taken place without us, for us, and against us. It is the *justification* of the obedient Son of God who is simultaneously the Son of Man, and even the Father's own justification. For the Father claims his own always gracious right to his always threatened creature, as a new creation and for the sake of his creature. In anticipation, God allows our and the whole world's redemption, which is grounded in reconciliation, to begin with the resurrected crucified One (cf. 118–19 and IV/3.1:315ff.).

Yet this aspect is merely touched upon by Barth in IV/1. More important is that the resurrection and, in a limited sense, the appearances of the risen Jesus Christ overcome the (not only temporal) "wide, ugly ditch" (Lessing) between then and now, in favor of a real simultaneity (Kierkegaard) between Jesus Christ and us. Based on the resurrection, which forever actualizes his *Stellvertretung* that ends on the cross, Jesus

Christ is the one eternal mediator. In his resilient real presence (cf. IV/1:349), he offers and reveals himself as the fulfillment of reconciliation, through the Holy Spirit, who already participates in the work of incarnation and through whom Jesus Christ becomes present to other human beings.

This is developed in IV/3.1:§69 as the *transition* of Jesus Christ, the one *Word of God* (cf. the first thesis of the *Barmen Declaration*) to us, as his self-representation, self-communication, and even proof of himself (!). Therefore, reconciliation, accomplished once for all in Jesus Christ, awakens a practical recognition in human beings by changing and converting them. Barth even calls this subjective reconciliation a "secondary event" of salvation (IV/3.1:220). With this revised notion of Christ's prophetic office, Barth battles against a free-floating doctrine of the Holy Spirit but also explicitly—though unfortunately in a rash or ambivalent manner compared to his talk of "immunity," "doubtless," "crystal clear," "axiomatic," and "uncontradictable" (74, 80ff.)—against Feuerbach's projection theory. Likewise, the transformation of the *circulus vitiosus* into a *circulus virtuosus* is far too quick (86ff., with a problematic appeal to Anselm).

Using the concept of the "closed circle," Barth struggles boldly, sometimes too boldly, on different fronts that are still relevant today. He also demonstrates in IV/2 clear ecumenical openness and in IV/3 a marked critical openness to the world (cf. especially the idea of the Light and the lights). Yet, apart from immanent tensions, interpretive and logical problems remain. After all, Barth's doctrine of reconciliation is already a theory of not only juridical but also ontological *Stellvertretung* in his doctrine of election (II/2), though he never clearly explains the concept. Apart from questions already indicated, Barth vacilates conceptually in regard to the *reality* of the reconciliation Jesus Christ accomplished once for all. This becomes clear in his occasional distinctions between "virtually"/"effectively" and "actually"/"actively" (e.g., IV/1:120) or between *de iure* and *de facto* (e.g., IV/3.1:279). These distinctions indicate again that we deal with an as-yet-unfinished-process of the exclusive-inclusive history of reconciliation, which aims at a final redemption and completion of *all creatures*. Barth often loses sight of how this can and shall be brought about, through a reconciliation that is not only a reaction to human sin—in spite of his doctrine of the temporal and eternal "divine preserving" of all creatures as the middle status between creation and redemption (III/3:§49.1) and in spite of his difficult doctrine of "nothingness" (§50).

B. Klappert, *Versöhnung und Befreiung* (1994); B. L. McCormack, "The Ontological Presuppositions of Barth's Doctrine of the Atonement," in *The Glory of the Atonement*, ed. C. Hill and F. James (2004), 346–66; K. H. Menke, "Karl Barth," in *Stellvertetung* (1991), 168–93; H. Ruddies, "Christologie und Versöhnungslehre bei Karl Barth," *ZDTh* 18, no. 2 (2002): 174–89; G. Thomas, "Der für uns 'gerichtete Richter,'" *ZDTh* 18, no. 2 (2002): 211–25.

J. CHRISTINE JANOWSKI

Reformed Tradition   Though Barth was raised in a leading Swiss Reformed theological family, and was acquainted with the works of *Calvin* and Zwingli from his student days, he began to be seriously preoccupied with Reformed *theology* only when he left pastoral work in 1921 to take up a chair teaching the subject in Göttingen. During his four years there, he lectured on Reformed historical theology, treating the Heidelberg Catechism, Calvin, the Reformed Confessions, Zwingli, and *Schleiermacher*, and worked out his first comprehensive account of Christian doctrine, the so-called *Göttingen Dogmatics*; he also lectured extensively on

New Testament texts. The texts of most of these lectures have been published posthumously in the last twenty years, and are having some impact on the interpretation of Barth. At first, Barth's knowledge of the Reformed tradition was slight, and he worked assiduously to master the materials. His reading was intense but unsystematic, driven by the needs of the classroom and by his own developing theological agenda. He was often prone to treat aspects of later Reformed thought as a declension from the magisterial figures of the early period, an interpretation adopted from Heppe's *Reformed Dogmatics*, which served as his entry into the world of Calvinist scholasticism. His studies did not make him into a confessional Reformed theologian, and he never pretended to historical professionalism. Rather, the texts of Calvin and his heirs exposed Barth to major themes of classical Christian *dogmatics*, and furnished him with concepts and arguments with which to articulate the theological sensibilities he had discovered as a pastor, and to begin building a theology to outbid Protestant *liberalism*.

A number of important trajectories of Barth's later thought may be traced back to his early interpretations of Reformed theology. He gave a radical account of the Reformed Scripture principle in which Scripture relativizes the *church* and its theology by bearing contingent *witness* to divine *revelation* as a pure gift prior to human experience, aspiration, or religious and moral activity. He was unsympathetic, however, to the elaborate theologies of biblical *inspiration* in later Reformed thought, fearing that they stabilized and naturalized the event of revelation. The rule of Scripture in church and theology led Barth to assert the relativity of the Reformed Confessions; unlike the Lutheran confessional documents, the early Reformed creeds and catechisms are occasional and unsystematic, subservient to Scripture as the supreme norm, and so commanding only provisional respect. Barth laid much emphasis upon the ethical character of the Reformed conception of Christianity. Where the Lutheran tradition was dominated by the pure divine act of *justification*, the Reformed retained a sense of the human historical *world*, and envisaged the Christian *religion* as a mode of soteriologically driven moral engagement—though Barth again worried that later Reformed theology detached human moral striving from divine agency, and so drifted into moralism. The moral character of Reformed Christianity attracted Barth in part because of his earlier sociopolitical interests, and became a deep structuring element in the *CD*.

Through his work on the Reformed tradition in this formative period, Barth felt his way into an account of the relation of *God* and *creation*. At times he drew a very sharp distinction between divine and created in the wake of his profound dissatisfaction with the apparent immanentism of Ritchlian theology, and spoke sympathetically of Zwingli's extrinsicism, which resonated with Barth's eschatological (possibly Platonic) instincts and which Barth never completely left behind. Yet he was also critical of abstract opposition of God and the world, and devoted much attention to topics in theology that probe the relation of God to created forms such as sacramental theology or *incarnation*.

When in his maturity Barth came to work on the *CD*, he was not attempting a confessional dogmatics of one or other version of the Reformed tradition. This vast work is open to and shaped by a great range of sources beyond the Reformed tradition, patristic, medieval, and modern; it is driven by much more than Reformed confessional debates and developments; and it shows extraordinary independence of mind. It is, therefore, Reformed more at the level of instinct. What the Reformed tradition provides is a set of texts as conversation partners (most of all Calvin and the later scholastics), raw material for Barth's considerable innovative talent, some basic theological orientations (such as the nonnecessity of the world for God, and the primacy of revelation), and an idiom in which to express himself.

In the course of the *CD*, Barth undertook some very large-scale revisions of the Reformed tradition. His account of divine election in *CD* II/2, for example, breaks with the conception of a double divine decree, and instead focuses on Christ as himself both electing God and elect creature. Behind this lies Barth's resistance to a theology of God's eternal being insufficiently related to God's temporal acts (this remains a controversial topic in the interpretation of Barth). Or again, in *CD* IV, Barth's treatment of *covenant* criticizes traditional Reformed federal theology, with its staged history of the covenants, as historicizing, and prefers to concentrate on Christ as himself the fulfillment of both sides of the covenant relation. Yet Barth nearly always departs from the tradition only after long argument and attentive listening, which, he often insisted, is essential to theological responsibility.

Though deeply influential on some leading Reformed theologians (Berkouwer in Holland, T. F. Torrance in Scotland, Otto Weber in Germany), Barth's dogmatic work often proved controversial. Adherents of stricter versions of confessional Reformed Christianity frequently criticized him for concessions to liberalism, for the deficiencies of his reading of the scholastics, or for the lack of an adequate *natural theology*. Some Roman Catholic reception of Barth, by contrast, found him still trapped by Reformed separation of *nature* and supernature, and unwilling to admit the participation of creaturely forms in the communication of divine life. Barth's work is of such scope that these critiques, warranted to some degree, rarely undermine it. He is perhaps best viewed as a theologian of classic stature, who transcends the strand of Christianity by which he was inspired and shaped, and on which he continues to exert a formative influence.

K. Barth, *GD*; idem, *ThC*; idem, *ThRefC*; M. Freudenberg, "Das reformierte Erbe erwerben," *ThZ* 54 (1998): 36–54; F. Schröter, "Bermerkungen über den reformierten Character des theologischen Ansatzes Karl Barths," in *Antwort*, ed. E. Wolf, et al. (1956), 148–55: J. Webster, *Barth's Earlier Theology* (2005).

JOHN WEBSTER

Religion   Although religion is among the most ancient human institutions, the *concept* of religion is a modern invention, a product of the secularization of Western society since the Enlightenment. Like other modern theologians, Barth includes a treatment of religion in his *dogmatics*, although he does so in a way that puts him radically at odds with most other theologians of the twentieth century. The notion of religion is prominent in the earliest of Barth's writings after his break with the theological *liberalism* of his teachers. At that time, for example, in his essay "The Strange New World within the Bible" (1917; ET: "New World"), religion claims his attention because it was so important in liberal *theology*. But from the start Barth took pains to distinguish between human religion and God's *revelation* in *Jesus Christ*.

By the time he began work on the *CD* in the 1930s, Barth's critique of liberal religion had developed into a sophisticated and subtle *theology* of religion, presented in its most systematic form in *CD* I/2:§17. Unfortunately, its central concept, *Aufhebung*, was misleadingly translated as "Abolition" in the *CD*, that is, "The Revelation of God as the Abolition of Religion," ignoring its dialectical meaning and leaving the utterly false impression that Barth simply rejects religion out of hand and thinks that Christianity is not a religion at all (see revised translation of *CD* §17, titled *On Religion*). What Barth has done is to borrow a technical term from Hegel's idealist *philosophy* and adapt it to his own theological purposes. The new translation employs *sublimation* for *Aufhebung*, but no single English term can capture the multivalence of the German verb *aufheben*, whose literal meaning is "to lift up," while having two other, seemingly contradictory, figurative uses. On the one hand, it can be used negatively to mean: "suspend," "annul," or "abolish." On the other hand, however, *aufheben* can be employed positively to mean: "preserve," "save," or "store up." Hegel seized on the ambiguity of this common German expression to capture the dialectical logic of what he calls the "negation of the negative," in which the negative or antithesis of a particular thesis is itself negated in such a way that the sublimated concept both includes and overcomes its own antithesis.

Barth finds the concept ideally suited to express the theological relationship of religion to revelation. Thus the claim that God's revelation in Jesus Christ is the sublimation of religion involves two dialectically related moves: (1) in the light of God's revelation, all human religion (*including* the Christian religion!) is shown to be faithlessness (*Unglaube*), the idolatrous attempt of man "to justify and sanctify himself before a willfully and arbitrarily devised image of God"; *and* (2) revelation, which is "hidden" in human religion, nevertheless appears in the *church* as "the site of the true religion to the extent that through *grace* it lives by grace."

Barth sets the context in the first of the three subsections of §17, "The Problem of Religion in Theology," by showing that Christianity is one species of religion alongside the other world religions. Even while emphasizing that revelation appears in this religious form, he eschews any attempt to demonstrate on nontheological grounds either the uniqueness or the superiority of the Christian religion. Yet to deny the religious nature of Christianity would be to deny revelation itself. This situation poses the theological problem of religion: how is it to be understood in the light of revelation? Beginning as early as the Protestant orthodoxy of the seventeenth century, there has been a creeping tendency in modern theology to reverse the priority by making religion the criterion of revelation rather than the other way around: an error that Barth dubs the *heresy* of *religionism*.

In the second subsection, "Religion as Faithlessness," Barth develops the negative thesis that religion is the great concern of *godless humanity*: it represents the human *resistence* to God's self-revelation and must therefore be removed before the true word of revelation can be heard. Barth always rejected the common view of human religion as a preparation for, or anticipation of, revelation, the open hand waiting to be filled by God's *truth*. (A clenched fist would be a more fitting image.) Religion, therefore, must be fully transformed, it must be destroyed and reconstituted—in a word, sublimated—before it can become the vessel of revelation. One can observe in the *history* of religion how its self-contradictory nature inevitably leads to its breakdown. The conservative form of the crisis is mysticism, which denies the external forms of religion in order to affirm its inner spiritual meaning; the more radical form is atheism, which attempts a wholesale denial of religion. Both forms of critique ultimately fail, serving only to clear the ground for new religious movements to arise and to fall victim to the same inevitable process.

The sublimation of religion promised in the title of §17 finally takes place in the third subsection, "The True Religion," which opens with a telling *analogy*: "we can talk about 'true' religion only in the sense in which we talk about a 'justified sinner.'" The negative moment of the dialectic is not removed even by the claim that Christianity is the true religion, since, as Barth writes, "No religion *is* true. . . . [It] can only *become*

true"—not through any human achievement but solely by the grace of God. "Like the justified man," Barth insists, "the true religion is a creature of *grace*" (*OR*, 85). Here Barth's theology of religion depends on maintaining the balance between two opposing claims: (1) that Christianity is, by the grace of God, the true religion; and (2) that Christians can nevertheless make no claims for themselves and have, in fact, repeatedly failed to give God the glory by trying to claim credit for what can only be the gift of God. In this way, the church comes again and again under the judgment of God without ceasing to be the locus of true religion. Barth uses the example of Pure Land Buddhism, thought by many to be a non-Christian religion of pure grace, to underscore the fact that the truth of the Christian religion rests not on its character as a religion of grace but solely on the name Jesus Christ. The concrete reality of the *incarnation* is the ultimate touchstone of religious truth.

K. Barth, *OR*; J. A. Di Noia, "Religion and the Religions," in *Cambridge Companion to Karl Barth*, ed. J. Webster (2000), 243–57; G. Hunsinger, *How to Read Karl Barth* (1991); J. Mangina, *Karl Barth* (2004); B. L. McCormack, *Karl Barth's Critically Realistic Dialectical Theology* (1995); J. Webster, *Barth* (2000).

GARRETT GREEN

Resurrection of Jesus Christ

Unlike those who attempt to understand the resurrection of *Jesus Christ* from the dead as a fabrication or a mythological depiction of a universal *truth*, Barth sees it as the utterly real and unique event of the return from death and self-presencing of Jesus Christ to his disciples. It is both historical and beyond *history*. While a locatable event within first-century Palestine, the resurrection is at the same time a history-making event of the same order as the divine act of *creation* that brought human *time* and space into being. The resurrection is the unique event within history that encloses and renews history's origin and end. It is the absolute miracle, the "impossible possibility," which occurs only by the will and act of *God*, beyond all creaturely powers and processes. As a pure act of God the resurrection is the primal form and content of *revelation*. Thus, according to Barth, the New Testament writers rightly resisted the urge to attempt to circumscribe it as a purely inner-worldly historical event. The resurrection can never be "proven" by historical-critical *science*, which concerns itself exclusively with so-called objective historical events. Every such attempt necessarily reduces the resurrection to an unrecognizable falsification.

The resurrection is the quintessential *revelation* of God in Jesus Christ: Jesus comes again in "the mode of *God*" (*CD* III/2:448). Whereas in his life from Bethlehem to Golgotha the true deity of Jesus Christ was veiled, in his resurrection the paradox is removed and his divine identity is fully and irrevocably disclosed. In the resurrection of Jesus Christ the man Jesus is revealed to be the Christ, the Son of God (Rom. 1:4). Thus the resurrection entails the unveiling of the existential unity of the Jesus of Nazareth and the second person of the *Trinity*. Barth speaks of the resurrection of Jesus Christ as the unsurpassable origin of all Christian knowledge: "Everything else in the New Testament contains and presupposes the resurrection. It is the key to the whole" (III/2:443). As "the axiom of all axioms" (IV/1:346) the resurrection is, for Barth, so fundamental that it alone provides the sufficient basis for academic *theology*. The resurrection of Jesus Christ from the dead is the *noetic* center, and, if not the *material* center, at least the *logical* point of departure and controlling element with which all further theological reflection must be congruent.

The resurrection constitutes the Father's absolute *vindication of the Son* (IV/1:283–357). In the Father's act of raising him from the dead, the divine character, life, and work of Jesus of Nazareth is revealed. And this constitutes the scandal of the gospel, for it means that the same Jesus Christ, who has acted definitively as representative and savior of all men and women in his death, is now risen and present in all the ontological force of that action. In view of the radical inclusiveness and finality of the death of Jesus, Barth marvels at the reality of the resurrection. Barth's thought accentuates both the utter impossibility of this transition except as an act of God and the fact of this transition as the scandal of the gospel of Jesus Christ. Barth thus seeks to understand the resurrection *dogmatically* as the essential link between *Christology* proper and soteriology. The doctrine of the resurrection of Jesus Christ has to do with the *evangelical* problem: the movement of Jesus Christ in his completed reconciling being and action (*extra nos* and *pro nobis*) to us in our as yet opposed and unaffected anthropological sphere.

Barth's resurrection discourse, from beginning to end, is a sustained effort to understand the gospel of Jesus Christ in the light of the decisive *movement* of the crucified Lord to others. He holds firmly to the conviction that the resurrection is the event, the way, and the power of the turning of Jesus Christ, in all that he had accomplished for us from Bethlehem to Golgotha, to us. Barth thus takes the resurrection to be the *transition* of Jesus Christ *in nobis*. In the resurrection of Jesus Christ from the dead God has elected not to permit the fullness of *reconciliation* to remain distant and concealed from us. Rather, in his resurrection, the crucified Lord has drawn near to us once again, revealing himself and in him our own true selves. Included in his self-revelation is his inalienable relatedness to us, into which we are caught up and by which we are transformed.

Barth thus develops the doctrine of the resurrection as the inauguration of the radical presence of our reconciled human being in Jesus Christ through the power of the *Holy Spirit* (IV/2:264–77). That is, Jesus Christ in the completed work of reconciliation does not still need to be made real and present and pertinent; by virtue of his resurrection he already is this in the most radical way. It is in the power of the Spirit of the Lord that the transition to the free subjective apprehension of the reconciliation, already secured in Christ, is accomplished. The truth of the reconciling being and action of Jesus Christ culminating (in his crucifixion) presses for subjectivization in other human beings (in his resurrection). From this it is to be noted that the problem of the transition has its original form and basis in the triune being of God. The problem of the transition between the existence of the one man Jesus and all other men and women has its antecedent in the relation of the Son to the Father in the Holy Spirit—the life of the Spirit is in the differentiation and unity of the Father and the Son. It is on the basis of the revelation of God in Jesus Christ, as the crucified Lord turns and moves out to others in the power of his Holy Spirit, that we begin to understand the inner relations of the divine being.

In addition, the resurrection of Jesus holds decisive *eschatological* importance for Barth (IV/3.1:274–367). It is the absolutely new coming of the very one who came before, and with him, the concretely real presence of the future of *salvation*. He sees the resurrection as the first of the three forms of the Parousia, all of which make up the one coming again and self-revealing of Jesus Christ. The resurrection, as the primordial form of the Parousia, contains its own unfolding (in the age of the Spirit) and consummation (in the final Parousia). See *eschatology.*

K. Barth, *RD*; R. D. Dawson, *The Resurrection in Karl Barth* (2007); P. D. Molnar, *Incarnation and Resurrection* (2007); J. Webster, *Barth's Earlier Theology* (2004).

R. DALE DAWSON

Revelation   The formal structure given to the concept of revelation by Barth in *Rom* II remained unchanged to the end of his life. The material content by means of which that structure was rendered concrete, however, did change—more than once. Understanding the nature of those changes is important not only to those with a specialized interest in Barth studies but also to those seeking to grasp the significance of Barth's *theology* for the first time.

Before entering into issues surrounding the development of Barth's concept of revelation, however, it is worth pointing out here at the outset that revelation for Barth is God's "self-revelation." Revelation is not, in the first instance at least, the divine bestowal of information about *God*; it consists rather in the self-giving of God to the human knower so that what is known in revelation is God himself, God in his being and, indeed, in his very essence. That such self-giving had to find its center in the incarnate life was clear to Barth from very early on, though the significance that he attached to that move would eventually deepen as a result of christological innovations introduced late in his career (a subject to which we will return). For now, it is important only to point out that attachment to the concept of God's self-revelation marked Barth's thinking on this subject as distinctively modern. As Wolfhart Pannenberg put the point, "Only in the philosophy of German idealism do we first find the thought of a self-revelation of God in the sense of the strict identity of subject and content. . . . God is either revealed as himself, just as he is revealed to himself, or he is not revealed at all, at least in the strict sense. Later, perhaps by way of [Philip] Marheineke, Karl Barth took over this linking of the thought of God's self-revelation with that of uniqueness, and he used it in opposition to all ideas of a second source of the knowledge of God." We turn then to the development of Barth's understanding of divine self-revelation.

In his *Romans*, the concern to safeguard the ontological *otherness* of God precisely in the event of his self-revelation absorbed almost the whole of Barth's attention. He achieved this by means of a formal dialectic of veiling and unveiling. His thought was this: revelation is not and does not become a predicate of (or quality that is made proper to) the medium through which it occurs. That is, that which God chooses to be the medium of his self-revelation has no capacity or suitability intrinsic to itself that enables it to perform this service. Nor does it receive such a capacity as a sort of permanent addition to its list of attributes. In and of itself, therefore, the medium is not a medium at all; it is only a *veil* that conceals God from view. If the medium is truly to become a medium, a miracle must occur. The veil must be lifted—by God from God's side. An unveiling must take place in and through a veil that, in itself, remains a veil.

The point will be made clearer by looking at the actual process of revelation. In *Romans* Barth understood the medium of God's self-revelation to be the crucifixion (*ER*, 160), with the following qualification. In and of itself, the death of Jesus of Nazareth is a human death like any other; a brutal death, to be sure, but others were crucified at that time and their deaths were not revelatory. So the death of Jesus as an event in human history had no capacity as such to bear adequate *witness* to the being and *truth* of God. What made it to be so was the light cast upon it by the *resurrection of Jesus Christ* (*ER*, 30, 97). But precisely here two further comments are in order.

First, resurrection is not something that can be produced by the forces operative in *nature* and history. If resurrection takes place, then the only explanation for it must be that God (i.e., a *supramundane* agency) has acted in space and *time* as the direct cause of an event. That means that the event in which light is shed on the true identity of the one who was crucified and the true meaning of the crucifixion originates (causally speaking) in a point lying outside the realm of nature and history. Thus an objective act of God is required if the event of Christ's death is to be made revelatory. But that also means that the resurrection is an utterly unique event (not to be compared to any other). Second, there were no eyewitnesses of the event itself. There were eyewitnesses of the resurrected One, but precisely here a further problem arises. There is some evidence to suggest that the eyewitnesses were not able to recognize the risen Christ as the Jesus who was placed in a tomb apart from *a further divine act*. They had to be enabled to "see" that the one before them was, in fact, the resurrected Jesus and not someone else (cf. Luke 24:31). And so it remains with those of us who come later, those of us who have not seen the resurrected One: the truth of the testimony of the eyewitnesses (and their disciples) in Scripture must be shown to us. A further divine act—this time, an act that is "internal" to the would-be recipient of revelation—must take place so that the true meaning of that which has been accomplished objectively is made known to us and received as truth subjectively.

Revelation so conceived is a *Trinitarian* event with two moments (one objective and one subjective). The Father reveals the Son's identity and the true meaning of his death by raising him from the dead, and we receive that revelation in that the Spirit awakens us to *faith* and obedience. There is thus an objective and a subjective condition of the possibility of revelation—conditions that we learn from the reality of revelation itself.

Thus far this is the understanding of revelation that is everywhere presupposed in *Romans*. One will have noticed that the focal point of revelation was a single (complex) event: crucifixion and resurrection. And Barth was at great pains at that time to speak of the revelation event as a vertical line that intersects a horizontal line at a single mathematical point (without before and after, in other words). To put it another way, revelation consists in an event that knows of no extension on the historical plane. This is but a poetic way of saying that it is not something that is immediately discernible. Revelation takes place in hiddenness; the veil must be "lifted" by God for unveiling to occur through the veil that is the crucifixion.

Three short years later, Barth would undertake his first cycle of lectures in dogmatic *theology*. As already suggested, the structure of his concept of revelation would remain the same. But now the material content would undergo significant expansion and correction—and this in two ways. First, Barth would develop for the first time a doctrine of the *incarnation*. *Romans* had no place for incarnation; the focus had been entirely on the complex event of crucifixion and resurrection. At this stage Barth would take a momentous step forward. By developing a doctrine of the incarnation, Barth was (at the same time) acknowledging that revelation occurs through a life history, which stretched from cradle to grave. For the first time, the category of *history* had intruded itself and been taken up into the concept of revelation. The second major advance had to do with the development of the concept of a "threefold form of the Word"; and that requires further comment.

The three forms of the **Word of God** are revelation (i.e., the incarnate Lord, *Jesus Christ*), Holy Scripture, and a *preaching* that is based on Holy Scripture. Of the utmost importance here is not, as is sometimes thought, their distinction, but their interrelatedness. What Barth is seeking here is a *unity-in-differentiation*. "The Word of God on which dogmatics reflects is . . . one in *three*, three in *one*: revelation, scripture, and preaching—the Word of God revelation, the Word of God scripture, the Word of God preached, neither to be confused nor separated. *One* Word of God, *one* authority, *one* truth, *one*

power—and yet not one, but *three* addresses. *Three* addresses of God . . . yet not three Words of God, authorities, truths, or powers, but one. Scripture is not the revelation but is *out of* the revelation; preaching is neither revelation nor scripture but rather *out of* both. But scripture is the Word of God no less than revelation and preaching no less than scripture. The revelation is out of God alone; the scripture out of revelation, preaching out of revelation and scripture. But no *prius* or *posterius* [and] therefore no *maius* or *minus*; the Word of God in the same majesty, the first, the second, the third: *unitas* in *trinitate* and *trinitas* in *unitate*" (*GD*, 14–15, rev.). As is clear in the passage, the only **analogy** to the unity of these three forms is tri-unity in God—which is why Barth uses Trinitarian **language** to describe the relation in question. Clearly, what Barth is after is a concept of the "participation" (212) of the second form in the first and the participation of the third form in the first and the second.

It should also be obvious that Barth's concept of revelation has undergone significant expansion here. No longer is it a single event that is the locus of revelation. Barth's understanding of the original and originating locus of revelation has now itself become a combination of the God who speaks from beyond history in the incarnation and who continues to mediate that speaking through a historical entity: the Christian canon of Old and New Testaments. The first and second forms of the Word belong together, which is why the third form proceeds from both. The participation of the second form in the first is a participation in the event of the Word itself, the event of God's speaking in and through the life, death, and resurrection of Jesus Christ. Expressed less formally: the prophets and the apostles belong to the "qualified history" (*GD*, 60) that is revelation itself. To them was granted a share in that event. For that reason, the **Bible** stands on the divine side of the great chasm that separates the divine from all things human *precisely in its humanness.*

That the Bible is the Word of God is a "paradox" (*GD*, 215), for how could anything human be God's Word? Barth knows all the questions one might ask here. And yet he does not hesitate to affirm, with *Calvin*, that "Recognition of the authority of the Bible coincides with the recognition of God as its author" (222). To be sure, he rejects as "deplorable" the idea that the writers of Scripture "simply took down divine dictation" (217), which he links to the seventeenth-century concept of *inspiration*. Whether this characterization of the seventeenth-century conception is right or not, Barth's point in setting it forth would remain: any attempt to make revelation to be directly identical with the words of Scripture would make revelation something immediately and directly given to human control, a conclusion that he wished to avoid at all costs. Barth is content to say: "The Spirit of *truth* speaks to us from the words of the prophets and apostles as their own true author. They spoke and wrote by the Spirit as they came to share in the Spirit of revelation" (223). None of this does anything to alter the human, historical character of the texts found in Scripture. The vocabulary and the stylistic features that vary from one writer to another are not received through inspiration (56). Again, it is in their humanness and frailty that they are the norm that governs all that may be said and done in the *church*. "The Reformation stands or falls with its Scripture principle" (212). Indeed, "Protestantism" (by which Barth means the Protestant church of his day) "stands or falls" with it (205).

What Barth has established here is a dialectical conception of the relation of revelation and the Bible. The dialectic of veiling and unveiling that was fundamental to the conception of revelation in Barth's *Romans* is here preserved. The Bible is not *as such* revelation (i.e., abstracted from the revelation relation, making it to be one historical set of documents alongside others). But in that the Spirit who first engendered it takes up its witness anew, making these human words to be a fit medium of the divine speaking, the true nature of the Bible is disclosed. And lest it be thought that Barth's view results in an "occasionalism" (i.e., the Bible only becomes the Word of God occasionally, once in awhile, or rarely), Barth tell us that he has chosen the Latin phrase *Deus dixit* in his attempt to refer to the divine speaking that is the presupposition of the Bible (*GD*, 58) because *dixit* is the perfect tense, which helps to indicate that the divine speaking is "an eternal perfect" (59), which means that it is repeated in each and every moment in which the church is given life. Still, that the Bible is not *as such* revelation does mean that it constitutes a "barrier" (59) between revelation and the church, so that the church may not apply to itself the authority that is proper to the Word of God alone.

Taking a step back, one should note that although there is a grain of truth in the American neo-orthodox belief that Barth was originator of their own view that the Bible *becomes* the Word of God, a great deal has been lost in translation. That the Bible becomes the Word of God does not mean that it is "essentially" something else until God acts. On the contrary, what the Bible is essentially is the Word of God. The Bible can only come to be God's Word for us because "it already *is*" (*GD*, 219, rev.). What the Bible "becomes" when it is received in faith and obedience is simply what it is. Where this becoming does not take place, the reason for it is to be found in the lack of faith and obedience on the part of a putative recipient. The fault does not lie on the objective side. And, in any event, what is given in such "becoming" is the one Word of God whose content never varies.

The participation of preaching in the address of God rests upon a participation in the Word mediated by Scripture, which means that preaching is two steps removed from the Word of God. Here too only a relation of indirect identity with the Word of God comes into consideration. Preaching becomes the Word of God in that it sets forth a witness to the primary witness of Scripture that the Spirit is pleased to honor by speaking in and through it.

Barth's doctrine of Scripture and its place in his doctrine of revelation remained unchanged in *CD* I/1 and I/2, though it did undergo considerable expansion. The final adjustment to be introduced into Barth's conception of revelation did not begin to emerge until IV/1 and was only completed with the account of the two "natures" of Christ in IV/2. Here again, no change was made to the formal structure of Barth's concept. The dialectic of veiling and unveiling remained in place. But Barth did make changes in his **Christology**, which meant that the objective moment of revelation was now understood less in terms of the abstract metaphysics of Chalcedon and more in terms of thoroughly actualized account of Christ's two "natures."

The actualization of the natures means at least two things. First, "hypostatic union" has been replaced by a "hypostatic uniting." The assumption of a human "nature" is not complete in a moment (i.e., in the conception of Jesus in the womb of the Virgin) but takes place throughout the course of the life of the earthly Jesus (IV/2:105–6). Second, there is for Barth no interpenetration of the "natures" since the "natures" (or, as Barth prefers, divine essence and human essence—IV/2:113) are not themselves substantially conceived. There is rather a single history in which both divine "essence" and human "essence" are communicated to the "person of the union," thereby making the God-human to be what he is. Alternatively expressed: the history of the humiliation of God and the exaltation of the human is the rendering concrete of the identity of the God-human as willed by God eternally in the *covenant* of *grace*.

In this way, the communication is itself made to be constitutive of the "person" of Christ (cf. IV/2:85).

The crucial point to be observed here is it is precisely the *imperceptible* nature of the communication of human attributes (and the experiences they make possible) to the Logos that now constitutes the material basis for the dialectic of veiling and unveiling. Who the subject of this human life finally might be is something that must be revealed by the Spirit, since the subject of both divine humiliation and human exaltation remains hidden to view. And that is how the revelational dialectic of Barth's *Romans* was kept in play by the late development of his Christology.

K. Barth, *CD* I/1–2; idem, *ER*; idem, *GD*; B. L. McCormack, *Karl Barth's Critically Realistic Dialectical Theology* (1995); idem, "The Being of Holy Scripture Is in Becoming," in *Evangelicals and Scripture*, ed. V. Bacote, L. C. Miguélez, and D. L. Okholm (2004), 55–75. W. Pannenberg, *Systematic Theology*, trans. G. W. Bromiley (1991).
BRUCE L. McCORMACK

Roman Catholicism Barth's intensive and continuous engagement of Roman Catholicism throughout his career takes place in the context of his quest for a way out of Protestant theology's identity crisis, vis-à-vis Protestantism *liberalism* or Neo-Protestantism. Barth considers Roman Catholicism an important dialogue partner on the way to recovering Protestant theology's identity. There are two intertwined, methodological ways of dealing with Roman Catholicism: criticism and learning. Barth's criticism of Roman Catholicism particularly appears as criticism of problematic elements within it that also took shape in Neo-Protestantism. Therefore, it coincides with the endeavor to cleanse Protestant *theology* of Roman Catholic teachings that in modified form were accepted into Protestant theology in the centuries after the Reformation.

However, Barth also believed that learning from Roman Catholicism is necessary because it is a "space" in which particular substantial elements of the Reformation/Protestant identity are better preserved than in Protestantism itself. In this sense, learning from Roman Catholicism is identical to diagnosing substantive problems within Protestant theology over the course of its history, which is especially evident in Neo-Protestantism. Along with subtle changes of emphasis toward the former (criticism) or the latter (learning), the mutual intertwining of these two methodological principles is reflected in Barth's engagement with Roman Catholicism throughout his entire opus.

The basic outlines of Barth's preoccupation with Roman Catholicism are formed during Barth's tenure as a lecturer at the University of Göttingen (1921–1924). Dealing with the issue of Protestant theology's identity crisis, Barth begins with investigating the theology of the Reformation period, the medieval theology with which the Reformers came into conflict. In doing so, he discovers that the problematic elements of medieval theology are not presented in Roman Catholicism exclusively, for which it is assumed that it follows medieval tradition, but also in modified shape in Neo-Protestantism, which considers itself as the definite Protestant break with the medieval theological traditions. As a result, Barth connects his preoccupation with medieval Roman Catholic theology with his criticism of Neo-Protestantism. Thus Neo-Protestant romanticism, the tendency toward the immediate, is seen as an analogy to the reasoning of medieval Catholic theology regarding the harmonious interpolation of *reason* and *revelation*, ecclesiastical and biblical authority, *nature* and *grace*, *time* and *eternity*, and what *Luther* criticized as *theologia gloriae*. In so far as original Reformation/Protestant theology is characterized by Luther's *theologia crucis*, the discontinuity between reason and revelation, ecclesiastical and biblical authority, nature and grace, time and eternity, it has little in common with both Roman Catholicism and Neo-Protestantism (*ThC*, 13–127).

Although the seminal idea that learning from Roman Catholicism is in the interest of Protestant identity is perceptible even in the early Göttingen writings, learning from Roman Catholicism as a methodological principle Barth appropriated concretely only at the end of the Göttingen period. This happened under the influence of the modification of Barth's understanding of the original Protestant identity. Among other things, Barth's dialogues with Erich Przywara (1923), Paul Tillich (1923), and Erik Peterson (1925) were motivating, as was, in particular, Barth's preoccupation with the Reformed *dogmatics* of the nineteenth-century theologian Heinrich Heppe. While Protestant identity in the early Göttingen writings is determined by discontinuity, uncertainty, and permanent crisis, Barth points out in his later Göttingen writings that the proper understanding of certainty belongs to the original identity of Reformation/Protestant theology. Such certainty is based on a proper understanding of the *Word of God* in the proclamation of the *church*. This modified understanding of Protestant identity receives its formative meaning for Barth's later theology in the *Göttingen Dogmatics*. Within the teaching of the threefold Word of God, Barth elaborates the Word of God in the proclamation of the church (*GD*, 14–15). The Word of God in the proclamation of the church is not self-understood, as if the church would simply stand in continuity with revelation, but its authenticity is rather measured in relation to Holy Scripture (211–29).

Barth contrasts such an understanding of the certitude of the Word of God with both Neo-Protestantism and Roman Catholicism, since both represent a kind of a historicization of revelation (210): Neo-Protestantism by emphasizing the continuity between revelation and religious experience (67–68), and Roman Catholicism by emphasizing the continuity between revelation and the church (202–3). Still, unlike Neo-Protestantism, which represents a complete betrayal of the Reformation (210–11), Roman Catholicism can serve as a learning "space" to Protestantism in search of its own identity. Moreover, although in a problematic way, the substantial elements of the original Reformation/Protestant theology have been preserved in Roman Catholicism: in the concept of the church's authority (240–41), the belief in the presence of the Word of God in the proclamation of the church (206), the understanding of the task of theology as *ministerium ecclesiasticum* ("C&T"). The stance on Catholicism as a learning "space" is reflected in the writings from the Münster period (1925–1930). In his essays "The Concept of the Church" (1927) and "Roman Catholicism: A Question to the Protestant Church" (1928) (both in *T&C*), Barth particularly focused on the similarities and differences in the concept of *notae ecclesiae* in Protestantism faithful to the Reformation and in Roman Catholicism.

Barth evokes the similarities, like the belief in God's presence as being constituent to the church, the belief in the authority of the church, and the belief in the significance of the church for *salvation* ("Roman Catholicism," 314ff.). In doing so, he reduces the differences between Protestantism faithful to the Reformation and Roman Catholicism to a different understanding of *grace* ("Concept of the Church," 280ff.; "Roman Catholicism," 322ff.). The doctrine of grace, which thus becomes a common denominator and a framework for the systematization of Barth's criticism of Roman Catholicism, has also to be seen as a framework for Barth's criticism of Neo-Protestantism, which merely represents a contemporary version of the medieval doctrine of grace ("Roman

Catholicism," 328; *VkA* IV, 192, 271, 281, 298ff.). The thematization of Roman Catholicism within the triangle of Protestantism faithful to the Reformation, Neo-Protestantism, and Roman Catholicism is also characteristic of Barth's *CD*.

As far as the first vertex of this triangle is concerned, a new element becomes discernible: Barth associates Neo-Protestantism with the theology of colleagues he previously considered to be kindred spirits, **Brunner, Bultmann,** Gogarten, and others. Barth characterizes their existentialist-theological system of thought as the anthropologizing of theology, classifying it in the same category as Neo-Protestantism (*CD* I/1:xii, 19–20, 26–27, 36–37, 128ff.). This reversal in regard to those he previously considered kindred spirits is already discernible during Barth's tenure in Münster. The framework for the systematization of Barth's criticism of Roman Catholicism (as well as Neo-Protestantism and the theology of Barth's former colleagues) within this modified triangle during Barth's Münster tenure becomes the *analogia entis* ("F&I," 34, 38ff., 57ff.; *HS&CL*, 3ff., 10ff.).

Barth considers his criticism of the *analogia entis* as a variation on his criticism of the Roman Catholic doctrine of grace. Barth's dialogue with Pryzwara in 1929 has certainly influenced this modification. The radical no of unadulterated Protestant theology to the Roman Catholic *analogia entis*, against which Barth puts an *analogia fidei* (I/1:237ff., 436ff.; II/1:226–27) has also to be understood over the entire opus of *CD* as a no to Neo-Protestantism and the existential theology of Barth's former fellow combatants (I/1:xii–xiii; II/1: passim).

K. Barth, *T&C*; B. Dahlke, *Die katholische Rezeption Karl Barths* (2010); E. Lamirande, "The Impact of Karl Barth on the Catholic Church in the Last Half Century," in *Footnotes to a Theology*, ed. H. M. Rumscheidt (1974), 112–41; A. Marga, *Karl Barth's Dialogue with Catholicism in Göttingen* and *Münster* (2010); L. Matošević, *Lieber katholisch als neuprotestantisch* (2005).

LIDIJA MATOSEVIC

Salvation   Salvation, as Barth understands it, means the original and basic will of *God*, from before the foundations of *creation* and unimpeded by any creaturely *sin* and rebellion, for *humanity* to reach the telos of its being, its ultimate end, in perfect and eternal communion and fellowship with God by sharing in the very triune life. Salvation then is the fulfillment of God's covenanted promise to be our God and for his human creatures to be his people accomplished by his own free and special act of *love* even in the face of human sin and alienation, that is, by the act of *election*. The coming of this salvation is the *grace* of God in its most proper sense and as such is the content and heart of the Christian message.

The *covenant* God has made, however, is with a humanity that has rejected its destiny for fellowship with God and in doing so corrupts its very creaturely existence. Humanity opposes and repudiates this gracious ordination to participation and fellowship in the divine triune life putting *hope*, rather, in merely creaturely sources of life and self-fulfillment. The object of God's redemptive *grace* is a fallen humanity, captive to *evil*, which must be rescued from its subjection to evil and whose being in sin must be judged so that the sin and corruption in him may be done away with forever and so may reach God's blessed ordained end. The fulfillment of the *covenant* then requires God's act of redemptive grace, which reconciles thankless, rebellious, and prideful humanity to himself. By its very nature then salvation involves both judgment and grace—a judgment not in opposition to or in tension with grace, but judgment for the sake of grace. God's No serves his Yes. God's No in response to our rejection of his Yes to us is perfectly consonant with and reinforces his Yes to us

in *Jesus Christ*, who triumphs over sin and death.

It is crucial to Barth that the reconciling grace to the end of salvation is the work of the one whole *Trinity*: Father, Son, and *Holy Spirit*. God the Father sends God the Son in the power of God the Spirit to reconcile the world to himself, to restore and fulfill the covenant broken by humanity. There is no opposition or division in God, but a oneness of action and oneness of being in accomplishing our salvation. The whole God is our Redeemer, not just the Son of God.

For Barth it is especially important to note that God's act of redemption to salvation is perfectly reflective of the very being of God. God saves because as Father, Son, and Holy Spirit, God is salvation. The acts and being of God entirely cohere so that the redemptive action of God does not merely reveal just one particular thing about God, but constitutes a self-revelation of who God is in his very triune Being. The reconciling work to the end of salvation arises out of the very nature and character of God as the one who loves in *freedom*. This act is not alien to God, but fully manifests the essence of his nature to be self-giving, even to that which is not God, even to that which is foolishly and pridefully against God. The almightiness of God in the highest is God's freedom to love and lift up from the depths. The omnipotent will of God is no naked, arbitrary, capricious will, but the sovereign exercise of his freedom to love, graciously judge, reconcile, and redeem his creatures. The love of God is such that the whole God, Father, Son, and Holy Spirit are, each in his own way, willing and able to suffer for us in our place and on our behalf. This exercise of God's own divine freedom to love his creatures to the end at his own expense is the manifestation of his glory.

This reconciling work of the triune God on behalf of fallen humanity is a work that must be accomplished for us by God from beginning to end. To that end, the Son of God, through whom all things came into existence and for whom all things were created, assumes our humanity and its entire fallen condition. The *reconciliation* is effected not just *by* Jesus Christ, one with God and one with humanity, but *in* Jesus Christ, in his own person. God in Jesus Christ has seized upon a recalcitrant humanity and through his life, death, crucifixion, *resurrection,* and *ascension* raised up the human mind, will, and very nature into perfect conformity with God's intentions to receive the salvation intended for it. In Jesus Christ we see the reconciliation of God and humanity achieved. In Jesus Christ we apprehend the perfect love of God for humanity and the perfect love of humanity for God—the fulfillment in his one person of the dual commandments that sum up the will of God: the love of God and the love of neighbor. That reconciliation of God and humanity in him is the reconciliation we receive from him, in the power of his Spirit, as the gift of his self-giving grace. Barth wants to make clear then that our salvation is not a particular thing that is given to us, or some stance or status external to us, but rather Jesus Christ himself is our salvation from God. We have salvation only as we have him, as we receive from him the gift of himself, truly God and truly human in right relationship of perfect loving union and communion. We are given the gift of sharing in the incarnate Son's own relationship with the Father in the power of the Spirit—and that is eternal life, our salvation.

It is only on the basis of who Jesus Christ is, one with Father and Spirit and one with us (the double *homoousion* of Chalcedon) that God is able to accomplish the work of our reconciliation. For only God can provide creatures with a share in his eternal life, and only a humanity reconciled to God can receive the gift of salvation. Jesus Christ, one with God and one with us, is the one true mediator who in his own person brings God and humanity together. This mediation, Barth wants us to recognize, is

a dual mediation. Jesus Christ mediates God to humanity bringing his Word, his will, indeed God's very presence to us. But the mediatorial ministry of Jesus Christ does not then reach a limit where now we are left on our own to make our own response on the basis of our own fallen, rebellious, and distrusting selves. Rather, Jesus Christ, as one of us, in our place and on our behalf, mediates us to God. As our substitute and representative, both, he regenerates in himself our captive, fallen, twisted, and broken humanity, setting it free from the power of sin, healing it, and offering up a perfect response of fully trusting repentance and faith to the Father in the power of the Spirit. And we by that same Spirit are given the gift of participating in his response to the gracious reconciling and saving work of the one triune God. Jesus Christ is both the Lord as Servant who brings the very presence and redeeming power of God to us and is, in his one undivided person, also the Servant as Lord who lifts us up in union with his own humanity to be seated with him at the right hand of God. The reconciling work is the work of God and the work of God as man, all in Jesus Christ for us and our salvation.

The reconciling ministry of Jesus Christ then involves not just the work of the cross, but extends from the moment of his conception in the womb of Mary, through his whole life and ministry of faithful obedience in the power of the Spirit, to the culmination of his earthly obedience in submitting to the judgment of sin upon our fallen humanity on the cross for the sake of our resurrection and ascension with him into eternal fellowship and communion with God. The reconciliation worked out in Jesus Christ involves not only a substitutionary death, but a substitutionary life in which we now may share. The *incarnation,* the person of Jesus Christ, is essential to the atoning work. The incarnation points to who Jesus Christ is and is the ontological foundation in relation to God and humanity for what he has accomplished for us. He is our salvation, from beginning to end, act and being.

The atoning work, as Barth grasps the Christian message, necessarily involves the judgment of the sinner. There can be no reconciliation unless the sin that has corrupted the very nature of humanity is done away with. The grace of God makes no exceptions, for exceptions—which would allow for the power of sin or the presence of corruption to remain in our human natures—would not be gracious and could not lead to our salvation. However, were we judged on our own, apart from Jesus Christ, we would be undone along with our sin. However, in Jesus Christ, because he, as Son of God and Son of Man, can do for us what we cannot do for ourselves (and yet as one of us in perfect communion with the Father and Spirit in his one person) we in him, are not done way with, but rather are separated from our sin, which is sent away and condemned, while we ourselves in him are rescued, forgiven, and restored. As Barth puts it, Jesus Christ the Judge is judged in our place as one of us, united to us. Only in this way can the essence of our sinfulness—our desire to judge ourselves, our neighbors, and God as if we were God—be cast out. Only the Judge judged in our place can take away and make impossible and unnecessary our prideful propensity to justify ourselves. In Jesus Christ the Judge is judged, and so we are justified in him and set free from the impossible task of justifying ourselves.

Furthermore, Barth recognized that Jesus Christ must be identified as both the Elect One and the Rejected One. Fallen humanity is neither rejected nor elected apart from Jesus Christ, as if he was merely a means to an end, a tool or instrument, to accomplish our salvation. Our election and rejection must be thought of as sharing in Jesus Christ's own election and rejection. In the economy of our salvation, accomplished not just by Jesus Christ but in Jesus Christ (*Calvin*), rejection/judgment is for the sake of election just as crucifixion is for the sake of resurrection and ascension. Jesus Christ is our salvation because he is the Elect One and we are given the gift of sharing in his election by the Spirit. It is in this way that Barth held election in Jesus Christ to be the sum of the gospel.

Barth, along with Calvin, wants to make clear that what Jesus Christ has accomplished is our whole salvation. That is, he has made real and actual in himself our *knowledge of God*, our *justification*, our *sanctification*, and our glorification/redemption. There is no aspect of our salvation that remains a mere potential that we somehow must make actual or real by our own efforts, even with the help of the Spirit. Our whole salvation is complete in all its dimensions now because Jesus Christ himself is our entire salvation. To have Christ is to have the whole of our salvation, a salvation that is whole in him. To be sure, we can differentiate, in the economy of our lives in Christ, among our justification, sanctification, and glorification, but they are all received by faith as the gift of participating in the regenerated humanity of Jesus Christ. We continue in the Christian life as we begin, with a trust that God will provide us our whole salvation from beginning to end and so live on the basis of the accomplished work of Christ. We live and obey by faith, hope, and love in the grace of God.

The *Christian life*, then, according to Barth, is a life in union with Jesus Christ in the power of the Spirit as members of his body and with the *vocation* of living lives of invocation, lives of *prayer*, where all that we do is participating in the ongoing *ministry* of Jesus Christ today. As those who are justified we can only regard ourselves now as forgiven sinners. Our lives in sin are in the past and have no power to determine our destiny—a destiny restored and secured for us in Jesus Christ. We really were lost sinners, but we are no longer. That really is our past, but it is not our future. The Christian life then acknowledges the past, but lives out of faith, hope, and love that comes from the future that Christ has for us. For who we are now is not who we were on our own, but we now are who we are only in union and communion with Jesus Christ. So Barth says, we no longer can take sin more seriously or as seriously as grace. For the *truth* and reality of who we are is coming to us from the future secured for us in the one who is to come again in vindicating glory, Jesus Christ.

K. Barth, *CD* I/2:§13; II/1:§§28–31; II/2:§§32–35; III/2:§45; IV/1–2; D. Bloesch, *Jesus Is Victor!* (1976); G. W. Deddo, *Karl Barth's Theology of Relations* (1999); A. Heron, "The Theme of Salvation in Karl Barth's Doctrine of Reconciliation," *Ex Auditu* 5 (1989): 107–22.

GARY W. DEDDO

Sanctification   If Barth's doctrine of *justification* is distinctive, his doctrine of sanctification is ground-breaking. Relative to familiar received traditions, whether Protestant or otherwise, there is nothing quite like it.

Sanctification, for Barth, is not so much about obtaining a new nature as it is about obtaining a new relationship, even though that relationship involves a total renovation of the whole person. Moreover, whereas *Calvin* (like many others) saw sanctification mainly as proceeding by degrees ("more and more"), Barth saw it mainly as an accomplished fact and an ongoing event ("once for all"/"again and again"). For Barth, sanctification was not merely inward but also outward, not simply individual but also communal, and finally not only communal but somehow also cosmic in scope.

The main reason for Barth's innovative approach was the priority he assigned to the idea of sanctification "in Christ" (for which he assembled considerable biblical evidence). Because sanctification, like justification, took place first of all apart from us in Christ, the grammar or logical structure of both

doctrines was much the same. It was not as though justification was something "instantaneous" in the life of *faith* while sanctification was in turn something "continual." On the contrary, each of them was instantaneous and continual in its own way. Justification and sanctification were each seen as a unitary, two-phased event involving a necessary transition from the "objective" aspect in Christ there and then to the "subjective" or "existential" aspect, taking place in us, or among us, here and now. In both cases, the objective was the ground of the subjective, even as the subjective was the fulfillment of the objective.

Justification and sanctification each brought out a different dimension of Christ's once-for-all work of *reconciliation*, and each in its own way stood for reconciliation as a whole, so that they were not two parts adding up to a whole. Justification and sanctification took place simultaneously, as Calvin taught, but their simultaneous occurrence was seen first of all as objective apart from us in Christ, as Calvin did not teach (or at least as he did not clearly emphasize). For Barth our sanctifying union with Christ was objective and passive by *grace* before it became active and subjective in faith working by *love*. Like justification, however, sanctification was also effected by Christ alone and grace alone, through faith alone. Works of love were a consequence, not a cause, of sanctifying grace.

In this context the differences between justification and sanctification as Barth saw them are instructive. Where justification focused mainly on Christ's cross, sanctification looked more to his resurrection. Where justification pertained to God's "downward" self-humiliation in Christ, sanctification involved our "upward" exaltation in Christ by the Spirit. Where justification dealt with *sin* as guilt, sanctification dealt with sin as a power of bondage. Where justification meant our eternal deliverance from divine condemnation, sanctification signified our eternal glorification in fellowship with *God*. Where justification served to humble us regarding our sin of pride, sanctification acted to rouse us from our sin of sloth.

The following account traces Barth's doctrine of sanctification in *CD* IV/2:499–613.

1. *Justification and Sanctification* (499–511). Sanctification, like justification, was not primarily psychological, moral, or otherwise mundane. On the contrary, it was primarily spiritual. Although it involved us as whole persons, it took place on an entirely different and superior plane. Traditional Protestant proposals about the *ordo salutis* (order of salvation), as Barth saw them, missed this fundamental point. In one way or another, they tended to reduce the spiritual to the psychological, and the mysterious to the mundane. They missed "the *simul* of the one event" of "redemptive occurrence" as it encounters us in different "moments" (502). Illumination, *vocation*, justification, sanctification, perseverance, glorification, and so on are not discrete or sequential "stages" of salvation so much as interlocking aspects of our union with Christ.

Barth drew upon the "Chalcedonian pattern" to explain how justification and sanctification are related. That is, he drew explicitly (and in the original Greek) on Chalcedon's distinctive terminology. Justification and sanctification, he proposed, are related (a) "without confusion or change," (b) "without separation or division," and (c) finally according to a principle of asymmetrical order.

a. Justification and sanctification occur in abiding distinction ("without confusion or change"). They are not identical nor are they interchangeable. Neither can be explained by the other. Nor can the one take the place of the other. Salvation from sin as guilt (justification) is not the same as salvation from sin as sloth (sanctification), nor is faith as humility the same as faith roused to action in love. These are different, irreducible moments of one and the same

saving event. And again, they are not two "parts," but two depictions of an indivisible whole.

He then mentions examples of confusion. In Roman Catholicism and modernist Protestantism (e.g., *Bultmann*), justification merges with sanctification, so that justification is regarded as the beginning of a sanctifying process in us. On the other hand, in the younger *Luther*, Zinzendorf, and Kohlbrügge, sanctification disappears into justification so that it has no independent significance in itself. Both errors have a common root in that both highlight salvation's subjective side at the expense of its objective occurrence apart from us in Christ.

b. Justification and sanctification occur in inseparable unity ("without separation or division"). Justification and sanctification cannot be separated because they are "only two moments and aspects of one and the same action" (505). Justification without sanctification tends toward an "indolent quietism," whereas sanctification without justification degenerates into "illusory activism" (505). *Forgiveness of sins* necessarily means liberation from sin's power, while the new human actions empowered by grace are never without their sinful elements, thus needing continual forgiveness. As God turns to us sinful creatures (justification), our conversion to God cannot be lacking (sanctification). They are two aspects of a single promise. As justification means "I will be your God," sanctification means "You shall be my people." They occur together like thunder and lightning.

c. Justification and sanctification are ordered to one another in a complex way (double asymmetry). Should justification be seen as materially superior to sanctification, or should it be the reverse, so that sanctification would be materially superior to justification? A double perspective is needed. From one point of view, justification is the fundamental ground while sanctification is merely the consequence. On the basis of justification, and not without it, the faithful are "called and given a readiness and willingness for discipleship, for conversion, for the doing of good works, for the bearing of the cross" (507–8). In this sense justification takes priority over sanctification.

From another angle, however, the situation is reversed. Here justification is simply the precondition for sanctification, which is ordained as the ultimate fulfillment. Forgiveness, although necessary, takes place finally for liberation in service to God. From a teleological standpoint, sanctification takes priority over justification.

In the end, both perspectives—ground/consequence and precondition/telos—are needed. In the nature of the case it is not possible to choose between them. The result is a double asymmetry. "We can and must give the primacy," Barth concluded, "now to the one and now to the other, according to the different standpoints from which we look" (511).

2. *The Holy One and the Saints* (511–33). Sanctification here and now serves to liberate the faithful from sin's power despite their in some sense remaining sinners. They are fully sanctified in Christ though not yet fully in themselves. In sanctification their remaining sinfulness is continually overridden by grace. They are continually "set apart" by grace for service to God and their neighbors (and in that sense made "holy") in a way that they are incapable of in themselves. Sanctification is the description of this *history* in which grace breaks the power of sin. In it the faithful are unified as a community, not just renovated as individuals. But the sole saving agent in this history is Christ in his office as King, as the Royal Man. He is the Holy One who constitutes the saints.

Sanctification means being roused from sloth to *freedom*. What rouses the sinner from sloth is an encounter with the *Word of God*. The Word is spoken with authority and power, and the Holy One who speaks it is Christ the Royal Man. "He does so forcefully, not merely in words but in acts, in his whole existence, and all-comprehensively in his death" (523). Through this Word the sinner is disturbed, summoned, and called to obedience. The life of sloth—with all its stupidity, inhumanity, dissipation, and weary resignation—can and must be left behind.

The faithful are not only roused by the Word but are also given direction. They are turned from foolishness to wisdom, from callousness to compassion, from anxiety to courage, and from apathy to works of love. "It is in this way that the Holy One creates the saints. It is in this way that he shares with them, in supreme reality, his own holiness; man's new form of existence as the true *covenant*-partner of God" (523). The slothfulness of the faithful is rejected and driven out by Christ.

Christ gives them a share in his holiness by giving them a share in himself. Sanctification from sloth to freedom means *participatio Christi* (participation in Christ). The faithful are made holy by a holiness not their own. "They do not belong to themselves, but to him. They are saints, not *propria* [with their own holiness], but *aliena sanctitate, sanctitate Jesu Christi* [with the holiness of another, the holiness of Jesus Christ]. They are holy in the truth and power of his holiness" (518). They are given a share here and now in what they already are in him (saints!) and in what they are destined to be fully in the age to come.

3. *The Call to Discipleship* (533–53). "The call issued by Jesus is a call to discipleship" (533). It is a call that is both substantive and effective. It teaches those who hear it what to do, and it gives them the power to do it. It is by looking to Jesus that they learn what to do, and by receiving his grace that they are equipped for it. They are called to follow Jesus in discipleship, to lift themselves up from their sloth, and to make use of the freedom that he gives them.

The call to discipleship binds the faithful to Jesus, not to a system of ideas. They are not bound to a program, ideal, or law, but to their living Lord, the Royal Man. They are called to faith in the form of obedience. There is no discipleship to Jesus apart from loyalty and obedience.

The call to discipleship is new each morning. It is always a summons to take a definite first step. "It always involves the decision of a new day; the seizing of a new opportunity which was not present yesterday but is now given in and with the call of Jesus" (538). Inevitably the faithful are called to turn away from themselves as those caught in the sins of yesterday. As the New Testament puts it, they deny themselves. Self-denial means doing what is proposed to them by Jesus. It may be something great or something small. "But its performance is laid upon us, not by ourselves, but by the One who has called us to himself, who has willed and chosen us as his own" (540).

The call to discipleship means breaking with false loyalties. Sole allegiance is claimed by God's kingdom, that is, by "the *coup d'état* of God proclaimed and accomplished already in the existence of the man Jesus" (543). Those whom Jesus calls to himself are required to stand firm by the kingdom he reveals, the kingdom as accomplished in him. This kingdom involves a drastic break—a protest and an onslaught—from the *world* as it exists in contradiction to God and the evils rejected by God's will. The faithful are not called to accomplish this break, for it is already accomplished in and through the Royal Man. But they are called (and this is a tall order) to correspond to God's kingdom as its witnesses with their lives.

The faithful can only live as witnesses to Christ by breaking with adverse cultural forces. "If we are his disciples we are freed by him from their rule. This does not mean that we are made superior, or set in a position of practical neutrality. It means that we can and must exercise our freedom in relation to them" (544). Breaking with them is a matter of "public responsibility" (545). No matter how costly it may

be, the faithful are called to deny them the ultimate loyalty they may claim (whether openly or secretly). Among the forces that assume the form of absolutes, Barth mentions possessions, social status, the resort to force, the family, and not least *religion*. "We will always know that it is his voice which calls us," Barth concludes, "from the fact that in what is demanded of us, we shall always have to do with a break with the great self-evident factors of our environment, and therefore of the world as a whole" (552). Sanctification is countercultural or it is not sanctification at all.

4. *The Awakening to Conversion* (553–84). The power by which we are moved from a state of slumber to a state of wakefulness, and so from sloth to freedom, can only be understood as a "divine mystery and miracle" (553). We are awakened by the power of grace, which capacitates us in spite of our incapacity. It awakens us from "the sleep of death" (555) in order that we may turn from ourselves to God.

Sanctification consists in fellowship with Christ as the Royal Man, who equips us beyond ourselves for discipleship. The dynamics of this occurrence cannot be described without paradox. The awakening that occurs is at once a creaturely and yet also a divine action. It is both "wholly creaturely and wholly divine" (557). Yet the initiative comes entirely from God: "Thus there can be no question of co-ordination between two comparable elements, but only of the absolute primacy of the divine over the creaturely. The creaturely is made serviceable to the divine and does actually serve it. It is used by God as his organ or instrument. Its creatureliness is not impaired, but it is given by God a special function or character. Being qualified and claimed by God for co-operation, it co-operates in such a way that the whole is still an action which is specifically divine" (557).

In this event there are thus two acting subjects, but only one Saving Agent. Freedom for God, and therefore from sloth, is a freedom available only as it is given, but as given it is there to be used.

This freedom for conversion involves the whole person in relation both to God and neighbor. It is a matter of heart, hand, and mind. And it is not something purely private, for it requires taking public responsibility. Nor is it confined to only one period in a person's life. On the contrary, it is a lifelong process in which a holy life is to be acquired "with growing sincerity, depth and precision" (566). It means halting at those points where we go wrong, and advancing toward those points where we are summoned. It means turning again and again from our old *humanity* to the new; the old that has died with Christ and the new that is risen in him. We are both of these simultaneously—*simul peccator et sanctus* (575). And we are both of them not partially but totally, though the old is past (yet still present) even as the new is already ours (though still future).

We do not find this new humanity, and therefore our true conversion, in ourselves. We find them only in Christ. "It is in his conversion that we are engaged," because in his life-history he has made us his own (583). "It is in his birth, from above, the mystery and miracle of Christmas, that we are born again. It is in his baptism in the Jordan that we are baptized with the Holy Spirit and with fire. It is in his death on the cross that we are dead as old human beings, and in his resurrection . . . that we are risen as new human beings" (583, rev.).

It is the Royal Man himself who is and who effects the great conversion of the world to God. In it the faithful are given a share, by being its participants and witnesses, as they look toward its manifestation in all things.

5. *The Praise of Works* (584–98). The expression "the praise of works" can be understood in two ways. It can mean "the works that God praises," or "the works that praise God." The works praised by God are those that please him in some way, while those by which he is praised are good for the very rea-

son that they praise him. This twofold usage suggests that the two meanings are inseparable.

A good human work is one that declares the good work of God. The good work of God occurs in the history of the covenant, which includes his works of *creation*, reconciliation, and redemption. Human works are good only as they relate to God's goodness in this covenantal history. Human good works can be good without being perfect or free from all sin. "We conclude that even a sinful man in his sinful work— and we are all sinners and all our works are sinful—may declare the good work of God, and therefore, even as a sinner and in the course of sinning, do a good work" (589).

The faithful receive the capacity to declare the goodness of God despite their sin. "Works can be good only as they declare what God has done and accomplished—the goodness in which he has turned to us human beings and given himself for us. That works are capable of this declaration does not alter the fact that they are the sinful works of great or little sinners" (590, rev.). Human works are made good by a goodness not their own despite their failings. A goodness is imparted to them from above. Such works of *witness* and praise are called forth and sanctified by God.

Human good works not only declare the goodness of God, they also participate in it by being taken into his service. Human beings are selected by God to be his witnesses. They are brought into God's service and empowered for specific actions. "In this sense, and on all these presuppositions, we must say of humankind's sanctification that it already takes place here and now in works which are really good, i.e., which are praised by God and praise him" (596, rev.).

6. *The Dignity of the Cross* (598–613). Sanctification not only means doing good works. It also means suffering with dignity. Sometimes it means suffering for the sake of Christ, while at other

times it means bearing some more general form of affliction in fellowship with him. But whatever form it may take, whether specific to faith or not, sanctification means never suffering without *hope*. For Christ, with Christ, and in his hope, the faithful receive power to live above their circumstances. Learning to suffer with dignity is both a sign and a means of their sanctification.

"The cross is the most concrete form of the fellowship between Christ and the Christian" (599). No one can be a disciple of Christ without being drawn into his passion. All those who confess his name, "if they are to be disciples of the Rejected and Crucified, must take up their own cross and therefore in their own place enter into the passion of Jesus, the shameful passion of One who is despised and rejected" (599). The dignity of their cross derives from him.

The cross of Jesus must not be confused with that of the faithful. He alone suffered and died for the sins of the world. Their cross may attest his saving work, but it in no way reenacts or contributes to it. Their cross may correspond to his, but always and only at a distance. "The relationship between the two is irreversible" (600).

The cross of the faithful is not something they should seek or induce. It will come to them. It is not to be affirmed for its own sake. It is simply to be endured in spite of itself. But the Lord will turn it for their good (603).

The suffering of the faithful is the fulfillment of their sanctification. The Lord will stand by them in their suffering and turn it for their good. It can be used to keep them in humility, to teach them to accept what punishment they deserve for their sins, to strengthen them in faith and obedience, and to confirm them in the love of Christ. By their suffering in this way, they will be purified and strengthened.

Certain forms of suffering take precedence. "In the New Testament the cross means primarily persecution" (609). But it reaches out from there to include all earthly forms of affliction and distress. Our only concern, writes Barth, is that we should not suffer as those without hope, "which means without the comfort and promise of suffering with Jesus. It must be our constant prayer, not only when adversity comes but in the good days which precede it, that this [failure] should not happen, that the Holy Ghost should make us free to accept and therefore to bear the appointed cross, i.e., to make it our own" (613). The faithful do so in the knowledge of resurrection hope that their suffering is not without a greater end. And in this knowledge lies their sanctification.

C. B. Anderson, "The Problem of Psychologism in Karl Barth's Doctrine of Sanctification," *ZDTh* 18, no. 3 (2002): 339–54; T. Greggs, *Theology against Religion* (2011); G. Hunsinger, "The Mediator of Communion," in *Disruptive Grace* (2000), 148–85; W. Jenkins, *Ecologies of Grace* (2008), 153–80; D. L. Migliore, "Participatio Christi," *ZDTh* 18, no. 3 (2002): 286–307; K. Sonderegger, "Sanctification as Impartation in the Doctrine of Karl Barth," *ZDTh* 18, no. 3 (2002): 308–15.

GEORGE HUNSINGER

Schleiermacher

Barth began his career as a liberal theologian, and his turn to *dialectical theology* did not occur overnight. After two years in the pastorate, he still praised Schleiermacher for adjusting the insights of the Reformation to the religious individualism and historical relativism of the modern *world* and called him "one of the deepest Christian thinkers of all times" (*P-1913*, 26). But in 1915 such sentiments gave way to growing doubts. In May 1921, during his work on *Rom* II, Barth mused that he would begin his teaching career as professor of *theology* with a "declaration of war at this church father" (*B–Th Br* I, 489). For the next decade, he engaged Schleiermacher with polemical excitement. The reason is well known. Barth's Schleiermacher confused theology with anthropology, concentrating on the piety and God-consciousness of human beings instead of *God* and God's *revelation* in *Jesus Christ*.

Barth's opposition was severe. Nevertheless, he acknowledged his opponent's genius and theological achievement. He called Schleiermacher "intelligent, instructive and generous," where the "useless crowd" of other theologians in the 1920s was "stupid, clumsy, inconsistent and timorous." Schleiermacher "is in almost everything he undertakes a *master*, to whom one has to take off one's little hat" (*B–Th Br* II, 207). Repeatedly Barth cautioned other dialectical theologians, especially Emil *Brunner*, against an overly triumphant attitude. In turn, Brunner thought that Barth's view on the relation between *creation* and redemption came "quite close—excuse me—to Schleiermacher, for whom redemption also is not a re-[storation] but an ultimate revelation of the divine life-reality" (*B–Br Br*, 145).

In his famous lectures on nineteenth-century Protestant theology (1932–1933), Barth cautioned against a general condemnation: "Anyone who has never loved here and is unable to love here again and again may not hate here either" (*PTh*, 427, rev.). Evidently, Barth's students at the time were rather dismayed by such an approach. They favored a clear-cut dismissal of Schleiermacher's theology as heretical. Yet their teacher called Schleiermacher a "giant among the theologians" and stated that it is wiser to acknowledge his place *within* the church (*B–Th Br* III, 143 n. 9). Barth concluded that Schleiermacher's focus on the Christian pious self-consciousness was intended to lead to a "pure theology of the *Holy Spirit*" and of the human being who receives God's grace through God alone (*PTh*, 471, rev.). At the same time, Barth suspected that Schleiermacher's conception of the relation between God and humankind conflicted with the full affirmation of Christ's divinity and implied that Christ is merely the predicate of the pious human subject. While Barth had been always aware of the difficulties in the attempt to overcome Schleiermacher, he now relativized his earlier polemical stance and put it into historical perspective. This position he would hold until the end of his life.

Throughout the *CD*, Barth kept Schleiermacher's theology at a distance. After a series of harsh reproaches in connection with attacks on *natural theology* in I/1–II/1, his remarks became more conciliatory. Shortly before his death, Barth summarized his position (see "Postscript"). He remained convinced that his original intuition of the necessity to overcome Schleiermacher's theology was correct, but he wondered whether his persistent criticism could have been more successful if it had focused on pneumatology, a topic of central importance in Schleiermacher's theology, instead of *Christology*.

On the whole, Barth's theological evaluation of Schleiermacher "is sometimes negative, sometimes positive, and often ambiguous" (Collins, 213). The thesis that he fundamentally broke with Schleiermacher is simplistic, even though Barth himself contributed to the perception that the two belong to opposite theological camps. It is not without irony that such a perception is also common among those who favor Schleiermacher and think that Barth is the one who has to be "overcome."

It hardly needs to be said that Schleiermacher should no longer be read through Barth's eyes. Such a reading only obscures the continuity of shared theological concerns. Occasionally, similarities between the two theologians have been noticed. In 1986, Barth's relation with Schleiermacher was "increasingly being recognized as one of serious dialogue rather than total rejection" (Gunton, 292). Several studies on the subject were published in the last two decades, but Barth's position prior to the *CD* has not been adequately recognized. As I have argued (in *Barth and Schleiermacher*), the comparison of Barth's position in different stages of his development can lead to a more nuanced description of his relation to Schleiermacher.

Methodologically, a concentration on the central texts by both theologians and the way in which each of them handles the subject matter at hand is useful. While many interpreters have recognized the importance of locating Barth's theology in the context of the Reformed tradition, they too often remain content with the conventional view that Barth rejected Schleiermacher's "anthropological presuppositions." Such contentment, however, prevents one from recognizing, for instance, that Schleiermacher's distinction between God and the world is even more radical than Barth's. In general, resemblances between the two theologians are most clearly visible in Barth's earlier theology, with its pneumatological focus on the event in which a human being is met by God's *revelation*. For example, the anthropocentric outlook of traditional views on *election* and predestination motivated Schleiermacher as well as the early Barth to search for a new approach. Both theologians criticized the classical concept of a twofold divine decree for two predetermined groups of persons and argued that the dialectic of election and reprobation is part of the historical realization of God's kingdom. Reprobation is not an end in itself but always remains open and oriented toward election for *salvation*, which is the steadfast goal of God's acting (cf. *GD*, §18).

Further research will also have to take into account the background of Barth's assessment of Schleiermacher. How did liberal theologians at the beginning of the twentieth century, like Barth's teacher Wilhelm *Herrmann* or Ernst Troeltsch, view Schleiermacher,

what did they accept or reject in his theology, and which Schleiermacherian tradition did Barth oppose? An answer to these questions will enable us to understand better the extent to which both Schleiermacher and Barth were modern theologians.

In sum, Barth's theology is not merely a repudiation of Schleiermacher but also an expansion of his predecessor's work in a new framework. Even where Barth seeks to break new ground, he often shares ideas and suggestions first brought into play by his predecessor. Further attempts are needed to identify links between Barth and Schleiermacher in order to sharpen our perception of their respective appropriation of the dogmatic tradition and to tease out the systematic-theological consequences for our own time.

K. Barth, "Schleiermacher"; A. Collins, "Barth's Relationship to Schleiermacher," *Studies in Religion* 17, no. 2 (1988): 213–24; M. Gockel, *Barth and Schleiermacher on the Doctrine of Election* (2006); C. Gunton, "Karl Barth and the Western Intellectual Tradition," in *Theology beyond Christendom*, ed. J. Thompson (1986), 285–301; B. L. McCormack, "What Has Basel to Do with Berlin?" *PSB* 23, no. 2 (2002): 146–73; C.-D. Osthövener, *Die Lehre von Gottes Eigenschaften bei Friedrich Schleiermacher und Karl Barth* (1996); R. J. Sherman, *The Shift to Modernity* (2005) .

MATTHIAS GOCKEL

Science The relation between *religion* and science was not a dominant theme in Barth's work. Barth apparently came in his mature *theology* to regard preoccupation with that relationship as a hallmark of theological *liberalism*. Nevertheless, Barth asserted after his break with liberalism that theology is a science. His defense of that claim remains controversial, however, particularly since many have missed its eschatological dimension (see *eschatology*).

In his early years, Barth worked in the line of his favorite Marburg professor, Wilhelm **Herrmann**. Herrmann contended that religion and science constitute different kinds of knowledge. On the one hand, scientific knowledge is lawful, mechanical, and objective. On the other, religious knowledge is experiential, living, and subjective. Barth expressed an analogous perspective in a lecture titled, "Religion und Wissenschaft," which he delivered in Safenwil in 1912 (*VkA* II, 418–38). In his lecture, he asserted that religion and science are distinct not quantitatively but qualitatively. He rejected any "either-or" between religion and science as misunderstanding the essence of both (437).

Barth's perception of science darkened during the Great War. He called into question the widespread assumption that scientific progress was leading toward the *kingdom of God* and pointed out the destructive potential of modern technology. The publication of *An die Kulturwelt!* in October 1914 by ninety-three prominent representatives of the German arts and sciences strengthened his impression that the sciences—like the rest of modern culture—had fallen from God. In *Rom* I (1919) Barth described science as a kind of idolatry, a superficial knowledge alienated from the reality of God. His study of Franz Overbeck would sharpen his sense that theologians had lost their way by accommodating their distinctly eschatological form of knowledge to the secular sciences. In *Rom* II (1922) he hinted at the possibility of theology as science, but only as eschatological event.

In the postwar period, Barth received an appointment as an extraordinary professor at the University of Göttingen in Germany. He now faced the challenge of justifying the presence of a faculty of theology at the university. What right does theology have to coexist with secular disciplines? In an epistolary debate with Adolf von **Harnack** in 1923, Barth defended himself against the accusation that he was "contemptuous of scientific theology" (*Beginnings*, 165–87). Harnack contended that theology must conform itself to the prevailing norms of scholarly objectivity in order to retain its position at the university. Barth, by contrast, asserted that theology is objective only insofar as it bears witness to its object, the **Word of God**.

In the period around 1930, Barth entered into debate with the philosopher Heinrich Scholz (1884–1956) about the possibility of a theological science. Scholz presented his challenge to the idea of theology as a science in a 1931 article titled, "Wie ist eine evangelische Theologie als Wissenschaft möglich?" According to Scholz, there are certain "uncontested" minimal requirements for labeling any discipline as a science. The "propositional postulate" requires that a scientific body of knowledge be expressible in noncontradictory propositions. The "coherence postulate" demands that any putative science relate to a single domain of objects. Finally, the "controllability postulate" stipulates that any science purporting to describe reality must be empirically testable in some manner. Scholz asserted that any theology that failed to satisfy these three postulates, and most particularly the last, would have to withdraw its claim to be scientific (Scholz, 48).

Barth responded to Scholz in CD I/1. While he did not quibble with Scholz's definition of science, he refused to accommodate theology to its criteria. "Theology can only say point-blank that this concept is unacceptable to it" (9). Barth proceeded to make claims about the relation between theology and the other sciences that continue to provoke perplexity among his interpreters. On the one hand, he asserted: "All sciences might ultimately be theology" (7). On the other, he claimed that theology as a discipline distinct from the other sciences "can have no epistemological basis" (7) and might be "superfluous" if the other sciences took up its task (5). In any event, theology cannot adopt the methods of the other sciences. "The only way which theology has of proving its scientific character," Barth concluded, "is to devote itself to the task of knowledge as determined by its actual theme and thus to show what it means by true science" (10). In general, philosophers of science have sided with Scholz rather than Barth. Wolfhart Pannenberg and H. M. Kuitert have continued Scholz's line of critique, arguing that Barth turned theology into an arbitrary expression of subjectivity by refusing to test its claims against objective standards. T. F. Torrance, by contrast, has defended Barth's contention that scientific cognition must conform itself to the nature of its object, discovering in his methodology an analogy to the construction of physical theories.

In the preface to *CD* III/1, Barth articulated his doctrine of **creation**. He admitted: "It will perhaps be asked in criticism why I have not tackled the obvious scientific question posed in this context." He elusively responded that he had come to realize that "there can be no scientific problems, objections or aids in relation to what Holy Scripture and the Christian Church understand by the divine work of creation" (ix). However, he suggested that others might fruitfully explore the "twofold boundary" between scientific study of the natural world and theological inquiry into the work of God the Creator (x).

A recurring theme in Barth's reflection on theology and science from first to last is resistance toward scientific pretensions to develop a "theory of everything." By claiming that theology is a science, Barth introduced an eschatological proviso toward scientific aspirations to describe reality exhaustively. Theology reminds the sciences of their limits and thereby keeps the scientific enterprise humble and human.

H. M. Kuitert, *Filosofie van de theologie* (1988); W. Pannenberg, *Theology and the Philosophy of Science* (1976); H. Scholz, "Wie ist eine evangelische Theologie als Wissenschaft möglich?" *ZZ* 9 (1931): 8–53; T. F. Torrance, *Karl Barth* (1962).

CLIFFORD B. ANDERSON

Sin   Barth's doctrine of sin is marked by seven characteristics. First, the question of how sin is recognized as such is decisive, according to Barth, for any theological assessment of its reality. He claims that sin can be truly known only through *faith* in *Jesus Christ*. For this reason, he dissented from the theological tradition that taught that true knowledge of sin came from a law of *God* abstracted from true faith in the gospel of Jesus Christ. Without faith in the gospel human beings evade the condemnation of God's law and become trapped in illusions regarding sin. "Access to the knowledge that he is sinner is lacking to man *because* he is a sinner" (*CD* IV/1:360–61). It takes an encounter with God's victory over sin in the life and death of Jesus Christ to understand fully the true nature of sin.

Second, humans are made free from sin through faith in Jesus Christ. Sin as it is understood in faith is "forgiven sin" (II/2:768). Thus the nature of sin must be described only by looking back at a human past that God has brought to an end. Seen in retrospect, sin appears to be absurd and meaningless human conduct that has no future.

Third, therefore, Barth understands sin as a form of *nothingness* (III/3:289–368). On the one hand, this concept expresses the meaninglessness of sin *before God*. It is something that has no ongoing existence before God because it emerges out of nothing. On the other hand, this concept emphasizes the power with which sin's annihilating force seizes human life. Human beings who sin effectively destroy their relationship to God and all the other structured relationships in which God created them.

Fourth, Barth called this human act and attitude an "impossible possibility" or even an "ontological impossibility" (III/3:354–55). In stating it this way he wanted to indicate that sinning has roots neither in God nor in the nature of *humanity* as created by God. Rather, God calls human beings into existence in order to live in relationship with God, with their fellow human beings, with themselves, and with their time (see III/2). Their *freedom* should be understood as freedom to lead their lives within these relationships. When they sin, they misuse their freedom; they senselessly and irrationally destroy the structures of their creaturely existence. They themselves are *responsible* for this. It is for this reason that Barth broke with the Augustinian and Reformation idea of "inherited sin." As Barth sees it, the concept of sin dissolves that of "inheritance," and the concept of "inheritance" dissolves that of "sin" (IV/1:500–501). If the Christian doctrine of sin makes reference to Adam's act in the primal biblical *history*, it does so only in the sense that everyone who sins does the same as Adam did. Adam is simply *"primus inter pares"* (509).

Fifth, on the basis of these presuppositions, Barth explicated his doctrine of sin in a distinctive way within the framework of the doctrine of *reconciliation* (see IV/1–3). What he does here is unparalleled in the history of the Christian doctrine of sin. In his presentation, sin appears as an absurd, essentially impossible—and yet actual—human turning against the care of God for his creatures in Jesus Christ. The true God, Jesus Christ, *humbles* himself for the benefit of sinful humanity. The sinner in his *arrogance* wants to be God (IV/1:413–78). The *truly human one*, Jesus Christ, exalts the human race to true humanity in the relations created by God within which it exists. The sinner in his *sloth* resists such an honoring of his humanity (see IV/2:403–82). The true *witness*, Jesus Christ, testifies to himself. The proud and indolent sinner evades this witness and falsifies it with the *lie* (see IV/3.1:434–60). While Barth has all human beings in view in his ac-

count of arrogant and slothful humanity, his characterization of sin as falsehood points to the specifically Christian form of sin (IV/3.1:451). Here the doctrine of sin becomes a critique of Christian *religion* that, as religion, strives to dispose of the free event of God's grace for sinful humanity.

Sixth, the consequence of sin is to bring human beings into a hopeless situation. Human pride is followed by the "fall" into alienation from God, which no one is able to evade (IV/1:478–513). Sloth leads to the "misery" of human "stupidity," "inhumanity," "dissipation," and "worry" into which sinful human beings are always sinking ever more deeply (IV/2:483–98). Falsehood sees to it that human beings seriously fear "condemnation" (IV/3.1:461–80). In Barth's view, sin in all its forms is human *guilt*, which no one but God himself can put right (IV/1:491). From the outset, Barth's doctrine of sin was conceived in light of the God who forgives human guilt. So it is not surprising that it should lead to an expression of *hope* that the judgment of Jesus Christ at the end of time might be a judgment of *grace for all human beings*. Barth has been reproached with the charge that the entire construction of his doctrine of sin promotes the idea of the *apokatastasis panton* (Origen) that the early church rejected. Yet, understood as an affirmation of the inevitability of the salvation of all human beings, Barth rejected this idea. However, understood as an *expression of hope* in Jesus Christ the Judge with whom we are well familiar, he did not deny it.

Finally, whosoever God frees from the power of nothingness becomes capable of resisting sin and its effects. The foundational act of such resistance is the concrete prayer, "deliver us from **evil**." In his *ethics* of reconciliation, Barth depicted the **Christian life** as one in which praying human beings become capable of resistance to sin without overestimating themselves (see CL). They cannot remain inactive when they pray that

God may liberate the *world* from the power of sin. Thus Barth's doctrine of sin has immediate ethical and political consequences. By faith in God and in the knowledge of the nothingness of sin, Christians never take sin—and the power at work in it that threatens to destroy creatures and the whole *creation*—to be a "final reality which cannot be altered" (*CL*, 212). Rather, they know themselves to be empowered daily by God to use their relative human capacities to fight against the "destruction" of creaturely existence by sin. They will never come to terms with the "corruption and evil of the world" (271).

Yet these ethical and political consequences are not the point of Barth's doctrine of sin. Rather its point is to direct Christendom to the fact that the humane grace of God *outpaces* sin's absurd effort to destroy human life and indeed the whole creation. In faith, Christians are able to participate in this outpacing. In so doing, they themselves in their lives and in their conduct will make visible the nothingness of sin in this world.

N. T. Bakker, "Die Sünde in der Kirchlichen Dogmatik," *ZDTh* 9, no. 1 (1993): 9–18; E. Busch, *The Great Passion*, trans. G. W. Bromiley (2004), 199–218; M. Jensen, *The Gravity of Sin* (2007); W. Krötke, *Sin and Nothingness in the Theology of Karl Barth* (2005); J. Mangina, *Karl Barth on the Christian Life* (2001), 91–124.

WOLF KRÖTKE

State   In a key essay written in 1946, Barth defined the state in geographic terms: "the commonality of all the people in one place, region, or country in so far as they belong together under a constitutional system of government that is equally valid for and binding on them all, and which is defended and maintained by force" ("CCCC," 150). The purpose of the state is to protect and safeguard *humanity* by upholding (a) the *freedom* of individuals and (b) the peace of the community. To unpack this definition, one must investigate the *theology* that informs it.

State—An Order of the Covenant: In his doctrine of **election**, Barth argued that Christ elected himself to be Lord of all humans. As a result, every person is subject to God's **providence**; God elects neither groups nor nations, but individual persons (II/2:313–14). For this reason, God's primary providential concern is not the upholding of a particular state, but the preservation of human lives for the hearing and *preaching* of the gospel. Thus it is not an order of *creation* or a result of natural law, but a "genuine and specific order of the *covenant*" (III/4:303).

Church and State: By depicting the state as an order of the covenant, Barth established an intrinsic connection between **church** and state, criticizing Reformed theologians for treating them as separate spheres of God's dominion ("C&S," 102–3). He pictured the relation as two concentric spheres, whose center is the providence of God. Both the church and the state find their common origin and common center as orders of divine **grace**, through which God preserves and upholds human life so that the gospel may be proclaimed ("CCCC," 156).

For this reason, the just state takes seriously its relationship to the Christian church. It does not attempt to replace the church or to make itself an object of human *worship*; rather it protects humans from the threat of anarchy and chaos and provides the church freedom and *time*: "time for preaching the gospel; time for repentance; time for *faith*" (156).

While Barth listed commonalities between church and state, such as the basis in covenant and their particular laws and authorities (153), the key difference between them lies at this point: the church knows its Lord is Christ and freely proclaims his rule; the state is ignorant of its own basis for existence and of its service for the purposes of God (169).

Laws of the State: Because the state (like the church) arises from the covenant of God, the command of God is likewise central to its existence. Barth explained, "Ruling grace is commanding grace. The Gospel itself has the form and fashion of the Law" (*CD* II/2:511). God's command serves as the basis for good human laws. According to Barth, the law of the state enjoys validity and force because of divine law (IV/2:724). Yet the law of the state addresses the human only in material relationships: regulating one's assimilation into society and one's duties; protecting human life, possessions, and honor; and determining the liberties that are allowed or denied (724). Barth suggested that three primary forms uphold the law of the state: (1) legislation, which establishes the legal system and laws that are binding on all; (2) the government and its administration, which applies the legislation; and (3) the administration of justice, which makes decisions on the application of the law in cases that are doubtful or conflicting ("CCCC," 150–51).

Analogue to the Kingdom of God: By arguing that the state is an order of the covenant, Barth (a) offered clear support for the existence of the state, (b) articulated a close relation between church and state; and (c) provided a basis for Christian obedience to the laws of the state. He went so far as to argue that the state may unknowingly serve as an analogue of the **kingdom of God**. While the state (like the church) could never be equated with the kingdom of God, inasmuch as it fulfills its purpose of upholding human life (by treating the poor with equity, for example), the state corresponds to the kingdom of God.

The Unjust State: Yet in his clear Yes spoken on behalf of the state, Barth spoke a corresponding No toward unjust states. In the Yes of Romans 13, the church is responsible to subordinate itself to the state. However, the state becomes "demonic" when it attempts to make itself Lord, embraces an inhumane ideology, or renounces its true dignity, function, and purpose (i.e.,

serving the person and work of **Jesus Christ**) ("C&S," 118). It becomes the state of Revelation 13, "the Beast out of the abyss" (119), which Barth likened to Hobbes's Leviathan: "the all-wise, all-knowing, all-powerful, and . . . all-good commonwealth or state" (*CL*, 220). While in the modern era the Leviathan may be seen in totalitarian states and dictatorships, no state is immune from the tendency to become "at least a little Leviathan" (221). Barth explained, "The demonism of politics consists in the idea of 'empire,' which is always inhuman," and can be discerned in monarchist, democratic, and socialist states (220).

The responsibility of the church is to "subordinate" itself to the state by making its knowledge of Jesus the Lord its criterion for discerning between the just and the unjust state ("CCCC," 162). In accordance with these judgments, the church "will offer its support here and its resistance there" (163). Barth modeled this discernment in the **Barmen Declaration** (1934), which affirmed the lordship of Jesus Christ in direct criticism of perceived subservience of the "Germans Christians" to the Nazi regime. Likewise, in the 1935 hearing that resulted in his dismissal from the University of Bonn, Barth stated that his refusal to give the required oath of loyalty and salute to Hitler was "my duty on behalf of the state." He called his judges to likewise resist totalitarianism, for "if they did not do that, they should realize that they were making Hitler a god incarnate and offending most seriously against the First Commandment" (*B–Th Br* III , 800–801). Barth sought to witness to the state as he believed that it was ordained to exist: as an order of the covenant of God intended to uphold human life and maintain peace and freedom so that the church could proclaim the gospel of Christ.

K. Barth, *AS*; idem, *BarThE*; idem, "C&S"; idem, "CCCC"; idem, *CSC*; idem, *HSGML*; idem, *LGB*; M. Barth, "Current Discussion on the Political Character of Karl Barth's

Theology," in *Footnotes to a Theology*, ed. H. M. Rumscheidt (1974), 77–94; G. Hunsinger, ed., *Karl Barth and Radical Politics* (1976); F. Jehle, *Ever Against the Stream*, trans. R. and M. Burnett (2002).

STEPHANIE MAR SMITH

Theology Barth's concept of theology developed over the course of his career, but his use of the term is characterized more by constancy in definition and intent than by change. Some of the most important theological disagreements he had early on with others (e.g., with **Harnack**, and later with his colleagues in **dialectical theology**, Gogarten, **Brunner**, **Bultmann**, and later also with Tillich and others), centered precisely on the content of this term and what it seeks to describe. One way to view Barth's achievement as a theologian is simply to note the extent to which his efforts gave theology a more explicitly theological definition, resulting in an altered landscape for the whole discipline.

To understand what Barth means by "theology," one might begin by stipulating what he does not mean. Theology for Barth does not mean the study of *religion*, or *ethics*, or *faith*'s reflection on itself or its own experience, or the offering of religious or moral explanations for what is deemed otherwise inexplicable, or the religious analysis of human existence. Nor does Barth think that "theology" is the reordering of the contents of the biblical narrative into a systematic or coherent set of logical propositions.

For Barth, theology happens when the *church* seeks to speak responsibly and therefore, faithfully, of the triune *God* whose *revelation* in *Jesus Christ* as attested in Scripture precedes and makes possible all our efforts to think or speak of God (I/1:11). Barth believes God has spoken (*Deus dixit!*) and God speaks. Before God is an object of our knowing, this God is Subject, so that our knowledge of the triune God, as with

other forms of Christian discipleship, is always a matter of following, and following not merely as a form of mental exercise but as the "following after" of Christian discipleship. Theology is made possible because God's speaking, like all of God's ways and works, is gracious, preceding our words yet not drowning them out. In seeking and creating fellowship with us, the God who is revealed to be beyond our comprehension renders himself knowable to us, and in such a way that our knowing of God, though always indirect, is nevertheless true knowledge and truly of God (II/1:204ff.).

Theology is necessary because the church, which is commissioned by God to proclaim the good news of Jesus Christ, can do so faithfully only when its proclamation reflects the *grace* of God's own self-giving. In this sense, theology is not to be characterized as an undertaking of religious virtuosos or interested academicians but as the modest yet happy offering of the church's own obedience, in which the church is called to examine the degree to which its *language* about God corresponds to God's self-revelation as attested in Scripture. Were the church not commissioned to proclaim the good news of Jesus Christ, there would be no reason for theology in Barth's view (I/1:81).

Barth describes theology as a "*science*," and often as a "peculiarly beautiful science." In claiming that theology is a science, Barth is neither attempting to justify the place of theology within the universe of knowledge, nor is he insisting that the rigor of theological investigations measures up to the criteria of what the universe of knowledge in other places calls a science (I/1:9ff.). Rather, he is simply stating that theology, like other forms of human knowing, seeks to understand its object in accordance with that object's self-giving. It is a "peculiarly beautiful science" (II/1:656) because the object it seeks to understand is the eternally rich God whose active self-giving radiates *joy* and delight in the knowledge of the believer (see *EvT*, passim).

Barth's emphasis on the subjectivity of God marked a major shift in the way theology understood itself in the twentieth century, recovering as it did the significance of the doctrine of the **Trinity** for thinking faithfully about God. The God who seeks and creates fellowship with us in Jesus Christ is the God who is able to do so, the God who is self-related and self-differentiating, whose faithfulness toward us is grounded not in what we think is possible but in the reality of God's own triune life. Theology is, therefore, from the very beginning both Trinitarian and christocentric.

Theology, for Barth, is for the sake of *preaching* but it is not the same thing as preaching. The church is called to preach the gospel, not theology. Yet there is no preaching of the gospel without theology, that is, there is no "untheological" proclamation of this Word. Theology exists to assist the church in the faithful study and preaching of Scripture's *witness* to Jesus Christ. To that extent, theology for Barth is always theology of the **Word of God**. As such, theology is inherently evangelical, catholic, and reformed in its character. It is evangelical in that it understands its work as bearing witness to the reality of the living Lord Jesus Christ, helping the church proclaim and live in the light of his gracious rule that embraces the whole *world*. It is catholic in that it exists not, primarily, as the work of an individual genius explaining difficult matters to a skeptical or even hostile *culture*, but as the work of the whole church, the listening and teaching church, that is called as a matter of Christian discipleship to think faithfully, and in the company of the apostles and prophets and their many children to speak the gospel in our own day. In this respect, it is worth noting how carefully Barth listens to others, how deep and broad his conversations are with theologians ancient and modern, Protestant and Catholic, and how energetically he engages with phi-

losophers and other thinkers in the *CD*. Finally, theology, for Barth, is reformed in that it regards its work as tentative, not finished, always subject to the lordship of Jesus Christ, and ever in need of his correction. Here too Barth's understanding of theology is characterized by his careful and lengthy *exegesis*, always seeking to discern in the words of Scripture the Word made flesh.

Barth occasionally preferred to use the term *theo-anthropology* to describe the content of theology (*EvT*, 12; *HG*, 11). His use of this neologism was not entirely whimsical. He thought that in light of God's self-giving in Jesus Christ, Christian theology could not be understood as having "only" God for its content. That would imply that the real work of theology was to connect this transcendent God to creaturely reality. But that would be to ignore what God has already done in Jesus Christ. For the God of Jesus Christ is precisely the God who refuses to be God without us, so that to know God is to know the incarnate God, who has drawn intimately near to us already. That is why, for Barth, theology is finally doxology, a gift in which our knowledge comes to speech in the happy praise and service of God.

———

G. Hunsinger, *Disruptive Grace* (2000), 319–37; J. Mangina, *Karl Barth* (2004), 29–56; B. L. McCormack, *Karl Barth's Critically Realistic Dialectical Theology* (1995), 327–70; idem, *Orthodox and Modern* (2008), 21–108; H. M. Rumscheidt, *Revelation and Theology* (1972).

THOMAS W. CURRIE

Thurneysen   Eduard Thurneysen, a Swiss Reformed theologian, was born the youngest of twins on Oct. 7, 1888, in Walenstadt (Canton St. Gallen) in the family of a minister. Two early losses left a mark on Thurneysen's life: his twin brother died three months after their birth, and his mother passed away in 1891. In 1892 his father was appointed as a hospital chaplain in Basel, where Thurneysen grew up. The second marriage of his father in 1893 did not bring harmony into the family.

Trying to reduce the domestic tension, Thurneysen's stepmother took him to Bad Boll in 1904 and introduced him to Christoph Blumhardt. This proved a crucial encounter for Thurneysen. Blumhardt's openness and candid interest toward his interlocutor greatly influenced Thurneysen's own view on pastoral work. His choice for studying *theology* was inspired by Blumhardt as well. He started his studies in 1907 in Basel under Bernhard Duhm and Paul Wernle. In the Basel fraternity "Zofingia," he met Karl Barth, who became his lifelong friend. In 1909 Thurneysen continued his studies in Marburg, where he attended courses by Wilhelm *Herrmann*, Adolf Jülicher, Wilhelm Heitmüller, Martin Rade, and Hermann Cohen. Together with Barth, Karl Bornhausen, and Wilhelm Loew, he formed a study group on Ernst Troeltsch and his school.

After graduating, Thurneysen worked in Zurich as a secretary at the YMCA (1911–1913). In these years he met Leonhard Ragaz and Hermann Kutter, and the future friend and sponsor of the *dialectical theology*, Rudolf Pestalozzi. While Barth gradually developed into an academic systematic theologian, *Seelsorge* or *pastoral care* was the driving force behind Thurneysen's life mission and theological work. From 1913 to 1920 Thurneysen served as a minister in Leutwil-Dürrenäsch (Canton Aargau), from 1920 to 1927 in St. Gallen-Bruggen (Canton St. Gallen), and from 1927 to 1959 at the Münster Cathedral of Basel. The seven years of his ministry at Leutwil were marked by an intensive, intimate collaboration with Barth, so that Thurneysen may be called the second most important representative of the early dialectical theology. They exchanged pulpits, traveled together (e.g., on Easter 1915 to Bad Boll to visit Christoph Blumhardt), read the same

books, visited each other frequently to discuss theological questions, and corresponded almost daily. In 1916 Thurneysen married Marguerite Meyer (Nov. 28, 1893–Oct. 24, 1995). Five children were born to this happy marriage. The Barth and Thurneysen families used to play music together. Marguerite was a pianist; Nelly Barth was a violinist.

Initially, Thurneysen was more impressed than Barth by liberal theology. Yet the First World War and the conditions of the laborers in Aargau showed them that any existing form of theology (including that of the religious socialists, the Blumhardts, or *Schleiermacher*) was insufficient. Their common conclusion, which led to the writing of both editions of Barth's *Römerbrief*, was that theology needed a new foundation. "So close has been our co-operation that I doubt whether even the specialist could detect where the one leaves off and the other begins," Barth wrote in his foreword to *Rom* II (*ER*, 15). Thurneysen read each chapter of Barth's manuscript, made suggestions for improvements, and wrote additions to many pericopes, most of which Barth used verbatim.

A scientific estimation of Thurneysen's role in the revision of *Rom* II remains difficult, as approximately only 10–20 percent of all his commentaries have been preserved. Thurneysen's manuscript on Romans 13, for example, which Barth integrated in his text, has not yet been traced (see *B–Th Br* I, 507, 517, 519). A careful examination of the many letters and passages that Thurneysen did not publish in their *Briefwechsel* could perhaps shed more light on the question of his contribution to *Rom* II as well as on other important church-historical and biographical issues they discussed. At the same time, when Barth started to rewrite his *Romans*, Thurneysen started to work on his own project, a lecture on Dostoevsky, which he held to great acclaim on April 2, 1921, at the student conference in Aarau, and then revised for publication. In a very different style than Barth's, but sometimes in a similar idiom, Thurneysen addresses themes that characterize early dialectical theology: the crisis of *history, culture,* and *humanity* (illustrated by Dostoevsky's characters), the effort to usurp the place of *God,* and the ultimate futility of such efforts in face of the *"wholly other"* God. Barth saw *Dostoevsky* as a counterpart to *Rom* II and urged Thurneysen to publish the book as soon as possible. Albert Lempp (Kaiser-Verlag), with whom Thurneysen established an important contact for the dialectical theology, published it six months before *Rom* II.

Though not as intensive, Thurneysen's collaboration with Barth continued in the following years in publishing the periodical *Zwischen den Zeiten* with Friedrich Gogarten and Georg Merz (in fact, the idea for the title came from Thurneysen) and the series *Theologische Existenz heute*. Thanks to his tact, wisdom, modesty, and loyalty, throughout Barth's life Thurneysen often acted as an intermediary both on theological and personal levels (see *B–Th Br* I–III; the third volume includes Thurneysen's correspondence with Charlotte von Kirschbaum).

Thurneysen's main theological contribution was to practical theology with an emphasis on the doctrinal presuppositions and theological and psychological content of pastoral counseling. His monographs *Die Lehre von der Seelsorge* (1946) and *Seelsorge im Vollzug* (1968) remain influential among practical theologians. He was awarded an honorary doctorate at the universities of Giessen (1927) and Aberdeen (1934), and became a lecturer (1929) and associate professor for practical theology, with homiletics as a special assignment (1941) at Basel University. After his retirement (1959) he was active as a visiting professor in Hamburg, Wuppertal, and Berlin until 1966. During his last years, Thurneysen edited, assisted by his wife, the first two volumes of his correspondence

with Barth. Thurneysen died in Basel on September 21, 1974.

R. Bohren, *Prophetie und Seelsorge* (1982); idem, *Wort und Gemeinde*, ed. R. Bohren and M. Geiger (1968); S. Lorberg-Fehring, *Thurneysen—neu gesehen* (2006); G. Rim, *Gottes Wort, Verkündiging und Kirche* (2000); E. Thurneysen, *Dostoevsky,* trans. K. R. Crim (1964); idem, *A Theology of Pastoral Care*, trans. J. Worthington and T. Wieser (1962).

KATJA TOLSTAJA

Time For Barth, "time" is a concept whose function is much like that of *eternity,* namely, as a theological term, not as a precise philosophical idea or scientific reality. In short, there is no such thing as Barth's "concept of time." The lack of specificity in such an interpretive banner leads inexorably to rhetorical excess whenever it is unfurled. Barth does, however, speak of time in certain characteristic ways, for example (and perhaps not exhaustively), time as given by *God* in *creation,* time as unredeemed *humanity* experiences it, and time as may be experienced when known in God's *grace* through *Jesus Christ.*

That second manner of describing time, the time of unredeemed humanity, may be understood as a middle state between the other two. It is time apart from God and unfulfilled by eternity. Barth calls this kind of time by several different names: "lost time," "empty time," and, perhaps most theologically evocative, "wounded time," that which is in need of healing by Jesus Christ.

All of these terms express, in different ways, the same fundamental character of the same kind of time. This is time as it is not intended to be, time that is far from ideal. Without God, time simply cannot be what it should be. The human being who is lost will experience time itself as lost. Such time is in need of healing, just as those who exist in that time are in need of healing. This kind of time can hardly even be called "time," for it has so little substance, but abides primarily in its discontinuity, and exists in its lack of existence.

Clearly, such metaphors as "lost" or "empty" or "wounded" time express not scientific assertions but theological convictions. For Barth's theological purposes, particularly in *CD* III, "time" is less a physical entity than the manner in which one exists. Both time and eternity are the means by which these two very different categories of beings, God and the human being, exist with and over against their "environment," or all that is not them.

Barth, then, understands human time to be fundamentally flawed, as long as such time and those who experience it are isolated from God. Yet such time is described mostly in a way that expresses well the fundamental character of time as it really is: flowing, ever changing, a mode in which "past" and "future" do not exist because they are not "present." Speaking of our own "relatively real" time, Barth says, "In contradistinction from eternity time is just this division into present, past and future" (III/1:71). This would appear to be what most people mean by "time." Barth, however, seems to be taking the position that the true character of time is not found in "our" time's lack of existence, but rather in something else, something abiding. Time's true character is seen in a tri unity found within the being of God, in whom there is a (supreme) kind of beginning, middle, and end in which those distinctions do not give way to each other but endure together.

This "coinherence" of past, present, and future within God is the very same as that which characterizes the relationship of Father, Son, and *Holy Spirit*. Barth's understanding of eternity's temporality is expressly and deeply a Trinitarian understanding of eternity. God, in God's eternity, is not timeless but "temporal," because God is the triune God.

Yet it is clear that "temporal" means something different here than what it

typically means. Eternity may be "temporal," but not in the same way that creatures are temporal. What, then, does Barth mean when he speaks of God's "temporality"? It all rests on Barth's apparent insistence that "time" can mean more than just the "time" that we know, in which past, present, and future are alienated from one another. Commonly speaking, time *is* the coming into existence of things that had not been, after which they cease to be. There may be a continuity of moments that, in our perception, memory, and anticipation form a whole that we designate by the singular noun *time*. Yet we do not pretend that the reality is different from our experience, namely, that the past exists no longer, the future not yet, and the present is but the quantum distance between the two. Barth, however, wants to assert a theological definition of time that is different from our common understanding that arises out of our own experience, a definition that applies supremely and truthfully only to God.

Thus when Barth speaks of God's temporality, he has not collapsed the distinction between Creator and creature, but rather has sought to express God's *freedom* vis-à-vis time. God's threefold eternality/temporality is the device Barth uses to express a positive relationship of God to time that is recognizably Christian.

Time, then, is described by Barth in various ways. Several of them emphasize the limitations of time as experienced by human beings, and highlight the difference between Creator and creature. What becomes apparent from those passages where he emphasizes that distinction and describes human time according to its imperfections is that such imperfections do not define what time really is. Rather, for Barth, time is defined not by its imperfections, but rather by the character of God's time. Barth conceives of something he understands as "time" in which Before, During, and After exist all at once, without one passing away and giving way to another. For Barth, God has something like (indeed, something superior to) our time, with its contours of past, present, and future. Yet for God these contours endure and do not pass away. Whereas we merely experience time, God possesses time: the time unique to God, and for that reason also the time we experience, which, by God's free act of *grace*, is healed of its imperfections, delivered from its alienation.

K. Barth, *CD* II/1:608–40; III/2:437–640; E. Busch, *The Great Passion*, trans. G. W. Bromiley (2004), 264–88; D. Griswold, "Perichoretic Eternality" (PhD diss., Southern Methodist University, 2010); G. Hunsinger, "Jesus as The Lord of Time According to Karl Barth," *ZDTh* (supplement series) 4 (2010): 113–27; R. H. Roberts, "Karl Barth's Doctrine of Time," in *Karl Barth*, ed. S. W. Sykes (1979), 88–146.
DANIEL M. GRISWOLD

Trinity   By placing the doctrine of the Trinity "at the head of all *dogmatics*," even as he recognized that in doing this he was in an "isolated" position in relation to dogmatic *history* (CD I/1:300), Barth stressed that the driving force of his *theology* was the triune *God* alone. Since the doctrine of the Trinity arises as a faithful explication of Scripture, which witnesses to God's utterly unique self-revelation within history that cannot be "understood as any sort of *revelation* alongside which there are or may be others" (I/1:295), Barth insisted that dogmatics takes its questions *only* from Scripture.

As the sole subject and object of revelation attested in Scripture, "*God* reveals Himself. He reveals Himself *through Himself*. He reveals *Himself*" (I/1:296). Three inseparable questions: the nature of revelation, how revelation comes about, or what its result is, are shaped by the fact that God is the content of revelation, since God's being and act are one; we encounter the eternal Father, Son, and Holy Spirit so that it is

and always remains God himself who initiates, sustains, and completes true *knowledge of God* as "an event enclosed in the mystery of the divine Trinity" (II/1:181; cf. 205). Revelation is not simply informational, but is God's reconciling act drawing us into fellowship or communion through *faith* and by *grace*; hence Barth neither emphasizes revelation at the expense of communion with God nor suggests that revelation is primarily the impartation of knowledge. Rather, revelation means that God is not only there for us in the *Holy Spirit* but we are there for God (I/1:480; II/1:273–75); knowledge of God and fellowship with God are factually inseparable.

Above all, Barth would only allow God's Word and Spirit to claim our attention since "God is known through God and through God alone" (II/1:44). Though he began with revelation, Barth did not exclude starting with *justification, sanctification,* or ecclesiology, as long as the source of these doctrines was clearly recognized as the "ontological Trinity" and the basis was a clear doctrine of the Holy Spirit (*TT*, 50–51; *HG*, 24–25). Still, the controlling center of dogmatics always remains the triune God acting for us in the economy, because "What God reveals in Jesus and how He reveals it, namely, in Jesus, must not be separated from one another according to the New Testament" (I/1:399).

Knowledge of God/Human Experience: Since knowledge of God comes through God alone and is in no way based on human knowledge or experience (II/2:3), it is unassailable from without. Everything depends on acknowledging God's lordship, which "consists in the fact that He is in Himself from *eternity* to eternity the triune God" (II/1:47). Hence, "We cannot say anything higher or better of the 'inwardness of God' than that God is Father, Son and Holy Spirit, and therefore that He is *love* in Himself without and before loving us, and without being forced to love us. And we can say this only in the light of the 'outwardness' of

God to us, the occurrence of His revelation" (I/2:377).

Because Barth believed the immanent Trinity is the indispensable premise of the economic Trinity (I/1:479) but could not be reduced to the latter (II/1:260–61), there is no depth grammar that could be used for Trinitarian description that even momentarily bypasses this particular triunity. Father and Son are not freely chosen symbols of human fatherhood and sonship but are descriptive of who God really is (I/1:432). Barth affirmed the *filioque* to stress that the immanent and economic Trinity is identical in content; that the Holy Spirit "is the Spirit of both the Father and the Son" *ad intra* and *ad extra*; that we have no direct mystical access to God that bypasses his historical mediation in Christ; and that biblical texts speaking of the Spirit proceeding from the Father cannot be isolated from those that say he is the Spirit of the Son (I/1:479–81).

Since actual knowledge of God is real only as our human act is begun, upheld, and completed miraculously by God himself, it cannot be traced to anything within our own experience or knowledge. It occurs only in faith, which itself derives from the Holy Spirit, who opens us to God "from above" (I/1:242, 341) and is the Spirit of the Word (I/1:464ff., III/3:263–64). Consequently, "The Holy Spirit is no less and no other than God Himself, distinct from Him whom Jesus calls His Father, distinct also from Jesus Himself, yet no less than the Father, and no less than Jesus, God Himself, altogether God" (I/1:459). Faith means acknowledgment of Christ's true deity so that any attempt to demonstrate Christ's divinity or the divinity of the Holy Spirit by analyzing our experience or belief would actually deny that it is the Holy Spirit who creates faith (I/1:460; I/2:258–59). "The Holy Spirit speaks by the *Word of God*. . . . The Spirit can never be observed or imprisoned by the creature, and therefore by the Christian, but in all His majesty He will always be a free Spirit and therefore the Holy Spirit" (III/3:255). "The Holy Spirit . . . does not come from us but to us. . . . He does not come to us from our own environment but from above. The Holy Spirit is the wisdom and power of the Word of God . . . guidance by the Spirit means obedience to the Word of God" (III/3:264).

Therefore, "The Holy Spirit does not first become the Holy Spirit, the Spirit of God, in the event of revelation" (I/1:466). The work of the Holy Spirit, then, "is not the created *world*" (I/1:470) but the love of the Father and Son in eternity. Thus, God loves us in an act of communion, love and gift that is his from all eternity.

Knowledge of God/Dogmatic History: Barth believed the doctrine was not treated first historically because the **church**'s thinking generally was dictated by views that did not actually begin and end with God's givenness in revelation (I/1:300; II/1:261). To begin with some general concept and attempt to understand the revelation that took place in Jesus Christ makes the doctrine of the Trinity irrelevant. To first ask: How do we know God? Does God exist? What is God? and finally, Who is our God? would leave open the question of who God really is who meets us in revelation, thus undermining what makes the Christian doctrine of God Christian, namely, the triune God himself acting *ad extra* (I/1:301).

The Word of God himself who exists antecedently with the Father and the Holy Spirit from all eternity and acts within history is and remains the norm for proper Trinitarian thinking: "the content of the doctrine of the Trinity . . . is not that God in His relation to man is Creator, Mediator and Redeemer, but that God in Himself is eternally God the Father, Son and Holy Spirit . . . [God acting as Emmanuel] cannot be dissolved into His work and activity" (I/2:878–79; cf. I/2:34–37; II/1:309, 313). Such a statement is in marked contrast to those who argue that speaking in immanent Trinitarian terms refers only to God's presence within the economy. "We have to say that, as Christ is in revelation, so He is antecedently in Himself. Thus, He is antecedently in Himself light of light, very God of very God, the begotton [sic] of God and not His creature. We have to take revelation with such utter seriousness that in it as God's act we must directly see God's being too" (I/1:428).

Barth carefully distinguished without separating the immanent and economic Trinity (I/1:172) to stress that while we meet God's essence in his works *ad extra*, God never becomes a prisoner of what he does for us as creator, reconciler, and redeemer but loves us freely: "Though the work of God is the essence of God, it is necessary and important to distinguish His essence as such from his work, remembering that this work is grace, a free divine decision" (I/1:371). For Barth the doctrine of the Trinity arose historically from a focus on "the second person of the Trinity, God the Son, the deity of Christ" (I/1:315).

Analogia Entis: Therefore, the *analogia entis* or the attempt to know God apart from his self-revelation in Jesus Christ always involved idolatry (II/1:260ff.). All theocentrism that is not simultaneously christocentric is excluded because to know Jesus Christ is to know God, and to bypass Jesus Christ is to bypass God acting for us within the economy (I/1:415; II/1:319–20; IV/1:48). Jesus, the Son of God, is not merely an example or an ideal, but the exalted Lord who gives direction to our lives; that precisely is the work of the Holy Spirit—to enable us to live in and from Jesus, as the "new and true and exalted [persons]" we are in him (IV/2:362–63). Because Jesus' divinity is to be seen as "definitive, authentic and essential," (I/1:400), "we have to accept the simple presupposition on which the New Testament statement [concerning his divinity] rests, namely, that Jesus Christ is the Son because He is. . . . With this presupposition all thinking about Jesus, which means at once all thinking about God, must begin and end" (I/1:415).

False theocentrism arises whenever the root of the doctrine of the Trinity (revelation) is ignored or bracketed by other considerations. That there is no court of appeal beyond God's revelation in Jesus Christ is summarized in saying "God reveals Himself as the Lord" (I/1:306). God is ontically and noetically free and has his life in himself: "He is the ground without grounds, with whose word and will man can only begin without asking Why, so that in and with this he may receive everything that deserves to be called true and good" (307). God revealing himself as the Lord is the sole root of Trinitarian doctrine. And "the God who has revealed Himself according to the witness of Scripture, is the same in unimpaired unity and yet also the same thrice in different ways in unimpaired distinction" (307); this God is the subject who cannot become an object that we can control (381).

Barth insisted that we know God the Creator as the "Father Almighty" precisely through his Son who, as the incarnate Word, reveals to us that God is not some timeless world principle but the one who determined to love us in his inner life as Father, Son, and Spirit, and does so in his Word and Spirit as "Emmanuel"—God with us (III/1:24). Hence, "Men did not seek out God for common life in this unity, but God sought out man. And God did not need this unity, but man was wholly and utterly in need of it. He lives, because God lives, because God lives for him, and it is God's free will to live for him" (III/1:26).

Christian life itself is shaped by the Trinity. Just as "the three trinitarian modes of the divine being do not limit and complete each other as parts of the Godhead, but are the one God in a threefold identity . . . so the faith and obedience and *prayer* of the Christian are the one Christian attitude, and they are all individually that which the others are as well" (III/3:246). Only a type of modalism, unaware of the *perichoretic* relations of the Father, Son, and Spirit, could play off against one another faith, obedience, and prayer instead of seeing that all three signify our life in Christ.

Scripture and the Trinity: For Barth the doctrine of the Trinity is not found directly within the **Bible** but is based in the biblical attestation of revelation as the revelation of the Father, Son, and Holy Spirit who is creator, reconciler, and redeemer and is known as such through the events of Good Friday, Easter, and Pentecost. By stressing that the root of the doctrine is revelation, Barth affirmed that dogmatic thinking, which takes place within faith, acknowledges the lordship of Jesus Christ, the divinity of the Holy Spirit, and the transcendence and love of God the Father. We are dealing with God himself as revealer "and not, as Modalists in all ages have thought, with an entity distinct from Him" (I/1:311). Hence, "God is who He is in the act of His revelation. God seeks and creates fellowship between Himself and us, and therefore He loves us. But He is this loving God without us as Father, Son and Holy Spirit, in the *freedom* of the Lord, who has his life from Himself" (II/1:257).

Because God is really free and has his life in himself, he is also free to act decisively as our helper, friend, and savior as only God can. He is thus unencumbered by our **sin** and unbelief and is not a prisoner of his freedom because he is in reality the Lord of his own inner life (IV/2:344–45). The triune God is in no way subject to any logical or other necessity—he does not even need his own being in order to be the triune God, because he already has it and is it.

What needs existence cannot be God (II/1:306). This must be stressed in face of claims that in his doctrine of **election** Barth changed his position on God's freedom so that he should have realized that by electing to be God for us, God simultaneously determined to be triune with the result that he could no longer maintain that God would have been triune without becoming creator, reconciler, and redeemer. Nothing could be further from the truth. For Barth it is

because God is first the triune God that everything else such as election, **creation, reconciliation,** and redemption can occur: "The triune life of God which is free life in the fact that it is Spirit, is the basis of His whole will and action even *ad extra*, as the living act which He directs to us" (IV/2:345). Even in the controversial sections of IV/1 where Barth speaks of super- and subordination, command and obedience within the immanent Trinity, he actually appeals to his earlier presentation of God's freedom in I/1 to support his doctrine of reconciliation (IV/1:204). Barth never ceased insisting that God "would be no less and no different even if they all [creatures] did not exist or existed differently" (II/1:311; IV/1:201). Indeed, "From all eternity God could have . . . remained satisfied with Himself and with the impassible glory and blessedness of His own inner life. But He did not do so. He elected man as a covenant-partner" (II/2:166; IV/2:346). Suggestions that Barth's doctrine of the Trinity needs to be revised in light of his doctrine of reconciliation unfortunately neglect the fact that for Barth, God's triunity is not constituted by any of his gracious actions *ad extra* (even in anticipation); God really did humiliate himself for our benefit in the **incarnation** but without ceasing to be God (IV/1:204ff.).

Revelation and Modalism: Barth is often accused of modalism or a tendency toward modalism. This charge comes mainly from the fact that he objected to using the word *person* to describe Father, Son, and Holy Spirit partially because of his fear of tritheism, but also because he understood that no one could really explain *how* God can be three persons, one being: "We can state the fact of the divine processions and modes of being. But all our attempts to state the How of this delimitation will prove to be impossible" (I/1:476) because this delimitation is established for us only as an act of God himself in the economy. Barth was no modalist. All his thinking, particularly his presentation of the *perfections of God*, bears the mark of God's inherent unity in trinity: "the point from the very first and self-evidently is both the oneness of God and the threeness of God, because our real concern is with revelation, in which the two are one" (I/1:342). God's omnipresence, for instance, illustrates that both inward and outward God is present to himself "in the triunity of His one essence" and "present to everything else as the Lord of everything else" in a way that demonstrates that "presence does not mean identity, but togetherness at a distance." Inwardly "it is the togetherness of Father, Son and Holy Spirit at the distance posited by the distinction that exists in the one essence of God," while outwardly "it is the togetherness at a distance of the Creator and the creature." Hence God has his own space or place and must not be conceived in a nonspatial manner, which would deny his unique triunity (II/1:468). God's eternity as pre-temporal, supra-temporal, and post-temporal in a manner corresponding to the unity in distinction of the Father, Son, and Holy Spirit (II/1:608–40) also undercuts any sort of modalism. George Hunsinger rightly thinks "modalism can be charged against Barth only out of ignorance, incompetence, or (willful) misunderstanding" (191).

Opera trinitatis ad extra sunt indivisa, Perichoresis (Circumincessio), Appropriation: These three expressions structured Barth's Trinitarian thinking. Barth believed the church doctrine of the Trinity was formulated in a way that explicitly ruled out all forms of subordinationism, including Arianism, adoptionism, as well as modalism (I/1:381–82). The former attempts to draw the divine subject, the Lord, into human subjectivity and thus to make God the kind of subject we are, leaving us with many gods and no real Lord. The latter suggests that God's being somehow lies behind the Father, Son, and Holy Spirit revealed in the economy. "Modalism finally entails denial of God" (I/1:382). *Opera trinitatis ad*

extra sunt indivisa implies that "Father, Son and Spirit are distinguished from one another by the fact that without inequality of essence or dignity, without increase or diminution of deity, they stand in dissimilar relations of origin to one another" (I/1:363). And while only the Son became incarnate, the Father and Spirit were not absent from the events of reconciliation. One will thus acknowledge that God is one precisely as Father, Son, and Holy Spirit, Creator, Reconciler, and Redeemer and that we know this in a manner appropriate to our human situation as this has been set up in the world by revelation and not as "the alleged *vestigia trinitatis*" (I/1:373). Barth's reconstruction of Thomas Aquinas's doctrine of appropriation aims to assert that while certain actions of God *ad extra* are assigned to the Father, Son, or Spirit, this must never deny God's presence in all his modes of being. Moreover, because the three "modes of being" are so completely intertwined, one cannot really know God's oneness at all unless all three persons of the Trinity are in view (*perichoresis*); indeed, "none exists as a special individual" (I/1:370). Because all the works of the Trinity are one, there can only be one divine subject and not three as often happens in social doctrines of the Trinity.

Barth's doctrine of the Trinity is at once simple and complex: simple because his thinking takes seriously the fact that Jesus really is the Son of God, begotten of the Father before all worlds, and that as such he enters history from outside in order to reconcile and redeem the world (I/1:426–27). But it is also complex because the Spirit, who enables us to participate in the union of the Father and Son in knowledge and love through faith, meets us and enables that participation in a myriad of ways throughout history according to his own sovereign love. Barth's Trinitarian theology is a masterpiece of twentieth-century thought that will continue to influence theology because it is a faithful pointer to Jesus Christ, the living Lord of history, the one who is worshiped and glorified together with the Father and Spirit.

P. Collins, *Trinitarian Theology, West and East* (2001); G. Hunsinger, *Disruptive Grace* (2000); E. Jüngel, *God's Being Is in Becoming,* trans. J. Webster (2001); P. D. Molnar, *Divine Freedom and the Doctrine of the Immanent Trinity* (2002); A. Torrance, "The Trinity," in *Cambridge Companion to Karl Barth,* ed. J. Webster (2000), 72–91.

PAUL D. MOLNAR

Truth A concern with a truth singular, final, comprehensive, and infinitely rich, communicated in and through Jesus the **Word of God,** is everywhere in Barth's work. No other theologian before or since has focused so relentlessly and untiringly on this truth as the "one thing needful" for **theology, faith** and life. Yet, prior to the final complete volume of the *CD,* the words *true* or *truth* barely feature in the chapter headings and introductory theses of this monumental work (§§17, 26, and 27 are the only minor exceptions). It is in *CD* IV/3, the third part of Barth's *Doctrine of Reconciliation,* that the word *truth* comes into its own as it is employed systematically—in conjunction with terms such as *prophet, witness, light,* and *falsehood*—to bear the weight of the entire argument. At the heart of this particular argument is a concern to relate the one truth of Jesus to the many truths and many falsehoods encountered within the ordinary secular *world* and indeed the *church.*

Underlying *CD* IV is the traditional doctrine of Christ's threefold office as prophet, priest, and king. Barth engages with these in reverse order, and so arrives at Christ's prophetic office in IV/3. Jesus is "the True Witness" (Rev. 3:14) because he is himself "the truth" as well as the way and the life (John 14:6). His prophetic truth speaking encompasses not just his teaching, as in *Calvin,* but his entire history from **incarnation** to *ascension.* He is alive, and as such he is "the *Light* of Life" (§69.2; cf. John 8:12). That is, his life or history reveals and declares itself to us as the truth that it embodies. In Jesus the truth is not concealed or obscure but radiant and eloquent.

Jesus is the truth as he is the light of the world, and we are not to seek for truth or light elsewhere. Yet, Barth argues, that does not mean that our human existence in the world is bereft of all lesser truths and lesser lights. The world, and not the church alone, is the place of Jesus' lordship, and the church may expect to hear true words addressed to it from the secular sphere that are grounded in the one truth and yet distinct from it (IV/3.1:110–36). Similarly, outside the sphere of human discourse, the world we inhabit is illuminated by lesser lights grounded in the one true light, basic structural characteristics of the created order that make it partially but really intelligible to us (136–51).

Jesus as the True Witness is foreshadowed by the Old Testament figure of Job, to whom Barth devotes four lengthy excursuses (IV/3.1:383–88, 398–408, 421–34, 453–61). When YHWH finally addresses Job (Job 38–41), it is by way of creaturely rather than divine truths. Job's friends demonstrate that the falsehood that truth both provokes and exposes can take the form of the sincerest piety. The truth embodied in Jesus and foreshadowed in Job cannot be appropriated once for all as a secure possession. Yet this truth comprehends the existence not only of Christians but of all human beings without exception. There is no place where its manifold witness to itself is lacking.

K. Barth, *ER,* 44–45, 51–52, 58, 80; E. Busch, *The Great Passion,* trans. G. W. Bromiley (2004), 128–51; G. Hunsinger, *How to Read Karl Barth* (1991), 67–184; idem, "Truth as Self-Involving," in *Disruptive Grace* (2000), 305–18.

FRANCIS WATSON

Universalism Universalism (*apokatastasis* = restoration) is the Christian doctrine that asserts the ultimate *salvation* of all *humanity* while denying the Christian doctrine of eternal punishment. Many have claimed that Barth's *theology* logically and necessarily leads to universalism, a conclusion Barth strongly denied throughout his life, desiring rather to affirm God's *freedom* in the matter and refusing to speculate on the eternal destiny of humanity. Yet, despite his protestations, Barth could write that "there is no good reason why we should not be open to this possibility . . . of an *apokatastasis* or universal *reconciliation* . . . [which should lead the *church*] to *hope* and pray cautiously and yet [distinctly for both its possibility and reality] . . . in the direction of the work of a truly eternal divine patience and deliverance." Barth concludes that this is appropriate in light of God's compassion and mercy in *Jesus Christ* (*CD* IV/3.1:478). Yet earlier in the *CD* he had written that "the Church will then not preach an *apokatastasis*, nor will it preach a powerless *grace* of Jesus Christ or a human wickedness which is too powerful for it. . . . It [the church] will preach the overwhelming power of grace and the weakness of human wickedness in the face of [grace]" (II/2:477).

Throughout his theology, Barth affirms the centrality of the person and work of Jesus Christ within his Trinitarian perspective. The foundation for this is established in his doctrine of *revelation* and his doctrine of the *knowledge of God*, in which Barth continually speaks of the objective and subjective reality and possibility of divine revelation in relationship to a true knowledge of *God*. This is all centered on God's self-revelation in Jesus Christ.

In his doctrine of *election*, Barth speaks of election as the act of a God who loves in perfect freedom, revealed in Jesus Christ as the electing God and the elected man, thereby affirming the Chalcedonian doctrine of the *incarnation*, as well as offering a reorientation to Calvin's double predestination. The doctrine of election for Barth is the divine Yes to humanity. Jesus Christ is the electing God as the eternal Son of God, who has elected himself to be the Son of Man, who has elected all humanity to himself. As the elected man, Jesus Christ is the one who truly lived in perfect obedience as God's *covenant* partner and as God's faithful *witness*. All of sinful humanity is taken up in Jesus Christ, elected by him and through him, to be justified by grace and sanctified into holiness and to serve as faithful witnesses to the gospel of Jesus Christ, which at its heart is a gospel of divine grace.

G. C. Berkouwer called this the "triumph of grace" in the theology of Barth. Barth himself preferred the phrase that he had learned from Johann and Christoph Blumhardt, *Christus Victor*, to speak of God's ultimate triumph and victory in Jesus Christ, over all that is in opposition to the eternal purposes of God revealed and fulfilled in Jesus Christ.

In his multivolume and incomplete doctrine of reconciliation, Barth returns to speak of Jesus Christ as "true God, true man and true witness," which he calls "the humanity of God." In a major excursus within his doctrine of reconciliation (IV/2:511ff.), Barth divides humanity into those who are in Christ *de jure* and those who are in Christ *de facto*. By this Barth seems to articulate that while Jesus Christ as the electing God and the elected man on behalf of all humanity has elected, reconciled, justified, sanctified, and redeemed all humanity *de jure* in his first coming, the election, reconciliation, *justification, sanctification,* and redemption of all humanity in Christ has yet to be fully realized *de facto*. This will only take place in his second coming as an eschatological reality and possibility. In the meantime, humanity is divided between those who are in Christ *de facto* and those who are in Christ *de jure*; the task of those who are in Christ *de facto* is to bear faithful witness to the electing and reconciling work of Jesus Christ in order that all may recognize in fact (*de facto*) who they already are *de jure*. This demonstrates a consistency in Barth's argument from the objective (*de jure*) to the subjective (*de facto*) within his doctrine of reconciliation that is present throughout the *CD*, beginning with his doctrine of revelation.

In his essay "The Humanity of God," Barth addresses the issue of universalism again. First, he questions the language of "outsiders" and "insiders" of the Christian *faith* that is often used in Christian witness to the kerygma of the Christian gospel. Barth prefers to speak of "'outsiders' who are really only 'insiders' who have not yet understood and apprehended themselves as such." Yet he also speaks of the need for "the most persuaded Christian [to] recognize himself as an 'outsider.'" He then asks, "Does this mean universalism?" to which he offers a threefold response. First, theology should not "panic" in light of the word *universalism* as if it is something to be feared. Second, theology should be stimulated in its thinking by Col. 1:19 and other texts that speak of God reconciling all things to himself in Jesus Christ, and that those texts have what Barth calls "a good meaning." Lastly, Barth raises the question concerning the so-called danger that universalism poses, whether the danger of theological gloom and skepticism on the one hand or the danger of "the unbecomingly cheerful indifferentism or even antinomianism" of certain understandings of the doctrine of universalism. He concludes by calling on theology to see and understand the reality of the humanity of God in greater ways than has been seen or understood before. He unequivocally states: "we have no theological right to set any sort of limits to the loving-kindness of God which has appeared in Jesus Christ" (*HG*, 58–62).

Most critics of Barth point to his christocentric monism, his overly objectivist doctrine of election, and his

optimistic and hopeful doctrine of reconciliation as being the primary contributors to their conclusion that Barth's theology logically and necessarily leads to universalism. However, Donald Bloesch may provide the most meaningful assessment to Barth's theology in this matter: "Barth transcends the polarity between universalism and particularism in that he denies both of these as rational principles or even as necessary conclusions of faith" (Bloesch, 70–71). On the one hand, Barth asserts the sovereignty and freedom of God in Jesus Christ that is revealed and fulfilled in Jesus Christ, while on the other hand affirming the importance of faith for knowing and experiencing the grace of God in Jesus Christ. Barth refused to be drawn into speculative theology concerning the eternal destiny of humanity since to do so would place human limits on the grace of God in Jesus Christ. Furthermore, for Barth, God's ways remain a mystery on this side of the eschaton, especially the mystery of divine election and humanity's final redemption. It seems apparent that while he would not affirm universalism as a *dogma* of Christian faith, he did affirm the all-inclusive reconciliation of all things to God in Jesus Christ as something to be hoped for and prayed for in light of who we know and experience God to be in Jesus Christ.

K. Barth, *HG*; G. C. Berkouwer, *The Triumph of Grace in the Theology of Karl Barth*, trans. H. R. Boer (1956); D. Bloesch, *Jesus Is Victor!* (1976); B. D. Burton, "Faithful Witness to the Uniqueness of Jesus Christ," *Theology Matters* 1, no. 6 (1995): 1–8; B. L. McCormack, "So That He May Be Merciful to All," in *Karl Barth and American Evangelicalism*, ed. C. Anderson and B. L. McCormack (2011), 227–49.

BRYAN BURTON

Vocation   In the Middle Ages *vocation* (calling or vocation) was a term reserved for priests, monks, and nuns.

The Reformers insisted on the contrary that anyone can have a vocation. *Luther* translated the word as *Beruf* (job), and *Calvin* wrote that ordinary people should find a "singular consolation" in the thought that "no task will be so sordid and base, provided you obey your calling in it, that it will not shine and be reckoned very precious in God's sight" (*Institutes* 3.11.6). Barth applauded this democratization but worried at the identification of vocation with job. For one thing, it leaves out children, the unemployed, the elderly, and others who do not have a job. Is there nothing that God calls them to do with their lives? Even more, the New Testament never uses *klēsis*, the word we translate as "vocation," to refer to a job.

Rather, Barth said, in New Testament usage every human being's vocation is *to become a Christian*. In one sense, *all* have already been called in Christ: "in *Jesus Christ* as the eternal beginning of all God's ways and works, no man is rejected, but all are elected in Him to their *justification*, their *sanctification* and also their vocation" (*CD* IV/3.2:484). Yet Barth acknowledged, "There are countless men whose justification, sanctification and vocation in the *history* of Jesus have not yet taken place in their own history" (486). That does not mean that they have no calling, however, but only that vocation for them is still in the future.

Here appear at least two of the most important recurring themes in Barth's *theology*. First, Barth's near *universalism*. *Everyone* already has justification, sanctification, and vocation in Christ. Therefore, "As Christians and therefore as those who are called we are constrained to be absolutely open in respect of all other men without exception" (493). Atheists, Buddhists, the worst of sinners—it is impossible that anyone should be without the vocation to become a Christian. On the other hand, vocation is not something in which those who are called are "ordained for pure passivity ... merely left gaping

at the One who discloses Himself to them" (542). Vocation requires human response. Therefore we cannot quite rule out the possibility that what Barth elsewhere calls "the impossible possibility" of *sin* might lead some to reject their vocation.

This is so especially because, second, what Barth said about vocation, like much else in his theology, follows what George Hunsinger has called the basic Chalcedonian character of Barth's *Christology*: Barth recognized Christ's full *humanity* and full deity but gave a kind of priority to the deity. In Christ, deity has precedence and initiative; humanity has subsequence and absolute dependence. So in human vocation, a proper theological understanding must recognize *both* that we are all called in Christ *and* that our calling is incomplete without an appropriate human response. But the first of those factors is more important than the second. Thus, while we cannot simply say that everyone has been called and that is the end of the story, the fact that we are called in Christ is ultimately more important than the nature of our response.

In Christ, to repeat, every human being is called to become a Christian. But humans are not called to be Christians for their own sake, for some "indescribably magnificent private good fortune ... opening to them the gates of Paradise which are closed to others" (567). Vocation is not about personal benefit. Rather, "to be called means being given a task" (573). Specifically, "The essence of their vocation is that God makes them His witnesses" (575). Witnessing to the *grace* of Christ is what Christians are called to do.

From the character of that calling, several consequences follow. First, because Christian *witness* is witness to God's *grace*, it follows that, as can be seen in the Gospels, Jesus never calls "those who are already righteous ... are ... the uncalled from whom He can only dissociate and whom He can only pass by, turning instead, and most surprisingly, to the sinner in the tax-office" (588). Second, because this witness must go out and address the *world*, to be a witness is to exist "in affliction." If Christians are not oppressed by their environment and feel they have nothing to fear from a hostile world, then they ought to ask themselves if they are genuine Christians at all (619). Third, however, if their witness is to be credible, then it cannot leave them despairing but must be liberating. "A troubled Christian is by definition not a Christian," for a true Christian must have "personal *joy*, making him a bright and merry Christian" (662). Thus, for instance, Christians are drawn out of solitariness into fellowship, out of indecision into action, and out of anxiety into *prayer*.

His doctrine of vocation represents one of the theological innovations in the grand structure of Barth's doctrine of reconciliation (*CD* IV). He began with the threefold form of Christology: the deity, the humanity, and the unity of those two natures in one person. Correspondingly, he identified three forms of sin (pride, sloth, and falsehood), three forms of grace (justification, sanctification, and vocation), three works of the *Holy Spirit* (the gathering of the Christian community, the upbuilding of the Christian community, and the sending of the Christian community), and three forms of individual's experience of the atonement (*faith, love,* and *hope*).

While the whole scheme is original to Barth, most of its triadic elements are familiar from the history of theology—but not the addition of vocation to Reformation discussions of justification and sanctification. Barth claimed that earlier theology had ignored "certain insights into Christian *salvation*. . . . : life in the present, in expectation of the *kingdom of God*, in the rest and unrest which this causes" (IV/1:146). Christians are called to *witness*, and therefore vocation corresponds to the *sending* of the Christian community out into the world; they witness to the *truth*, and

therefore this form of grace parallels *falsehood* as a form of sin.

———

K. Barth, *CD* III/4:595–647; IV/3.2:481–680; G. Hunsinger, *Disruptive Grace* (2000); W. C. Placher, ed., *Callings* (2005); D. J. Schuurman, *Vocation* (2004).
WILLIAM C. PLACHER

Wholly Other   No phrase is more famous yet more misunderstood in Barth's *theology* than the phrase "wholly other." Barth acknowledged he did not coin it but it was "in part taken over and in part newly invented!" (*HG*, 42) when he used it throughout *Rom* II (1922) to describe God's absolute transcendence over all things, including all human thoughts, desires, and expectations. For Barth it indicates the "'infinite qualitative distinction' between *time* and *eternity*," which, he said, bears "negative as well as positive significance: '*God* is in heaven, and thou art on earth'" (*ER*, 10). It means God's being is utterly distinct, *totaliter aliter*, completely different than all creaturely phenomena and noumena and on such bases is totally underivable, unintuitable, and uninferrable.

Though Barth described God's will as "wholly other" (*ganzlich andere*) in 1916 ("Righteousness," 24), it appears he began to refer to God as "*das ganz andere*" only in his Safenwil sermons of 1919–1920 and in his address, "Biblical Questions, Insights, and Vistas," which he delivered on April 17, 1920, in Germany (ET: "Vistas"), where the phrase had come into vogue through Rudolf Otto's *Das Heilige* (1917). In this address, Barth notes its popularity but clearly means something different by it ("Vistas," 75–76). He had read Otto's book only a few months earlier and reported to Eduard *Thurneysen* on June 3, 1919, that he had done so with "considerable joy." He appreciated the "numinous" quality of Otto's "wholly other," that it could not be understood rationally and thus its potential for overcoming Ritschlianism, yet he rejected its basic "psychological orientation" and its failure to do justice to its subject matter, "the divine in God" (B–Th Br., 330).

In Rom II Barth emphasizes that "das ganz Andere" is not really that which is wholly other but rather he, or the one, who is wholly other (Rom II, 186, 258, 265, 431–32). In 1922 he stated: "If we take the word 'different' [anders] seriously, what does it mean to confront something totally different? If we are not finally to be guilty of mere bombast, can the totally different be one thing in contrast to this or that other different thing? What do 'new' and 'old' mean when it is a matter of this new thing, when it is a matter of the knowledge of God in this theology?" (ThC, 16). For Barth we cannot know that God is "wholly other" merely apophatically, but only dialectically; not by piling up negations, but only through revelation; not on the basis of metaphysics, but only through the veiling and unveiling of God's mysterious presence. However, many still interpreted the phrase abstractly, that is, undialectically or in idealistic terms to express theological skepticism or the nongivenness of the divine according to the "iron law" of philosophers (CD I/2:750–51). To them it implied divine aloofness or absence. Such definitions, Barth said, "might just as well fit a dead idol" (HG, 72).

Barth took some responsibility for this misunderstanding. Although he had found the concept fascinating, he claimed he had not identified it with the God of the Bible "without examination." Yet he conceded: "We viewed this 'wholly other' in isolation, abstracted and absolutized, and set it over against man, this miserable wretch—not to say boxed his ears with it—in such fashion that it continually showed greater similarity to the deity of the God of the philosophers than to the deity of the God of Abraham, Isaac, and Jacob" (HG, 45). Barth did not "intend any such thing," but he acknowledged: "we did not know how to carry through with sufficient care and thoroughness the new

knowledge of the deity of God which was so exciting to us and to others" (44). Justice, he admitted, was not done to the incarnation (I/2:50), "the humanity of God," nor to the fact that "God in the highest does not mean a wholly other, who has nothing to do with us; rather . . . it means he who from out of the highest has come down to us" (DiO, 37, rev.).

Nevertheless, Barth defended his use of the phrase. We may have been "only partially in the right," but given the wholesale anthropologization of theology and radical domestication of God's transcendence that had occurred over the previous two hundred and fifty years, he insisted it played an important albeit antiseptic, critical, and polemical role (HG, 38ff.). He tried to disabuse the impression that the phrase necessarily implies "the swallowing of immanence by transcendence" (43). For Barth, God is radically transcendent and also radically immanent, but only as an act of his freedom. He also continued to qualify his understanding of the "wholly other" from existentialists who, with varying degrees of assurance, claimed to encounter "It" in various "frontier situations" (III/2:114ff.). Indeed, in affirming that God is "literally" the Father and not "a 'He' that is a mere cipher ascribed with more or less knowledge to an 'It' concealed behind it," Barth declared in his last years: "An 'It,' even though it might be the supreme 'It,' the Holy or Wholly Other (Otto), the Encompassing (Jaspers), could not be addressed as a 'Thou' and affirmed as an 'I,' or could be so only symbolically, so that this would not be the 'Thou' or 'I' that Christians have in mind when they speak of God" (IV/4:52ff.). To Barth, affirming that God is "wholly other" was, in short, simply another way of saying that "God is God" and as such is free and unsearchable (Rom. 11:33).

K. Barth, CD III/2:114ff.; idem, DiO, 35–41; idem, HG; I. Dalferth, "Representing God's Presence," IJST 3, no. 3

(2001): 237–56; B. L. McCormack, *Karl Barth's Critically Realistic Dialectical Theology* (1995), 241ff.

RICHARD E. BURNETT

Witness Few concepts were more significant in the aftermath of Barth's break with *liberalism* than the concept of witness. Following *Schleiermacher*, Barth had previously read the biblical prophets and apostles primarily as *sources* of piety. Yet after reading Paul's Epistles around 1915, Barth understood them primarily as witnesses. Shortly thereafter, he hung above his desk a picture of Grünewald's *Crucifixion* with John the Baptist's oddly elongated finger pointing "in an almost impossible way" to Jesus on the cross with the words underneath, "He must increase, but I must decrease." Barth interpreted John's oddly elongated finger as indicative of the decisive factor in all true human witness to *Jesus Christ*, namely, a miracle. Grünewald's picture remained in front of Barth's writing desk his entire career, reminding him of what witnessing means.

"Witnessing means pointing in a specific direction beyond the self and on to another" (*CD* I/1:111). The prophets and apostles "do not speak and write for their own sakes, nor for the sake of their deepest inner possession or need; they speak and write, as ordered, about the other" (112). They do not make themselves witnesses, but are made witnesses. *God* makes them witnesses by making himself the subject of their testimony. Certainly they are "conditioned by their historical and biographical situation, by their particular speech and outlook" (I/2:817). But what distinguishes them from the "interested spectator, or the narrating reporter, or the reflective dialectician, or the determined partisan" is that they are "not answering a question which comes from [themselves], but one which the judge addresses to [them]. . . . They are in the position and are called to give informa-tion upon a question put to them from without. . . . Their starting-point is this speaking and acting of God . . . who now as Judge asks of them nothing but the truth concerning this reality, concerning His own speaking and acting which has taken place once for all." They are made witnesses only because God Himself is the first, true witness. As "eyewitnesses of those deeds done . . . and *hearers of the Word* spoken in their time," they "were destined, appointed, and elected for this cause by God" and "commanded and empowered by him to speak of what they had seen and heard" (*EvT*, 26).

These "primary witnesses" give "direct information" to a wider circle of "secondary witnesses" who "can only confirm and repeat" what they have heard, and "for *dogmatics* as for *Church* proclamation everything depends on hearing" these first witnesses aright (I/2:818). A secondary witness may "possess a better astronomy, geography, zoology, psychology, physiology, and so on than these biblical witnesses possessed; but as for the *Word of God*, he is not justified in comporting himself in relationship to those witnesses as though he knew more about the Word than they" (*EvT*, 31). He is not "a high-school teacher authorized to look over their shoulder benevolently or crossly, to correct their notebooks, or to give them good, average, or bad marks. Even the smallest, strangest, simplest, or obscurest among the biblical witnesses has an incomparable advantage over even the most pious, scholarly, and sagacious latter-day theologian." Evangelical *theology* "must agree to let *them* look over its shoulder and correct its notebooks" (32).

Bearing witness is rooted in the praise of God and *love* of neighbor (I/2:§18). It has three decisive forms "equally complete and adequate in themselves and yet all three are equally indispensable" (441): word, deed, and attitude.

If I have been helped then I must say something to my neighbor by way of "a declaration of this knowledge." I must speak a *word*. Yet I must not make my story of need the main theme, nor the experiences, states, and events in which I have felt "an alleviation or even a removal of my need" (442). This would put my experience of help at the center instead of the help itself, Jesus Christ. "This name, and in the strict sense only this name, . . . is what we know about help in need" (443). Indeed, "The only word which is praise of God and a witness to the neighbor is a word which is praise of Jesus Christ and witness about him." Witnessing thus means more than what I do with my lips, but not less. But if I believe what I say, "then I must act" (445).

The second form of witness is *deed*. The witness of word is itself "the most concrete act" (444), and the witness of deed does not replace it. It is another form of the same duty. It interprets my word. My word or deed as such cannot bear real witness. But by "helping the sick life of another to rather better health, of lightening a little the burden he has to carry, of comforting him a little in his trouble, of bringing a bit of *joy* into his sadness" (447), I set up a sign that awaits divine disclosure.

The third form of witness is *attitude*. However "clear and true my word may be and however helpful in itself my action," there is no witness if my attitude, mood, or disposition do not reflect "my own subjection to the lordship of Jesus Christ" (447–48). My indifference, self-centeredness, or impatience in speaking or acting may reflect a "heathen or legal" rather than "evangelical attitude," which demands my "whole life." "I have no power to make an impression by the witness of my person. But that does not alter the fact that I am summoned to give . . . the witness of my person and attitude," and "there is much we can do in relation to our inward and outward attitude" (449).

A witness is limited and cannot make things happen. "A witness will not intrude on his neighbor. He will not 'handle' him. He will not make him the object of his activity, even with the best intention. Witness can be given only when there is respect for the freedom of the *grace* of God, and therefore respect for the other man who can expect nothing from me but everything from God" (440). Because true witness requires a miracle, the self-witness of Jesus Christ, "the true Witness," our witness as such "will always be a matter of doubt" (700).

Yet "whether strong or weak, willing or unwilling, successful or unsuccessful, the Christian is a witness, irrespective of whether the miracle occurs" (IV/3.2:609) by virtue of God's promise, "You shall be my witnesses" (Acts 1:8). Christian existence is not primarily about seeking one's own salvation or enjoying the benefits of the gospel. It is about being a witness. "The *ministry* of witness is the primary determination of Christian existence" (618). It is "the essence" of our vocation as Christians (575). As the church does not exist for its own sake, but for the sake of the *world* (763ff.), so Christian existence "is not an end in itself" (648), but is directed outwardly. In what makes one "a Christian the first concern is not with his own person. He is referred, not to himself, but to God who points him to his neighbor" (652). Hence we are not witnesses because we are Christians; we are Christians because we are witnesses, because of the commission and appointment we have been given (653–54). Finally, a true witness will always be "disturbing" to those around and be marked by unavoidable affliction (§71.5) yet also joyful liberation (§71.6).

K. Barth, *CD* IV/3.2:554ff., 676ff.; idem, *EvT*, 26–36; E. Busch, *The Great Passion*, trans. G. W. Bromiley (2004), 145–51, 253–63; J. Mangina, *Karl Barth* (2004).

RICHARD E. BURNETT

Word of God   *What* the Word of God is cannot be known apart from *who God* is, Father, Son, and *Holy Spirit*, and who God is cannot be known apart from

God's own self-revelation in his Word, that is, apart from him who assumed human flesh, *Jesus Christ*. "The Word of God is uncreated reality, identical with God Himself. Hence it is not universally present and ascertainable, not even potentially" (*CD* I/1:158), nor is it "given to us in the same way as natural and historical entities" but only as God speaks (132). God has spoken and continues to speak, and where this reality is known the *church* is born, and *how* God has spoken and continues to speak is acknowledged in threefold form: as preached, written, and revealed.

The Word of God preached. "The *preaching* of the Word of God is the Word of God," says the Second Helvetic Confession. How so? By an event in which God speaks for himself through weak, corrupt, fallible human *language*. When this happens, and it can happen not only in "sermons from the pulpit" but when we "'preach' to ourselves in the quiet of our own rooms" (*GD* ,16), it entails: (1) that beyond all "scientific or artistic" criteria, all "circumstances or scales of value," all "personal convictions" or "motives," God's Word has been proclaimed by *God's own commission*, command, or sending (I/1:89–90); (2) that God's Word "sets itself" up as its *own theme* "where we cannot possibly set it," and "presents and places itself as an object over against us and the whole *world* of all our objects" by God's own "self-objectification" (91–92); (3) that beyond all criteria of human judgment whereby we can and must judge the truthfulness of other words, God's Word *judges by its own criterion of truth*, which "cannot be anticipated and never passes under our control." However subject we are to other judgments, its "judgment alone is absolutely binding and inviolable" (93); (4) and, finally, beyond all motives, themes, and judgments, and all "human willing and doing" (yet not setting these aside, either), it entails "primarily and decisively" a "divine willing and doing." Thus when God speaks his Word through human subjects it hap-

pens not contrary to their *humanity* as created or by "obliterating the human subject," but "through the new robe of righteousness thrown over it" in a "new event" of *God's own speaking* (95). In other words, "when human talk about God is for us not just that, but also and primarily and decisively God's own speech," it is a miracle (93). Yet if church proclamation becomes the Word of God it happens not in isolation but only in recollection of *revelation* once enacted. What is the basis for such recollection? Not a revelation "originally immanent in the existence of every man" (99) nor in an "unwritten spiritual-oral tradition" (105), otherwise the church would be "in dialogue with itself"; but in "an authority irremovably confronting the Church" and as a reality distinct from yet "absolutely constitutive" (102) of it—the *Bible*.

The Word of God written. The Bible serves as the normative authority (canon) in the church not because it is written or because the church says so but "because it imposed itself upon the Church as such, and continually does so" (107), and it does so because it *is* the Word of God. Barth never said, as some have alleged, that the Bible is not the Word of God but only *contains* the Word of God. Rather he insists: "the true Church, stands or falls by the fact that . . . it understands exclusively the statement that the Bible is the Word of God" (I/2:546). The Bible is the Word of God by virtue of the content to which it attests, by virtue of its promise: "The promise given to the Church in this Word is the promise of God's mercy which is uttered in the person of Him who is very God and very Man" (I/1:107–8) and this promise extends to the words of the prophets and apostles (see *inspiration*). "When the Church heard this word—and heard it only in the prophets and apostles and nowhere else—it heard a magisterial and ultimate word which it could not ever again confuse or place on a level with any other word" (108). And the Church continues to hear this Word through these words. "As the Word of God in the sign of this prophetic-apostolic word of man, Holy Scripture is like the unity of God and man in Jesus Christ. It is neither divine only nor human only. Nor is it a mixture of the two, nor a *tertium quid* between them. But in its own way and degree, it is very God and very man, i.e. a *witness* of revelation which itself belongs to revelation" (I/2:501).

That God takes the human words of the apostles and prophets and speaks his own Word through them is a continuous event. It has occurred and continues to occur not because of anything inherent in the apostles or prophets themselves or their words, but solely because of God's decision. Some have suspected that subjectivism underlies such talk and has led others to ask whether for Barth the Bible is the Word of God even apart from this event. But to ask such a question in light of this event is for Barth to play games with the Word of God, to treat it *in abstracto*, as a possibility instead of a reality, and rather than unmasking subjectivism actually reflects it or a false objectivism (I/2:530–31). Contrary to many of his opponents (and proponents), Barth never advocates that upon reading Scripture we should "Listen *for* the Word of God" instead of "*to* the Word of God," as if the Bible is not the Word of God unless some sort of existential light goes on in the individual hearer or "our attitude to it could be constitutive for its reality" (I/1:117). To claim that the Bible is the Word of God, Barth acknowledges, is a *confession* of *faith*, but "it is a statement which, when venturing it in faith, we accept as true even apart from our faith and beyond all our faith and even in face of our lack of faith. We do not accept it as a description of our experience of the Bible. We accept it as a description of God's action in the Bible, whatever may be the experiences we have or do not have in this connection. . . . The Bible, then, becomes God's Word in this event, and in the statement that

the Bible is God's Word the little word 'is' refers to its being in this becoming. It does not become God's Word because we accord it faith but in the fact that it becomes revelation to us. But the fact that it becomes revelation to us beyond all our faith, that it is God's Word even in spite of our lack of faith, is something we can accept and confess as true to us and for us only in faith" (110).

That "the Bible is the Word of God" and "becomes the Word of God" or that Scripture's "being" is in "becoming" may sound contradictory, but it reflects an ontology based on the life of God's own being, a being "ever at work and ever at rest" (Augustine), in which there is eternal constancy and eternal movement or procession (see *actualism*). But that one may "say of proclamation and the Bible that they are God's Word, that they continually become God's Word" (118), is not to say the Bible becomes something it is not. Rather it "becomes again and again what it is" (109) and not merely occasionally, as neo-orthodox interpreters suggest, but "continually." Thus "in the event of God's Word revelation and the Bible are indeed one, and literally so" (113). Nor for Barth does the Bible "contain" or "hold" the Word of God. The Word of God is not a predicate, property, or attribute of the Bible because *the Word of God is God* and "God is not an attribute of something else, even if this something else is the Bible" (I/2:513). Rather it is the Word of God that holds the Bible and as such (and only as such) is it: (1) "held up on high"; (2) "held in place"; and (3) "held in store" (I/1:117–18) in virtue of God's free decision.

The Word of God revealed. "This independent and unsurpassable origin of the Word of God that comes to us is what we have in view when we speak of its third form, or materially we should rather say its first form, i.e. its form as the Word of God revealed" (120). What the Bible and church proclamation are "derivatively and indirectly," the Word of God revealed is "originally and directly" (117–18). Whereas the speakers in the former are both God and humans, the speaker in the latter is God himself and God alone. Whereas the former are witnesses to revelation and as such belong to revelation, the latter is revelation itself. Whereas the former requires continuous repetition and confirmation to be what it is as the Word of God, the latter does not (I/2:513). In contrast to the humanity of the prophets and apostles, the humanity assumed by the Word of God revealed was taken up into glory and "does not differ from the person of Jesus Christ" (I/1:119). "Where we say 'Word of God revealed,' then in distinction from the 'written' and 'preached' of the two other forms of the Word of God, 'revealed' does not belong to the predicate. It is simply a paraphrase, a second designation of the subject. If 'written' and 'preached' denote the twofold concrete relation in which the Word of God is spoken to us, revelation denotes the Word of God itself in the act of its being spoken in time. Above this act there is nothing other or higher on which it might be based. . . . It is the condition which conditions all things without itself being conditioned" (118).

Yet to say the Word of God revealed is "revelation itself," "directly" and "unconditionally," refers to the person of Jesus Christ, not to his humanity as such. Even the hypostatic union does not imply "direct identification" between Christ's divinity and Christ's flesh as such. There remains a fundamental distinction between "creaturely reality itself and as such and the reality of the Creator . . . even in the person of Christ" (I/2:499). And if such a distinction remains in the hypostatic union, particularly following, as Barth does, the consistent pattern of Reformed *Christology* wherein "the divine and human natures of Christ remain distinct and unimpaired in their original integrity *after* their union in one Person" (McCormack, 70), such a distinction surely remains between the Word of God and the Bible and preaching where no such

union is implied. All three forms of the Word of God come veiled in creaturely form. Each creaturely form shares an indirect identity with revelation, which means in each form assumed by the Word the human element remains human and the divine remains divine.

Unity-in-differentiation. Because the Bible does not teach nor does the Church confess three different Words of God, but rather the one *incarnation* of the one Word of God, one Word in threefold form, Barth emphasizes the unity of these forms rather than their distinction. "In this threefold form and not otherwise—but also as the one Word only in this threefold form—the Word of God is given to us and we must try to understand it conceptually. It is one and the same whether we understand it as revelation, Bible, or proclamation. There is no distinction of degree or value between the three forms" (I/1:120), no "more or less" when it comes to the power and authority of the actualized forms (121). Since the Word of God revealed "never meets us anywhere in abstract form," but "only indirectly, from Scripture and proclamation," we know it only in relation to the other two forms. Likewise we do not know the Word written apart from the Word revealed and proclaimed or the Word proclaimed apart from the Word revealed and written. Thus to say that Barth distinguishes revelation or the Word of God from Scripture and preaching and to leave it at that is only half right. It misses the *indissoluble* unity-in-differentiation and interrelatedness for which "there is," Barth claims, "only one *analogy*," the *Trinity*.

Barth develops his doctrine of the Word of God in light of extensive *exegesis*, the theology of the ancient fathers and Reformers, and many insights from "Protestant Orthodoxy, which," he says, "at the peak of its development had no liking for talk about the distinction between the forms of the Word of God and the fluidity of their mutual relations, emphasised the more zealously something which is equally true and instructive in itself, namely, their unity" (I/1:123). Though he did not invent the concept of a threefold form of the Word (it emerged in the Reformation and was already partially developed, e.g., Bullinger's *Decades*), Barth's effort to think through how these three forms relate, which he develops in the first two half-volumes of the *CD*, is widely regarded as among his greatest contributions. Unfortunately, however, most treatments of Barth's doctrine of the Word focus primarily on the issue of form (as here), whereas Barth devotes significantly more attention to "The Nature of the Word of God" (125–86), "The Knowability of the Word of God" (187–247), and to exegesis of passages such as John 1:14 (I/2:132–71), and so on. Justice cannot be done to these sections here, but the upshot is: God's Word is at the same time his act. The Word is conceptual and personal, propositional and existential yet cannot be reduced to any concept, idea, or principle. "God's Word is not a thing. . . . It is neither a matter nor an idea. It is not 'a truth,' not even the very highest truth. It is *the* truth as it is God's speaking person, *Dei loquentis persona*" (1/1:136). Against its commodification, Barth insists God's Word is "living and active," not primarily a "what" but a "who," not an "it" but a "him," "the divine, creative, reconciling, redeeming Word which participates without restriction in the divine nature and existence, the eternal Son of God" (I/2:132). Against its domestication and the perennial temptation "that members of the Church may want the Word of God without God, bringing it under their power and understanding, and applying it according to their own good pleasure" (807), Barth insists God's Word is sovereignly free.

K. Barth, *CD* I/1:§§3–7; 1/2:§§15, 19–21; idem, *GD*, §§1–13; T. Hart, "The Word, the Words and the Witness," in *Regarding Karl Barth* (1999), 28–47; B. L. McCormack, "The Being of Holy Scripture Is in Becoming," in *Evangelicals and Scripture*, ed. V. Bacote, L. C. Miguélez, and D. L. Okholm (2004), 55–75.

RICHARD E. BURNETT

World   Though the term occurs frequently in his writings, Barth provides no explicit treatment of the concept of "world." He has theological reasons for doing so that he states at the beginning of *CD* III/2 in chapter 10, introducing his theological anthropology. This chapter follows immediately upon the volume that treats the **creation** as a whole, and Barth anticipates criticisms challenging the fact that he is jumping directly from the creation as God's work to the human being without paying attention to the created *world* in which human life takes place. Barth responds: "The reason why there is no revealed or biblical worldview characteristic of and necessary to the Christian *kerygma* is that faith in the **Word of God** can never find its theme in the totality of the created world. It believes in **God** in His relation to the man who lives under heaven and on earth; but it does not believe in this or that constitution of heaven and earth" (*CD* III/2:8). "The Word of God is concerned with God and man. It certainly gives us an ontology of man. . . . But the Word of God does not contain any ontology of heaven and earth themselves" (6). Barth restricts **theology** to treating God, the human being, and their relationship. The world is not an independent topic for theology. Barth finds support for this contention in the fact that there is no specific term for our notion of "world" in Old Testament Hebrew (cf. III/3:420: "The Old Testament does not use the term 'world' to denote the sum of the reality distinct from God and posited by Him"). Instead, Genesis 1 speaks of "heaven and earth," which indicates, in Barth's eyes, a focus on the relationship between God and **humanity**.

Therefore, when Barth speaks throughout his writings of the world, he uses the word in terms of this relationship. The first broader occurrence is the essay about "The New World in the Bible" (1917). As the title suggests, it deals with the new world, the good world, the world of God that is hoped for in the *Bible*. This new world begins already to grow in our world. With its organic imagery in terms of a steady process, the essay foreshadows *Rom* I, which was published two years later.

In *Rom* II (1922) Barth no longer holds to a "process *eschatology*" but emphasizes the present crisis, the sinful state of affairs, and the distance between God and humankind. Barth's notion of world in the new edition fits perfectly into this changed general paradigm. Now the focus lies on the *old* world. Instead of being God's world, it is the "world of man" (*Rom* II, 145), it is *our* world, a "world of contradiction" (cf. *GD*, 160), which means the world in so far as it has abandoned its creator, the world as determined by *sin*. "This world, because of being *our* world, is the world in which sin has entered" (*Rom* II, 147). We find a definition in this sense in Barth's interpretation of Romans 5:12: "What is the world? The world is our entire being, as it is and continues to develop under the domination of sin" (*Rom* II, 146).

Far from the common understanding of being just a neutral place where life unravels, the world in Barth's view is a *theological* category for human life *as it is*. The world is "God's creation as it is in its totality" (*CL*, 116). The world is not only *our* world, but we *are* ourselves the world, as far as we live under the domination of sin. And this domination reaches very far. It is important for Barth to avoid constructing a distance between the world and the *church*. The church, rather than representing heaven on earth, is itself part of the world and dominated by sin. The distinction between world and church is only a relative one. "The World and the Church are what they are only because they are related to one another. Neither can say

that the other is excluded absolutely. What is absolute is simply the fact that both are opposed to God" (*ER*, 401).

The last claim is, in all its negativity, not the last word Barth has to say about the world. In its close junction with the church, the world continues, in spite of its seeming separation from God, to be a place of God's presence in Christ. This continuing presence is stressed particularly in the later works of Barth, for example, in a talk he gave in 1963: there is no separation between the church and the world because Christ is present in both (*G-1963*, 162–63). One might mention here the famous "doctrine of lights" ("Lichterlehre") from *CD* IV/3 that was written in the 1950s. But actually the same idea of a worldly presence of God in Christ is already invoked by Barth as early as 1938 in *CD* II/1, where Barth speaks of God's immanence, with Christ being "the principle and basis of all divine immanence" in the world (II/1:317).

We see, then, that the world is entirely involved in the story of creation, sin, and redemption. This gives the world an ambiguous character, as is underlined in the text that is arguably the most comprehensive treatment of the notion of world in Barth's writings, *CL*, 116–32. In this passage, Barth is not only highlighting the ambivalence in the relationship the world has with God (118): God is objectively known in the world, but subjectively unknown. Furthermore, Barth is, once again, relativizing the distance between the world and the church in making them two concentric circles with regard to their respective *knowledge of God*. The church is the inner circle, and therefore entirely part of the world.

In sum, two elements in Barth's notion of the world are worth highlighting. First, the world is an entirely *theological* concept, reflecting the relationship between God and humanity. Barth has no interest in a cosmology. Second, with regard to its relation to God, the world is a *dialectical* notion: full of sin, but, just *as it is*, a place of God's presence.

K. Barth, *CD* III/2:3–19; idem, *CL*, 116–32; idem, "New World"; N. Biggar, *The Hastening That Waits* (1993), 146–61; G. S. Cootsona, *God and the World* (2001); F. Lohmann, *Karl Barth und der Neukantianismus* (1995); O. Weber, "Kirche und Welt nach Karl Barth," in *Antwort*, ed. E. Wolf, et al. (1956), 217–36.
FRIEDRICH LOHMANN

Worship Barth's most sustained treatment of Christian worship (*Gottesdienst*) appears in *Knowledge of God and Service of God*, which are his Gifford Lectures from 1937–1938. He addresses the issue as well in *CD* IV/3.2. Barth envisions worship that is recognizably Reformed in its artistic austerity and its focus on hearing the **Word of God**. At the same time, he insists that a Reformed worship service is primarily an act of **God**, incomplete without **baptism** and the **Lord's Supper**, and only secondarily a human activity.

The primary basis for the church's worship is the presence of **Jesus Christ**, who "wishes the *church* to be as He is and to continue as He continues." In Christian worship God effects his intention that the church should come into being and continue to exist, while the church itself also actively hears and obeys the Word of God. Thus the service is primarily God's work and it has no other purpose or justification. "The church service is in the first instance primarily, in origin and substance, divine action, and is only then human action secondarily, by derivation, and as an accident of the former" (*KGSG*, 192).

Baptism and the Lord's Supper provide the limits and center of the service of worship, which also includes *preaching*, praise, and *prayer*. The words and sacramental elements used in the service are important not in themselves, but as the particular testimonies God has chosen. Barth makes a particular point that even the media of the service, that is, the water, bread, wine, and words, are God's own choice and "are in no sense at the mercy of man's imagination or his likes and dislikes" (199). Baptism testifies "that we are ingrafted in Jesus Christ, to be made partakers of his justice." The Lord's Supper bears *witness* that "he remains in [us] and [we] in him" (195). Barth sees worship as a movement from baptism to hearing the Word of God to the Lord's Supper. That Reformed worship ordinarily does not include sacraments is a serious problem. "As a rule we hold such outwardly incomplete services as if it were perfectly natural to do so. What right have we to do that?" (211).

If the presence of Jesus Christ is the primary ground of the service of worship, the secondary ground is the obedience of the church, and on this basis the service occurs as human action. Generally speaking, the human action required of the church is to hear the Word of God. This hearing takes a number of forms, including praise, prayer, and preaching. "The hearing of the Word of God forms the real action of the church and in the last resort everything depends on its taking place around the centre characterized by the two sacraments" (212).

In speaking of human action in the service of worship, Barth tends to focus on preaching. Preaching is "the proclamation of God's *revelation*" (196). Through preaching, Holy Scripture, which "refuses to be silent," clarifies and corrects the church's understanding of its origin and destiny. The **Holy Spirit**, "who does not let himself be quenched," requires that preaching occur (196–97). Barth understands preaching as an act of worship, and not a separate act. It is to be done with sincerity and humility, by which he means openness and submissiveness to God's Word (214–15). If preaching is not a sacrament in Barth (and it is not), a sacramental logic nevertheless characterizes it. The words of the sermon, with the sacramental elements, are to be received, "not as ordinary water, ordinary nourishment and ordinary words, but as water, nourishment and words which bear a testimony" (214).

In *CD* IV/3.2 Barth includes preaching, praise (by which he means primarily congregational song), and prayer within a longer list of the ministries of the church. Here he makes explicit that preaching is an integrated part of the service of worship: "When preaching does not proceed deviously but comes quickly to the point; when it does not engage in confusing analysis or tedious expansion but . . . is concise and pointed; when in this way it declares and expounds the Gospel . . . , then it, too, is a liturgical act" (869).

Likewise the praise of God in the service of worship is a specifically liturgical act, and not a mere preliminary. "The Christian community sings," and indeed its singing is essential to its existence, as "the community which does not sing is not the community." It is "one of the indispensable basic forms of the ministry of the community" (866–67).

Whereas preaching and praise (among other ministries) are primarily speech, prayer is primarily action (882). It is primarily a work of the community, and here again is an act of corporate worship, not "a ritual addition to liturgical action but an integral part of it, of no less dignity than praise and preaching" (884).

Barth is concerned that nothing distract the congregation from hearing the Word of God and responding with praise. Because he believes that in the sermon "Jesus Christ himself" speaks to the community, "the presence of artistic representations of Jesus Christ is not desirable in the places of assembly." An interpretation of the Second Commandment may underlie this misgiving, but he does not refer to it as a warrant. Rather, such "static works" will inevitably attract the eye and attention of the congregation away from the task of hearing Christ himself speak, binding their minds to the artist's conception of Christ, which is inevitably inadequate to the reality of Christ himself. Similarly, he is concerned that organ accompaniment to congregational singing may merely "conceal the feebleness with which the community discharges the ministry of the *vox humana* committed to it" (867).

In 1962, during a visit to the United States, Barth suggested that baptism, preaching, and the Lord's Supper be brought into a visible, liturgical unity through the use of a table set in the center of the congregation gathered in the round, which could be used variously as a pulpit, table, and font. Here again he insists, "Images and symbols have no place in a Protestant church building." The reason is genuinely theological and not mere legalism: "Not only the congregation gathered for worship, . . . but also and above all the congregation busy in everyday life represents the person and work of Jesus Christ. No image and no symbol can play this role" ("P&A").

K. Barth, *CD* IV/3.2:865ff.; idem, *KGSG*, 192–215; idem, "P&A"; M. Boulton, *God against Religion* (2008).

MICHAEL D. BUSH

Bibliography

Aagard, Johannes. "Some Main Trends in Modern Protestant Missiology." *Studia theologica* 19 (1965): 238–59.

Anderson, Clifford B. "The Problem of Psychologism in Karl Barth's Doctrine of Sanctification." *ZDTh* 18, no. 3 (2002): 339–54.

Anderson, Ray. *The Shape of Practical Theology: Empowering Ministry with Theological Praxis.* Downers Grove, IL: InterVarsity Press, 2001.

Asprey, Christopher. *Eschatological Presence in Karl Barth's Göttingen Theology.* Oxford: Oxford University Press, 2010.

Bakker, Nicolas T. *In der Krisis der Offenbarung: Karl Barths Hermeneutik, dargestellt an seiner Römerbrief-Auslegung.* Neukirchen-Vluyn: Neukirchener Verlag, 1974.

———. "Die Sünde in der Kirchlichen Dogmatik: Höhepunkte aus der Sündenlehre Karl Barths." *ZDTh* 9, no. 1 (1993): 9–18.

Balthasar, Hans Urs von. *The Theology of Karl Barth.* Translated by John Drury. San Francisco: Holt, Rinehart, and Winston, 1971.

———. *The Theology of Karl Barth: Exposition and Interpretation.* Translated by Edward T. Oakes. San Francisco: Ignatius, 1992.

Barth, Markus. "Current Discussion on the Political Character of Karl Barth's Theology." In *Footnotes to a Theology: The Karl Barth Colloquium of 1972.* Edited by H. Martin Rumscheidt, 77–94. Waterloo, Ont.: Corporation for the Publication of Academic Studies in Religion in Canada, 1974.

Baxter, Christina. "Barth a Truly Biblical Theologian?" *TynBul* 38 (1987): 3–27.

Beintker, Michael. *Die Dialektik in der "dialektischen Theologie" Karl Barths. Studien zur Entwicklung der Barthschen Theologie und zur Vorgeschichte der "Kirchlichen Dogmatik."* Munich: Kaiser, 1987.

Bender, Kimlyn J. *Karl Barth's Christological Ecclesiology.* Aldershot: Ashgate, 2005.

———. "Karl Barth's Doctrine of the Church in Contemporary Anglo-American Ecclesiological Conversation." *ZDTh* 21, no. 1 (2005): 84–116.

Berkouwer, G. C. *The Triumph of Grace in the Theology of Karl Barth.* Translated by Harry R. Boer. Grand Rapids: Eerdmans, 1956.

Biggar, Nigel. *The Hastening That Waits: Karl Barth's Ethics.* Oxford: Clarendon, 1993.

Bloesch, Donald. *Holy Scripture: Revelation, Inspiration and Interpretation.* Downers Grove, IL: InterVarsity Press, 1994.

———. *Jesus Is Victor! Karl Barth's Doctrine of Salvation.* Nashville: Abingdon, 1976.

———. *A Theology of Word and Spirit.* Downers Grove, IL: InterVarsity Press, 1992.

Bohren, Rudolf. *Prophetie und Seelsorge: Eduard Thurneysen.* Neukirchen-Vluyn: Neukirchener Verlag, 1982.

Bohren, Rudolf, and Max Geiger, eds. *Wort und Gemeinde: Probleme und Aufgaben der praktischen Theologie. Eduard Thurneysen zum 80. Geburtstag.* Zurich: Evangelischer Verlag, 1968.

Bosch, David. *Transforming Mission: Paradigm Shifts in Theology of Mission.* Maryknoll, N.Y.: Orbis, 1991.

Boulton, Matthew. *God against Religion: Rethinking Christian Theology through Worship.* Grand Rapids: Eerdmans, 2008.

———. "'We Pray by His Mouth': Karl Barth, Erving Goffman, and a Theology of Invocation." *MTh* 17, no. 1 (2001): 67–83.

Bracher, Karl D. *The Age of Ideologies: A History of Political Thought in the Twentieth Century.* Translated by Ewald Osers. New York: St. Martin's, 1984.

Brunner, Emil. *Die Mystik und das Wort: Der Gegensatz zwischen moderner Religionsauffassung und christlichem Glauben dargestellt an der Theologie Schleiermachers.* Tübingen: Mohr Siebeck, 1924.

———. *The Divine Imperative.* Translated by Olive Wyon. Philadelphia: Westminster, 1937.

———. *God and Man.* Translated by David Cairns. London: SCM, 1936.

———. "The New Barth: Observations on Karl Barth's *Doctrine of Man.*" Translated by John C. Campbell. *SJT* 4 (1951): 123–35.

———. *Wahrheit als Begegnung.* Berlin: Furche Verlag, 1938.

———. *The Word and the World.* London: SCM, 1931.

Buckley, James J. "Christian Community, Baptism and Lord's Supper." In *The Cambridge Companion to Karl Barth.* Edited by John Webster, 195–211. Cambridge: Cambridge University Press, 2000.

Bultmann, Rudolf. *Jesus.* Tübingen: Mohr Siebeck, 1926.

———. "New Testament and Mythology: The Problem of Demythologizing the New Testament Proclamation." In *New Testament and Mythology and Other Basic Writings.* Edited and translated by Schubert M. Ogden, 1–43. Philadelphia: Fortress, 1984.

———. "What Does It Mean to Speak of God?" In *Faith and Understanding* I. Edited by Robert W. Funk. Translated by Louise Pettibone Smith, 53–65. Philadelphia: Fortress, 1969.

Burgess, Andrew. *The Ascension in Barth.* Aldershot: Ashgate, 2002.

Burnett, Richard E. *Karl Barth's Theological Exegesis: The Hermeneutical Principles of the Römerbrief Period.* Tübingen: Mohr Siebeck, 2001. Repr., Grand Rapids: Eerdmans, 2004.

Burton, Bryan D. "Faithful Witness to the Uniqueness of Jesus Christ." *Theology Matters* 1, no. 6 (1995): 1–8.

Busch, Eberhard. *The Barmen Theses Then and Now.* Translated by Darrell and Judith Guder. Grand Rapids: Eerdmans, 2010.

———. *The Great Passion: An Introduction to Karl Barth's Theology.* Translated by Geoffrey W. Bromiley. Grand Rapids: Eerdmans, 2004.

———. *Karl Barth and the Pietists: The Young Karl Barth's Critique of Pietism and Its Response.* Translated by Daniel Bloesch. Downers Grove, IL: InterVarsity Press, 2004.

———. *Karl Barth: His Life from Letters and Autobiographical Texts.* Translated by John Bowden. 1976. Repr., Grand Rapids: Eerdmans, 1994.

———. *Karl Barth und der Pietismus: Stadien eines Weges* (Bad Salzuflen: Arbeitsgemeinschaft Mädchen-Bibel-Kreise, 1987).

Capper, John. "Joy in the Church Dogmatics? A Neglected Theme." In *Karl Barth: A Future for Postmodern Theology?* Edited by Geoff Thompson and Christian Mostert, 98–121. Adelaide,

Australia: Australian Theological Forum, 2000.

Chalamet, Christophe. *Dialectical Theologians: Wilhelm Herrmann, Karl Barth and Rudolf Bultmann.* Zurich: Theologischer Verlag, 2005.

Chung, Sung Wook. *Admiration and Challenge: Karl Barth's Theological Relationship with John Calvin.* New York: Peter Lang, 2002.

Clough, David. *Ethics in Crisis: Interpreting Barth's Ethics.* Aldershot: Ashgate, 2005.

Cochrane, Arthur C. *The Church's Confession under Hitler.* 2nd ed. Pittsburgh: Pickwick, 1976.

Collins, Alice. "Barth's Relationship to Schleiermacher: A Reassessment." *Studies in Religion* 17, no. 2 (1988): 213–24.

Collins, Paul M. *Trinitarian Theology, West and East: Karl Barth, the Cappadocian Fathers, and John Zizioulas.* Oxford: Oxford University Press, 2001.

Cootsona, Gregory S. *God and the World: A Study in the Thought of Alfred North Whitehead and Karl Barth.* New York: Peter Lang, 2001.

Couenhoven, Jesse. "Karl Barth's Conception(s) of Human and Divine Freedom(s)." In *Commanding Grace: Studies in Karl Barth's Ethics.* Edited by Daniel L. Migliore, 239–55. Grand Rapids: Eerdmans, 2010.

———. "Law and Gospel, or the Law of the Gospel: Karl Barth's Political Theology Compared with Luther and Calvin." *JREth* 30 (2002): 181–205.

Crisp, Oliver. "Karl Barth and Jonathan Edwards on Reprobation (and Hell)." In *Engaging with Barth: Contemporary Evangelical Critiques.* Edited by David Gibson and Daniel Strange, 300–322. London: T&T Clark, 2009.

Cunningham, Mary K. *What Is Theological Exegesis? Interpretation and Use of Scripture in Barth's Doctrine of Election.* Valley Forge, PA: Trinity Press International, 1995.

Dahlke, Benjamin. *Die katholische Rezeption Karl Barths: Theologische Erneuerung in Vorfeld des Zweiten Vatikanischen Konzils.* Tübingen: Mohr Siebeck, 2010.

Dalferth, Ingolf. "Karl Barth's Eschatological Realism." In *Karl Barth: Centenary Essays.* Edited by S. W. Sykes, 14–45. Cambridge: Cambridge University Press, 1989.

———. "Representing God's Presence." *IJST* 3, no. 3 (2001): 237–56.

Dawson, R. Dale. *The Resurrection in Karl Barth.* Aldershot: Ashgate, 2007.

Deddo, Gary W. *Karl Barth's Theology of Relations: Trinitarian, Christological, and Human: Toward an Ethic of Family.* New York: Peter Lang, 1999.

Demson, David E. *Hans Frei and Karl Barth: Different Ways of Reading Scripture.* Grand Rapids: Eerdmans, 1997.

Di Noia, J. Augustine. "Religion and the Religions." In *The Cambridge Companion to Karl Barth.* Edited by John Webster, 243–57. Cambridge: Cambridge University Press, 2000.

Drewes, Hans-Anton. "Auseinandersetzung mit Adolf von Harnack." In *Karl Barth in Deutschland* (1921–1935). Edited by Michael Beintker, Christian Link, and Michael Trowitzsch, 190–203. Tübingen: Theologischer Verlag, 2005.

Driel, Edwin Chr. van. *Incarnation Anyway: Arguments for Supralapsarian Christology.* New York: Oxford University Press, 2008.

Ebeling, Gerhard. "Karl Barths Ringen mit Luther." Pages 428–573 in vol. 3 of *Lutherstudien.* Tübingen: Mohr Siebeck, 1985.

Etzelmüller, Gregor. ... *zu richten die Lebendigen und die Toten: Zur Rede vom Jüngsten Gericht im Anschluss an Karl Barth.* Neukirchen-Vluyn: Neukirchener Verlag, 2001.

Farrow, Douglas. *Ascension and Ecclesia: On the Significance of the Doctrine of the Ascension for Ecclesiology and Christian Cosmology.* Edinburgh: T&T Clark, 1999.

Flett, John G. *The Witness of God: The Trinity, Missio Dei, Karl Barth, and the Nature of Christian Community.* Grand Rapids: Eerdmans, 2010.

Ford, David. "Barth's Interpretation of the Bible." In *Karl Barth: Studies of His Theological Method*. Edited by S. W. Sykes, 55–87. Oxford: Clarendon, 1979.

Frei, Hans W. "An Afterword: Eberhard Busch's Biography of Karl Barth." In *Karl Barth in Re-View: Posthumous Works Reviewed and Assessed*. Edited by H. Martin Rumscheidt, 95–116. PTMS 30. Pittsburgh: Pickwick, 1981.

———. *The Eclipse of Biblical Narrative*. New Haven: Yale University Press, 1974.

Freudenberg, Matthias. "Das reformierte Erbe erwerben: Karl Barths Wahrnehmungen der reformierten Theologie vor 1921." *ThZ* 54 (1998): 36–54.

Gadamer, Hans-Georg. *Wahrheit und Methode*. 2nd ed. Tübingen: Mohr Siebeck, 1965. Translated by Joel Weinsheimer and Donald Marshall as *Truth and Method*. New York: Crossroad, 1989.

George, Timothy. "Running Like a Herald to Deliver the Message: Barth on the Church and Sacraments." In *Karl Barth and Evangelical Theology: Convergences and Divergences*. Edited by Sung Wook Chung, 191–208. Grand Rapids: Baker Academic, 2006.

Gerrish, Brian A. "The Lord's Supper in the Reformed Confessions." In *Major Themes in the Reformed Tradition*. Edited by Donald K. McKim, 245–58. Grand Rapids: Eerdmans, 1992.

Gibson, David. *Reading the Decree: Exegesis, Election and Christology in Calvin and Barth*. London: T&T Clark, 2009.

Gignilliat, Mark. *Karl Barth and the Fifth Gospel: Barth's Theological Exegesis of Isaiah*. Aldershot: Ashgate, 2009.

Gockel, Matthias. *Barth and Schleiermacher on the Doctrine of Election: A Systematic-Theological Comparison*. Oxford: Oxford University Press, 2006.

Gollwitzer, Helmut. *Reich Gottes und Sozialismus bei Karl Barth*. Munich: Kaiser, 1972.

Gorringe, Timothy. "Crime, Punishment, and Atonement." In *Commanding Grace: Studies in Karl Barth's Ethics*. Edited by Daniel L. Migliore, 136–61. Grand Rapids: Eerdmans, 2010.

———. "Culture and Barbarism: Barth amongst the Students of Culture." In *Conversing with Barth*. Edited by John C. McDowell and Mike Higton, 40–52. Aldershot: Ashgate, 2004.

———. *Furthering Humanity: A Theology of Culture*. Aldershot: Ashgate, 2004.

———. *Karl Barth: Against Hegemony, Christian Theology in Context*. Oxford: Oxford University Press, 1999.

Greggs, Tom. *Theology against Religion: Constructive Dialogues with Bonhoeffer and Barth*. London: T&T Clark, 2011.

Griswold, Daniel. "Perichoretic Eternality: God's Relationship to Time in Karl Barth's *Church Dogmatics*." PhD diss. Southern Methodist University, 2010.

Gunton, Colin. "Karl Barth and the Western Intellectual Tradition." In *Theology beyond Christendom: Essays on the Centenary of the Birth of Karl Barth*. Edited by John Thompson, 285–301. PrTMS 6. Allison Park, PA: Pickwick, 1986.

———. "The Triune God and the Freedom of the Creature." In *Karl Barth: Centenary Essays*. Edited by S. W. Sykes, 46–68. Cambridge: Cambridge University Press, 1989.

Guretzki, David. *Karl Barth on the Filioque*. Aldershot: Ashgate, 2009.

Hailer, Martin. *Die Unbegreiflichkeit des Reiches Gottes: Studien zur Theologie Karl Barths*. Neukirchen-Vluyn: Neukirchener Verlag, 2004.

Harnack, Adolf von. *History of Dogma*. Translated by N. Buchanan. New York: Dover, 1961.

Hart, John W. *Karl Barth vs. Emil Brunner: The Formation and Dissolution of a Theological Alliance, 1916–1936*. New York: Peter Lang, 2001.

Hart, Trevor. "The Word, the Words and the Witness: Proclamation as Divine and Human Reality." In *Regarding*

Karl Barth: Toward a Reading of His Theology, 28–47. Downers Grove, IL: InterVarsity Press, 1999.

Hartenstein, Karl. "Was hat die Theologie Karl Barths der Mission zu sagen?" *ZZ* 6 (1928): 59–83.

Hauerwas, Stanley. "On Honor: By Way of a Comparison of Barth and Trollope." In *Dispatches from the Front: Theological Engagements with the Secular,* 58–79. Durham, NC: Duke University Press, 1994.

Healy, Nicholas M. "Karl Barth's Ecclesiology Reconsidered." *SJT* 57 (2004): 287–99.

Heidtmann, Dieter. *Die Engel: Grenzgestalten Gottes: Über Notwendigkeit und Möglichkeit der christlichen Rede von den Engeln.* 2nd ed. Neukirchen-Vluyn: Neukirchener Verlag, 2005.

Hendry, George S. *Theology of Nature.* Philadelphia: Westminster, 1980.

Heron, Alasdair. "The Theme of Salvation in Karl Barth's Doctrine of Reconciliation." *Ex Auditu* 5 (1989): 107–22.

Herrmann, Wilhelm. *The Communion of the Christian with God: Described on the Basis of Luther's Statements* (1892). Translated by J. Sandys Stanyon. Philadelphia: Fortress, 1971.

Holmes, Christopher R. J. *Revisiting the Doctrine of the Divine Attributes: In Dialogue with Karl Barth, Eberhard Jüngel, and Wolf Krötke.* New York: Peter Lang, 2007.

———. "The Theological Function of the Doctrine of the Divine Attributes and the Divine Glory, with Special Reference to Karl Barth and His Reading of the Protestant Orthodox." *SJT* 61 (May 2008): 206–23.

Hunsinger, Deborah. "Becoming Bilingual: The Promise of Karl Barth for Pastoral Counseling." PhD diss. Union Theological Seminary, New York, 1993.

———. *Theology and Pastoral Counseling: A New Interdisciplinary Approach.* Grand Rapids: Eerdmans, 1995.

Hunsinger, George. *Disruptive Grace: Studies in the Theology of Karl Barth.* Grand Rapids: Eerdmans, 2000.

———, ed. *For the Sake of the World.* Grand Rapids: Eerdmans, 2004.

———. *How to Read Karl Barth: The Shape of His Theology.* New York: Oxford University Press, 1991.

———. "Jesus as The Lord of Time According to Karl Barth." *ZDTh* (supplement series) 4 (2010): 113–27.

———. "Justification and Justice: Toward an Evangelical Social Ethic." In *What Is Justification About? Reformed Contributions to an Ecumenical Theme.* Edited by John Burgess and Michael Weinrich, 207–30. Grand Rapids: Eerdmans, 2009.

———, ed. *Karl Barth and Radical Politics.* Philadelphia: Westminster, 1976.

———. "Karl Barth's Christology: Its Basic Chalcedonian Character." In *The Cambridge Companion to Karl Barth.* Edited by John Webster, 127–42. Cambridge: Cambridge University Press, 2000.

———. "A Tale of Two Simultaneities: Justification and Sanctification in Calvin and Barth." In *Conversing with Barth.* Edited by John C. McDowell and Mike Higton, 68–89. Aldershot: Ashgate, 2004.

Hütter, Reinhard. "Karl Barth's 'Dialectical Catholicity': *Sic et Non.*" *MTh* 16, no. 2 (2000): 137–57.

Janowski, Bernd. *Die Welt als Schöpfung.* Neukirchen-Vluyn: Neukirchener Verlag, 2008.

Jehle, Frank. *Emil Brunner: Theologe im 20. Jahrhundert.* Zurich: Theologischer Verlag, 2006.

———. *Ever Against the Stream: The Politics of Karl Barth, 1906–1968.* Translated by Richard and Martha Burnett. Grand Rapids: Eerdmans, 2002.

Jenkins, Willis. *Ecologies of Grace: Environmental Ethics and Christian Theology.* New York: Oxford University Press, 2008.

Jensen, Matt. *The Gravity of Sin: Augustine, Luther and Barth on homo incurvatus in Se*. London: T&T Clark, 2007.

Jenson, Robert. *Systematic Theology*. 2 vols. New York: Oxford University Press, 1997–1999.

Johnson, Keith. *Karl Barth and the Analogia Entis*. London: T&T Clark, 2010.

Jones, Paul Dafydd. *The Humanity of Christ: Christology in Karl Barth's Church Dogmatics*. London: T&T Clark/Continuum, 2008.

Jüngel, Eberhard. *God's Being Is in Becoming: The Trinitarian Being of God in the Theology of Karl Barth. A Paraphrase*. Translated by John Webster. Grand Rapids: Eerdmans, 2001.

———. *God as the Mystery of the World*. Translated by Darrell Guder. Grand Rapids: Eerdmans, 1983.

———. *Justification: The Heart of the Christian Faith*. Translated by Jeffrey F. Cayzer. Edinburgh: T&T Clark, 2001.

———. *Karl Barth: A Theological Legacy*. Translated by Garrett E. Paul. Philadelphia: Westminster, 1986.

———. *Karl Barths Lehre von der Taufe: Ein Hinweis auf ihre Probleme*. Zurich: Evangelischer Verlag, 1968.

———. "Theses on the Existence, Essence, and Attributes of God." Translated by Philip G. Ziegler. *TJT* 17 (Summer 2001): 55–74.

Kant, Immanuel. *Critique of Pure Reason*. Translated by Norman Kemp Smith. New York: St. Martin's, 1929.

Kegley, Charles W., ed. *The Theology of Emil Brunner*. New York: Macmillan, 1962.

Kirschstein, Helmut. *Der souveräne Gott und die heilige Schrift: Einführung in die biblische Hermeneutik Karl Barths*. Aachen: Shaker, 1998.

Klappert, Bertold. *Versöhnung und Befreiung. Versuche, Karl Barth kontextuell zu verstehen*. Neukirchen-Vluyn: Neukirchener Verlag, 1994.

Klempa, William. "Barth as a Scholar and Interpreter of Calvin." In *Papers Presented at a Colloquium on Calvin Studies*. Edited by John H. Leith, 31–44. Davidson, NC: Davidson College, 1994.

Knappe, Wilhelm. "Karl Barth und der Pietismus." *Licht und Leben* 39 (1927): 499–501, 515–18.

Kooi, Cornelis van der. *As in a Mirror: John Calvin and Karl Barth on Knowing God: A Diptych*. Translated by Donald Mader. Studies in the History of the Christian Tradition 120. Leiden: Brill, 2005.

Korsch, Dietrich. *Dialektische Theologie nach Karl Barth*. Tübingen: Mohr Siebeck, 1996.

Kraus, Hans-Joachim. "Das Problem der Heilsgeschichte in der 'Kirchlichen Dogmatik.'" In *Antwort: Karl Barth zum siebzigsten Geburtstag*. Edited by Ernst Wolf, Charlotte von Kirschbaum, and Rudolf Frey, 69–83. Zurich: Evangelischer Verlag, 1956.

Krötke, Wolf. "The Humanity of the Human Person in Karl Barth's Anthropology." In *The Cambridge Companion to Karl Barth*. Edited by John Webster, 159–76. Cambridge: Cambridge University Press, 2000.

———. *Sin and Nothingness in the Theology of Karl Barth*. Translated by Philip G. Ziegler. Studies in Reformed Theology and History 10. Princeton: Princeton Theological Seminary, 2005.

Kuitert, Harry M. *Filosofie van de theologie*. Leiden: M. Nijhoff, 1988.

Küng, Hans. *Justification: The Doctrine of Karl Barth and a Catholic Reflection*. Translated by Thomas Collins, et al. 40th anniversary ed. Louisville, KY: Westminster John Knox, 2004.

La Montagne, D. Paul. *Barth and Rationality: Critical Realism in Theology*. Eugene, OR: Wipf & Stock, 2012.

Lamirande, Emilien. "The Impact of Karl Barth on the Catholic Church in the Last Half Century." In *Footnotes to a Theology: The Karl Barth Colloquium of 1972*. Edited by H. Martin Rumscheidt, 112–41. Waterloo, Ont.:

Corporation for the Publication of Academic Studies in Religion in Canada, 1974.

Lane, Anthony N. S. *The Unseen World: Christian Reflections on Angels, Demons, and the Heavenly Realm.* Grand Rapids: Baker, 1996.

Lauber, David. *Barth on the Descent into Hell: God, Atonement, and the Christian Life.* Aldershot: Ashgate, 2004.

Lewis, Alan E. *Between Cross and Resurrection: A Theology of Holy Saturday.* Grand Rapids: Eerdmans, 2001.

Lindemann, Walter. *Karl Barth und die kritische Schriftauslegung.* Hamburg-Bergstedt: Evangelischer Verlag, 1973.

Link, Christian. "'Leben um der Gerechtigkeit willen': Die Wirklichkeit des Geistes nach der Kirchlichen Dogmatik von Karl Barth." In *Komm, Heiliger Geist: Das Wirken des Geistes nach Karl Barth; eine kleine Festschrift für Gerhardt Langguth.* Edited by Peter Eicher, et al., 49–67. Karlsruhe: Evangelische Akademie Baden, 1990.

———. *Schöpfung.* Gütersloh: Gütersloher/Mohn, 1991.

Lohmann, Friedrich. *Karl Barth und der Neukantianismus: Die Rezeption des Neukantianismus in 'Römerbrief' und ihre Bedeutung für die weitere Ausarbeitung der Theologie Karl Barth.* Berlin: de Gruyter, 1995.

Lohse, Bernard. *A Short History of Christian Doctrine.* Translated by F. Ernest Stoeffler. Philadelphia: Fortress, 1966.

Lorberg-Fehring, Sönke. *Thurneysen— neu gesehen.* Marburg: Tectum, 2006.

Mangina, Joseph. "Bearing the Marks of Jesus: The Church in the Economy of Salvation in Barth and Hauerwas." *SJT* 52 (1999): 269–305.

———. *Karl Barth on the Christian Life: The Practical Knowledge of God.* New York: Peter Lang, 2001.

———. *Karl Barth: Theologian of Witness.* Aldershot: Ashgate, 2004.

Marga, Amy. *Karl Barth's Dialogue with Catholicism in Göttingen and Münster: Its Significance for His Doctrine of God.* Tübingen: Mohr Siebeck, 2010.

Marquardt, Friedrich-Wilhelm. *Die Entdeckung des Judentums für die christliche Theologie. Israel im Denken Karl Barths.* Munich: Kaiser, 1967.

Marshall, Bruce. *Christology in Conflict: The Identity of a Saviour in Rahner and Barth.* Oxford: Blackwell, 1987.

Matošević, Lidija. *Lieber katholisch als neuprotestantisch. Karl Barths Rezeption der katholischen Theologie 1921–1930.* Neukirchen-Vluyn: Neukirchener Verlag, 2005.

McCormack, Bruce L. "The Being of Holy Scripture Is in Becoming: Karl Barth in Conversation with American Evangelical Criticism." In *Evangelicals and Scripture: Tradition, Authority and Hermeneutics.* Edited by Vincent Bacote, Laura C. Miguélez and Dennis L. Okholm, 55–75. Downers Grove, IL: InterVarsity Press, 2004.

———. "Grace and Being." In *The Cambridge Companion to Karl Barth.* Edited by John Webster, 92–110. Cambridge: Cambridge University Press, 2000.

———. "Graham Ward's Barth, Derrida and the Language of Theology." *SJT* 49, no. 1 (1996): 97–109.

———. *Karl Barth's Critically Realistic Dialectical Theology: Its Genesis and Development 1909–1936.* Oxford: Clarendon, 1995.

———. "The Ontological Presuppositions of Barth's Doctrine of the Atonement." In *The Glory of the Atonement: Biblical, Historical and Practical Perspectives.* Edited by Charles Hill and Frank James, 346–66. Downers Grove, IL: InterVarsity Press, 2004.

———. *Orthodox and Modern: Studies in the Theology of Karl Barth.* Grand Rapids: Baker, 2008.

———. "So That He May Be Merciful to All: Karl Barth and the Problem of Universalism." In *Karl Barth and American Evangelicalism*. Edited by Clifford Anderson and Bruce L. McCormack, 227–49. Grand Rapids: Eerdmans, 2011.

———. "What Has Basel to Do with Berlin? The Return of 'Church Dogmatics' in the Schleiermacherian Tradition." *PSB* 23, no. 2 (2002): 146–73.

McDowell, John C. *Hope in Barth's Eschatology: Interrogations and Transformations beyond Tragedy*. Aldershot: Ashgate, 2000.

———. "Much Ado about Nothing: Karl Barth's Being Unable to Do Nothing about Nothingness." *IJST* 4, no. 3 (2002): 319–35.

McGlasson, Paul. *Jesus and Judas: Biblical Exegesis in Barth*. Atlanta: Scholars Press, 1991.

McGrath, Alister E. *Iustitia Dei: A History of the Christian Doctrine of Justification*, 2 vols. Cambridge: Cambridge University Press, 1986.

McKelway, Alexander J. *The Freedom of God and Human Liberation*. Philadelphia: Trinity Press International, 1990.

McLean, Stuart. "Creation and Anthropology." In *Theology beyond Christendom: Essays on the Centenary of the Birth of Karl Barth*. Edited by John Thompson, 111–42. PrTMS 6. Allison Park, PA: Pickwick, 1986.

———. *Humanity in the Thought of Karl Barth*. Edinburgh: T&T Clark, 1981.

Mechels, Eberhard. *Analogie bei Erich Przywara und Karl Barth. Das Verhältnis von Offenbarungstheologie und Metaphysik*. Neukirchen-Vluyn: Neukirchener Verlag, 1974.

Menke, Karl Heinz. "Karl Barth: Christi Stellvertretung als Inbegriff der 'analogia fidei.'" In *Stellvertetung. Schlüsselbegriff christlichen Lebens und theologische Grundkategorie*, 168–93. Freiburg: Johannes, 1991.

Metzger, Paul. *The Word of Christ and the World of Culture: Sacred and Secular through the Theology of Karl Barth*. Grand Rapids: Eerdmans, 2003.

Migliore, Daniel L. "Editorial: Reappraising Barth's Theology." *ThT* 43, no. 3 (1986): 309–14. (Special issue celebrating the centennial of Barth's birth.)

———. "Freedom to Pray." In Karl Barth, *Prayer: 50th Anniversary Edition*. 95–113. Louisville, KY: Westminster John Knox, 2002.

———. "Participatio Christi: The Central Theme of Barth's Doctrine of Sanctification." *ZDTh*, 18, no. 3 (2002): 286–307.

———. "Reforming the Theology and Practice of Baptism." In *Toward the Future of Reformed Theology*. Edited by David Willis and Michael Welker, 494–511. Grand Rapids: Eerdmans, 1998.

Mikkelsen, Hans Vium. *Reconciled Humanity: Karl Barth in Dialogue*. Grand Rapids: Eerdmans, 2010.

Molnar, Paul D. *Divine Freedom and the Doctrine of the Immanent Trinity: In Dialogue with Karl Barth and Contemporary Theology*. Edinburgh: T&T Clark, 2002.

———. *Incarnation and Resurrection: Toward a Contemporary Understanding*. Grand Rapids: Eerdmans, 2007.

———. *Karl Barth and the Theology of the Lord's Supper: A Systematic Investigation*. New York: Peter Lang, 1996.

———. "Love of God and Love of Neighbor in the Theology of Karl Rahner and Karl Barth." *MTh* 20, no. 4 (2004): 567–99.

Neder, Adam. *Participation in Christ: An Entry into Karl Barth's Church Dogmatics*. Columbia Series in Reformed Theology. Louisville, KY: Westminster John Knox, 2009.

Niebuhr, H. Richard. *Christ and Culture*. New York: Harper & Row, 1951.

Nimmo, Paul T. *Being in Action: The Theological Shape of Barth's Ethical Vision*. London: T&T Clark/Continuum, 2007.

———. "The Orders of Creation in the Theological Ethics of Karl Barth." *SJT* 60, no. 1 (2007): 24–35.

Ogletree, Thomas. *Christian Faith and History: A Critical Comparison of Ernst Troeltsch and Karl Barth*. Nashville: Abingdon, 1965.

Osthövener, Claus-Dieter. *Die Lehre von Gottes Eigenschaften bei Friedrich Schleiermacher und Karl Barth*. Berlin: de Gruyter, 1996.

Otto, Rudolf. *Das Heilige*. Breslau: Trewendt & Granier, 1917. ET: *The Idea of the Holy*. Translated by John. W. Harvey. 2nd ed. New York: Oxford University Press, 1950.

Outka, Gene. *Agape: An Ethical Analysis*. New Haven: Yale University Press, 1972.

Palma, Robert. *Karl Barth's Theology of Culture: The Freedom of Culture for the Praise of God*. PTMS, ns 2. Allison Park, PA: Pickwick, 1983.

Palmer, Russell. "Karl Barth and the Orders of Creation: A Study in Theological Ethics." PhD diss. University of Iowa, 1966.

Pannenberg, Wolfhart. *Analogie und Offenbarung. Eine kritische Untersuchung zur Geschichte des Analogiebegriffs in der Lehre von der Gotteserkenntnis*. Göttingen: Vandenhoeck & Ruprecht, 1977.

———. *Systematic Theology* I, trans. Geoffrey W. Bromiley (Grand Rapids: Eerdmans, 1991).

———. *Theology and the Philosophy of Science*. Translated by Francis McDonagh. Philadelphia: Westminster, 1976.

Pauw, Amy P. "Where Theologians Fear to Tread." *MTh* 16, no. 1 (2000): 39–59.

Pfleiderer, Georg. *Karl Barths praktische Theologie. Zu Genese und Kontext eines paradigmatischen Entwurfs systematischer Theologie im 20. Jahrhundert*. Tübingen: Mohr Siebeck, 2000.

Placher, William C., ed. *Callings: Twenty Centuries of Christian Wisdom on Vocation*. Grand Rapids: Eerdmans, 2005.

———. *Unapologetic: A Christian Voice in a Pluralistic Conversation*. Louisville, KY: Westminster John Knox, 1989.

Price, Daniel J. *Karl Barth's Anthropology in Light of Modern Thought*. Grand Rapids: Eerdmans, 2002.

Price, Robert B. *Letters of the Divine Word: The Perfections of God in Karl Barth's Church Dogmatics*. London: T&T Clark, 2011.

Przywara, Erich. *Analogia Entis: Metaphysik*. Munich: Kösel & Pustet, 1932.

Purves, Andrew. *Reconstructing Pastoral Theology: A Christological Foundation*. Louisville, KY: Westminster John Knox, 2004.

Rae, Simon. "Gospel, Law and Freedom in the Theological Ethics of Karl Barth." *SJT* 25 (1972): 412–22.

Rendtorff, Trutz. "Radikale Autonomie Gottes: Zum Verständnis der Theologie Karl Barths und ihrer Folgen." In *Theorie des Christentums: Historisch-theologische Studien zu seiner neuzeitlichen Verfassung*, 161–81. Gütersloh: Gütersloher Verlagshaus, 1972.

Rim, Gol. *Gottes Wort, Verkündigung und Kirche. Die systematisch-theologischen Grundlagen der Theologie Eduard Thurneysens*. Münster: LIT, 2000.

Roberts, Robert H. "Karl Barth's Doctrine of Time: Its Nature and Implications." In *Karl Barth: Studies of His Theological Method*. Edited by S. W. Sykes, 88–146. Oxford: Clarendon, 1979.

Ruddies, Hartmut. "Christologie und Versöhnungslehre bei Karl Barth." *ZDTh* 18, no. 2 (2002): 174–89.

Ruether, Rosemary Radford. "The Left Hand of God in the Theology of Karl Barth: Karl Barth as a Mythopoeic Theologian." *JRT* 25 (1968–1969): 3–26.

Rumscheidt, H. Martin, ed. *Adolf von Harnack: Liberal Theology at Its Height*. San Francisco: Harper & Row, 1989.

———, ed. *Karl Barth in Re-View: Posthumous Works Reviewed and Assessed*. PTMS 30. Pittsburgh: Pickwick, 1981.

———. *Revelation and Theology: An Analysis of the Barth-Harnack Correspondence of 1923*. Cambridge: Cambridge University Press, 1972.

Santmire, H. Paul. *The Travail of Nature: The Ambiguous Ecological Promise of Christian Theology.* Philadelphia: Fortress, 1985.

Sauter, Gerhard. *Gateway to Dogmatics: Reasoning Theologically for the Life of the Church.* Grand Rapids: Eerdmans, 2003.

———. *What Dare We Hope? Reconsidering Eschatology.* Harrisburg, PA: Trinity Press International, 1999.

———. "Why Is Karl Barth's Church Dogmatics Not a 'Theology of Hope'? Some Observations on Barth's Understanding of Eschatology." *SJT* 52 (1999): 407–29.

Schleiermacher, Friedrich. *The Christian Faith.* Translated By H. R. MacKintosch. Edinburgh: T & T Clark, 1928.

———. *On Religion: Speeches to Its Cultured Despisers.* Translated by Richard Crouter. Cambridge: Cambridge University Press, 1996.

Scholder, Klaus. *The Churches and the Third Reich.* Translated by John Bowden. 2 vols. Philadelphia: Fortress, 1988.

Scholz, Heinrich. "Wie ist eine evangelische Theologie als Wissenschaft möglich?" *ZZ* 9 (1931): 8–53.

Schröder, Caroline. "'I See Something You Don't See': Karl Barth's Doctrine of Providence." In *For the Sake of the World.* Edited by George Hunsinger, 115–35. Grand Rapids: Eerdmans, 2004.

Schröter, Fritz. "Bermerkungen über den reformierten Character des theologischen Ansatzes Karl Barths." In *Antwort: Karl Barth zum siebzigsten Geburtstag.* Edited by Ernst Wolf, Charlotte von Kirschbaum, and Rudolf Frey, 148–55. Zurich: Evangelischer Verlag, 1956.

Schultze, Harald. "Gebet zwischen Zweifel und Vertrauen." *Evangelische Theologie* 30, no. 3 (1970): 133–49.

Schuurman, Douglas J. *Vocation: Discerning Our Callings in Life.* Grand Rapids: Eerdmans, 2004.

Schwöbel, Christoph. "Theology." In *The Cambridge Companion to Karl Barth.* Edited by John Webster, 17–36. Cambridge: Cambridge University Press, 2000.

Seifrid, Mark A. "The Subject of Rom. 7:14–25." *Novum Testamentum* 34 (1992): 313–33.

Shapiro, Lou. "Karl Barth's Understanding of Prayer." *Crux* 24, no. 1 (1988): 26–33.

Sherman, Robert J. *The Shift to Modernity: Christ and the Doctrine of Creation in the Theologies of Schleiermacher and Barth.* London: T&T Clark, 2005.

Simon, Carolyn J. "What Wondrous Love is This? Meditations on Barth, Christian Love, and the Future of Christian Ethics." In *For the Sake of the World: Karl Barth and the Future of Ecclesial Theology.* Edited by George Hunsinger, 143–58. Grand Rapids: Eerdmans, 2004.

Smail, Thomas. "The Doctrine of the Holy Spirit." In *Theology beyond Christendom: Essays on the Centenary of the Birth of Karl Barth.* Edited by John Thompson, 87–110. PrTMS 6. Allison Park, PA: Pickwick, 1986.

Smart, James D. *The Divided Mind of Modern Theology: Karl Barth and Rudolf Bultmann 1908–1933.* Philadelphia: Westminster, 1967.

Smend, Rudolf. "Nachkritische Schriftauslegung." In *Parrhesia: Karl Barth zum achtzigsten Geburtstag.* Edited by Eberhard Busch, Jürgen Fangmeier, and Max Geiger, 215–37. Zurich: EVZ, 1966.

Smith, Steven G. "Karl Barth and Fideism: A Reconsideration." *AThR* 66 (1984): 64–78.

Sonderegger, Katherine. "For Us and for Our Salvation." In *Commanding Grace: Studies in Karl Barth's Ethics.* Edited by Daniel L. Migliore, 162–75. Grand Rapids: Eerdmans, 2010.

———. "Sanctification as Impartation in the Doctrine of Karl Barth." *ZDTh* 18, no. 3 (2002): 308–15.

———. *That Jesus Christ Was Born a Jew: Karl Barth's "Doctrine of Israel."* University Park, PA: Pennsylvania State University Press, 1992.

Soulen, R. Kendall. *The God of Israel and Christian Theology*. Minneapolis: Fortress, 1996.

Spinks, Bryan D. "Karl Barth's Teaching on Baptism: Its Development, Antecedents and the 'Liturgical Factor.'" *Ecclesia Orans* 14 (1997): 261–88.

Sykes, S. W., ed. *Karl Barth: Studies of His Theological Method*. Oxford: Clarendon, 1979.

Tanner, Kathryn. "Creation and Providence." In *The Cambridge Companion to Karl Barth*. Edited by John Webster, 111–27. Cambridge: Cambridge University Press, 2000.

———. *God and Creation in Christian Theology: Tyranny or Empowerment?* New York: Blackwell, 1988.

Thadden, Rudolf von. *Die Krise des Liberalismus zwischen den Weltkriegen*. Göttingen: Vandenhoeck & Ruprecht, 1978.

Thomas, Günter. "Chaosüberwindung und Rechtsetzung Schöpfung und Versöhnung in Karl Barths Eschatologie." *ZDTh* 21, no. 3 (2005): 259–77.

———. "Der für uns 'gerichtete Richter'. Kritische Erwägungen zu Karl Barths Versöhnungslehre." *ZDTh* 18, no. 2 (2002): 211–25.

Thompson, John. *Christ in Perspective: Christological Perspectives in the Theology of Karl Barth*. Grand Rapids: Eerdmans, 1978.

———. *The Holy Spirit in the Theology of Karl Barth*. Allison Park, PA : Pickwick, 1991.

Thurneysen, Eduard. *Dostoevsky*. Translated by Keith R. Crim. Richmond: John Knox, 1964.

———. *A Theology of Pastoral Care*. Translated by Jack Worthington and Thomas Wieser. Richmond: John Knox, 1962.

Torrance, Alan. "The Trinity." In *The Cambridge Companion to Karl Barth*. Edited by John Webster, 72–91. Cambridge: Cambridge University Press, 2000.

Torrance, T. F. "Justification: Its Radical Nature and Place in Reformed Doctrine and Life." *SJT* 13 (1960): 225–46.

———. *Karl Barth: An Introduction to His Early Theology, 1910–1931*. London: SCM, 1962.

———. *Karl Barth: Biblical and Evangelical Theologian*. Edinburgh: T&T Clark, 1990.

———. *Space, Time and Resurrection*. 1976. Repr., Edinburgh: T&T Clark, 1998.

Vanhoozer, Kevin. "A Person of the Book? Barth on Biblical Authority and Interpretation." In *Karl Barth and Evangelical Theology: Convergences and Divergences*. Edited by Sung Wook Chung, 26–59. Grand Rapids: Baker Academic, 2006.

Ward, Graham. *Barth, Derrida and the Language of Theology*. Cambridge: Cambridge University Press, 1995.

Ward, Timothy. *Word and Supplement: Speech Acts, Biblical Texts and the Sufficiency of Scripture*. Oxford: Oxford University Press, 2002.

Watson, Francis. "The Bible." In *The Cambridge Companion to Karl Barth*. Edited by John Webster, 57–71. Cambridge: Cambridge University Press, 2000.

Weber, Otto. *Karl Barth's Church's Dogmatics*. Translated by Arthur C. Cochrane. Philadelphia: Westminster, 1953.

———. "Kirche und Welt nach Karl Barth." In *Antwort: Karl Barth zum siebzigsten Geburtstag*. Edited by Ernst Wolf, Charlotte von Kirschbaum, and Rudolf Frey, 217–36. Zurich: Evangelischer Verlag, 1956.

Webster, John. *Karl Barth*. London: Continuum, 2000.

———. *Barth's Earlier Theology*. Edinburgh: T&T Clark, 2004.

———. *Barth's Ethics of Reconciliation*. Cambridge: Cambridge University Press, 1995.

———. *Barth's Moral Theology: Human Action in Barth's Thought*. Edinburgh: T&T Clark, 1998.

Welker, Michael. "From Fighter against the 'Roman Heresy' to Leading Thinker for the Ecumenical Movement." *SJT* 57, no. 4 (2004): 434–50.

Willimon, William. *Conversations with Barth on Preaching*. Nashville: Abingdon, 2006.

———. *The Early Preaching of Karl Barth*. Louisville, KY: Westminster John Knox, 2009.

Winn, Christian T. Collins. *"Jesus Is Victor!" The Significance of the Blumhardts for the Theology of Karl Barth*. PrTMS 93. Eugene, OR: Wipf & Stock, 2009.

Wolf, Ernst. "Die Rechtfertigungslehre als Mitte und Grenze reformatorischer Theologie." *EvTh* 9 (1949–1950) 298–333.

Wolterstorff, Nicholas. "Barth on Evil." *Faith and Philosophy* 13 (1996): 584–608.

Wyschogrod, Michael. "Why Was and Is the Theology of Karl Barth of Interest to a Jewish Theologian?" In *Abraham's Promise*. Edited by R. Kendall Soulen, 211–25. Grand Rapids: Eerdmans, 2004.

Yocum, John. *Ecclesial Mediation in Karl Barth*. Aldershot: Ashgate, 2004.

Zahn-Harnack, Agnes von, ed. *Adolf von Harnack*, 2 vols. Berlin: de Gruyter, 1951.

Lightning Source UK Ltd.
Milton Keynes UK
UKOW04f2033120913

217111UK00005B/661/P

9 780664 225308